L1

CONFLICT OF LAWS AND EUROPEAN COMMUNITY LAW

With special reference to the Community Conventions
on private international law

PROBLEMS IN
PRIVATE INTERNATIONAL LAW

General Editor

R.H. GRAVESON

CBE, QC, Ph. D, LL.D (London), LL.D (Sheffield),
SJD (Harvard), LL.D h.c. (Ghent), D. Jur h.c. (Freiburg-i-Br),
LL.D h.c. (Uppsala), LL.D h.c. (Louvain),
Emeritus Professor of Private International Law
King's College
University of London

Volume 3

NORTH-HOLLAND PUBLISHING COMPANY
AMSTERDAM · NEW YORK · OXFORD

CONFLICT OF LAWS
AND EUROPEAN COMMUNITY LAW
With special reference to the Community Conventions
on private international law

IAN F. FLETCHER, M.A., LL.B., Ph. D. (Cantab), M.C.L. (Tulane)
Of Lincoln's Inn, Barrister-at-Law
Senior Lecturer in Law, University College of Wales, Aberystwyth

1982

NORTH-HOLLAND PUBLISHING COMPANY
AMSTERDAM · NEW YORK · OXFORD

© North-Holland Publishing Company — 1982

ISBN North-Holland: 0 444 86376 1

Publishers:
North-Holland Publishing Company
Amsterdam · New York · Oxford

Distributors for the U.S.A. and Canada:
Elsevier Science Publishing Company, Inc.
52 Vanderbilt Avenue
New York, N.Y. 10017

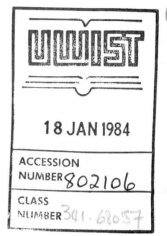
Library of Congress Cataloging in Publication Data

Fletcher, Ian F.
   Conflicts of laws and European community law.

   (Problems in private international law ; 3)
   Includes index.
   1. Conflict of laws--European Economic
Community countries.   I. Title.   II. Series.
Law   340.9   82-2270
ISBN 0-444-86376-1   AACR2

PRINTED IN THE NETHERLANDS

To my Mother

Table of Contents

Introduction to the Series

Our age has seen a development in private international law of a scale, variety and depth not experienced since the nineteenth century. The subject has acquired practical importance and an international dimension through the participation of many countries in conferences at governmental level, through the increasing use of legislation to deal with problems hitherto left to the courts and juristic writers, and through an increased frequency of occasions for invoking its principles to deal with the complexities of modern life.

The development of this subject in scale may be instanced by the attention given to it in the Conventions of the Hague Conference of Private International Law, the European Economic Community and the Council of Europe. The very existence of the special regime of private international law established by the European Economic Community, for example, creates its own problems of the duality of systems of private international law in member states, if not beyond. We now meet regional groupings of systems for various purposes. In variety we find new problems in many fields including torts, credit and the problems relating to children. In the dimension of evolution, hitherto insufficiently recognised, the systems of private international law of western civilisation, founded as they are on common cultural values and standards of Roman law or the common law, the Christian faith and the Holy Roman Empire, can no longer ignore other systems which fail to conform to these standards, as was often done in the nineteenth century.

These and other factors point out to the need for an explanation in depth of areas of private international law in the light of modern conditions. They require a degree of specialisation which may be thought inappropriate in a general text on the subject. A clear answer to this particular need lay in the introduction of a series of monographs, each dealing with an aspect or series of problems in the subject to which special treatment could be devoted.

Under these circumstances it seemed most useful to arrange a marriage of each author with the subject of his choice, not only to ensure the authority of the statement but to provide a medium in which the author could deal fully with a matter in which he had a special interest or qualification, whether academic or practical. It is on the basis of these two main considerations that the authors of the respective volumes have been invited to contribute. Within the broad limits of editorial policy each author is free to deal with his subject as he thinks best. His opinions are entirely his own, but it may not be simply coincidence that many others will probably share them.

The general policy behind this series will already have appeared. It is to present topics of importance and interest to those concerned with private international law in practice, in the universities or in government. It is not difficult to think of a number of such topics of an almost equal degree of urgency, and while each volume will be complete in itself one can envisage the series eventually covering most of the area of private international law and thus constituting a comprehensive and authoritative statement. The general approach is to compare relevant systems of private international law, not only because of the added value of a wider view of problems in this area, but also because of the special interest or qualification of the authors, and although each one is free to include within his horizons any legal system he may regard as relevant, the general basis of approach in this series is private international law as found within the British Isles, the European Economic Community or the U.S.A. The constraints of space compel all our authors to be selective in their area of comparison but it is hoped that this need for selection will add to rather than detract from the value of their work.

R.H. Graveson

Preface

Of the numerous, legally-significant developments which have resulted from the formation of the European Communities, those taking place in the field of private international law have perhaps been among the least noticed. This prolonged state of obscurity seems destined shortly to come to an end, however, since the first of the Community Conventions specifically negotiated for the purpose of harmonising the Member States' rules of private international law is presently poised to enter into force in the United Kingdom, having already been in force for several years between the original Six Member States of the Community. It would therefore seem that the time is ripe to review the theoretical and practical implications for private international law arising from the creation of the European Communities, and of the unique legal system to which the Founding Treaties have given birth. In addition to surveying this scene in a general way, it also seems appropriate to explore in detail the provisions contained in the Community Conventions on private international law, most of them concluded pursuant to the provisions of Article 220 of the Treaty establishing the European Economic Community, which either are, or shortly will be, in force throughout the EEC. By means of these Conventions, important and extensive changes will be brought about, affecting the law and practice in each Member State, including of course the United Kingdom, in matters of conflict of laws. As will be seen the majority of these changes — but by no means all of them — will represent an improvement upon the *status quo*. But the novelty and complexity of some of these new provisions can appear not a little disconcerting upon first acquaintance. The present work is therefore offered as a modest contribution towards the gaining of a better understanding of the new system of European private international law which is gradually being ushered into place.

The opportunity to write this book as a contribution to the series dealing with problems in private international law arose thanks to the kind initiative of Professor R.H. Graveson, the General Editor of the series. I am happy to acknowledge the encouragement and the perceptive advice which I have received from Professor Graveson, both in and beyond his capacity of editor, during the unavoidably extended time in which the book was researched and written. I also owe very considerable debts of gratitude to Dr. W.M. Hauschild, Head of Division in the Commission of the European Communities, to Mr. K.M. Newman, of the Lord Chancellor's Office, and to Professor A.L. Diamond, formerly of the Law Commission, each of whom has given me invaluable help and guidance over a period of several years. My further thanks are extended to my colleagues within the Department of Law at the University College of Wales, Aberystwyth, who helped to alleviate the burden of my teaching responsibilities during the final phase of the writing of this book. Additionally, it is a pleasure to take this opportunity to express my wholehearted appreciation of the indispensable contribution made by Mrs Christine Davies, who together with Mrs Eileen Pryce and Mrs Anne Watkin Jones produced the finished typescript with breathtaking speed and accuracy.

The last individual acknowledgement, and by no means the least of them, is to my wife. She not only took pains to secure for me the tranquil environment essential to the completion of any extended academic project, but also rendered me active assistance in many forms, including reading through the typescript in its entirety and, by her comments and suggestions, helping to purge this book of some at least of its all too many faults. Needless to say, the responsibility for those which survive is mine alone.

Much of the research for this book was undertaken with the help of a Fellowship provided by the Council of Europe for work in the field of European Integration. The funds thus generously made available enabled me to travel extensively for the purpose of using the collections of materials in libraries and institutes in several European countries, and also to visit and to meet the staff and officials of the Court and Commission of the European Communities, of the Permanent Bureau of the Hague Conference on Private International Law, and of the Council of Europe itself. I am most grateful for the patience and helpfulness extended to me by all concerned.

Aberystwyth   Ian F. Fletcher
July 1981

Table of Cases

Court of Justice of the European Communities

National Courts

United Kingdom

Table of Community Treaties

Table of Community Conventions

Judgments Convention (Convention of 27 September 1968, as amended)

**Convention on the mutual recognition of companies
(convention of 29 February 1968)**

Convention on the law applicable to contractual obligations (convention of 19 June 1980)

Draft convention on bankruptcy and related matters

List of Principal Works Cited

Anton , A.E., Private International Law (Edinburgh, 1967).

Bathurst, M.E. (Ed.), Legal Aspects of an Enlarged Community (1972).

Battifol, H. and Lagarde, P., Traité de Droit International Privé (6th edn. 1974).

Blom-Cooper, L., Bankruptcy in Private International Law (London, 1954) (also published in (1955) 4 I.C.L.Q. 170).

Bonell, J., Fletcher, I.F. and Fontaine, M., Les Conditions d'Ouverture des Procédures de Faillite et des Procédures Analogues (Brussels, 1979, E.C. Commission Doc. III/D/223/80-FR, 2 vols.).

Bourel, P., and others, The Influence of the European Communities upon Private International Law of the Member States (Brussels, 1981).

Bredimas, A., Methods of Interpretation and Community Law (Amsterdam: North-Holland, 1978).

Brown, L.N. and Jacobs, F.G., The Court of Justice of the European Communities (1977).

Campbell, A., Common Market Law (1973).

Camps, M., Britain and the European Community 1955—1963 (Princeton U.P., 1964).

Cheshire, G.C. and North, P.M., Private International Law (10th edn. 1979).

Cohn, E.J. (Festschrift): Liber Amicorum E.J. Cohn (1975).

Collins, L., European Community Law in the United Kingdom (2nd edn. 1980).

Cook, W.W., The Logical and Legal Bases of the Conflict of Laws (1942).

Coppens, P. (Ed.), Idées Nouvelles dans le Droit de la Faillite (Travaux de la Quatrième Journée d'Etudes Juridiques Jean Dabin) (Brussels, 1969).

Cork, K. (Chairman), Report of the Department of Trade Advisory Committee 1976 (Cmnd. 6602) ("The Cork Report").

Council of Europe: Practical Guide to the Recognition and Enforcement of Foreign Judicial Decisions in Civil and Commercial Law (Strasbourg, 1975).

Dalhuizen, J.H., Compositions in Bankruptcy (Amsterdam, 1968).

Dalhuizen, J.H., International Insolvency and Bankruptcy (New York, 1980. 2 vols.).

David, R., The International Unification of Private Law, in: International Encyclopaedia of Comparative Law, vol. 2, ch. 5.

Dicey, A.V. and Morris, J.H.C., The Conflict of Laws (10th edn. 1980, 2 vols.).

Droz, G.A.L., Compétence Judiciaire et Effets des Jugements dans le Marché Commun (1972).

Ehrenzweig, A.A., Specific Principles of Private International Law (1968, II) 124 Hague Recueil des Cours 179.

Ehrenzweig, A.A., Private International Law, vol. 2, special part (1973).

Falconbridge, J., Conflict of Laws (2nd edn. 1954).

Farnsworth, A., The Residence and Domicile of Corporations (1939).

Feld, W., The European Common Market and the World (1967).

Fletcher, I.F., Law of Bankruptcy (Plymouth, 1978).

Ganshoff, L., Droit de la Faillite dans les Etats de la CEE (Brussels, 1969).

Goldman, B., European Commercial Law (1973).

Graveson, R.H., Conflict of Laws (7th edn. 1974).

Graveson, R.H., Cohn, E.J. and Graveson, D., The Uniform Laws on International Sales Act, 1967 (London, 1968).

Haas, E.B., The Uniting of Europe (1958, revised edn. 1968, Stanford, California).

Hallstein, W., United Europe (1962).

Hallstein, W. (transl. C. Roetter), Europe in the Making (1972).

Hallstein, W., (Festschrift): Probleme des Europäischen Rechts (1966).

Holleaux, D., Compétence du Juge Etranger et Reconnaissance des Jugements (1970).

Jacobs, F.G. and Durand, A., References to the European Court (1975).

Jacobs, F.G. (Ed.), European Law and the Individual (Amsterdam: North-Holland, 1976).

Kahn-Freund, O., General Problems of Private International Law (1974, III) 143 Hague Recueil des Cours 147, also published separately (The Hague, 1976).

Kapteyn, P. and VerLoren van Themaat, P., Introduction to the Law of the EEC (1973).

Lando, O. (Ed.), European Private International Law of Obligations (1975).

Lasok, D., The Law of the Economy in the European Communities (1980).

Lipstein, K., The Law of the European Economic Community (1974).

Lipstein, K. (Ed.), Harmonisation of Private International Law by the EEC (1978).
Lysen, G., Non-Contractual Liability of the European Community (1976).
Marquand, D., Parliament for Europe (1979).
Miller, J R , Partnership (1973)
Morandière, J. de la, (Festschrift): Etudes Offertes à J. de la Morandière (1964).
Morris, J.H.C., The Conflict of Laws (2nd edn., 1980).
Nadelmann, K., Conflict of Laws, International and Interstate (1972).
Rabel, E., The Conflict of Laws, a Comparative Study (2nd edn. 1958–1960, 4 vols.).
Rabel, E., Das Problem der Qualifikation (Darmstadt, 1962).
Robertson, A.H., Characterisation in the Conflict of Laws (1940).
Savigny, F.K. von, System des heutigen Römischen Rechts (1848), vol. VIII, transl. Guthrie (1869, 2nd edn. 1880).
Schmitthof, C., European Company Law Texts (1974).
Schmitthof, C. (Ed.), Harmonisation of European Company Law (1973).
Schonfield, A., Europe, Journey to an Unknown Destination (1973).
Schmitt, H.A., The Path to European Union (Baton Rouge: L.S.U. Press, 1962).
Soumampouw, M., Les Nouvelles Conventions de la Haye (vol. 1, 1976, vol. 2, 1980).
Stein, E., Harmonisation of European Company Laws (1971).
Trochu, M., Conflits de lois et Conflits de jurisdictions en matière de la Faillite (Paris, 1967).
Valentine, D.G., The Court of Justice of the European Coal and Steel Community (The Hague, 1955).
Valentine, D.G., The Court of Justice of the European Communities (London, 1965, 2 vols.).
Van der Gucht, J., Droit de la Faillite dans les Six Pays du Marché Commun (Brussels, 1964).
Vischer, F., Internationales Vertragsrecht (Bern, 1962).
Vitta, E., International Conventions and National Conflicts Systems (1969, I) 126 Hague Recueil des Cours 113.
Weser, M., Le Traité Franco-Belge du 8 Juillet 1899 (Paris, 1951).
Weser, M., Convention Communautaire sur la Compétence Judiciaire et l'Exécution des Décisions (Brussels, 1975).
Wolff, M., Private International Law (2nd edn. 1950).
Wyatt, D. and Dashwood, A.A., The Substantive Law of the EEC (1980).

PART I

General Part

CHAPTER 1

Introduction

1. International Legal Unification: Two Kinds of Diversity

It has been well said that the ultimate purpose of conflict of laws is self-extermination: that our task is to work towards the withering away of the state of chaos which exists as the result of the innumerable disparities between different legal systems, both in their rules and in their methods.[1] While the difficulties created by the existence of these disparities between domestic legal systems are too numerous and too notorious to require detailed elaboration here,[2] the realist must perforce acknowledge that any aspirations towards the eradication of even the most troublesome examples of this phenomenon are best conceived in regional, rather than global terms if they are to enjoy any reasonable prospect of fulfilment at all, even within a relatively extensive time-scale. This is due in large part to the self-evident fact that negotiations are more easily conducted among a small number of participants than among a large number. Moreover, regionally-based developments profit from the important further fact that countries which are physically proximate to each other will in most cases share a considerable proportion of common heritage in their legal, social, political and economic traditions, thereby simplifying the task of devising an acceptable, common rule for all concerned. It is also frequently the case that countries which are neighbours will find that their contemporary outlook and policies, based upon their perception of national interest and destiny, will contain a great deal of common ground, thereby enhancing the prospects of achieving consensus in negotiations. However, with relatively few exceptions (foremost among which we must list the European Communities, with whose achievements this book is mainly concerned) even regionally-based efforts aimed at the harmonisation of substantive law are neither numerous nor particularly comprehensive at the present time, with developments tending rather to take place on an *ad hoc* basis with a view to eradicating certain specific difficulties.[3] Even if it were the case that, over an extended period of time, the

substantive laws of the world were destined gradually to become standardised into perhaps a dozen regional "types", the resultant position would
effectively be no more than a distillation of the problems which currently
subsist, and the task would remain of somehow bridging the legal gulfs that
would exist between consolidated positions adopted by the various groupings. Thus, we must conclude that the final eradication of all disparities
between the substantive laws of the different countries of the world is likely
to take place, if at all, at such a distant point in time that it is unrealistic to
seek to order our present affairs upon the assumption that it will come to
pass.

In the meantime, in a less-than-perfect legal world, the science of private
international law remains the practical instrument whereby, on a day-to-day
basis, solutions are sought to the problems, both real and notional, which
arise whenever the significant elements in a given case render it necessary to
have regard to the provisions of more than one system of law. Unfortunately, but perhaps inevitably, the development of private international law itself
has to some extent undergone a diversification and particularisation reflect-
ing the individual characteristics and traditions of the different "law districts" (or "countries", to use the term customarily employed by common
lawyers) of which the legal world is composed. Although these differences
sometimes consist only of variations in one or two significant matters of
detail, their effects can in certain cases be far-reaching. There is thus no
single *corpus* of rules and procedures to be referred to by means of the
expression "private international law", but instead there exists a plurality of
distinct *corpora* of such rules and procedures, each of which has been developed by and within one of the individual law districts of the world according
to local experience and circumstances, and which represents the idiosyncratic response of the legal system in question to the perceived problems
ensuing from the fact that its domestic law differs from that of every one of
its neighbours in some material way or other. Hence, we encounter the
paradox that the result of *bona fide*, but uncoordinated efforts to surmount
the unwelcome practical consequence of plurality of domestic laws has been
the creation of a plurality of systems of private international law. Confusion
worse confounded! Therefore, while the arduous but essential task of eliminating the *raison d'être* of private international law is being pursued by
means of a variety of programmes aimed at producing the eventual harmonisation of the relevant provisions of some, if not all, of the most important
systems of domestic law,[4] there is much scope for simultaneous action within the sphere of private international law itself.

2. Unification of Private International Law

Enormous practical, as well as theoretical, benefits would ensue from the substitution of a unified practice in the area of private international law among the states of those countries whose subjects' affairs most frequently give rise to problems of conflict of laws. The elimination of the need to consider not merely which domestic laws may possibly have a bearing upon a given case, but also which systems of private international law may in some way come to be applied in the process of achieving a solution to the case, would produce a radical simplification of the calculations involved in the ordering of human and corporate affairs. But as with efforts to secure the unification of the domestic laws of nations, so in the case of the attempted harmonisation of private international law both intuition and experience indicate that the greatest prospect of short- or medium-term success is enjoyed by those projects pursued by a comparatively discrete group of countries amongst whom there already exists a relatively high degree of common interest, outlook and tradition.[5] Thus, numerous instances exist of bilateral treaties concluded in relation to such particular matters as the enforcement of foreign judgments,[6] while a far smaller number of multilateral treaties have been concluded between groups of countries possessing some kind of regional affinity.[7] On the whole, attempts at creating multilateral Conventions between countries drawn from several different regions of the world have met with uneven success so far. Some impressive results have emerged from the continuous work of the Hague Conference on private international law which now enjoys a membership in excess of thirty states, and whose Conventions are in fact open to accession by other states which have not as yet become members of the Conference. However, a survey of the patterns of signatures and ratifications of the twenty-six Hague Conventions so far opened for signature reveals at once the practical limitations to the universal acceptance of any Convention of even the narrowest scope and content: none of the Hague Conventions has yet been ratified by all of the Member States of the Conference, while some Conventions, despite their having been open for signature for several years, have as yet received no ratifications at all, or have received fewer than the requisite minimum of ratifications necessary to bring them into force. Again, it may be observed that none of the Member States of the Hague Conference has to date become a ratifying party to even as many as 50% of the Conventions which have been produced, and that several indeed have as yet failed to lodge ratification, or even become signatories, to even one Convention.[8] This is by no means intended to denigrate the achievements of the Hague Conference, merely to emphasise the extreme difficulty of the task upon which it is engaged, and to provide support for the assertion made above concerning the empirical advantages of regionally-based unification projects pursued by a relatively small number of participants. It is again noteworthy that the States which have individually attained the highest incidences of ratifications of the Hague Conference Conventions are predominantly the European nations which composed the original nucleus of membership of the organisation.[9]

In view of what has been said thus far it might well be argued that for the immediate future it is preferable, both tactically and in terms of the most productive employment of human and material resources, for the greater proportion of international effort to be expended in pursuit of the unification of private international law, at least in a regional context.[10] In theory, progress in this sphere should generally be easier to achieve than in the case of attempts to unify substantive law, in that the latter, *ex hypothesi*, necessitate the contemplation of change of an integral character, concerning legal rules which will apply to all parties in all circumstances. Rules of private international law, on the other hand, are by their very nature destined to affect only a small proportion of cases, namely those containing an international element, while leaving untouched the individual substantive rules of law of the participating states. Moreover, a great deal of common ground already exists at the level of principle in the realm of private international law: there is doctrinal consensus, for example, that every effort should be made to eliminate arbitrariness of result attributable solely to such possible variables as the *forum* chosen for litigation. Scholars as far apart both in time and in ideological standpoint as Savigny and the authors of the American Second Restatement are united at least in their aspiration to secure the basic objectives of "certainty, predictability and uniformity of result",[11] albeit divergences quickly appear when the respective theorists begin to elaborate their proposals for the rules and techniques whereby this common goal is to be attained. *Quot doctores, tot sententiae.* The unhurried course of free-ranging debate among academics is as unlikely to arrive at a unified conclusion in the foreseeable future as it has failed to do in the measurable past, and indeed the experience of recent decades has been to see the proliferation of diverse theories and methodologies, especially those of transatlantic origin, rather than the converse process of *rapprochement* and synthesis for which we are here arguing. Also, at the level of international negotiations for the purpose of concluding multilateral Conventions, as exemplified by the deliberations of the Hague Conference on private international law, or of the Member States of the Council of Europe, the final product often reflects the currently unbridgeable abyss which separates different national, or sometimes regional, traditions: [12] even where a consensus can be achieved among a majority of the participants, the probability remains that several of the States whose representatives helped formulate some hard-fought compromise will see fit to refrain from actually becoming parties to the Convention which embodies it, whilst those States for whom even the original compromise was unacceptable will, *a fortiori*, be disinclined to accede to the Convention. The fact that the States which participate in the work of the two organisations mentioned retain the ultimate freedom to choose whether or not to become ratifying parties to any Conventions which are concluded as a result of the negotiations in which they participate, is probably responsible for the disappointing statistics of accessions and ratifications to many Conventions, as mentioned above. At the same time, however, the arrangement has a certain practical justification in that it ensures that the negotiations need not become deadlocked indefinitely through the intransigence of parties whose legal traditions and institutions appear too difficult to reconcile with those of the members of any consensus which may be emerging. In sum, the results of efforts pursued in circumstances where States retain a complete final discretion whether or not to become bound by any Conventions emerging as the fruits of negotiations, while by no means inconsiderable, have to date been disappointingly uneven. It is not merely that, as already stated, many Conventions have yet to enter into force, but even those which have received the requisite minimum number of ratifications are in very many instances in force between only a minority of the members of the organisation under whose auspices they were negotiated. [13] It would appear, therefore, that the optimum conditions for the successful conduct of international negotiations for the harmonisation of areas of private international law, and for the expeditious carrying into force of Conventions resulting from those negotiations, are to be found when they are conducted among a comparatively small group of States, regionally proximate to each other and sharing to a high degree both a common heritage and a common contemporary outlook. The prospects for such success are further enhanced whenever there exists among these same States an established framework for continuous, multilateral co-operation, at governmental and other levels, as exemplified by the institutional arrangements which it is appropriate to create among the States participating in a free trade area or customs union.

The foregoing considerations perhaps serve to explain why, in the realm of conflict of laws and in particular in the context of efforts aimed at the harmonisation thereof, the foundation and development of the European Economic Community represents arguably the most significant development to have occurred during the present century. Although a variety of similar organisations have been established in several regions of the world during the latter part of the twentieth century,[14] it would be no exaggeration to assert that the EEC, which can already claim distinction as the original example and pattern for such regional ventures in post-War international co-operation by means of supra-national institutions, at the same time constitutes by far the most successful and accomplished example of the *genre* to have flourished to date. This is true both in a general sense,[15] and also in relation to our particular concern here, namely the conflict of laws. Not only has the Treaty of Rome,[16] together with its related Treaties,[17] given rise to a new, and in many ways unique, legal order which has added a totally new dimension to the operation of conflict of laws, but also those self same Treaties and that self same legal order, contain the requisite ingredients for bringing about a progressive transformation, and the ultimate harmonisation, of the greater part of the private international law of the Member States of the European Communities. This book attempts to deal with these related themes, and to show how the satisfactory solution to the age-old problems of reconciliation and harmonisation of laws, including the rules of private international law, is indeed integral to the very conception and purpose of the Common Market which lies at the centre of the Community legal order. It will, however, be a matter of insistence throughout this present work that the processes of legal unification and harmonisation taking place within the European Communities do not, and cannot, take place *in vacuo*, but must be perceived and appraised in the context of a wider, global framework of legal diversity, both on the plane of municipal law and also on that of private international law. Whatever the short-term, and immediate, benefits accruing locally within the Member States of the European Communities in consequence of harmonising developments occurring simultaneously within their substantive and conflicts law, the outer world and its unresolved legal problems remain matters of very real moment. It is submitted that the ultimate interests of neither side are best served by the consolidation of the laws of the European region in a manner and form which almost provocatively ignores, not only the present, legitimate claims and interests of the legal systems of third States to enjoy parity of status and effect at all stages of the conflicts process, but also the need to create possibilities for future reconciliation between the currently-entrenched positions of the various legal "families" and traditions to be encountered in the world today, a problem to which reference has already been made above.[18] What is here advocated, therefore, is an attitude of permanently-raised consciousness among the participants in the European, and indeed in any other regionally-based programme of legal integration, so that they maintain a sensitivity to the external implications of developments taking place internally within the organisation or Community to which they belong, and furthermore make every effort to create and encourage, rather than to suppress or discourage, opportunities for enhancing progress towards inter-regional legal harmony.

3. The European Communities and Legal Unification

The European Communities comprise at present three distinct, Treaty-based international organisations administered, since 1967, through a unified institutional structure. [19] While the EEC Treaty, being by far the broadest of the three in scope and objectives, constitutes the main vehicle for legal, economic, social and political integration among the Member States, the role of the other two Communities, which are each specialist organisations dealing with what are in reality functionally discrete sectors of activity, should not altogether escape our notice. Although the three Treaties differ from one another in numerous ways by virtue of the different subject matters to which they respectively relate, and also, as between the Treaty establishing the European Coal and Steel Community and the two Rome Treaties, in certain important respects touching the powers and functions of the Community Institutions themselves, it is nevertheless possible to affirm the existence of a common core of elements which confer a sense of unity of character upon the three Communities, and also lend validity to certain generalised statements referring simultaneously to all three. The source of these common elements is to be found in the expressions both of motivation and aspiration which are contained in the Preambles to, and the initial few Articles of, each of the founding Treaties. [20] There on the one hand, the original signatories commemorated their appreciation that the resolution of age-old rivalries and periodical conflicts among the nations of Europe could be attained only through constructive collaboration in organised ventures with an avowedly integrationist purpose, while, on the other hand, they placed on record their expectations and intentions that, by means of the Communities and Institutions which they were bringing into existence, further concrete and positive advantages would ensue for all the Member States and their populations in the form of enhanced living and working conditions, greater and more uniformly-distributed prosperity, and the eventual approach to union among the peoples of Europe through the elimination of all divisive barriers to the economic, social and political progress of the participating countries. The principles and objectives consequently specified for each of the three Communities [21] accordingly constitute the outline for a functional approach to European unity, embarked upon by States whose respresentatives discerned and attested to a sense of solidarity and shared destiny among the constituent States of Europe. [22] However, and most significantly, no specific expression was inserted at any point in the texts of any of the Treaties to indicate the precise nature, particularly in political and constitutional terms, of the eventual "unity" which the Treaties were calculated to bring about. The reticence, not to say ambiguousness, with regard to the final, ulterior objective underlying the entire venture undoubtedly reflects an admixture of prudence and *dissensus* on behalf of those involved at the time, but with the passing years, which have been accompanied by great changes in national, regional and global affairs and fortunes at every level, the possibility of attaining Community-wide unanimity concerning the *terminus ad quem* has appeared to grow increasingly remote. [23] Despite this, the language of the Treaties remains sufficiently open and permissive to provide legal justification for the continued pursuit of integrationist programmes in many areas, including that of the law itself, both along lines actually specified or authorised by explicit Treaty provisions and also in accordance with policies which, if not expressly sanctioned by any particular Article of one of the Treaties, may be seen to be implicitly sanctioned by reason of their constituting a necessary prerequisite, or sometimes even an incidental complement, to the accomplishment of any of the objectives for which the Communities were established. [24] Legal unification in the context of the European Communities therefore derives its impetus from a plurality of factors and considerations. In the first place, it is frequently to be seen as the necessary counterpart to some Community policy which, although ostensibly non-legal in character, depends for its proper implementation upon the substitution of a unified law throughout all the Member States. [25] Secondly, in areas of a more clearly legal character, the unification of the national laws of the Member States may be expressly required by the provisions of one of the Treaties, as in the case of many matters connected with the right of persons to move freely and to take employment throughout the Community, or with the right of establishment or the freedom to provide services. [26] But in a third, and more general way, the unification and harmonisation of the M n-ber States' laws may be seen as an instrument whereby the larger, ultimate objective of European union is to be achieved. The traditional nexus between individual, state autonomy and a distinct and in many ways idiosyncratic legal system belonging to that State, provides a point of attack for those intent upon progressively weakening the identity and powers of the State while correspondingly strengthening those of the Community: to the extent that legal distinctions of every kind can be eliminated as between the Member States of the Community, a distinctive feature of statehood — and indeed a very important buttress of the State itself — can be made to disappear. [27] Increasingly it will be tempting to regard the Community as a jurisdictional unity, as a single legal entity, rather than as ten separate but associated forensic units. When, eventually, the Community reaches a stage where it functions as a single legal unit, or at least as a federalised legal system, the psychological and material foundations for political unity will be well and truly laid. Hence, it is in accordance with the integrationist philosophy with which they are imbued that at numerous points the Treaties contain provisions to facilitate, and even to require as a matter of obligation, the progressive unification of the laws of the Member States. Such unification may be brought about by direct means through Community regulations which, as will shortly be explained, [28] have the special characteristic of assuming the force of law in all Member States immediately upon their enactment, a characteristic which is technically termed "direct applicability". [29] In addition, the Treaties make provision for legal unification to be pursued by indirect means either by means of directives [30] or by other processes, including Conventions concluded among the Member States. [31] In the case of such indirect modes of bringing about unification of laws, the Treaties speak variously of the "approximation", the "co-ordination" or the "harmonisation" of the domestic laws or administrative rules of the Member States, using these terms almost interchangeably. [32] In many instances, these provisions are included within particular sections or chapters of the Treaties dealing with specific matters of Community policy, and are so expressed as to indicate that the harmonising measures in question are intended to be complementary to the policy with which they are associated. [33] In addition, however, the Treaty establishing the European Economic Community bestows a more concrete embodiment upon the general, philosophical attitude to the process of legal unification *per se*, first by including it specifically among the activities of the Community listed in A. 3, and secondly by devoting a separate chapter to the matter under the title of "Approximation of Laws". [34] In each instance, the Treaty employs limitative modes of expression to confine the harmonisation measures thus sanctioned to such as are necessary for the proper functioning of the Common Market. Thus, A. 3(h) speaks of "the approximation of the laws of Member States *to the extent required for the proper functioning of the Common Market*", while A. 100 empowers the Council, acting unanimously on a proposal from the Commission to "issue directives for the approximation of such provisions laid down by law, regulation or administrative action in Member States as *directly affect the establishment or functioning of the Common Market"* (emphasis added in each case). Likewise in the even wider provisions of A. 235 of the EEC Treaty,[35] authorising the Community to assume powers to fill any *lacuna* in the Treaty itself, words of apparent restriction are included to the effect that the action for which the Community seeks to create enabling powers must be *"necessary* to attain, in the course of the operation of the Common Market, *one of the objectives of the Community"* (emphasis again added). Since, as has already been noted, the Treaties maintain a discreet silence in matters of detail concerning the ulterior goal or goals of the Communities, and the exact form which these are to take, the language used in all three of the provisions just quoted effectively leaves a generous margin for flexibility of interpretation in practice. Moreover, the notions of "necessity" and "extent required" must, in the final analysis, be matters of subjective evaluation on the part of those empowered to take the relevant measures. Thus, the rate of progress, and to a not inconsiderable extent the form and substance also, of Community-inspired development in the area of harmonisation of the laws of the Member States may be said to depend upon a complex interaction of the perceptions, attitudes and intentions of the various parties involved, chief among whom are the Commission of the European Communities, which has the responsibility for initiating the proposals necessary to "trigger" the harmonisation process, and the Governments of the Member States acting through their representatives in the Council of Ministers, which is the body formally empowered to transform the Commission's proposals into measures carrying the force of law.[36] Despite many vicissitudes and even crises which have beset the Community at various periods since its inception,[37] the process of legal unification has been maintained across virtually the entire spectrum of operation of the Community Treaties, albeit with varying intensity and completeness as between the different sectors thereof.

4. Harmonisation of Private International Law within the European Communities

By far the greater part of the Community's achievements in legal harmonisation have been in the realm of municipal law, the area which, theoretically at least, is the more difficult to harmonise, even on an exclusively regional basis, because of the profound consequences which changes in their substantive law may entail for the States involved and also because of the need for all concerned to review meticulously the implications of any change in one aspect of the law for every related aspect of their domestic legal system. But even a finally-accomplished harmonisation of the rules of substantive law of the Member States would leave the Communities still short of their necessary goal, legally speaking. For the rational and orderly functioning of the Common Market, free from every vestige of distortion-producing elements, would require the putting into effect of logically-devised, standardised rules for the assumption of jurisdiction by local courts throughout the Community in respect of every species of legal action or proceeding falling within the Communities' widely-drawn realm of competence. Such jurisdictional arrangements would need to be complemented by further arrangements which would ensure that the judgments or orders emanating from Community courts of competent jurisdiction received "full faith and credit" through being recognised and enforced everywhere throughout the Community, by means of whatever court, tribunal or officer may prove appropriate in the circumstances. Furthermore, the final completion of the optimum legal organisation of the European Communities would be brought about only by the introduction of unified rules for choice of law, and standardised procedures and approaches in all matters relating to conflict of laws, [38] to be applied by all courts throughout the Community. Thus, all aspects of the conflicts process — namely rules governing respectively the assumption of jurisdiction, the choice of law, and the recognition and enforcement of "foreign" judgments, including those of sister courts — may be said to be within the compass of the long-term programme of legal unification to be carried out in fulfilment of the objectives of the European Communities. Given the initial premises on which the Communities were established, the inevitability of these conclusions seems inescapable. The underlying logic was once succinctly expressed by Dr. H.C. Ficker, speaking in the context of the harmonization of the company laws of the Member States, in the following terms:

"Differences in the Member States' legislative and administrative provisions affect the establishment or functioning of the Common Market. They hamper the free circulation of goods, persons and capital, provoke distortion in competition making unequal the burdens on the competing national industries and are, therefore, obstacles for the development of the Common Market *to the same extent* as the maintenance of tariff borders or of different national policies in the various economic fields. Therefore, these differences have to be abolished". [39]

Such arguments are equally applicable to each and every aspect of the conflict of laws: to the extent that differences exist between the rules and practices prevalent in the respective Member States with regard to the assumption of jurisdiction, or once jurisdiction has been assumed, with regard to the choice of the applicable law, infinite possibilities arise for variations in the outcome of cases which are in principle similar, or even virtually identical, to each other, depending exclusively upon which of the Member States happens to become the *forum* for litigation. Such a situation is undoubtedly one in which "distortion" is operative, in the sense employed by Community law, both because the incidence of such disparities runs counter to the basic principle of unity and uniformity which is required to prevail in favour of all persons across the Community,[40] and also because it will tend to create, in relation to each category of legal matter or proceeding, a "hierarchy of preference" among those parties who are at liberty to select, or even to pre-select, the eventual *forum* for litigation of any disputes and who will contrive to arrange matters to their personal advantage, which may well coincide with a material disadvantage inflicted upon the other party or parties. That such "business" should be thus artificially attracted to attach itself to the legal system, if not also the courts, of any one Member State in preference to those of its partners would be generally, and rightly, deplored: the availability of any such "haven of convenience" cannot be reconciled with the notions of open and fair competition, and of equality of conditions and opportunities for competing, which represent the fundamental precepts upon which the Common Market is established. So, too, in the matter of the recognition and enforcement of judgments throughout the Community. It would be plainly intolerable if uneven conditions prevailed in this area, so that, for example, a judgment creditor seeking to enforce the judgment of a court of Member State A in Member State B (where the judgment debtor's assets may happen to be concentrated) were to experience far greater difficulty and expense than his counterpart who seeks to enforce in State A, or for that matter in State C, a judgment of a court of State B. To the extent that Member State B by virtue of its practice in relation to the enforcement of foreign judgments represents a "haven" for judgment debtors within the Community, the conditions for free play of rights and remedies throughout the Common Market undergo distortion. An incidental, but probable, consequence of the existence of such a "judgments haven" would be that assets would come to be deliberately situated there for no other reason than to render them less amenable to execution: the so-called "Delaware Syndrome", familiar to American company law has, after all, its counterparts in many other compartments of the law.[41] Once again, any such situation may be characterised as one of "distortion" according to the criteria by which the European Communities are governed.

To sum up, it may be fairly claimed that the terms and objectives on and for which the European Communities were created not merely facilitate, but actually necessitate the continuous promotion of legal unification among the Member States, with regard both to their municipal and their private international law. In the case of the latter, unification is to be seen not solely in terms of a *pis aller*, to be resorted to whenever some intractable difficulty appears to preclude all hope of achieving consensus on harmonisation of the Member States' substantive laws, but indeed as a major end in its own right whose accomplishment is logically and functionally complementary to the unification of municipal law. To a certain extent the draftsmen of the Treaty establishing the EEC anticipated the need for harmonisation of private international law by the Member States in the course of fulfilling the objectives of the Treaty, and in A. 220 they made provision for the unification of certain aspects by means of negotiated Conventions to become a matter of obligation for the Member States. A. 220 provides as follows:

"Member States shall, so far as is necessary, enter into negotiations with each other with a view to securing for the benefit of their nationals:
— the protection of persons and the enjoyment and protection of rights under the same conditions as those accorded by each State to its own nationals;
— the abolition of double taxation within the Community;
— the mutual recognition of companies or firms within the meaning of the second paragraph of Article 58, the retention of legal personality in the event of transfer of their seat from one country to another, and the possibility of mergers between companies or firms governed by the laws of different countries;
— the simplification of formalities governing the reciprocal recognition and enforcement of judgments of courts or tribunals and of arbitration awards."

In Part II of this book the Conventions which have so far emerged, in concluded or in draft form, pursuant to A. 220, will be examined in detail. For the purposes of Part I, however, it is necessary to emphasise that the provisions of A. 220 in themselves are determinative neither of the permissible limits within which unifying developments in the realm of private international law may take place in fulfilment of the objectives of the Community, nor of the possible or appropriate modes by which such developments may be accomplished. While Conventions concluded between Member States, aided and encouraged in their negotiations by the Commission and other Community Institutions, may furnish a suitable means for achieving significant advances in harmonisation of areas of law in which the Member States frequently start from positions of considerable remoteness from one another, they also suffer from numerous disadvantages. Chief among these are the extreme ponderousness of the negotiations themselves, an aspect which has tended to become more pronounced as the membership of the Communities

has grown. Furthermore the atmosphere of confidentiality which traditionally surrounds inter-governmental negotiations has tended to permeate the
proceedings concerned with the formulation of the Community Conventions
under A. 220 and this has often hindered the prospects for submitting the
evolving draft proposals to suitably rigorous criticism and comment by a
sufficiently wide community of interested and informed persons and bodies.
Lastly, the relatively reduced role and status of the Community Institutions
(principally the Commission) in such negotiations can have unfortunate consequences, in that the maintenance of a "balanced" and *"communautaire"*
approach to the problems of unification, and the simultaneous need to strive
to secure the best possible provision in functional terms, may be lost sight of
whenever the course of negotiations is allowed to be influenced by considerations of *Realpolitik*, or of national or governmental *amour propre*. Another important consideration, requiring a high degree of skill in co-ordination, is the need to ensure that the developments in harmonisation of private
international law are fully compatible with the simultaneous or pending
developments in harmonisation of substantive law, and vice versa. For these
reasons perhaps, among others, the resultant products of the programme
being followed pursuant to A. 220 are in certain respects flawed and unsatisfactory, and it is probable that alternative modes of harmonisation of private
international law by means of Regulations or Directives may be favoured
increasingly in the future. [42]

5. Parallelism

Whatever the means by which harmonisation is ultimately introduced into
the rules of private international law employed by the Member States of the
EEC, *inter se*, there will remain the question of the rules which are to be
applied by them in cases which either do not fall into the proper realm of
the Community at all, or do so only in part. A further problem concerns
those cases in which only some, or even none, of the parties, or of the
material elements of the case, are linked with the Community, albeit the
subject-matter itself notionally falls within the area in which the Treaties are
operative. In such circumstances, it is possible to envisage the Member
States' legal systems operating several sets of parallel rules of private international law, to be employed according to the exact circumstances of any case:
a unified Community rule would perforce regulate any case falling exclusively within the realm of Community law *ratione personae*, and *ratione materiae*, but some other (and perhaps unharmonised) rule might be employed

where the subject-matter lay outside the ambit of the Treaties,[43] or where the connecting factors in the case were exclusively associated with extra-Community jurisdictions. However, yet a further set of rules (harmonised or otherwise) might be needed to deal with cases of a hybrid character, either in terms of their subject matter or in terms of their associations by virtue of relevant connecting factors. Some of the implications of the emergent phenomenon of parallel systems of conflicts rules will be reviewed and considered in the final chapter of Part I;[44] in the preceding chapter we shall explore the types of legal conflicts which are capable of arising by virtue of the fact that the creation of the European Communities brought into existence a new and independently-established legal system ("the Community legal order") which therefore lays claim to participate in the various events and processes which contrive to give rise to "conflicts" of laws. From the foregoing discussion in this chapter regarding the nature and purposes of the European Communities, we have already obtained some intimation of the fact that the Community legal order, like the Community to which it belongs, is nothing if not out-of-the-ordinary. We must therefore prepare ourselves for some un-common encounters in the course of examining the provisions and implications of Community law in the realm of conflict of laws, both as contained in and applied to Community law itself, and as imposed upon or insinuated into the laws, practices and policies of the Member States.

NOTES

1. This idea was memorably expressed to the author by the late Professor Sir Otto Kahn-Freund.
2. See, for example, the expositions of the basic problems of private international law in Dicey and Morris, The Conflict of Laws (10th edn. 1980), ch. 1; E. Rabel, The Conflict of Laws, a Comparative Study (2nd edn. 1958—60); O. Kahn-Freund, General Problems of Private International Law (1974, III) 143 Hague Rec. des Cours 147 (reprinted separately, 1976); A.A. Ehrenzweig, Specific Principles of Private International Law (1968, II) 124 Hague Rec. des Cours 179.
3. Besides the work being done within the European Community, important contributions to the unification of private and commercial law are being made by, *inter alia*, the Council of Europe; the International Institute for the Unification of Private Law (UNIDROIT); the United Nations Commission on International Trade Law (UNCITRAL); the Hague Conference on Private International Law; and the Commission International de L'Etat Civil. For a detailed survey of the work and achievements of these bodies, see R. David, *The International Unification of Private Law*, in International Encyclopaedia of Comparative Law (1969), vol. 2, ch. 5, esp. part II.
4. See the published documentation relating to the achievements of the organisations

mentioned in note 3 *supra*. Collected Conventions and Agreements (European Treaty Series), 1971-   ; the Collected Conventions and Papers of UNIDROIT appeared in four volumes between 1948 and 1956 as Unification of Law, followed thereafter by annual Yearbooks; see also the Collected Conventions and Recommendations of the Commission International (Frankfurt, 1972).

5. *cf*. David, *op. cit. supra* n. 3, at p. 142.

6. For details of such treaties see, for example, M. Weser, Convention Communautaire sur la compétence judiciaire et l'exécution des décisions (Brussels, 1975); Nadelmann (1967) 67 Col. L. Rev. 995, also published in Conflict of Laws, International and Interstate (1972) at p. 238.

7. The most notable examples to date are the Montevideo Treaties of 1889; the Havana Treaty of 1928 (Codigo Bustamante); the Scandinavian Convention of 1931–1953; the Benelux Convention of 1951, revised 1966 and 1969. For more detailed survey and comment, see E. Rabel, the Conflict of Laws, a Comparative Study, vol. 1 (2nd edn. 1958) at pp. 29–46; E. Vitta, International Conventions and National Conflicts Systems (1969, I) 126 Hague Rec. des Cours 113, at 133 *et seq*.; O. Kahn-Freund, General Problems of Private International Law (1974, III) 143 Hague Rec. des Cours 147 (reprinted separately 1976), ch. II, esp. pp. 187–196 (= pp. 41–50); A.N. Makarov, Sources of Private International Law (1970) Int. Encyc. Comp. Law, vol. III, ch. 2. For texts of the aforementioned treaties, and comments, see (1943) 37 A.J.I.L. Supp. 149 (Montevideo Treaties); 86 L.N.T.S. at 120 and 254 (Codigo Bustamante); 139 L.N.T.S. 181, and Philip (1959, I) 96 Hague Rec. des Cours 241 (Scandinavian Conventions); (1952) 1 I.C.L.Q. 426; Meijers (1953) 2 A.J.C.L. 1; Nadelmann (1970) 18 A.J.C.L. 406 (Benelux Convention).

8. *cf*. M. Soumampouw, Les Nouvelles Conventions de la Haye (1976) at p. 299 *et. seq*.: "Situation actuelle".

9. *viz*. Netherlands (14 Ratifications; 5 Signatures), France (15R; 2S), Portugal (10R; 6S), Belgium (10R; 4S), Luxembourg (8R; 9S), Germany (8R; 2S), Austria (8R; 2S), Switzerland (11R; 1S), Norway (9R; 1S), Finland (7R; 3S), United Kingdom (7R; 1S), Italy (6R; 8S), Sweden (8R), Denmark (7R).

10. *cf*. Drobnig (1967) 15 A.J.C.L. 204, 229: "The ultimate superiority of a uniform substantive rule has to be balanced off against the greater price in terms of time and effort necessary for its development". For a more recent statement of his views by the same author, see his contribution to The Influence of the European Communities upon Private International Law of Member States, ed. by P. Bourel and others (Brussels, 1981) at pp. 1–12.

11. *cf*. Savigny, System des heutigen Römischen Rechts (1848), vol. 8, transl. Guthrie (1869, 2nd edn. 1880), esp. at pp. 68, 133 and 139–47; and A.L.I. Restatement of the Law, Second, Conflict of Laws, § 6(2)(f).

12. One most striking illustration is furnished by the various approaches to the long-standing problem of the rival allegiances to "nationality" and "domicil" as a basic connecting factor in establishing the applicable law for a variety of purposes, and even for the purpose of founding judicial jurisdiction. Thus, the Hague Convention of 15 June 1955 to regulate conflicts between national and domiciliary law has to date attracted but 2 Ratifications, plus a further 3 Signatures, while earlier attempts to devise a reconciliation between these two, fundamentally opposed traditions were even less successful. One might also instance the failure of the early Hague Conventions on aspects of family law and personal status (produced between 1893 and 1905) to command wide or continuing acceptance due principally to the use of the "nationality" principle. The 5th and 6th Sessions (in 1925 and 1928) actually failed to conclude any conventions at all. See Vitta, *op. cit. supra* n. 7, at pp. 133–44, and also De Winter (1969, III) 128 Hague Rec. des Cours 357,

esp. at 419—23. In more recent times, the use of the compromise concept of "habitual residence" has at least enabled the two traditions to achieve a *modus vivendi*.

13. The Conventions of the Hague Conference are here primarily in contemplation, but the statement is also true to a considerable extent in relation to the Conventions of the Council of Europe. Some notable exceptions in each case include the Hague Convention of 1 March 1954 on Civil Procedure (15 Ratifications; 12 Adhesions); the Convention of 24 October 1956 on the Law Applicable to Maintenance Obligations towards Children (12 Ratifications; 2 Signatures; 1 Adhesion); the Convention of 15 April 1958 on the Recognition and Enforcement of Decisions Concerning Maintenance Obligations towards Children (14 Ratifications; 2 Signatures; 4 Adhesions); the Convention of 5 October 1961 on the Conflict of Laws relating to the Form of Testamentary Dispositions (13 Ratifications; 5 Signatures; 9 Adhesions); and the Convention of 15 November 1965 on the Service Abroad of Judicial and Extra-Judicial Documents in Civil and Commercial Matters (16 Ratifications; 2 Signatures; 4 Adhesions). Of the Conventions produced by the Council of Europe, undoubtedly the most successful has been the European Convention on Human Rights of 4 November 1950, ratified now by all 21 Member States of the Council of Europe. For further discussion of the problems of non-ratification, see David, *op. cit. supra* n. 3, at pp. 147—48.

14. For developments in Latin America and the Caribbean, see Griffin and Ffrench-Davis (1965) 4 J.C.M.S. 1; Schmitter (1971) 9 J.C.M.S. 1; Wionczek, *ibid.* at p. 49; Avery and Cochrane (1972) 11 J.C.M.S. 85; Hall and Blake (1978) 16 J.C.M.S. 211; Payne (1981) 19 J.C.M.S. 255. For developments in Africa and the Arab world, see Diab (1965) 4 J.C.M.S. 238.

15. For surveys of the achievements of the European Communities, both in comparative and in absolute terms, see W. Feld, The European Common Market and the World (1967); E.B. Haas, The Uniting of Europe (1958); W. Hallstein, United Europe (1962).

16. This is the expression popularly, and traditionally, applied to the Treaty Establishing the European Economic Community, originally signed in Rome on 25 March 1957 (herein referred to as ECT).

17. The other principal Treaties include the Treaty Establishing the European Coal and Steel Community, originally signed in Paris on 18 April 1951 (herein referred to as CST), and the Treaty Establishing the European Atomic Energy Community (EURATOM), originally signed in Rome on 25 March 1957 (herein referred to as EAET). The three Communities established by the Paris Treaty together with the two Rome Treaties are herein collectively referred to as "the European Communities" or, for the sake of convenience, as "the Community". The principal amendments to the three basic Treaties include the two Accession Treaties, of 22 January 1972 and 28 May 1979, respectively, whereby, in all, four new Member States (Republic of Ireland, Denmark, United Kingdom and Greece) joined the original six Members (Belgium, France, Germany, Holland, Italy and Luxembourg).

18. *supra* at p. 4.

19. The Treaty Establishing a Single Council and a Single Commission of the European Communities (generally referred to as the Merger Treaty) was signed in Brussels on 8 April 1965, and came into force on 1 July 1967. The creation of a unified Court of Justice, Assembly and Economic and Social Committee was earlier accomplished by the Convention on Certain Institutions Common to the European Communities, signed in Rome on 25 March 1957.

20. See CST: Preambles and Arts. 1—6 inclusive; ECT: Preambles and Arts. 1—8 inclusive; EAET: Preambles and Arts. 1—3 inclusive.

21. See CST Arts. 2, 3; ECT, Arts. 2, 3; EAET Arts. 1, 2.

22. *cf.* the following statement by A. Spinelli, formerly a member of the Commis-

sion: "Customs unification is not the objective for which the Community exists but an instrument for achieving certain other goals ... . The objective which the various governments set themselves is that of unifying their peoples' destinies, giving them a prospect of solidarity, of integration, of interdependence and of belonging, different from that which existed in the past ... and in order to move in this direction it was considered important to begin the Common Market with the customs union" – Brussels Conference, December 1977, "Customs Union today and tomorrow", E.C. Doc. CB-24-78-047-EN-C.

23.   A comprehensive survey of this subject, and of the vast literature devoted to it, would transcend the objectives of the present book. However, lawyers will find much of interest in E.B. Haas, The Uniting of Europe (London 1958, revised edn. Stanford, Calif. 1968); W. Hallstein (transl. C. Roetter), Europe in the Making (London, 1972); M. Camps, Britain and the European Community 1955–1963 (Princeton U.P., 1964), esp. chs. 1–3; H.A. Schmitt, The Path to European Union (L.S.U. Press, Baton Rouge, 1962); D. Marquand, Parliament for Europe (London, 1979); A. Schonfield, Europe: Journey to an Unknown Destination (London, 1973). For consideration of the functional and teleological approaches employed by the European Court of Justice in interpreting the Treaties, see H. Kutscher, Methods of Interpretation as seen by a judge at the Court of Justice (Judicial and Academic Conference, 1976) (Luxembourg, 1976); A. Bredimas, Methods of Interpretation and Community Law (Amsterdam, North-Holland, 1978), esp. pt. II, chs. II and III.

24.   See especially A. 235 ECT (= A. 203 EAET), the so-called "bootstrap" provisions of the Rome Treaties. A. 95 CST is somewhat less ample in its terms and scope.

25.   For example, under the Common Transport Policy (ECT Pt. 2, Title IV), and in particular measures adopted pursuant to A. 75. See, for example, Reg. 543/69 (O.J. 1969, L 77/49); Reg. 1463/70 (O.J. 1970, L 164/1); Reg. 2828/77 (O.J. 1977, L 334/5), concerning, *inter alia*, the harmonisation of provisions relating to control devices ("tachygraphs"), considered in Case 128/78, *Commission* v. *United Kingdom* [1979] E.C.R. 419, [1979] 2 CMLR 45. The Community secondary legislation relating to transport is collected in Encyclopaedia E.C. Law, vol. C, part C.16.

26.   See ECT, Arts. 48(2), 49 and 51; 52, 54, 56 and 57; 59, 63, 65 and 66.

27.   It follows that those who, conversely, wish to promote a revival of the identity of state- or nationhood, or some other species of autonomy, within a region which has been subsumed within a larger national unit, will logically seek to revitalise the distinctive characteristics of a separate legal system which at one time may have flourished there. The example of Scotland in recent years is a case in point.

28.   See Chapter 2, *post*, p. 29.

29.   See A. 189 ECT; A. 161 EAET. The counterpart of a Regulation under the CST is the General Decision: see A. 14 CST.

30.   See A. 189 ECT; A. 161 EAET for the technical definition of "Directive". The counterpart of a Directive under the CST is a Recommendation: see A. 14 CST.

31.   A. 220 ECT. See Chapter 2, *post*, p. 49, and Part II of this book *passim*.

32.   See ECT, Arts. 3(h), 6(1), 27, 40(2)(b), 54(3)(g), 56(2), 57(2), (3), 66, 70(1), 99, 100(1), 105(1), 111(1), 112(1), 117, paras 1 and 2. For a review of attempts to attribute a specific meaning to each of the terms used, see Van Ommeslaghe (1969) Cah. Dr. Eur. 495 at 513–16, esp. footnotes 39 and 40.

33.   *cf*. ECT, Arts. 27 (customs); 40(2)(b) (agriculture); 54(3)(g) (companies or firms); 56(2), 57(2), (3) and 66 (rights of establishment and of provision of services); 70(1) (free movement of capital); 99 (taxation); 105(1) (balance of payments); 111(1), 112(1) (commercial policy); and 117 (social policy).

34.   ECT, A. 3(h) together with Pt. 3, Title I, Ch. 3 (Arts. 100–102). See generally Pipkorn in The Influence of the European Communities upon Private International Law

of the Member States, ed. by P. Bourel and others (Brussels, 1981) at pp. 13—46, and the Bibliography contained *ibid.* at pp. 47—48.

35. Mentioned *supra*, n. 24.

36. See, respectively, A. 100(1) and A. 235 ECT.

37. Notably the crisis of 1965—66, during the period of the French boycott of the sessions of Community Institutions, which resulted in the conclusion of the "Luxembourg Accords" of 28 and 29 January 1966 (E.C. Bull. 1966, no. 3, at pp. 9, 10). Subsequent adherence to these Accords on the part of the Council of Ministers has effectively caused the indefinite suspension of the Treaty rules providing for the enactment of community legislation by means of majority voting (see ECT, A. 148; EAET, A. 118; CST, A. 28) whenever the Government of any of the Member States chooses to declare the matter in hand to be one affecting "very important interests" of the State concerned.

38. It is here envisaged that procedural rules, and also such fundamentally important matters of forensic technique as characterisation, would perforce require to undergo harmonisation.

39. "The E.E.C. Directives on Company Law Harmonisation", in C. Schmitthof (Ed.), Harmonisation of European Company Law (London, 1973), at p. 66 (emphasis added).

40. See esp. ECT, Arts. 3(h), 5 and 7.

41. A "neutral" illustration may be taken by referring the reader to the case of Switzerland: numerous considerations of a legal, as well as of a purely monetary or financial, character clearly underly the widespread use made of that country as a "haven" for the deposit of valuable assets. Foremost among the legal considerations which influence such depositors, both individual and corporate, in their choice are strict rules of Swiss law concerning confidentiality in matters between Swiss banks and their clients, whether domestic or foreign.

42. For one example of the use of Directives to accomplish the harmonisation of rules of private international law, alongside related rules of substantive law, see the Directives on Life and Non-life Insurance Services, O.J. 1979, L 63 (Dir. 79/267 EEC) and O.J. 1973, L 228/3 (Dir. 73/239 EEC). See also the report of the English and Scottish Law Commissions on the choice of law rules contained in the Draft Second Directive on Non-life Insurance.

43. The recognition of foreign divorces and legal separations might suggest itself as an example of a matter falling outside the ambit of the Treaties. See, however, the argument to the contrary, *post* Chapter 2, p. 46.

44. Chapter 3, *post*.

New Dimensions in the Conflict of Laws: The Nature and Significance of the Community Legal Order

In this chapter it is proposed to consider the special nature and characteristics of the Community legal order, and its implications from the standpoint of conflict of laws. It will be argued·that three varieties of conflicts may be identified, namely those of a special type arising between the national and the Community legal order in which the latter system is perforce required to prevail; conflicts between the laws of the Member States; and conflicts occurring between the Community legal order and the general body of legal systems of the world, whether members of the Community or not. The three types of conflict will be considered in turn.

1. Conflicts between the National Legal Order and that of the Community. The Evolution of the Community Legal Order

The Paris Treaty of 1951, establishing the European Coal and Steel Community, makes provisions for the creation, along with other Community institutions, of a Court of Justice,[1] whose role and function are laconically described in A. 31 of the Treaty in the following terms:

"The Court shall ensure that in the interpretation and application of this Treaty, and of rules laid down for the implementation thereof, *the law is observed*" (emphasis added).

Each of the two Rome Treaties of 1957 likewise establishes a Court of Justice,[2] whose purposes are summarised even more succinctly, but in terms effectively corresponding to those contained in the Paris Treaty, by means of identically worded Articles, as follows:

"The Court of Justice shall ensure that in the interpretation and application of this Treaty the law is observed."[3]

The task of discovering and expounding the meaning to be ascribed to these key provisions of the three founding Treaties has been pursued by the Court itself which, thanks to the rational arrangement introduced by the Convention on Certain Community Institutions Common to the European Communities,[4] is constituted as a single entity invested with the jurisdiction and duties separately conferred by the provisions of each of the three respective Treaties upon the Court of Justice for which its terms make provision. Thereby, a continuity and consistency has been achieved in the realm of judicial regulation of the three Communities, so that despite the presence of certain significant differences between the legally important provisions of the earlier Treaty and the later two,[5] a general picture of the Court's role and function can be formed using elements of decisions taken at various times under the provisions of all three Treaties, or under the secondary legislation derived from them. Indeed, the character assumed by the Court of Justice in its first period of existence from 1953 to 1957,[5a] when it constituted the Court of Justice of the Coal and Steel Community alone, has proved to be a crucial one for several reasons. First, the radical nature of the powers conferred under the terms of the Coal and Steel Treaty upon the institutions of that Community, and upon the High Authority in particular, so transcended the limits of previous experience and practice in the field of international institutions as to furnish the immediate basis for a reappraisal of the fundamental assumptions upon which international treaty law had formerly been based. In particular, the "classical doctrine" whereby no international treaty could enjoy the force of law *proprio vigore* within the domestic legal order of the high contracting parties was necessarily called into question. It was manifestly the case that the high contracting parties to the Paris Treaty had conferred upon the High Authority, acting either alone or in conjunction with the Council of Ministers, the capacity and power to operate in an autonomous manner in administering the provisions of the Treaty and in implementing the policies and programmes formulated thereunder. Nor could it be doubted that those acts of the High Authority which were issued in the form of general decisions, within the meaning of A. 14 CST, enjoyed throughout the Community a force as law which could not be questioned in or challenged by proceedings in the national courts of the Member States: under the Treaty, sole jurisdiction to review or to rule upon the validity of acts of the Community Institutions was strictly reserved to the Court of Justice (Arts. 33, 38 and 41 CST). Moreover, under the Paris

Treaty the power enjoyed by the High Authority to issue instructions or orders of a legally binding character was plainly made exercisable not merely *vis-à-vis* the Member States of the Community but also, in a direct manner, *vis-à-vis* industrial enterprises engaged in the production and marketing of coal and steel [6] These latter were unquestionably the creatures of, and subject to, domestic law of some Member State or other, and yet at the same time it was clearly the case that the Communities' legal acts were capable of reaching them in a direct way which, under "orthodox" theories of international law, should not have been possible. This state of affairs was sufficiently exceptional to induce writers and analysts to employ, if not actually to coin for the first time, the special term "supranational" to designate the exceptional character of the Community as an institution possessed of a legal personality and capacity able, within its sphere of competence, actually to override the legislative and executive powers of the individual Member States, and to penetrate the domestic legal order of each one of them so as to exert a dominant force upon certain of the legal rights of their subjects.[7] In practice, the subject-matter of cases brought before the Court of Justice under the Coal and Steel Treaty, both during the early, formative period and also since the Rome Treaties additionally came into force, has tended to be concentrated in the realm of "administrative law" proceedings in which the High Authority has been the defendant in actions brought either by Member States or by industrial undertakings to secure the annulment of Community acts alleged to be in violation of the law. This pattern is undoubtedly a consequence of the strongly centralised executive power with which the High Authority is invested under the Coal and Steel Treaty, but nevertheless the premiss upon which such actions were, and are, founded, especially when they are brought by an industrial enterprise as plaintiff, is that the supranational character of the Treaty is a fact of life. The practices developed, and the attitudes engendered, in the course of litigation concerning the implementation of the Coal and Steel Treaty have readily been carried over into the sphere of operation of the Rome Treaties, and in particular of the Economic Community Treaty. This latter Treaty, while creating a considerably less powerful and independent central executive, undoubtedly built upon the foundations of supranational institutional government established by the earlier Coal and Steel Treaty, and at the same time was designed to have application to a vastly broader spectrum of economic, social and political affairs than was its precursor. An important, and striking, consequence of the altered profile of the Economic Community Treaty, as compared with the Coal and Steel Treaty, has been the extensive dissemination of the incidence of litigious issues involving questions of Community law into the national *fora*, where they arise with increasing frequency in a steadily multiplying number of different contexts. Such proceedings, since they originate in some domestic court established within the framework of the legal system of one of the Member States, provide the venue for a direct confrontation between the respective legal orders, Community and national. It might be reasonably expected that, if left to themselves to resolve the problems engendered by such confrontations of conflicting legal rules arising in "domestic" proceedings, the national courts would tend to diverge from one another both in regard to the solutions furnished to problems of a basically similar nature, and — even more significantly — in regard to the interpretation placed upon the very same rule of Community law when considered in different jurisdictions.[8] Such developments, were they to occur, would violate one of the fundamental principles upon which the Community is based, namely the provision, contained in A. 7 ECT, enjoining Member States from differentiating in an arbitrary manner between the nationals of the Member States. Accordingly, the procedure for which provision is made by A. 177 ECT (substantially identical to A. 150 EAET)[9] has proved to be a vital one for securing the requisite unity and integrity of Community law, since the facility has thereby been created for the European Court of Justice to act as a common source of interpretation in all such matters.[10] The ambit of A. 177 ECT and A. 150 EAET is significantly broader than that of A. 41 CST, which merely provides that "the Court shall have sole jurisdiction to give preliminary rulings on the validity of acts of the High Authority and of the Council where such validity is in issue in proceedings brought before a national court or tribunal". This provision omits to empower the Court to give, much less to oblige national courts to seek, interpretative rulings on the provisions of the Paris Treaty itself, or on the provisions of acts of the institutions of that Community wherever the actual validity of such acts is not being called into question. The consequence of this omission has been that few occasions have arisen for national courts to have recourse to the procedure contained in A. 41 CST. By contrast, the two Rome Treaties contain identical provisions which not merely facilitate, but in certain situations actually require such references to be made. The two Articles are worded as follows:

"The Court of Justice shall have jurisdiction to give preliminary rulings concerning:
   (a) the interpretation of this Treaty;
   (b) the validity and interpretation of acts of the institutions of the Community;
   (c) the interpretation of the statutes of bodies established by an act of the Council, where those statutes so provide.
Where such a question is raised before any court or tribunal of a Member State, that

court or tribunal may, if it considers that a decision on the question is necessary to enable it to give judgment, request the Court of Justice to give a ruling thereon.

Where any such question is raised in a case pending before a court or tribunal of a Member State, against whose decisions there is no judicial remedy under national law, that court or tribunal shall bring the matter before the Court of Justice."

In the light of the carefully circumscribed role which is ordained for it by the very provisions of A. 177 itself, the Court of Justice has adopted a severely exact attitude towards its powers and functions in relation to the giving of preliminary rulings under A. 177 ECT (or, as appropriate, A. 150 EAET). Being conscious at all times of the fact that it is strictly confined to making pronouncements regarding the *interpretation* of *Community* law, the Court deems it improper to presume to tender interpretative utterances regarding domestic law proper, and furthermore insists that, even concerning Community law, its competence is restricted to the issuing of a disengaged ruling upon a pure issue of law. Hence, the European Court does not venture to concern itself either with any inquiry into the motives of the Court making the reference, or with the final task of application of Community law in the case in question, which remains the task and prerogative of the national court from which the reference has emanated. [11] Indeed, the Court of Justice goes so far as to insist that it is no part of its own function to determine whether the provisions of Community law which the national court has chosen to refer for interpretation have any proper bearing whatever upon the actual case which the national court is in the process of deciding: the sole concern of the Court of Justice is to interpret Community law as and when it is duly seized of such a question by virtue of a national court's having submitted a reference. [12]

Although, as has been suggested above, the Treaty imparts the ready indication that the Court's pronouncement is to be authoritative and decisive of the meaning and extent of the obligations which are created by Community law, and which it is incumbent upon national courts to apply as a matter of duty in fulfilment of the Treaty, the strictness of the Court of Justice in maintaining distinctions between the role and functions ascribed to itself and to the national courts is no mere exercise of pedantry, much less is it an empty sophistry. For the national court remains master of the totality of the proceedings of which the question of Community law forms but a part, and it is moreover necessary for the national court to undertake the often extensive exploration of all factual and evidentiary questions, with which the European Court of Justice is absolved from concerning itself. Nevertheless, the factual components of the case in issue, in so far as they have been established or ascertained at the time when the national court chooses to submit a reference to the European Court under A. 177, are certainly included in the latter Court's consideration of the question or questions formulated by the referring court: otherwise, the proceedings would assume a highly abstract and artificial character. Frequently the Court's ultimate interpretation may upon close analysis be seen to owe much to the actual facts of the instant case,[13] but in leaving the final task of application of Community law to the national court, the Court of Justice reaffirms the chosen demarcations of function and competence. Of course, it remains the case that fulfilment of the legal obligations created and imposed by the Community Treaties is a solemn duty for every Member State and for every officially established institution (such as courts or tribunals) functioning within the organised administration of every Member State. Indeed, the Court has gone so far as to speak of a "principle of co-operation laid down in A. 5 ECT".[14] It should therefore suffice for the European Court of Justice to perform the task of identifying and expounding the "pure" meaning of Community law upon any matter about which there exists any uncertainty: thereafter, the primary responsibility for ensuring that any given Member State, directly or via its institutions, properly implements its Treaty obligations is quite deliberately entrusted to a completely distinct Community institution, namely the Commission.[15]

The immediate virtues of the A. 177 arrangement have been the establishment of lines of communication, and of co-operation, between the national court and the European Court of Justice, and also of the means of ensuring a uniform application of Community law in all Member States.[16] As the history of the Communities' existence has lengthened, and as the numerous policies and programmes called for in the Treaties' several divisions have come to be put into effect by means of secondary legislation, so legal consciousness in every national jurisdiction of the Community has awakened to the implications of the potential impact of Community primary and secondary law upon the existing provisions and arrangements of the national legal order. With this awakened consciousness has come a steady acceleration in the frequency of the use made of the procedure for obtaining preliminary rulings. From comparatively modest beginnings during the period 1961–66, when an average of ten preliminary rulings were given each year, the growth of case law before the European Court of Justice in which its jurisdiction is invoked under A. 177 ECT (or A. 150 EAET) has been truly remarkable: between 1970 and 1974 the average number of such rulings was fluctuating between 30 and 50 per year, and in 1979 no less than 115 out of the total of 250 cases dealt with by the Court of Justice were proceedings brought under A. 177.[17] But of far greater significance than statistics regarding the use of

A. 177 is the actual character of the jurisprudence which has been developed as a result of that usage. Indeed, it would be no exaggeration to assert that proceedings under A. 177 ECT have regularly furnished the most convenient occasions for the progressive exposition of the very nature and quality of the Community legal order itself when considered in juxtaposition to possibly conflicting provisions of individual national legal orders. For it is in this context that the true qualities of the legal system created by means of the founding Treaties are revealed and shown to be operative not solely within the realm of public and administrative law, but also within the realm of private law, impinging upon the rights and relationships of individuals in an almost ubiquitous fashion.

(a) One Law or Two?

The task of "poldering in" the territory to be reclaimed by the Community from the legal waters formerly regarded by the national legal systems as *mare nostrum* was begun, appropriately enough, in a case referred for a preliminary ruling by an administrative tribunal in Holland, the *Tarrief-Commissie*. In its landmark ruling in the case of *Van Gend en Loos* v. *Nederlandse Administratie der Belastingen*,[18] the Court of Justice formulated for the first time the theory which has come to be known as the doctrine of direct effect, whereby it is averred that certain provisions of Community law (in the instant case, A. 12 ECT) if expressed with sufficient clarity and precision and if so formulated as to lead naturally to the conclusion that some legal right is intended to be bestowed upon some natural or legal person, may indeed be held to give rise to such rights and also to corresponding duties on the part of other natural or legal persons, or on the part of some Member State, to defer to those self same rights.[19] The notions of "right", and of its correlative concept "duty", are not mere abstractions existing in some theoretical vacuum. They are legal concepts whose formulation presupposes the existence of an applicable legal system by virtue of whose procedures for the awarding of remedies to and against the appropriate parties the identification and allocation of "rights" and "duties" is enabled to take place. In its ruling in the *Van Gend en Loos* case,[20] the Court of Justice furthermore asserted that the "rights" which arise by virtue of the doctrine of direct effect must of necessity be respected and enforced by the *national* courts of the Member States if they are to enjoy the full and proper character designed to be ascribed to them by the scheme and framework of the Treaty. The fact that, under the Treaty, certain procedures had been established for procuring the fulfilment by Member States of their obligations arising under the Treaty at

large (namely the procedures under A. 169 or A. 170 for infraction proceedings to be instituted either by the Commission or by some other Member
State) was held to be no obstacle to the existence of ancillary procedures for
ensuring that the "rights" which had arisen under Community law in favour
of individual subjects of the Member States of the Community were being
accorded immediate and appropriate effect wherever it became expedient to
assert them, such as in the course of litigation conducted in national courts.

In the key passage of its judgment in *Van Gend en Loos*, the Court
insisted:

> "The objective of the EEC Treaty, which is to establish a common market the function-
> ing of which is of direct concern to interested parties in the Community, implies that this
> Treaty is more than an agreement which merely creates mutual obligations between the
> contracting States.
>
> This view is confirmed by the preamble to the Treaty which refers not only to
> governments but to peoples. It is also confirmed more specifically by the establishment of
> institutions endowed with sovereign rights, the exercise of which affects Member States
> and also their citizens. Furthermore, it must be noted that the nationals of the States
> brought together in the Community are called upon to co-operate in the functioning of
> this Community through the intermediary of the European Parliament and the Economic
> and Social Committee.
>
> In addition the task assigned to the Court of Justice under A. 177, the object of which
> is to secure uniform interpretation of the Treaty by national courts and tribunals, con-
> firms that the States have acknowledged that Community law has an authority which can
> be invoked by their nationals before those courts and tribunals.
>
> The conclusion to be drawn from this is that the Community constitutes a new legal
> order of international law for the benefit of which the States have limited their sovereign
> rights, albeit within limited fields, and the subjects of which comprise not only Member
> States but also their nationals. Independently of the legislation of Member States, Com-
> munity law therefore not only imposes obligations on individuals but is also intended to
> confer upon them rights which become part of their legal heritage. These rights arise not
> only where they are expressly granted by the Treaty, but also by reason of obligations
> which the Treaty imposes in a clearly defined way upon individuals as well as upon the
> Member States and upon the Institutions of the Community." [21]

Later in its judgment the Court of Justice proceeded to consider the
argument advanced by three Governments in their intervening submissions in
the case, contending that the sole way in which the Court could validly be
seized of any question involving an allegation of infringement of the Treaty
by a Member State was in the context of proceedings brought under Arts.
169 or 170. The Court replied to this suggestion as follows:

> "The fact that ꞯese Articles of the Treaty enable the Commission and the Member States
> to bring before the Court a State which has not fulfilled its obligations does not mean
> that individuals cannot plead these obligations, should the occasion arise, before a nation-
> al court, any more than the fact that the Treaty places at the disposal of the Commission

ways of ensuring that obligations imposed upon those subject to the Treaty are observed, precludes the possibility, in actions between individuals before a national court, of pleading infringement of these obligations.

A restriction of the guarantees against an infringement of [here] A. 12 by Member States to the Procedures under Articles 169 and 170 would remove all direct legal protection of the individual rights of their nationals. ... The vigilance of individuals concerned to protect their rights amounts to an effective supervision in addition to the supervision entrusted by Articles 169 and 170 to the diligence of the Commission and of the Member States. It follows from the foregoing considerations that, according to the spirit, the general scheme and the wording of the Treaty, A. 12 must be interpreted as producing direct effects and creating individual rights which national courts should protect." [22]

Thus, the ruling of the Court of Justice in *Van Gend en Loos* established a sequence of linked propositions about the nature and quality of Community law, and about the manner in which it could be invoked and employed even in proceedings before national courts. Finally and, it must be stressed, perfectly consistently with its overall conception of the unique nature of the Community and of the Community's legal order, the Court's judgment contains the clear implication, which in later judgments was to be affirmed with increasing confidence, that in the event of any conflict between the provisions of any national law and those of Community law, the latter provisions must prevail and be given effect not merely by the European Court of Justice and by the courts of other Member States, but indeed by the courts of the very Member State whose domestic legal provisions exhibit a variation from the Community norm. [23] This further proposition, which effectively predicates the supremacy of Community law over national law where there is any inconsistency between their provisions or effects, was given more forthright articulation in the judgment of the Court in *Costa* v. *ENEL*, [24] in a passage which also deserves to be quoted at some length:

"By contrast with ordinary international treaties, the EEC Treaty has created its own legal system which, on the entry into force of the Treaty, became an integral part of the legal systems of the Member States and which their courts are bound to apply.

By creating a Community of unlimited duration, having its own institutions, its own personality, its own legal capacity and capacity of representation on the international plane and, more particularly, real powers stemming from a limitation of sovereignty or a transfer of powers from the States to the Community, the Member States have limited their sovereign rights, albeit within limited fields and have thus created a body of law which binds both their nationals and themselves.

The integration into the laws of each Member State of provisions which derive from the Community, and more generally the terms and the spirit of the Treaty, make it impossible for the States, as a corollary, to accord precedence to a unilateral and subsequent measure over a legal system accepted by them on a basis of reciprocity. Such a measure cannot therefore be inconsistent with that legal system. The executive force of Community law cannot vary from one State to another in deference to subsequent

domestic laws, without jeopardising the attainment of the objectives of the Treaty set out
in A. 5(2) and giving rise to the discrimination prohibited by A. 7." [25]

A little further on, the Court's judgment contains a further, key passage
which affirms both the separateness of the two legal orders, national and
Community, and the supremacy of the latter over the former in the event of
any conflict between them:

"The precedence of Community law is confirmed by A. 189, [26] whereby a Regulation
"shall be binding" and "directly applicable in all Member States". This provision, which is
subject to no reservation, would be quite meaningless if the State could unilaterally
nullify its effects by means of a legislative measure which could prevail over Community
law.

It follows from all these observations that the law stemming from the Treaty, *an
independent source of law*, [emphasis added] could not, because of its special and original
nature, be overridden by domestic legal provisions, however framed, without being
deprived of its character as Community law and without the legal basis of the Community
itself being called into question.

The transfer by the States from their domestic legal system to the Community legal
system of the rights and obligations arising under the Treaty carries with it a permanent
limitation of their sovereign rights, against which a subsequent unilateral act incompatible
with the concept of the Community cannot prevail. Consequently A. 177 is to be applied
regardless of any domestic law, whenever questions relating to the interpretation of the
Treaty arise."

It is here submitted that the tenor and purport of the Court's language in
the passages quoted above *in extenso* is to affirm the continued *distinctness*
of the two legal orders, national and community, while yet insisting upon
their having become "integrated" but not, it must be emphasised, "merged"
with each other as a consequence of the entry into operation of the terms of
the Treaty. [27] The potentiality for the occurrence of conflicts thus arises, in
the words of Advocate-General Lagrange in his opinion in *Costa v. ENEL*,
because of the "coexistence of two legal rules which both apply to the
domestic system, one deriving from the Treaty or the Community institutions, the other from the national legislature and institutions". [28] Further
confirmation for the position which is here being advanced is forthcoming
from the subsequent remarks of the Advocate-General in the same section of
his opinion:

"[T]he Treaty establishing the European Economic Community, as well as the other two
"European Treaties", creates its own legal system which, although distinct from the legal
system of each of the Member States, by virtue of certain precise provisions of the
Treaty, which bring about a *transfer of jurisdiction* to the Community institutions, partly
replaces the internal legal system." [29]

The process which therefore occurs is one of eclipse, or displacement, of the national law in any functional context in which the Treaty is properly applicable, rather than one of purported repeal, or annulment, of the national rule itself. The latter processes thus remain under the control of the national legislative institutions.[30] What the formulation advanced jointly by the Advocate-General and by the Court itself conveniently succeeds in doing is to supply a workable *modus vivendi* whereby the *necessary* developments entailed by the implementation of the Treaties may be accommodated within every Member State while each of the latter may be left to resolve in whatever way may be deemed most expedient any resultant anomalies which ensue from the fact that provisions of national law have ceased to be in correspondence with the provisions of Community law. To adapt the words of Advocate-General Lagrange it is required that Community law "must *predominate* until such time as the conflict is resolved".[31]

The conceptual formulations and, if one may so put it, the metaphorical imagery, employed in the *Costa* v. *ENEL* case were consistently redeployed by the Court in its judgments, and by the respective Advocates-General in their submitted opinions, in the ensuing succession of cases which have now established a *jurisprudence constante* upon these two, essentially related, questions, namely that of the supremacy of Community law over national law, and that of the operation of the doctrine of direct effect.[32] This notion has been developed by the Court of Justice to the extent of asserting that the supremacy of Community law must be acknowledged both in relation to every kind of ordinary national law, irrespective of whether the latter was enacted prior or even subsequent to the date on which the State in question became a member of the Community, and also in relation to fundamental provisions of the constitutions of the Member States, in so far as these may be found to be in conflict with provisions of Community law.[33] Throughout the course of this highly important sequence of case decisions, the Court of Justice remains emphatic upon the aspect of the "distinctness" of Community law from the national law of which it is nevertheless required to constitute an operative part. This seeming paradox gives rise at times to a certain amount of confusion, but has been explained by means of a nice distinction in an extra-judicial pronouncement of Advocate-General Warner, in the following way:

"It is not quite true, as is sometimes said, that Community law 'has become part of English law'...though it would be true to say that it has become 'part of the law of England' in the sense of being part of the law applicable in England."[34]

Thus, Community law, by virtue of its own very special nature and conception, commands supreme force within the domestic legal order of every

Member State. It does so *proprio vigore* and *ratione imperii*. It will continue to do so for as long as the Treaties remain in force in the form in which they were originally adopted. The laws of all the Member States have been profoundly changed, both substantively and administratively, as a consequence of the process which has just been described, and whose purport may be summed up in the following sequence of quotations extracted from judgments of the European Court of Justice in chronological order:

"[T]he municipal law of any Member State, whose courts request a preliminary ruling from this Court, and Community law constitute two separate and distinct legal orders." [35]

"[C]onflicts between the rules of the Community and national rules (in the matter of the law on Cartels) must be resolved by applying the principle that Community law takes precedence." [36]

"[T]hese provisions have conferred on individuals rights which the national courts must protect and which must prevail over conflicting provisions of national law even if the Member State has delayed in repealing such provisions." [37]

"So as to apply with equal force with regard to nationals of all the Member States, Community regulations become part of the legal system applicable within the national territory, which must permit the direct effect provided for in A. 189 to operate in such a way that reliance thereon by individuals may not be frustrated by domestic provisions or practices." [38]

"The effect of all these provisions without exception, is to impose duties on Member States and it is accordingly for the courts to give the rules of Community law which may be pleaded before them precedence over the provisions of national law if legislative measures adopted by a Member State in order to limit within its territory freedom of movement or residence for nationals of other Member States prove to be incompatible with any of those duties." [39]

"[T]he Member States may neither adopt nor allow national organisations having legislative power to adopt any measures which would conceal the Community nature and effects of any legal provision from the persons to whom it applies. ... The Member States may not, therefore, either directly or through the intermediary of organisations set up or recognised by them, authorise or tolerate any exemption from Community law." [40]

"Direct applicability ... means that rules of Community law must be fully and uniformly applied in all the Member States from the date of their entry into force and for so long as they remain in force. (Furthermore), in accordance with the principle of the precedence of Community law, the relationship between provisions of the Treaty and directly applicable measures of the Institutions on the one hand and the national law of the Member States on the other is such that those provisions and measures not only by their entry into force render automatically inapplicable any conflicting provision of current national law but — in so far as they are an integral part of, and take precedence in, the legal order applicable in the territory of each of the Member States — also preclude the valid adoption of new national legislative measures to the extent to which they would be incompatible with Community provisions.

A national court which is called upon, within the limits of its jurisdiction, to apply provisions of Community law is under a duty to give full effect to those provisions, if necessary refusing of its own motion to apply any conflicting provision of national legislation, even if adopted subsequently, *and it is not necessary for the court to request or await the prior setting aside of such provisions by legislative or other constitutional means*"[41] (emphasis added)

(b) The Growth of "Community Conflicts" Problems

The implications of the foregoing propositions from the point of view of private international law are, it is submitted, as follows. While it is perfectly true that the majority of the "landmark" decisions which have already been cited, or quoted from, in the present chapter properly belonged to the sphere of "public" law — more specifically to the sphere of legal relations between the individual and the state — this is by no means true of all of them. Some of the cases cited may properly be described as cases in which the rights conferred upon individuals by virtue of the provisions of Community law became a central issue in litigious proceedings between private parties. Cases of this type are continuing to arise, and indeed to do so with increasing frequency. Such a development was wholly predictable for, after all, if it is once established that the individual is entitled to assert a Community-created right against the authorities and agents of a given Member *State, a fortiori* that person ought to be able to maintain the same right against fellow individuals in any legal proceedings to which it has relevance. An early intimation of this propensity of Community law to affect the rights of individuals *inter se* was forthcoming in Case 13/61, *Bosch* v. *De Geus*,[42] which came before the Court of Justice for a preliminary ruling in relation to Dutch proceedings taking place between private parties in which the defendant, De Geus, had contended that the agreement on which the plaintiffs relied as the basis of their action at law was in conflict with A. 85(2) ECT and was thereby rendered void, albeit it might be regarded as lawful according to the provisions of Dutch domestic law concerning such agreements. Although the defendants' contention was unsuccessful in view of the precise circumstances surrounding the case, there is no doubt that the underlying point of principle was well taken.[43] A similar argument was invoked, and accepted in principle by the Court of Appeal in England, in *Application des Gaz S.A.* v. *Falks Veritas Ltd.*,[44] in which the defendants to an action claiming, *inter alia*, an injunction to restrain an alleged infringement of copyright claimed that the plaintiffs might be met by defences based on Arts. 85 and 86 ECT. In an interlocutory appeal, the Court of Appeal unanimously held that the defendants' pleadings could be amended so as to enable them to argue the merits of this defence founded upon an invocation of Community law. [45] Other cases which came before the English courts at a relatively early date following United Kingdom accession to the Communities, and in which issues of Community law were invoked in proceedings between private parties, included *H.P. Bulmer Ltd.* v. *J. Bollinger S.A.*; [46] *Löwenbräu München* v. *Grünhalle Lager International Ltd.*; [47] and *Schorsch Meier GmbH* v. *Hennin.* [48] In each of these cases the judgments of the English courts contain clear statements to the effect that rights originating from the Community Treaties must be regarded as forming part of the general panoply of legal principles governing relations between individuals, and that if it should transpire that the consequences predicated by any such "enforceable Community right" [49] lie contrary to the position which has hitherto obtained under domestic law, dominant effect is to be accorded to the Community-law right.

The foregoing expressions of principle voiced by the English judiciary in the early days of their practising acquaintance with the impact of Community law are in accord with the views of the European Court of Justice, as expounded in proceedings both of earlier and of more recent date. Although it is true that, by virtue of their very character, the provisions of Arts. 85 and 86 ECT were the first to lend themselves to this kind of application, the essential principle, once formulated and embodied within a lengthening *jurisprudence constante*, was quickly found to be applicable to numerous other provisions of the Treaties, and of Regulations also. [50] Thus, the not unexpected *dicta* contained in the judgment of the Court of Justice in Case 127/73, *Belgische Radio en Televisie* v. *SABAM*, [51] to the effect that "As the prohibitions of Arts. 85(1) and 86 tend by their very nature to produce direct effects *in relations between individuals*, these Articles create direct rights in respect of the individuals concerned which the national courts must safeguard", may be seen as seminal to the later rulings of the Court in proceedings concerning the effects of such provisions as Arts. 5, 7, 48, 52, 57, 59, 60 and 119 ECT. One of the principal landmarks of this jurisprudential development was Case 36/74, *Walrave and Koch* v. *Association Union Cycliste Internationale*, [52] in which the Court of Justice ruled that the prohibition of discrimination based on nationality contained in Arts. 7, 48 and 59 ECT was, in principle, capable of applying to professional sporting activities, viewed as an economic activity within the meaning of A. 2 of the Treaty, albeit that such prohibition does not affect the composition of sports teams, and in particular of national teams, whose formation is of purely sporting interest and as such has nothing to do with economic activity. Thus, leaving aside the special question of representative, international sporting competitions, the basic principle is established that the nationals of Member States enjoy an enforceable Community right to freedom from any discrimination based on nationality in relation to the taking up of employment, or to the provision of services or the exercise of freedom of establishment. [53] This right furthermore may be asserted directly against the actual party responsible for practising the discrimination in question, typically an existing or potential employer (whether established under the private or public law of a given Member State), or a body or authority possessed of the power to control the appropriate registration, or admission to membership of some professional body, of a would-be provider of services, or of one aspiring to become established in some profession or occupation. [54] The lawfulness of the behaviour or practices or operating rules of such parties may be tested in relation to the mandatory requirements of Community law, which in this respect introduces certain important overriding principles which are required to govern relationships between individuals, and which supersede any contrary provisions of national law whereby certain discriminatory or restrictive practices may hitherto have been sanctioned, if not even positively ordained.

A further development of considerable importance occurred when the Court of Justice delivered its ruling in the Case 43/75, *Defrenne* v. *SABENA*, [55] a case in which a retired employee of the Belgian national airline SABENA, retrospectively sought compensation in respect of pecuniary losses which she had suffered in terms of salary, allowance on termination of service, and pension as a result of the fact that female and male members of the air crew of SABENA performing identical duties did not receive equal pay. The main thrust of Miss Defrenne's argument was to the effect that, notwithstanding any provisions extant under Belgian law relating to terms of employment whereby it might be lawful to maintain such practices of material discrimination between male and female employees, all such practices had been deprived of their lawful validity by virtue of the unequivocal requirement of A. 119 ECT, to the effect that: "Each Member State shall during the first stage ensure and subsequently maintain the application of the principle that men and women shall receive equal pay for equal work." In ruling that this provision had become directly effective with regard to the original six Member States as from the end of the first stage of the transitional period (1 January 1962), and with regard to the three new Member States as from the date of entry into force of the Accession Treaty (1 January 1973), the Court of Justice furnished individual employees with a basis of legal claim henceforth maintainable directly against their immediate employers irrespective of whether the latter may have acted within limits permitted and sanctioned by national law with regard to the remuneration of their male and female employees. [56] Hence, in another sphere of legal relationships between individuals, an overriding principle of Community law has been declared to be invokable by the party in whose favour a legal right has been conferred.

The types of proceedings which have been described in the two immediately preceding paragraphs are, it is suggested, perfectly familiar to students of private international law. They involve legal issues arising in interpersonal relationships which, by virtue of some relevant connecting factor applicable to one or both of the parties, are simultaneously subjected to the effects of more than one system of law. In these instances, the two systems in question are the law of the European Economic Community on the one hand, and the law of one of the Member States of that Community on the other. Their simultaneous application to the relationship between parties may arise either *ratione personae*, because of the parties' personal attachment (by virtue of nationality or establishment) to the law of one or more Member States of the Community, or *ratione loci*, because of the territorial location of one or more of the legally-relevant matters or events which have a bearing upon the relationship, or *ratione materiae*, because of the very nature of the issue or issues involved, which may be of such a character as to render them properly subject to the provisions of those separate systems of law whose spheres of influence are in some way impinged upon. [57] The novel aspect of these cases, from the point of view of the conflicts lawyer, may be said to consist of two elements. First, there is the undoubted fact that Community law, in so far as it may purport to bear upon or regulate a given matter or relationship, does not necessarily presume to do so by means of a full set of legal provisions capable of displacing the provisions of any "rival" system of law *in toto*. An appropriate example is furnished by the provision of A. 119 ECT already referred to: apart from the question of equality of pay for men and women performing equal work, that provision of Community law by itself imports no further overriding rules into any contract of employment, which in other respects continues to be governed by the extant provisions of the national system of law by which it is otherwise regulated. [58] On the other hand, more extensive, though yet not fully comprehensive, legal provisions are compulsorily insinuated by Community law into the legal situation of persons eligible to invoke the basic Community freedoms of movement (as workers), of establishment or of the provision of services. [59] But even these latter provisions do not purport to exclude the continued operation and application of such provisions of the relevant national law as may not prove to be in conflict with the precepts of Community law. Thus, the ultimate legal position is arrived at by a process tantamount to one of *"dépeçage"*, in which the legal relationship between the parties is dismembered into numerous sub-components, each of which is regulated by national or Community law in accordance with the established principle of precedence, namely that where Community law applies *at all*, it does so to the exclusion of any contrary provisions of national law, but where Community law is silent, the national law may continue to regulate that aspect of the relationship.

It is in consequence of the proposition just stated that the second, novel element may be discerned, namely that the apparent "choice of laws", which occurs to be made whenever Community and national laws are at variance, is in reality a "non-choice", on account of the operation of the fundamental principle or theory that in such situations Community law *must* prevail, and must be accorded such effect by the national judge himself. The fact that Community law maintains a self-limiting concept of its own sphere of application produces the net effect of an interleaved combination of legal rights, not altogether unlike the historic interrelationship between the systems of Common Law and Equity whereby the latter supplemented (and, where necessary, ultimately supplanted) the former so as to produce convenient consequences in terms of the rights and remedies exercisable by the individual. While it is true, as a matter of historic record, that the first opportunities for testing and establishing the existence of rights conferred by Community law on individuals arose in the context of relations between the individual and the State, it should be apparent from the foregoing exposition that the same basic principle is involved in cases concerning the impact of Community law upon the relationships of individuals *inter se*, and that this type of case is potentially of extremely common occurrence, as the provisions of Community law proliferate and assume their intended, binding force. Increasingly, therefore, courts belonging to the national judicial hierarchy of the Member States of the Community will encounter the need to discern the impact of Community law upon the legal relationship between the parties to proceedings with which they are seized. They will need to become adept at discerning the limits of that impact, as well as its actual effect, so that their final determination will be based upon the application of rules and principles derived from Community law, together with such complementary provisions of national law as are left unimpaired by the incursions of the Community legal order. In effect, therefore, the end product will resemble that which can result from a sophisticated application of conflict of laws processes of an "issue-segregating" and "rule-selecting" type, in which no single system of law necessarily enjoys a monopoly of control over the rights and liabilities of the parties.

Thus, it is submitted that the doctrine of supremacy of Community law, from which all else effectively flows, entails the operation, on a continuous basis, of processes which, properly understood, belong to the realm of conflict of laws. Some cases, namely those raising questions of an inter-personal nature, are more readily recognisable as instances of conflicts of law, while others, which involve litigious issues arising between an individual and the State, represent a *nova species* of conflicts case adding a further dimension to the subject. The fact that the Court of Justice initially chose to express its fundamental idea (or *Grundnorm*) in a manner suggestive of a "once and for all accomplished event". ("The EEC *has created* its own legal system which, on the entry into force of the Treaty, became an integral part of the legal systems of the Member States" [emphasis added].) [60] should be taken as referring to the fact that the acceding States, at the moment of becoming members, formally committed themselves to acceptance of the legal consequences which, on a comprehensive appraisal of the terms of the Treaty as a whole, were clearly and inevitably destined to ensue for all concerned, and also to the fact that these effects were to remain continuously in force for the future. That one part of those consequences was the creation of an interconnecting bridge between the existing and continuing legal orders of the Member States, and the legal order of the Community which was then being established *de novo*, is undeniable. But it is strongly submitted that it nevertheless remains the case that the two legal orders — national and Community — also retain distinct identities, if for no other reason than that the regulation and development of the two are essentially separate. The Community legal system, and the substantive law of the Member States of the Community, are both distinct, growing things, which have undergone considerable development and mutation since the moment of the Communities' original inception. Although many of these developments are properly attributable to the realm of public law, traditionally so-called, it is nevertheless the case that developments are continuously taking place at both Community and national level in the realm of substantive, private law also, so that there is the constant possibility that a state of incompatibility may be created between them. Whenever such a situation arises, it is submitted that, in principle, the national judge is confronted by a problem of conflict of laws, albeit one whose determination is controlled by means of the pre-eminent rule, imposed by the Treaty, that each national system of law must ensure that Community law is fully and uniformly applied. Thus, it is incumbent upon the national system to make whatever accommodation may be necessary to enable this requirement to be fulfilled. But conflicting national laws are not necessarily annulled, repealed or cancelled *erga omnes* by virtue of

the development taking place at Community level: the Treaty merely requires that such laws be given effect in situations possessing a Community
character in such a way as not to violate the principles of Community law. In
situations containing no "Community" element, or connecting factor, it
would thus be perfectly possible for some rules of national law to be retained and applied, albeit their application in a Community context had been
rendered impermissible.

(c) Conclusion

The task of the national judge may therefore be summarised as follows: he
must respond to the onset of any new provision of Community law by
having regard to its possible implications for any part of his existing national
law which is of relevance in the proceedings before him; if necessary, any
uncertainty as to the purport of Community law must be clarified by means
of a ruling sought from the European Court of Justice, using A. 177 ECT.
The national judge must finally apply the Community law if it is, in his
judgment, properly applicable to the case confronting him, and he must do
so, where necessary, by means of a deliberate omission to give effect or
application to provisions of national law which otherwise have a bearing
upon the outcome, notwithstanding that these latter provisions may have
undergone no formal repeal or amendment by any national legislative organ.
The net *result* thus resembles the result which ensues from an "orthodox"
conflict of laws process in which a national judge, having applied the relevant
choice of law rule of the *forum* to an issue in which, say, the possible
alternative selections as *lex causae* are his own domestic law or that of State
X, concludes that the law of X must be applied in the circumstances. The
one major difference in a Community law situation is that, in theory, the
national judge does not have a true freedom to choose at all: his choice is
always pre-ordained to be exercised in favour of Community law.

An aura of predestination thus surrounds the process of interaction between Community law and national law. The resulting effect is therefore not
dissimilar to that which the late Professor Ehrenzweig was wont to describe
as the "operation of a superlaw". [61] This latter expression was employed for
the purpose of indicating the pre-eminent force exerted upon legal relationships by the provisions of some Treaty or Constitution which, in relation to
the proceedings in question, has already established the terms, and the
framework of rules, upon which any final decision is to be arrived at. Just
like the judge in a system regulated by a federal constitution, who must
respect the limitations which the notion of constitutionality imposes upon

his scope for reaching his decision, the national judge in the European Community exercises freedom of action only within certain defined limits. In crude terms he must, as an official agent of the State to which he belongs, ensure that his ultimate decision does not constitute a violation of its Treaty obligations on the part of the State in question. The fundamental distinction thereby produced is that Community law prevails over national law *ratione imperii*, whereas, in the view of the more enlightened modern writers in the field of private international law, the application of foreign law, in the absence of a "superlaw" such as a Treaty or Constitution, is considered to occur *imperio rationis*. [62] The analogy with the processes which take place within a federalised system must not be pursued too far at present, because it is far from being the case that the European Community has yet succeeded in transforming itself into such an entity. However, by virtue of the operation of the Treaty, many of the legal effects which would accompany the creation of a fully-formed federal system are already required to take place, and in particular the provisions of Arts. 5, 7 and 189 ECT clearly serve to establish the general principle of supremacy of Community law over provisions of individual national laws. It is true, on the one hand, that in the majority of cases the two systems so function as to be complementary to each other, as where it is left to the Member States to implement in accordance with their national styles and methods the requirements of Community secondary legislation, especially that which is enacted in the form of Directives. But, on the other hand, it is also true that there exists considerable potential for the two systems simultaneously to purport to regulate the same situations or circumstances, even in the realm of private law, and that this possibility is enhanced by the operation of the doctrine of direct effect, which has been formulated in the full consciousness that it will predicate results which cut across existing provisions of national law at every level.

To what extent, therefore, does the assertion that "conflicts of law" considerations are present in the case of conflict between the Community and national legal orders, yield practical consequences? The answer would appear to be that, in the case of what are here termed "Community conflicts", namely conflicts between the national law and Community law itself, any theoretical problems have been felicitously resolved by means of the successful assertion of the predominant character of the Community legal order. By complying with the requirement that, in such situations, Community law must prevail, national courts have enabled a state of affairs to emerge in which the *consequence* of employing the invariable resolution of legal conflicts demanded by the Community "superlaw" succeeds in masking all practical traces of the very existence of such conflicts at all. Thus, it is not the case that Community law falls to be regarded as foreign law in proceedings before national courts: [63] it is unnecessary to prove Community law by means of expert evidence, as is normally the case where a rule of private international law has led to the selection of the law of some country other than the *forum* as *lex causae*. The *fait accompli* of integration between the national and Community systems of law not merely enables, but indeed requires, the national court to apply Community law as part of its own law (that is, as part of the law applicable within its jurisdiction), despite the fact that, technically, Community law does not constitute part of the national law of the *forum*. [64] But the discreet manner in which this entire process of integration of two legal orders has been accomplished has perhaps concealed certain problems of a substantial nature, which ought not to continue to be ignored.

In the first place, there is the need to ensure that all national courts, at all levels, are alerted to the extensiveness of the impact which Community law has made, and is progressively making upon the law which they administer, so that they are constantly adjusting to the changing net situation in a way which is uniform to the entire Community. The second area of problems is a more profound, and even imprecise, one necessitating a review of the implications for national practice in relation to private international law amongst the legal systems of the Member States themselves. This somewhat complex — not to say controversial — question will be considered in the following section.

2. Conflicts Between the Legal Orders of the Member States Themselves

In the foregoing section the attempt was made to show how the impact of the Community legal order upon that of the Member States has the effect, in relation to inter-personal legal proceedings at least, of creating a new type of problem in the conflict of laws, attended by its own, specially-ordained rule for solution. It may be seen that as a consequence of this process of accommodation, or forced reception, of the effects of Community law by the national courts, in those cases whose elements, *ratione personae, ratione loci* or *ratione materiae*, necessitate the application of provisions of Community law as part of the final, juridical determination, a special set of hybrid rules, part Community inspired, part national, is rendered applicable. Thus, in many cases of the types which have traditionally been regarded as belonging to the realm of private international law, a new dimension has been introduced in as much as it has become necessary to have regard, initially, to the question whether a case containing multinational contacts falls to be determined with reference to Community law or not. Furthermore, a quite new category of "conflicts-type" cases has been established by reason of the fact that, even where the elements of a case, and the parties to it, appear to possess no juridically relevant connection with any foreign *country*, the impact of certain provisions of Community law may nevertheless have to be deferred to as being capable of influencing, or altering, the rights and duties of individuals as administered by their national courts. [65]

Therefore, in a new and special way, it has become essential to distinguish between two types of conflicts case, namely the "Community" type (which has previously been described) in which the application of some provision of Community substantive law is somehow required, and the "international" type, of more familiar and traditional incidence, in which the impact of Community substantive law is not apparently necessitated albeit the case does contain one or more "foreign elements" of a legally significant character. It may be noted at this stage, that such elements may on the one hand simply establish connections with the laws or legal systems of other Member States of the Community so that the case may be said to remain within the overall ambit of the Community, territorially speaking. Alternatively, the foreign elements in the case may serve to establish connections with the laws, or legal systems, of countries which do not belong to the European Communities at all. For the sake of convenience of reference it will be useful to apply the term "internal" or "intra-Community" conflicts to the former type of case, while the term "external" conflicts will be employed to denote the latter type in which the international contacts are with countries outside the EEC. [66] Thirdly, cases in which connections simultaneously arise with both third States and with some Member State other than the *forum* merit special consideration, and will be referred to as "hybrid" conflicts.

With regard to "internal" conflicts cases, A. 220 ECT contains limited provision for the progressive substitution of unified rules of private international law by the Member States acting together in fulfilment of a programme whose results, in the form of a series of concluded or draft conventions, are reviewed in the second part of this book. In relation to matters not specifically covered by express provisions of the Treaty, it is appropriate to enquire how far the Member States are intended to remain free to operate in accordance with their established, diversified traditions in cases of "internal" conflicts of laws. At the same time, it is also appropriate to consider whether, in cases of "external" conflicts, those same diversified traditions can entirely escape some sort of reappraisal in the light of the changed circumstances in which each of the States in question is now placed in consequence of its having joined a Community such as the EEC. Finally, it is necessary to have regard to the question of "hybrid" cases, as defined above.

(a) Internal (Intra-Community) Conflicts Cases

Leaving aside for the present the matters which have been, or which are destined to be, dealt with in accordance with the requirements of A. 220 ECT,[67] the question arises of the extent to which membership of the Community *per se* places all Member States under a duty to modify, or at least to review, their rules and procedures in matters of private international law, at any rate in those cases in which the parties concerned, or one of them at least, are subjects of any of the Member States, or in which the key issues (choice of *forum*; choice of law; the making available of any appropriate legal remedy, and the enforcement thereof) involve the exercise of a choice between the courts, or between the legal systems, of different Member States of the Community. At first sight, it may appear that in the absence of any express provisions of the basic Treaties themselves such developments could not be regarded as matters of legal *obligation* incumbent up on the Member States, so that, at best, it might be possible to regard them as *desiderata*, to be pursued on a purely voluntary basis out of considerations of mutual convenience or, perhaps, comity. However, it is here submitted that there are several valid reasons why this negative view is not sustainable, whereas the converse, namely that the issue is indeed one of obligation for the Member States, most assuredly is. In the first place, it is necessary to insist that the same considerations and arguments which underlay the inclusion within the ECT of a limited number of express provisions for the harmonisation of certain aspects of law, must logically be further applied to the majority of other aspects of private international law, despite the fact that these were not actually singled out for mention in the Treaty. As has been shown already,[68] the ultimate intention that the Community shall progressively come to function as a single legal and jurisdictional unit, coupled with the ubiquitous implementation of the "Community philosophy" founded upon the systematic eradication of every relevant type of "distortion-producing" factor, constitutes the primary motivation for, and justification of, the manifold Community programmes of harmonisation of substantive law, as well as of the matters mentioned in A. 220 ECT. In the case of the harmonisation of the substantive laws of the Member States there has been a perceptible, and inevitable, "spillover" in practice, far transcending the specific matters envisaged and identified by the redactors of the Treaties, so that a host of ancillary programmes have been devised drawing their inspiration from reasonable extrapolations which are capable of being made using the language of the Treaties as a starting point. So too with private international law, the logic of processes willed into motion by the founding fathers of the Community, and the principles they solemnly embodied in the Treaties, must together be pursued and applied with increasing sophistication, and in the light of accumulated experience. The inescapable consequence is that the aforesaid processes and principles will be discerned as being applicable, necessarily, to a far more extensive range of matters than were originally thought to be embraced by the Community's mantle of operation, while in addition the natural processes of change and evolution in circumstances which take place in the course of time will ultimately give rise to a further necessity for the re-interpretation of the static terms of the texts of the Treaties. Thereby, a *corpus* of policy and interpretation steadily develops, and eventually contributes a so-called "penumbra" to the Treaties proper, enabling them to continue to function by responding to changes, rather than eventually becoming imprisoned by them. If it is accepted that the Community legal order possesses these dynamic characteristics, it is important to maintain a constant review of the system as a whole, so that any implication which may hitherto have been ignored, or underestimated, may be given an appropriate re-assessment. In this respect, it is submitted that inadequate attention has hitherto been paid to the true significance of the development of the Community legal order from the aspect of the Member States' private international law, [69] perhaps owing to the fact that conflict situations of any given type arise relatively infrequently in practice. What strikes the present writer as especially significant, however, is the fact that as the substantive laws of the Member States become progressively more harmonised in consequence of the implementation of the different, Treaty-based programmes already alluded to, [70] those disparities between the rules of private international law of the Member States which retain their potential for significantly influencing the outcome of specific cases undergo a corresponding increase in importance. This is because, since the *apparent* conflicts between the potentially applicable rules of law of the different Member States have been transformed into "false" ones as a result of harmonisation, the residual capacity, inherent in the diverse, unreconstructed private international law rules and procedures of those same Member States, to cause the concrete result in a given case to vary according to the court seized of the matter, must perforce be stigmatised as a further species of "distortion" and, as such, be regarded as anathematical to the overall purposes for which the Community exists.

One may take as an example illustrative of the above contention the case where social security and other benefits are claimed by a person purporting to be the "spouse" of a deceased "Community worker" in whom, as a consequence of the now well-developed rules of Community primary and secondary law, a considerable number of rights had become vested at the time of death, including an eligibility to receive pension and other benefits in accordance with the principles established by Community, and not merely national, legislative provisions. Other relevant rights which would have become vested in the deceased would include the entitlement to continue to reside in the territory of the Member State where he or she was employed, and to exercise full civic and economic rights therein. [71] Many of these same rights attach by derivation to the spouse and dependent family of the Community worker irrespective of their own actual nationality, and are moreover capable of being enjoyed even after the death of the worker by virtue of whose lifetime activities they were originally acquired. [72] Despite the fact that the courts of all Member States are required to give uniform interpretation and application to the enacted rules of Community law relating to these matters, it nevertheless appears to have been left open to each Member State to employ a more idiosyncratic approach to the solution of such vital questions as whether a given person is to be recognised in law as possessing the status of "spouse", or "member of family" for the purposes in hand. [73] Thus, in addition to possible differences between the substantive laws of the Member States in relation to the definition of "spouse", "dependent" and "member of family" for the purposes of establishing an entitlement to benefit from the provisions of Community law, there is also considerable scope for further variation by virtue of the different approaches taken by the private international law of the several Member States wherever a case involves the making of some reference to the impact of foreign laws upon personal status. Supposing that the "spouse" in our hypothetical example had, prior to marrying the deceased, undergone proceedings of divorce or for the annulment of a previous marriage contracted with a former spouse (then still living), the recognition of the decree of divorce or nullity (assuming it to be a "foreign" one from the point of view of the *forum* in the instant proceedings) thus becomes an incidental question in relation to the present claim based upon the premiss that the applicant was the "spouse" of the deceased at the time of the latter's death. Comparable problems arise where it was the deceased who had been party to foreign divorce or nullity proceedings, or where any other question relating to the validity of the marriage between the applicant and the deceased is held to be referable to foreign law. It may thus be seen that any variations in practice between the Member States' rules of private international law in relation to (*inter alia*) the recognition of foreign divorce or nullity decrees, or upon the valid formation of marriage, [74] may have a decisive impact upon the outcome of the application here under hypothetical consideration, and may subject claimants whose personal circumstances and history are otherwise identical to an unequal legal treatment by virtue of the sole factor that their cases fall to be considered by the courts of separate Member States applying separate rules of private international law. Such possibilities inevitably run contrary to the aspirations voiced at the very outset of the Treaty of Rome, whereby it is made clear that the intention underlying the Community is to "lay the foundations of an ever closer union among the peoples of Europe" and "by common action to eliminate the barriers which divide Europe". Such disparities of outcome are, it is submitted, serious enough to attract the accusations of unfairness and improper distortion even where the applicant personally is not a national of any Member State of the Community, since it must be remembered that, retrospectively, the totality of the rights enjoyed by the Community worker (including the rights derivatively imparted by virtue of that status to the worker's spouse and dependents) has been seriously depreciated in the case of any adverse decision regarding the entitlement of the worker's spouse to enjoy the benefits for which provision is made by Community law. *A fortiori*, if the spouse is personally a national of any Member State of the EEC, the injustice thereby perpetrated surely assumes even greater proportions, as also it would do if, to take a further example, a living Community worker were to discover that the most intimate questions concerning the legal status attributed to his marital and family relationships were differently regarded, and consequently attracted different treatment, by the law in different national jurisdictions of the Community. [75] It is moreover submitted that it is insufficient answer, on behalf of any national legal system which may be shown to be capable of producing such results, that the rules of private international law in question are invariably applied in all cases coming before the courts of that country, so that there is ostensibly no discrimination between the nationals of the country in question and those of other Member States, a proceeding which would, of course, contravene the provisions of A. 7 ECT. This is because, here, it is the actual *results* produced by the application of the rules of law in force in the jurisdiction in question which are working contrary to the *overall* purposes of the Community by virtue of the very fact that they are in a state of variance from the equivalent rules applied in the systems of private international law administered in other Member States. To put it more comprehensively, it is the existence of some species of material variation between the systems of private international law of the Member States, viewed collectively, which is, under certain conditions, giving rise to such instances of improper distortion.

In the light of the foregoing, it is submitted that the Member States' developed rules and practices in private international law must be subjected to an overall reappraisal for the purpose of discovering possible ways in which they either do, or may, operate in a manner which effectively infringes the paramount principles on which the European Communities are established. In the end, it must be conceded that only the complete eradication of such disparities between the Member States' systems of private international law will eliminate altogether the possibility for distortion to occur in situations analogous to those which have been described above by way of example. Let there be recalled here the words already quoted in the previous chapter of this book, to the effect that "Differences in the Member States' legislative and administrative provisions affect the establishment or functioning of the Common Market", and that they constitute "obstacles for the development of the Common Market *to the same extent* as the maintenance of tariff borders, etc.", and that consequently they "have to be abolished".[76]

In relation to internal conflicts cases, as here defined (i.e. those containing no relevant connection with any system of law outside the Community) there can surely be no question but that the basic considerations previously discussed,[77] which necessitate the attainment of internal legal uniformity throughout the Community in matters of substantive law, impose a corresponding necessity to ensure that the results thus accomplished are not partially, or even totally, circumvented by reason of the capriciousness of which private international law is sometimes capable. Thus, it is here strenuously submitted that, among the obligations incumbent upon the Member States as a consequence of their having become members of the Community, and notwithstanding the absence of any express provision to that effect within the texts of the Treaties themselves, there exists a general obligation to accomplish the progressive harmonisation of their rules of private international law in their entirety, and likewise to co-ordinate their administrative practices in relation to private international law, to an extent sufficient to ensure the eradication of all possible sources of distortion in the determination of legal questions involving reference to the laws of two or more Member States. It is further submitted that, once it is conceded that an obligation does indeed arise within the context of the operation of the European Communities, appropriate authorisation already exists within the provisions of the ECT to furnish a valid basis for the implementation of any legislative measures which may be thought necessary in order to bring about the realisation of this goal. Such measures could take the form of Directives or Regulations enacted on the basis of Arts. 100 or 235, or of further Conventions concluded between the Member States in response to a suitably liberal interpretation of the spirit and purport of A. 220 ECT. Indeed, as will be demonstrated in Part II of this book, the latter Article already appears to have undergone precisely such an expansive construction, both in the course of realisation of its explicit requirements in relation to the negotiation of conventions governing the Reciprocal Recognition and Enforcement of Judgments,[78] and, *a fortiori*, in the process of responding to the more implicit authorisations alluded to therein, as in the case of the Convention of 19 June 1980 concerning Contractual Obligations.[79] Such concerted action on the part of the Member States is undoubtedly capable of reconciliation with the open language of the first indent to A. 220 ECT, which requires the Member States to secure for their nationals "the protection of persons and the enjoyment and protection of rights under the same conditions as those accorded by each State to its own nationals". But in the view of this writer, there is need for the Member States to go much further than they have so far done, and it is respectfully urged that they should also make genuine efforts to accelerate the rate of progress in this area which has, unquestionably, been disappointingly slow. Even ahead of, or for that matter even despite the absence of, further measures sponsored at Community level in the near future, it should be possible for the Member States, and in particular for the courts functioning within all ten States, to adopt a positive attitude towards the challenge which is here presented, namely that they should review, and where necessary revise, their own existing rules of private international law, endeavouring thereby to ensure, so far as they can, that these rules are so applied as to maximise the extent to which the results in cases of intra-Community conflicts are in conformity with the principal objectives of the Community. Such action at national level is perfectly in accord with the precepts voiced in A. 5 ECT, which, it will be recalled, provides that "Member States shall take all appropriate measures, whether general or particular, to ensure fulfilment of the obligations arising out of this Treaty, or resulting from action taken by the Institutions of the Community. They shall facilitate the achievement of the Community's tasks. They shall abstain from any measures which could jeopardise the attainment of the objectives of the Community". Likewise, the provisions of A. 7 ECT may once more be invoked in aid of any review or revision of law or procedure which is aimed at ensuring that the prohibition against any discrimination on grounds of nationality is fully respected on the part of every Member State.

It may be objected at this juncture that the foregoing exhortations to unilateral action on the part of the Member States may in some instances be self-defeating, if their net effect serves merely to proliferate the examples of diversity which already abound in the area of private international law. A further, practical objection may be based on the technical difficulties confronting a court sitting at national level, should it aspire to discover the existing state of the law in force in all nine sister states on the point at issue before it. Indeed, even should such information be obtained, in many cases the extreme diversity, and number, of the alternative positions adopted by the different Member States' laws may be such as to defy all hope of devising a *via media*, and it is not without significance, besides, that there would be no guarantee that any solution which commended itself to the judiciary of one Member State would find ready acceptance elsewhere. All of these difficulties must be acknowledged, and it may well be that in practice they combine to create intractable problems which no single national court alone could aspire to surmount. Nonetheless, it is submitted that the attempt to explore, and possibly to solve, the problems is always worth making, for at the very least it may serve to reveal the magnitude, and the practical reality, of what might otherwise be supposed to constitute merely theoretical difficulties commanding no special priority with regard to bringing about their eventual solution by concerted efforts. On the other hand, the national court experiencing difficulty in responding to the challenge posed by an internal conflicts problem could, and it is submitted should, enlist the assistance of the European Court of Justice by means of a reference pursuant to A. 177 ECT,[80] treating the question as one of Community law on which it is necessary to obtain a decision in order to enable the national court to give judgment. The resources of the Court of Justice are certainly such as to make it pre-eminently qualified to undertake the sort of comparative investigations which the question may well require, and it is to be noted besides that a further advantage of this procedure being employed is that the ruling of the Court of Justice, by taking its place within Community jurisprudence, will thereafter constitute a source of reference and inspiration for all courts in all Member States.

It is hoped that courts, and also those responsible for formulating national legislative policies, in the Member States will take seriously the obligation to review, and if necessary recast, their rules of private international law in the light of what has been stated above. No illusions need be entertained about the limitations inherent in any such efforts which take place within the confines of a single Member State, but nevertheless the utility of such exercises is by no means negligible, especially where they serve to furnish inspiration for the promotion of redoubled efforts to resolve problems by means of action to be taken at Community level.

(b)   "External" and "Hybrid" Conflicts Cases

It will be convenient to consider these two types of case together, since they raise common questions of principle which render it difficult, if not impossible, to argue that the two should be treated differently in practice. In the foregoing subsection of this chapter it has been possible to demonstrate, in the case of internal conflicts cases, that the maintenance of Member States' rules of private international law in their presently unharmonised state is directly responsible for the occurrence of inequalities and distortions which contravene precisely-defined, Community obligations. However, the same is not so readily demonstrable in the case of "external" conflicts in which, *ex hypothesi*, significant contacts exist in relation to only one Member State, or its legal system, while all the other legally-relevant ingredients form connections with third states, or with the legal systems of such states. Nevertheless, it is possible to predicate the necessity for the full harmonisation of the Member States' private international law also with regard to external cases, and hence, *a fortiori*, with regard to hybrid cases, upon several grounds. The first, but by no means the most compelling, reason for such harmonisation is simply derived from the logical and practical advantages of consistency and uniformity in the approach to functionally similar legal issues, which is here achieved by subjecting all cases — whether internal, external or hybrid — in which essentially the same issue of private international law is raised, to the same method and rule of solution irrespective of the whereabouts within the EEC of the *forum* of litigation. Such a solution would also have the convenient, further advantage of obviating the development of separate but parallel rules of private international law,[81] and hence possesses obvious, all-round attractions in terms of *elegantia iuris* as well as being a significant contribution to the cause of international legal unification.[82] Such a proceeding would undoubtedly also have favourable implications from the aspect of legal certainty and predictability, coupled with a general raising of confidence in the stability of established rights and expectations based upon sound, harmonised legal principles.

The foregoing considerations, however, could not of themselves suffice to do more than merely render it highly *desirable* that the Member States should harmonise their rules of private international law in relation to external and hybrid cases, and that they should furthermore do so by means of rules and approaches identical to those to be applied to internal cases, or at any rate as closely identical to the latter as proves to be expedient.[83] But it is here forcefully contended that this solution, far from being a mere *desideratum*, is in fact legally compulsory, and is a further manifestation of the obligations which flow, logically and inexorably, from the basic fact of Community membership, but which become progressively discernible only with the passage of time. Once it is recognised that the unique characteristics of the founding Treaties have bestowed upon Community law a dynamic and evolutionary potential, it becomes necessary to pursue to their proper conclusion all the implications of the essential principles which those Treaties enshrine. Accordingly, it has to be appreciated that the eradication of inequalities which operate as distorting factors affecting the functioning of the Common Market [84] cannot be carried out consistently unless regard is had to the *indirect*, as well as the direct, causes of distortion.

(c) Indirectly-Caused Distortion

Indirect forms of distortion, of the type inimical to Community law, are attributable to the disparities in Member States' private international law practices with regard to external cases on at least two broad grounds. In the first place, under certain circumstances parties may successfully avail themselves of the relative advantages offered by any idiosyncratic legal rules or practices prevalent within the jurisdiction of a given Member State. Such cases will constitute examples of distortion wherever it is demonstrable that the sole, or at any rate the paramount, consideration which has induced such parties to render themselves qualified to exploit the legal advantage in question was the very existence of the advantage itself. Here, distortion occurs by virtue of the artificiality of the connection thus established with the law or with the courts of the Member State in question, whether this connection is the result of the adroit use of choice-of-law or choice-of-forum clauses, or (in extreme instances) of a deliberate decision to reside or maintain a centre of corporate operations within, or to accomplish corporate formation under the law of, the Member State whose laws afford the advantage in contemplation. Under the circumstances described, "distortion" will not remain on the merely theoretical level, since it will be manifested in such concrete ways as an exaggeration in the use made of the courts, and of other legal services, within the Member State in question by parties who otherwise lack any compelling reasons for resorting to them. More serious, perhaps, is the possibility that enterprises, and therefore investment and other material elements, might be attracted into the jurisdiction of any Member State able to offer such "Delaware-type" potential. As the domestic laws of the Member States become progressively more uniform as a result of the fulfilment of other programmes set in motion by the Treaties, the scope for this "Delaware syndrome" to yield any worthwhile gains will be increasingly limited to instances where, through the operation of rules of private international law, access is obtained to the domestic laws of non-Member States which naturally remain untouched by any legal developments reforming and harmonising the internal laws of the Member States of the Common Market. In consequence, the gravitation towards the jurisdiction in question would be based primarily upon ulterior motives aimed perhaps at converting a legal advantage into an economic or competitive one.

The second ground on which indirect distortion may be identified follows on from the possibilities which have just been adumbrated, in that identifiable, material advantages may be derived by a given enterprise or entrepreneur through exploiting, in relation to matters otherwise connected exclusively with extra-Community activities, legal facilities which are not simultaneously available to be used by all other competitors operating throughout the Common Market in accordance with the legal regimes to which they are properly and naturally subject. The material gains which are accomplished in this way may, and indeed are likely to, have a "carry-over" effect in relation to the overall competitive position of the enterprise or person in question, and hence will come to have a bearing upon conditions of competition obtaining within the more limited confines of the Common Market itself. Thus, from this indirect source, an appreciable degree of distortion is imparted to competitive behaviour even within the Common Market.

By way of illustration of the possibilities for distortion which have just been suggested above, let it be supposed that there exists a situation in which the rules of private international law of Member States X, Y or Z would all require the application, as *lex causae*, of either their own internal law or at least that of the same non-member State, selected by means of identical choice-of-law processes, accompanied by the application of standardised policies in relation to such matters as the permissible limits within which the evasion of foreign (or domestic) public law may take place. Let it be further supposed that, by the private international law of Member States A, B or C, it is possible for the same situation to give rise to the application of the laws of various non-Member States, selected by means of a variety of choice-of-law processes accompanied by individualised policies and approaches to the questions of party autonomy in relation to choice-of-law, choice-of-forum, and the scope for the evasion of foreign and domestic public law. Within the former group of Member States the elimination of distortion, whether directly or indirectly caused, may be said to have been achieved through a combination of the harmonisation of domestic law, coupled with a unified approach in practice to matters of private international law. In each of the latter group of States, on the other hand, irrespective of the effects of

Community-inspired reforms concerning rules of domestic law, a capacity has been retained for furnishing the means by which, according to circumstances, selective advantages will be attainable by those in a position to secure the application of the private international law of State A, B or C as the case may be. This potential for the introduction of distortion is capable of arising at virtually any point in the conflicts process, from the rules for initial assumption of jurisdiction, via such stages as characterisation, *renvoi*, or the discovery and solution of "incidental questions", through to the final stages of the selection and application of the *lex causae* itself. Indeed, one would go so far as to assert that even the practice of the respective Member States with regard to the enforcement of the judgments of Courts of non-Member States must also undergo harmonisation, in view of the possibility that any discrepancies in this field may, in certain cases, create material inequalities between the positions enjoyed by competitors who are subject to the laws of different Member States with regard to overseas liabilities of a comparable commercial nature. [85]

What has been said thus far in relation to "external" conflicts cases can surely be reaffirmed, with even greater emphasis, with regard to "hybrid" cases, in which contacts exist with two or more different jurisdictions of the Common Market as well as with one or more countries outside. Here, not only are the arguments in favour of uniformity and consistency of approach manifestly stronger (in view, *inter alia*, of the fact that such cases give rise to distortion of a "direct", and not merely of an "indirect" kind), but also the need to make suitable provision for "hybrid" cases further reinforces the argument in favour of the adoption of harmonised rules of private international law to govern "external" cases, since otherwise any attempt to maintain distinctions between the two would inevitably give rise to results which would seem arbitrary, mechanistic and unjust. The two categories may therefore be seen as furnishing mutually-supportive grounds for receiving parity of treatment in accordance with the main argument here being advanced.

In the light of the foregoing considerations, it is submitted that the proposal made to the Commission on 8 September 1967 by the three Benelux countries [86] proposing nothing less than the complete unification of the rules of conflict of laws for the (then) six Member States, was a step which was both logically and legally necessitated by the nature of the Community and by the provisions of the basic Treaties. The venture which was born of this initiative was destined to transcend the limited provisions of A. 220 ECT, and took its inspiration from a wider appreciation of the true purport of the Treaties, read as a whole. It was fully consistent with the overall concept of a Common Market that the Member States, in collaboration with the Commission, should commence the search for identical rules of conflict which would apply both to Member States' relations *inter se* and in relations with non-Community States. While the enormity of the undertaking necessitated the adoption of a progressive approach, and of a schedule of priorities for working purposes, it must be borne in mind that, despite all the difficulties which have subsequently impeded the progress of those engaged upon this great task, nothing short of its total completion will be finally acceptable. For whilever private international law within the Common Market remains at best but partially harmonised, opportunities will survive for *"forum shopping"*, and for other species of legal artifice, to yield appreciable benefits for a fortunate few, under conditions amounting to distortion and thus constituting a continuing violation of Community law. Thus, the following statement by Mr. T. Vogelaar, made in the course of his opening address as chairman of the meeting of government experts convened in response to the Benelux proposal, remains as pertinent today as when it was uttered in February 1969:

"According to both the letter and spirit of the Treaty establishing the EEC, harmonisation is recognised as fulfilling the function of permitting or facilitating the creation in the economic field of legal conditions similar to those governing an internal market. I appreciate that opinions may differ as to the precise delimitation of the inequalities which directly affect the functioning of the Common Market and those having only an indirect effect. Yet there are still fields in which the differences between national legal systems and the lack of unified rules of conflict definitely impede the free movement of persons, goods, services and capital among the Member States." [87]

It is therefore submitted that the progressive, total unification of the rules of private international law which are to be applied by courts located within the Common Market remains one of the important tasks confronting the Member States, and the Institutions, of the Community as a matter of legal obligation derived from the Treaties. While conceding that practical consideration must give rise to selectivity of approach in the short and medium term, it is respectfully urged that this programme must be maintained in view of the integral significance of private international law in the operation of the Common Market, a significance which is destined to become more apparent with the passage of time, as the functional integration of Europe becomes progressively more complete.

(d)   Festina Lente: Limited Traces of Responsiveness to the Foregoing Arguments

The argument which has so far supplied the central theme of the present chapter has been based upon the conviction that the nature of Community law, properly understood, necessarily entails important modifications of private international law for all the participating States, both immediately and also in the longer term. A survey of events and developments within the jurisdiction of the United Kingdom courts subsequent to our taking up membership of the Communities reveals only a very limited state of awareness of the actual and potential impact of EEC law upon the everyday administration of our private international law. Even where such awareness is exhibited, the resulting responses on the part of some important members of the judiciary have been for the most part disappointing. One notable exception consists in a series of *dicta* uttered principally by Lord Denning M.R. on various occasions in the course of giving judgment in cases in which, usually, some question of Community law was present, and in which the learned Master of the Rolls took some pains to voice an acknowledgment of the broad legal consequences of Community membership from the standpoint of the law of the United Kingdom. Thus, in a now celebrated passage in his judgment in *Bulmer* v. *Bollinger*, [88] Lord Denning remarked that "when we come to matters with a European element, the Treaty is like an incoming tide. It flows into the estuaries and up the rivers. It cannot be held back ... ." [89] And in the course of his judgment, delivered on the same day in the interlocutory appeal in *Application des Gaz, S.A.* v. *Falks Veritas Ltd.*, [90] Lord Denning had observed:

"In the ordinary way, the national courts of various Member States can protect and enforce patents, trade marks, copyright and trade names by their own laws with their own remedies as they have always done. ... *But the national courts should not enforce such rights in any case where such enforcement would impede the free movement of goods within the Community between one Member State and another.*"[91]

Admittedly, the foregoing were cases involving questions of "Community" conflicts (i.e. cases involving the effects of possible conflict between Community law and national law) rather than questions of "internal" conflicts between the laws of more than one Member State, but it has already been argued in the course of the present chapter that "Community" conflicts may properly be regarded as belonging to the realm of conflict of laws, albeit as a novel species possessing certain novel characteristics. [92] Hence, it is suggested that propositions of a general kind concerning the impact of Community law upon national legal practice may be applied with equal validity to the more specific question of the essential adjustments in approach to the solution of conflicts problems (whether internal, external or hybrid), which are required of Member States by virtue of the immanence of the Community legal regime.

On at least two matters the English Court of Appeal and House of Lords have had the opportunity to review the implications of Community law from the standpoint of existing, well-established rules of English law bearing upon conflicts cases. The first matter concerned the possibility of an English court awarding judgment expressed in terms of some foreign currency, a possibility which had formerly been altogether excluded by reason of a series of precedents by courts up to and including the House of Lords itself, whereby it had repeatedly been held that the English courts lacked jurisdiction to order payment of money except in English currency.[93] However, in *Schorsch Meier GmbH* v. *Hennin*,[94] the Court of Appeal found in favour of the argument advanced by the plaintiff, a German company, that, by virtue of A. 106 ECT, damages in respect of breach of contract committed by the English defendant could be awarded in terms of German currency which, in the circumstances, represented the currency of the contract. All three members of the Court of Appeal, though expressing their views with varying intensity and generality, concluded that A. 106 ECT furnished a valid ground in law for no longer adhering to the established rule governing judgments in foreign currency in a case where the parties were citizens of Member States of the EEC, and the currency in question was that of one of the Member States. Thus, in the words once again of Lord Denning M.R. (with whose judgment Foster J. concurred), "The English courts would be acting contrary to the spirit and intent of the Treaty if they made a German creditor accept payment in depreciated sterling".[95] Indeed, the Master of the Rolls was prepared to go further, and to argue that this change in the law of England should not be considered to be confined to purely intra-Community cases, but should be treated as enjoying general effect in all cases, a proposition which in view of then extant authorities of the House of Lords in the *Volturno* and *Havana Warehouses* cases,[96] constituted a naked defiance of English rules of precedent as commonly understood and applied. The third member of the Court of Appeal, Lawton L.J., expressly refrained from investing his judgment with more ample aspirations than were strictly necessary in the light of the facts of the case before him, and indeed placed on record his unwillingness to appear to challenge the superior authority of the House of Lords.[97] He was, however, able to concur in the result in the instant case, on the basis of the argument that A. 106 must be taken to have effected a direct change in the law to be administered by English courts.[98] It was, with respect, unfortunate that the Court of Appeal, all three of whose members clearly placed much reliance on the assumption that A. 106 ECT was directly effective in the special sense understood by Community law,[99] nevertheless saw fit not to submit a reference to the European Court of Justice for the purpose of seeking confirmation of this key question regarding the proper interpretation of one of the provisions of the Treaty.[100] Moreover, since there was no appeal against the judgment of the Court of Appeal,[101] no further opportunity arose in those proceedings for testing the validity of the construction which the three members of the Court of Appeal chose to apply to A. 106. However, a few months after this not uncontroversial decision, the same general point of law arose again, in a case this time involving contacts lying outside the EEC, in *Miliangos v. George Frank (Textiles) Ltd.*[102] Before the Court of Appeal itself,[103] which purported to follow as precedent its own recent decision in the *Schorsch Meier* case, the conclusion was arrived at that English law had been altered in accordance with the broader of the two bases of decision (subscribed to by two of the three members of the Court) contained in that case. All three members of the Court in *Miliangos* held that it had become possible for English courts to order payment of sums expressed in foreign currency even in cases not subject to the overriding effects of A. 106 ECT.[104] When the case came on appeal before the House of Lords, however, the opportunity was taken to deliver critical remarks casting doubt upon both the propriety and the correctness of the approaches adopted by the Court of Appeal in deciding both the instant case and also that of *Schorsch Meier*.[105] In general, their Lordships were insistent that it was not open to the Court of Appeal to presume to declare decisions of the House of Lords to have been rendered inoperative, for that task remained the prerogative of the House itself,[106] while in relation to the particular question of the construction previously placed by the Court of Appeal upon A. 106 ECT, the House expressed the gravest of reservations and issued a firm admonition to the effect that any courts which might encounter such questions in future would be well advised to refer them to the European Court of Justice for clarification.[107] With this latter exhortation one can but express the most respectful of agreement in the circumstances under consideration. It must, nevertheless, be a matter of insistence that Community law (which was not strictly in point in the *Miliangos* case itself) must be conceded to be capable of asserting direct effects within the national legal order such that, existing precedents of the House of Lords notwithstanding, courts at all levels are instantly required to respond in fidelity to them.[108] To this extent only one may commend the spirit of allegiance to the principles of Community law on the basis of which the Court of Appeal *purported* to reach its unanimous conclusion in *Schorsch Meier*, while one may yet beg leave to deplore the imperfections in the method and approaches adopted in that decision for the purpose of ascertaining the meaning and authority to be ascribed to the Treaty provision in point. In its decision in the *Miliangos* case itself, the House of Lords in fact, by a majority of four to one, concluded that there were appropriate reasons for overruling the existing precedents of the House in relation to the awarding of judgments in foreign currency,[109] and accordingly English private international law was changed in line with the actual result arrived at in the Court of Appeal both in the instant case and in *Schorsch Meier*. Thus, in relation both to intra-Community conflicts and to external cases, a uniform rule of private international law has been introduced. Regrettably, the House of Lords chose to confine its attention to the broad issues of policy raised by the specific facts of the case it was deciding, wherein no question of Community law was directly in point. Thus, the opportunity was missed for a fuller exploration of what might constitute the optimum rule to be adopted out of consideration for the interests of Community legal development, a particularly unfortunate omission in view of the fact that the new rule laid down by their Lordships' majority decision could certainly be said coincidentally to operate in the best interests of the Community in this matter, for it serves to eliminate many of the arbitrary and unjust consequences which have previously been capable of occurring through such factors as disparities between, and fluctuations of, the relative exchange rates of the currencies both of Member and also of non-Member States.

If in the Miliangos case the House of Lords contrived merely to ignore any opportunities for incorporating considerations of Community obligation into the framework of their decision-forming processes, it must be recorded with regret that in the subsequent case of *The Siskina*[110] their Lordships, when faced with the necessity of considering them directly in the course of disposing of the appeal before them, appear to have exhibited a frankly unreceptive attitude to arguments similar to those which have been advanced in the present chapter. The case arose before the English courts in relation to litigation pending in Italy, before whose courts, according to a jurisdiction clause in the bill of lading, the main action was exclusively capable of being tried. It had become apparent that the defendants' sole asset, from which the plaintiffs might eventually hope to satisfy any judgment of the Italian court in their favour, consisted of the proceeds of an insurance policy payable in England. Accordingly, and perfectly reasonably, the plaintiffs sought to enlist the aid of the English courts by applying for a species of *saisie conservatoire* in the form of a so-called *Mareva* injunction[111] which, if granted, would prevent the defendants from disposing of the policy moneys pending the outcome of the Italian proceedings. The primary obstacle to the granting of the desired injunction lay in the form of wording employed in the relevant rules governing the jurisdiction of the English courts, [112] which in the circumstances would preclude them from assuming jurisdiction in any substantive claim which might be brought by the plaintiffs against the defendants. Consequently, since the *Mareva* injunction operated as an ancillary remedy in relation to substantive proceedings before an English court, it was technically impossible, on the basis of established legal practice, for such an injunction to be granted in the instant case. On this basis, Kerr J. at first instance [113] had refused to sanction the issue of a *Mareva* injunction, but on appeal to the Court of Appeal, [114] a majority of that court [115] were able to find grounds for allowing the injunction to be issued. On a further appeal to the House of Lords, however, [116] the latter Court insisted upon a strict and unvarying interpretation of existing rules concerning both the jurisdiction of English courts and their competence to issue *Mareva* injunctions, and accordingly the issue of such an injunction in the case in hand was held to be impossible. On the question of the possible relevance of Community law, and of its effects upon the central issue raised by the proceedings, it is interesting to contrast the attitudes of Lord Denning M.R. in the Court of Appeal [117] with those of Lords Diplock (with whose speach Lords Simon, Russell and Keith concurred) and Hailsham in the House of Lords. [118] In the former stage of the proceedings, the learned Master of the Rolls introduced, as one of the supporting reasons for his judgment to the effect that English law was here required to undergo modification, arguments based unequivocally upon the premiss that it had become incumbent upon the courts of the United Kingdom to take serious notice of the incidental legal consequences and requirements flowing from our membership of the EEC. Arguing along lines previously rehearsed some months earlier in his judgment in *Trendtex Trading Corporation Ltd.* v. *Central Bank of Nigeria*, [119] Lord Denning was insistent that provisions such as Arts. 3(h) and 100—102, as well as 220 ECT had given rise to a profoundly significant alteration in the spirit and approach required of English courts in relation to the performance of their functions. In the course of giving judgment in the *Trendtex* case, Lord Denning had said (in relation to the doctrine of sovereign immunity):

"Even if there were no settled rule of international law on the subject, there should at least be one settled rule for the nine countries of the European Economic Community. The Treaty of Rome is part of the law of England ... In view of those provisions [viz. Arts. 3(h) and 100—102] it seems to me that it is the duty of each of the Member States — and of the national courts in those States — to bring the law as to sovereign immunity into harmony throughout the Community. The rules applied by each Member State on the subject should be the same as the rules applied by the others."[120]

It is noteworthy besides that in his concurring judgment in the same case, Stephenson L.J. expressly endorsed the same general point of principle.[121] Although these remarks of both members of the court may strictly have constituted *obiter dicta* in the context in which they were initially uttered, they express a basic notion which, with respect, cannot be too often reaffirmed and, where possible, applied in practice. Hence, it was perfectly consistent for the Master of the Rolls to employ the same line of reasoning and approach in his judgment in *The Siskina*,[122] where considerations of the possible impact of Community law were fully relevant, and to make the following assertions:

"Now that we are in the Common Market *it is our duty to do our part in harmonising the laws of the countries of the Nine.* ... It is our duty to apply the Treaty according to the spirit and not the letter. ... Now under A. 220 it is the duty of the Member States to seek to secure the "reciprocal recognition" of the "judgments of courts". To do so in this case means that we should regard a determination by the Italian courts — one of the countries of the Common Market — with the same respect as a determination of the English courts: and that we should give our aid to the enforcement of it to the same extent as we would our own. In particular, we should take protective measures to see that the moneys here are not spirited away pending the decision of the Italian courts. ... In order to harmonise the laws of the Common Market countries, it is therefore appropriate that we should apply protective measures here so as to prevent these insurance moneys being disposed of before judgment."[123]

Neither of the two Lords Justices sitting with Lord Denning in the Court of Appeal was willing to express concurring sentiments in relation to this far-going proposition, and indeed Bridge L.J. in the course of his dissenting judgment expressly affirmed his conviction that, in the circumstances, it could not be said that the requirements of Community law led to the conclusions reached by the Master of the Rolls on the point at issue, nor did he feel that the Court was presently in possession of the resources necessary to undertake properly the task of elucidating the true requirements of Community law in this matter.[124] The strictures and reservations voiced by Bridge L.J. in the Court of Appeal were, if anything, amplified by the members of the House of Lords in their speeches delivered in the final appeal in *The Siskina*,[125] whereby it was decided to restore the judgment of Kerr J. denying the plaintiffs the injunction they had sought. In the leading speech, delivered by Lord Diplock,[126] the suggestion that courts should unilaterally seek for solutions furthering the progress of harmonisation within the Community was strongly refuted in the following passage:

"Under the Treaty the machinery for the harmonisation of the laws of Member States is to be found in A. 100. It is to be done not by individual Member States of their own initiative but pursuant to directives issued by a unanimous decision of the Council of the Communities on a proposal from the Commission and after consultation with the European Parliament and the Economic and Social Committee. There is little encouragement here for judges of national courts of Member States to jump the gun by introducing their own notions of what would be suitable harmonisation of laws concerning their jurisdiction and that of the courts of other Member States." [127]

With the greatest possible respect, the above passage fails to take sufficient account of the capacity of European Community Law to advance by means of jurisprudential developments, and not on the basis of laboriously-enacted, secondary legislation, or international conventions,[128] alone. In particular, in several notable instances the European Court of Justice has boldly proceeded to give effect to what it discerned to be the dictates of the basic Treaties, notwithstanding the fact that the enactment of various Directives expressly mentioned in the Treaty, or the taking of other deliberate actions on the part of the Community Institutions, had not taken place.[129] It must additionally be insisted that, in concentrating attention upon a single Article of the Treaty (A. 100), Lord Diplock has overlooked the implications borne by such other provisions as Arts. 3, 5 and 7, to say nothing of the more general conclusions which, as has been explained, are nowadays seen as flowing inevitably from a comprehensive and enlightened appraisal of the Treaty.

Perhaps the most effective rejoinder to the policy of judicial passivity, seemingly commended to all national courts by Lord Diplock and his brethren in *The Siskina*, is to be found within the judgment of the Court of Justice in Case 71/76, *Thieffry* v. *Conseil de l'Ordre des Avocats à la Cour de Paris*,[130] in which it is asserted that, once it has been discerned that a given right or freedom (in the instant case, freedom of establishment) forms one of the objectives of the Treaty, thereafter:

"In so far as Community law makes no special provision, these objectives may be attained by measures enacted by the Member States, which under A. 5 of the Treaty are bound to take "all appropriate measures, whether general or particular, to ensure fulfilment of the obligations arising out of this Treaty or resulting from action taken by the Institutions of the Community", and to abstain "from any measure which could jeopardise the attainment of the objectives of this Treaty".

Consequently, if the freedom of establishment provided for by A. 52 can be ensured by a Member State either under the provisions of the laws and regulations in force, or by virtue of the practices of the public service or of professional bodies, a person subject to Community law cannot be denied the practical benefit of that freedom solely by virtue of the fact that, for a particular profession, the Directives provided for by A. 57 of the Treaty have not yet been adopted."[131]

The jurisprudence of the Court of Justice has been consistent, and increasingly insistent, upon the matters of principle which are here being advanced with all possible vigour. There is also a small, but highly distinguished and significant, *corpus* of doctrinal literature[132] in which similar arguments are advanced to the effect that the onset of European Community Law is such as to require extensive reappraisal and adjustment by the Member States of their rules of private international law, even in areas which ostensibly seem far removed from the themes and topics expressly mentioned in the basic Treaties. A. 5 ECT may indeed be discernible as the key provision in this context, and at least one highly informed writer has gone so far as to assert that, given that the abolition of internal juridical frontiers and the creation of a single juridical domain represent characteristic elements of the Communities' overall objectives, national laws which detract from the effects of Community law, once the latter has become crystallised in some clearly-expressed form, will constitute a default by the State in question in respect of its Treaty obligations.[133] Since, as has been seen, the judgments of the Court of Justice itself are capable of bringing about exactly the sort of crystallisations of which we are speaking here, it is surely all the more vital that a national court, which has some intimations of the possible significance of Community law for the point at issue in proceedings before it, should provide the Court of Justice with the opportunity to pronounce upon the question in a preliminary ruling which can then serve as the basis for an authoritative final determination by the national court itself.

As further support for the thesis which has been argued at length above, one may invoke finally the general sanction accorded by the original six Member States to the essential proposition regarding the logical and legal necessity for the complete unification of the private international law of the Member States. This sanction was, it is submitted, implicit in their positive response to the proposal to this effect originally advanced by the Benelux countries.[134] In conclusion, therefore, it must be affirmed that, despite the disappointing pronouncements of the English House of Lords in the two main cases discussed above,[135] there are promising indications elsewhere, and no shortage of reinforcing arguments besides, which enable a cautious optimist such as the present writer to venture to hope that legal practice in the United Kingdom will gradually develop in accordance with the principles herein advocated.

3. Conflicts Rules Evolved by and for the Community Itself

In the light of what has been said thus far in the present chapter concerning the obligations springing from the Treaties in relation to the harmonisation of the private international law of the Member States, it is interesting to conclude with a survey of the conflicts rules which are already identifiable within the provisions of Community law itself. As has been suggested, Community law can lay claim to an independent existence entitling it to be considered as a member of the international "society" of legal orders, and thus capable of becoming involved in its own right in the "collision situations" which furnish the basis of private international law. Naturally, the special nature and purpose of Community law impart certain characteristics of an unusual — not to say exceptional — nature to some of the rules and solutions which are employed. For example, in view of the close functional relationship between the Community and its constituent members, it is inevitably the case that the main area of legal interaction in practice lies between the Community legal order and those (individually or collectively) of the Member States. In the first instance, therefore, Community law has, as we have seen,[136] formulated a highly individual solution to this special type of problem (herein designated as one of "Community conflict"), by means of the consistent, and irresistible, application of certain basic principles arrived at by regarding the founding Treaties as a species of "superlaw". Secondly, and as a natural extension of the same basic principles from which Community law derives its unique quality and coherence, it has transpired that a unified approach in all matters of private international law has become required of the Member States themselves, so that harmonised rules and practices will in time come to be employed by all national courts throughout the Common Market when dealing with both internal and external conflicts cases.[137] This harmonisation will progressively be achieved by means of the Conventions discussed in Part II of this book,[138] and also increasingly by means of other legally binding forms of Community act such as directives or regulations,[139] as well as through the jurisprudential interaction between the national and Community courts, along the lines discussed above. But in addition to these important areas of development, it is possible to discern a further one, consisting of conflicts rules evolved by and for the Community itself,[140] and primarily conceived as being applicable whenever the European Court of Justice itself is seized of a case in which a conflicts issue arises. However, in view of the presently limited competence of the Court to exercise plenary jurisdiction many issues which have a bearing upon the functioning of the Community itself as a legal entity will actually arise for consideration before national courts, and hence the application of the conflicts rule in question will be simultaneously affected by the same basic principles which regulate the scope for action by national courts whenever any question of Community law obligations arises.

(a)   Legal Personality and Capacity of the Community

One Treaty provision containing important consequences for the Community in its conduct of affairs is A. 211 ECT (= A. 185 EAET; A. 6(3) CST), which states that in each of the Member States the Community is to enjoy the most extensive legal capacity accorded to legal persons under their laws, and that it may, in particular, acquire or dispose of movable and immovable property, and may be a party to legal proceedings wherein the Commission shall serve as its representative. This provision, in conjunction with that contained in A. 210 (= A. 184 EAET; A. 6(1) CST) to the effect that the Community "shall have legal personality", serves to indicate that the Community is intended to have legal personality both in international and national law, and that in the latter sphere its personality is to be analogous to that of a corporation. At the same time, A. 211 has the further consequence of creating a uniform conflicts rule concerning the method of ascertaining the nature and extent of the legal capacity enjoyed by the Community by virtue of its possession and exercise of legal personality: the question is to be referred for solution to the law of the relevant Member State. Moreover, this rule would seem to be one which is required to be applied by the Community Court of Justice itself or by any national court before which there arises any question concerning the legal capacity of the Community.[141] However, the rule contained in A. 211 appears to beg one most important question by failing to specify which connecting factors are to be regarded as determining the Member State whose law is to be considered "relevant" in any given situation in which the legal capacity of the Community is in issue. It is presumably a residual task for the Court of Justice itself to endow this inchoate conflicts rule with full substance, and it would surely be in full accordance with the established practice of the Court in such matters if the appropriate subsidiary rules were to be formulated by reference to any rules which it may be possible to treat as expressive of "general principles" of law by virtue of the fact that they enjoy common, or widespread, acceptance among the Member States under their existing practices in private international law. However, there exists here a certain danger that logical solecisms of the "chicken and egg" variety might be perpetrated if the Court of Justice were to content itself with deducing some rule on the basis of such approaches as may *currently* be employed by the laws of the Member States in relation to the problem in hand. This is because, as has been argued above, all the Member States' rules of private international law must at some stage be subjected to review precisely for the purpose of ascertaining whether any reform or modification is predicated by the onset of Community law itself. Accordingly, any proceedings in which the Court of Justice encounters the necessity to consider such questions would be suitable occasions for the undertaking of a more rigorous course of enquiry in search of the *optimum* rule, and it is submitted that the Court ought not to feel confined to the adoption of such practices as might happen *at that time* to enjoy currency among the Member States. This is surely the occasion for the Court to search openly for the "best" or "most progressive" solution, and in this task it ought not to be limited to making its choice necessarily from among those solutions actually in use in at least one, or a number, of the Member States: the search for the best solution should be a truly comprehensive one. [142]

Further inspiration in the task of formulating appropriate conflict rules on such occasions could well be derived from an appraisal of the rules which have come to be embodied in those Community Conventions which may have been concluded by the time the matter undergoes judicial consideration, and with which it would clearly be desirable to retain a consistency of approach. Thus, it may now be possible to anticipate that any question of the Community's capacity to acquire immovable property situate within the Community should be referred to the *lex situs*,[143] and that questions of its capacity to acquire property (whether movable or immovable) which is subject to public registration should be referable to the law of the Member State in which the register is kept.[144] Questions concerning the Community's competence to acquire unregistered, movable property may be somewhat less amenable to solution by means of a singular rule (e.g. the *lex situs* may not be a uniformly satisfactory one, where it can be shown that the current *situs* of the property is a fortuitous one), and the same may perhaps be true of the otherwise straightforward-seeming suggestion that the basic question of characterisation of property (i.e. to determine whether it is movable or immovable) should likewise be referred to the *lex situs*.[145] Any question of capacity to enter into a contract would arguably have to be made referable to the law which would govern it,[146] assuming the contract to have been validly formed.[147]

The foregoing proposals have been put forward in contemplation of situations in which all legally relevant contacts are grouped within the Common Market, and hence it may safely be anticipated that if any serious difficulties are encountered in practice on account of true conflicts between the laws of the Member States regarding the Community's legal competence, it ought to prove possible to transform these into "false" conflicts eventually by means of further Community measures harmonising the relevant provisions of the domestic laws of the Member States. Such solutions are not available, however, whenever conflicts arise which involve the laws of non-Member States and hence here once again the special dilemma arises, namely whether the Community should adhere to uniform principles already developed for internal purposes, and proceed to dispose of such "external" cases through the application of the same rules, or whether on the other hand special rules should be created to avert any possibility that in a given situation the legal capacity of the Community to accomplish some desired objective should come to be denied on the footing that the law of the third country, referred to in accordance with conflicts rules formulated along the lines suggested above, fails to accord it the requisite capacity. Here once again it is submitted that the preferable course to be followed is for the Community legal system to aspire to operate on the basis of uniform rules of private international law as far as possible, without regard to whether under certain circumstances this will result in the application of the law of some non-Member State.[148] However, in order to avert the possibility that the Community itself might incur unnecessary inconvenience as a result of too rigid adherence to its own ideals in such matters, it must be conceded that, where the initiative rests with the European Court of Justice or with the Court of any Member State, a residual discretion should be exercisable in the name of Community public policy, to avoid the substantive application of the law of any non-Member State whose legal provisions on the matter in question are found to be *seriously* at variance with those obtaining among the Member States of the Community. It should be noted, however, that the mere fact that the law of a non-Member State is *somewhat* at variance with the laws of the Member States with regard to the capacity of legal entities cannot *per se* constitute a valid ground for excluding the application of the law of that State, since the possible continuance of some variation in this matter is specifically envisaged by the terms of A. 211 ECT with regard to the laws of the different Member States themselves.

(b)   Contractual Liability of the Community

A. 215(1) ECT (= A. 188(1) EAET) specifies that the contractual liability of the Community shall be governed by the law applicable to the contract in question. Although possessing the appearance of a general conflicts rule governing the interpretation of all contracts to which the Community is a party (irrespective of the identity of the other party or parties to the contract), this provision of itself is incapable of furnishing a complete solution to any questions arising from such contracts, since it offers no guidance on the method by which "the law applicable to the contract in question" is to be ascertained. Thus, a crucial aspect of the choice of law process is left unprovided for, and remains the task of the court seized of the proceedings in which any question of contractual liability arises. Such jurisdiction may be exercised by the Court of Justice itself only in the event of the contract containing an "arbitration clause", whereby the Court may be rendered competent in accordance with A. 181 ECT (= A. 153 EAET; A. 42 CST). In such cases it is to be expected that the Court will resort to its familiar practices to fashion a rule for finding the proper law of the contract. The search for a "common principle" within the laws of the Member States would readily yield a rule based upon the concept of "party autonomy",[149] but little else. Thus, absent a choice of law clause, it will be necessary for the Court to formulate additional rules to identify the "proper law", and it would again seem reasonable — and would make for overall consistency — if the Court were to regard as a further repository of "General Principles of Community law" the provisions of Conventions to which the Member States have together become parties, and in particular the Convention of 19 June 1980 on Contractual Obligations.[150] On the other hand, to the extent that the rules contained in that Convention may prove to be less than completely satisfactory in practice, it would perhaps be worthwhile for the Court to regard itself as free to develop alternative solutions where they can be shown to be better than the ones offered by the Convention.[151]

Where a contract is concluded without an "arbitration clause" invoking the jurisdiction of the Court of Justice, jurisdiction will be enjoyed by any other court validly nominated by means of a *forum* clause, or in the absence of any such clause, by any court whose own rules of jurisdiction[152] enable it to entertain proceedings relating to the contract. It is expressly provided by A. 183 ECT (= A. 155 EAET; *cf.* A. 40(3) CST) that in cases where jurisdiction has not been conferred upon the Court of Justice itself, disputes to which the Community is a party may be competently heard by the courts or tribunals of the Member States. Until the process of ratification and incorporation of the Convention on Contractual Obligations[153] is fully accomplished by all the Member States, their pre-existing rules of private international law will be applied whenever their courts are called upon to discover the proper law of a contract to which the Community is a party. However, once the Convention has entered into force in any Member State, the courts of that state will thereafter be required to determine the proper law of the contract in accordance with the rules specified in the Convention.

Finally, it may be observed that in contractual matters between the Community and its employees, the combined effect of Arts. 179 and 215(3) ECT (= A. 152 and 188(3) EAET; 40(2), last sentence, CST) is to invest the Court of Justice with jurisdiction under the terms of the Staff Regulations or Conditions of Employment, which also have the effect of determining the personal liability of its employees towards the Community.

(c) Non-Contractual Liability of the Community

A. 215(2) ECT (= A. 188(2) EAET) declares:

> "In the case of non-contractual liability, the Community shall, in accordance with the general principles common to the laws of the Member States, make good any damage caused by its institutions or by its servants in the performance of its duties."

The use, in accordance with civil law terminology, of the expression "non-contractual liability" ensures that this provision, though primarily concerned with questions of tortious liability, is also capable of covering such other matters as restitution. No further guidance is provided as to the method of determining whether a matter is to be classified as "contractual" or "non-contractual" for the purposes of subjecting it to the respective provisions of paragraphs (1) or (2) of A. 215. This is presumably a task to be undertaken by the court seized of jurisdiction, at an early stage in the proceedings. In the case of actions for damages under A. 215(2) ECT, it appears to be generally agreed that the Court of Justice enjoys exclusive jurisdiction, by virtue of the combined effects of Arts. 178 and 183 (= Arts. 151 and 155 EAET; *cf.* Arts. 34(1) and 40 CST).[154] Hence, the task of resolving any differences of opinion whether a given litigious issue should undergo classification as "contractual" or "non-contractual"[155] should be performed by the Court of Justice, mindful of the implications of its determination from the aspect of the practice of private international law in the Member States. For it would surely be in accordance with the best interests of the Community (and, incidentally, would be consistent with the thesis herein being advanced) if a uniform approach were to be followed by the Court of Justice and by national courts in relation to the exacting and crucial process of classification in private international law.[156] Therefore, as has been argued above,[157] the creation of unified solutions to problems of classification should be regarded as part of the overall programme of harmonisation of private international law within the Common Market.[158] But in view of the likelihood that such an undertaking will encounter numerous practical difficulties, the task of the Court of Justice in determining any issues of classification arising in proceedings under A. 215(2) ECT will need to be pursued with considerable delicacy, and should moreover be approached in such a way as to avoid the creation of a needless dichotomy between the categories of characterisation developed in relation to proceedings in which the Community is a party, and the categories utilised in practice whenever the same litigious issues arise in proceedings in which the Community is not involved. Therefore, it is suggested, the specific invocation within A. 215(2) itself of "general principles common to the laws of the Member States" should be interpreted in the most ample sense possible, in order to create an enlightened jurisprudence in relation to the determination of the non-contractual liability of the Community. In particular, it may be noted, the effect of this key phrase is to designate the *lex fori* as the mandatory *lex causae* in all suits of this nature, and in view of the further fact that jurisdiction therein is reserved exclusively to the European Court of Justice, it follows that the task to be pursued by the Court in such proceedings is not one of choice of law, but rather one of injecting a specific meaning and content into the phrase "general principles common to the laws of the Member States". In other words, it has been left to the Court of Justice to create by means of its jurisprudence the substantive law of the Community in the field of non-contractual liability.

Although a detailed consideration of the developments to date under A. 215(2) ECT would be out of place in the present work,[159] the response of the Court to this "praetorian" law-making role created for it by the Treaty is worth remarking upon, in view of the suggestions which have already been made above concerning the opportunities arising elsewhere under the Treaty for the Court to function creatively by means of a selective approach to "General Principles of law".[160] Since the laws of the (now) ten Member States fail to display any degree of common approach to questions involving the tortious liability of states or public authorities and their agents, doctrinal writers have not been slow to urge that the opportunity exists for the Court to play a formative role through the imaginative use of comparative techniques in discovering the best, and most suitable, legal principles and rules which at the same time remain sufficiently faithful to the generalised spirit of the legal traditions of the Member States.[161] In line with such suggestions, the developing jurisprudence of the Court is beginning to exhibit a somewhat eclectic (if uneven) character,[162] in its search for the correct point of balance between the interests involved. Thus, although its insistence so far upon the basic principle that liability is to be fault-based undoubtedly

operates in favour of the Community as defendant,[163] the Court has afforded some comfort to the individual seeking to recover damages from the
Community by deciding that the degree of fault on the part of the latter
which will suffice to give rise to liability is *simple* wrongfulness in relation to
the acts or measures in question, as opposed to *gross* fault (*faute lourde*),
which would be extremely difficult for any plaintiff to prove in practice.[164] On the other hand, it has been held essential that the plaintiff establish that he has suffered, or is definitely destined to suffer,[165] actual damage
which is causally attributable to the wrongful act of the Community,[166] and
the court has gone further in holding that even where such a *prima facie* case
can be made out, the plaintiff is not entitled to compensation unless the
damage has been sustained as a result of a sufficiently flagrant violation of a
superior rule of law for the protection of the individual.[167]

One area of difficulty in which matters of principle are involved concerns
the possibility of concurrent liability incurred by the Community together
with any Member State which, as is frequently the case, has been involved in
the actual implementation of some policy or programme for which the Community is ultimately responsible, and which causes wrongful damage to an
individual. The Treaties fail to make it clear whether, in such circumstances,
a Member State is to be regarded as the mere agent or servant of the Community, or whether the two are to be treated as joint or several tortfeasors.
It may be noted besides that a Member State (or its agents) may commit a
wrongful or illegal act in the course of attempting to administer a Community policy which, in itself, is perfectly lawful in every respect. The usual
practice of the Court has been to examine whether, in the circumstances,
primary liability should be said to rest with the Member State rather than
with the Community. Where this is the case, the individual is obliged to
pursue his remedy before the appropriate national courts, albeit the Court of
Justice may thereafter proceed to dispose of a further claim maintained by
the same plaintiff against the Community, and will endeavour by its judgment to ensure that the duality of proceedings does not give rise to excessive
− or exiguous − compensation *in toto*.[168] The situation which is thus
engendered is amenable to severe criticism on the grounds of the cumbersome nature of the compound procedures which the plaintiff is required to
undergo in order to recover full and adequate compensation, and in view of
the necessary wastage of expense and effort thereby entailed. Furthermore,
fundamental criticism may be levelled at this complex miasma of concurrent
or consecutive proceedings in that it lays the way open to grave disparities
and inequalities in terms of the actual prospects of recovery for litigants
placed in different jurisdictional circumstances. Thus, variations in approach

to these questions of compensation, as between the Community Court
(whose creative role has been explained above) and the national courts (applying, presumably, their established national laws on the matter in point)
may prove to be the basis of indefensible differences in the level of compensation recovered by different litigants who are victims of comparable, or
even identical, wrongs. Nor can this defective state of affairs be properly
cured by means of a policy on the part of the Court of Justice of providing a
"residual award" to attone for any shortfall in the compensation awarded by
the national courts.[169] Not every litigant may be able to afford the cost of
dual proceedings in order to secure in full measure whatever may ultimately
be considered by the Court of Justice to be due to him, while those who are
so able may still legitimately complain of the duplication of costs which this
circuitous procedure entails. Hence, it would seem preferable that all such
proceedings should be capable of being consolidated into the jurisdiction of
the Court of Justice and that the Community and the Member States should
there be liable to be sued jointly.[170]

*(d)   Assertion of Jurisdiction Against Parties Situated or Acting Outside the
Community*

Although the primary sphere of application of Community law, *ratione loci*,
lies within the geographical boundaries of the Community's constituent
Member States and, *ratione personae*, relates to persons who are resident
within (or, even, who are nationals of) one of the Member States,[171] this
does not necessarily represent the full potential ambit of Community law.
However, questions of the possible limits to the spacial application of Community substantive law escape any detailed attention in the basic Treaties,
and, correspondingly, the precise extent of the competence of the European
Court of Justice, or of other Community Institutions which are able to
exercise a judicial function, to assume jurisdiction over parties resident or
established outside the geographical boundaries of the EEC, or acting outside
the same, is nowhere clearly defined. Opportunities for the Court of Justice
to supplement these important omissions in the Treaties have arisen from
time to time, principally in relation to the application of Community law
concerning competition. The extremely open language of the principal provisions of the ECT,[172] upon which competition law is founded, appears to
impose no inherent spacial limitations upon the applicability of the law to
undertakings established inside or outside the EEC, and omits any reference
to the place of acting as a factor capable of operating to exclude the application of Community law, or to render the Commission or Court incompetent

to assume jurisdiction. Thus, A. 85 ECT refers to "all agreements between undertakings, decisions by associations of undertakings and concerted practices which may affect trade between Member States and which have as their *object or effect* the prevention or restriction or distortion of competition within the Common Market ...", while A. 86 speaks of "*any* abuse by one or more undertakings of a dominant position within the Common Market or in a substantial part of it ...".[173] Neither provision actually makes it a requirement that the undertakings in question be established within the Common Market, nor, in the case of A. 85(1), is it suggested that the agreements, decisions or practices in question must necessarily be concluded, taken or put into effect within the territory of the Common Market. Likewise, perhaps, it may be envisaged that the actions which constitute an "abuse of a dominant position" under A. 86 could actually take place outside the Common Market. What is of relevance, however, is the requirement that the actual or intended *effects* of the practices proscribed by the provisions of Arts. 85 and 86 must be experienced *within* the Common Market.

In view of the above, it may be confidently asserted that the jurisdiction of the Court of Justice (and also, in this instance, of the Commission) may be exercised in respect of undertakings which alternatively are established within, or act within, or whose actions, if external, achieve or are intended to achieve forbidden consequences within, the Common Market. It may furthermore be asserted that, in all such cases, the competition law of the Community will be applied as *lex fori* without reference to any question of other rules of law which may simultaneously have been applicable to the same actions or conduct by virtue of any alternative choice of law principles which might be invocable.[174]

(e) Enforcement of Community Judgments

All three of the basic Treaties incorporate provisions which render it obligatory for the judgments of the Community Court, or of the Commission or of the Council, to be enforceable within the territory of the Member States whenever they impose a pecuniary obligation upon any person other than a Member State itself.[175] Enforcement of such Community judgments is not, however, made the subject of a uniform procedure but is declared to be governed by "the rules of civil procedure in force in the State in the territory of which it is carried out".[176] However, a requirement is imposed by Community law to the effect that each Member State must designate an authority[177] which is empowered to issue orders for enforcement of Community judgments pursuant to a single formality of verifying the authenticity of the original decision. Once such an order for enforcement has been issued to the party who has applied for one in this manner, that party is able to proceed to enforce the Community judgment in accordance with national law as though this judgment had been a judgment or order of the national courts of the state in question.[178]

In contrast with the provisions which have been adopted in relation to the enforcement within the Member States of the judgments or orders of the courts of fellow Member States in civil or commercial matters,[179] the rules governing the enforcement of Community judgments incorporate only minimal opportunities for challenging the issue of an order of enforcement. It would appear that the sole ground on which the designated national authority may properly decline to issue the order in response to an application is where it proves to be possible to impugn the authenticity of the document purporting to embody the decision of a Community institution imposing a pecuniary obligation upon the party challenging the application.[180] However, the possible existence of more extensive grounds for opposition to enforcement is hinted at in each of the Treaties by means of the following paragraph: "Enforcement may be suspended only by a decision of the Court of Justice", while the two Rome Treaties go on to add a further proviso to the effect that: "The courts of the country concerned shall have jurisdiction over complaints that enforcement is being carried out in an irregular manner."[181] Jurisdiction is thus restrictively apportioned between the European Court and the national courts on the two respective issues. It would appear to have been left open to the courts in question to determine with what content they will invest the functions which have been bestowed upon them, but in the case of the Court of Justice, it would be appropriate for that Court to make available an order suspending enforcement of a Community judgment not only wherever an interested party makes a *bona fide* application for the interpretation or revision of the Court's own former judgment on which the proceedings for enforcement are based,[182] but also whenever it is possible to show that, *mutatis mutandis*, if the Community judgment had been a judgment to which the Convention of 27 September 1968 were applicable it would not have been entitled to recognition or enforcement by reason of one of the grounds specified in A. 27 of that Convention.[183]

4. Conclusion

The arguments which have been advanced, and the developments which have been described, in the course of this chapter have led the writer to entertain a number of convinced opinions which can be summarised as follows.

(1) From the very fact of their having acceded to the basic Treaties establishing the European Communities, the Member States must be taken to subscribe to the principal objectives set forth in those Treaties.

(2) It further appears that variations in the Member States' private international law rules are capable of giving rise to distortions which effectively derogate from the realisation of these principal objectives.

(3) Accordingly, it is submitted that the co-ordination of their rules of private international law, at least to the extent necessary to eradicate such distortions, must be considered as one of the obligations of Community membership incumbent upon the Member States.

4) In view of this, the Communities are legally justified in the taking of such measures as are appropriate to bring about the requisite co-ordination of the Member States' private international law rules, over and above the cases for which specific provision was included in A. 220 ECT itself.

(5) Moreover, in cases where such direct measures may not yet have been taken by the Communities, it is submitted that efforts should be made within the Member States themselves to review their rules of private international law, and to endeavour, so far as it can be accomplished, to ensure that these rules are so applied (and, if necessary, are so reformulated) as to maximise the extent to which they produce results in conformity with the principal objectives of the Communities. It is further submitted that this final precept constitutes a basic justification for any attempt, within the limits of its own competence, by a court in a Member State so to reformulate, or to modify, an established rule of the national private international law, as to produce a result which would be basically in conformity with the objectives herein referred to.

NOTES

1. CST, A. 7.
2. ECT, A. 4; EAET, A. 3.
3. ECT, A. 164; EAET, A. 136.
4. Signed at Rome on 25 March 1957, on the same day as the two Rome Treaties: see Arts. 3 and 4 thereof.
5. This divergence is alluded to in Chapter 1, *ante*, p. 9.
5a. The Court of Justice took up its duties under the Paris Treaty in 1953, and under the two Rome Treaties in 1958. The first case to be brought under the Coal and Steel Treaty was decided on 25 December 1954, Case 1/54, *Government of the French Republic* v. *High Authority* [1954–56] E.C.R. 1. The first case to be brought under the EEC

Treaty was not decided until as late as 15 July 1960: Cases 43, 45 and 48/59, *Lachmüller* v. *Commission* [1960] ECR 463.

6. For a detailed examination of the legal order established by the Coal and Steel Treaty, see D.G. Valentine, The Court of Justice of the European Coal and Steel Community (The Hague, 1955), and also by the same author, The Court of Justice of the European Communities (London, 1965, 2 vols.). The "orthodox" doctrine of public international law, namely that international agreements *cannot* create direct rights and obligations for private individuals, received its classic expression in the Advisory Opinion of the PCIJ in the *Courts of Danzig Case*, (1928), Series B, No. 15, at pp. 17–18.

7. See A. 6, CST: "The Community shall have legal personality. In international relations, the Community shall enjoy the legal capacity it requires to perform its functions and attain its objectives ... ."

8. *cf.* Case 166/73, *Rheinmühlen-Düsseldorf* v. *EVst* [1974] ECR 33, at p. 38, *para* [2]; [1974] 1 CMLR 523 at p. 577.

9. There are minor discrepancies between the wording of the two Articles in the official English versions of the Treaties, but these probably do not create any substantial differences of meaning. The sole variation between the official French versions of the two Articles lies in the use of the phrase "sauf dispositions contraires de ces statuts" contained in A. 150(c), in place of the phrase "lorsque ces statuts le prévoient" in A. 177(c).

10. Of the extensive literature relating to A. 177 ECT, the following will be found of particular value: F. Jacobs and A. Durand, References to the European Court (1975); L. Collins, European Community Law in the United Kingdom (2nd edn. 1980), ch. 3; N. Brown and F. Jacobs, The Court of Justice of the European Communities (1977), ch. 9; D. Wyatt and A. Dashwood, The Substantive Law of the EEC (1980), ch. 7; P. Kapteyn and P. VerLoren van Themaat, Introduction to the Law of the EEC (1973), ch. 6, section 2. See also Barav (1977) 2 EL Rev. 3; Freeman [1975] C.L.P. 176; Bebr (1977) 26 ICLQ 241.

11. See, for example, Case 13/61, *Bosch* v. *De Geus* [1962] ECR 45, [1962] CMLR 1; Cases 28–30/62, *Da Costa en Schaake N.V.* v. *Nederlandse Belastingsadministratie* [1963] ECR 31, [1963] CMLR 224; Case 20/64, *Albatross* v. *SOPECO* [1965] ECR 29, [1965] CMLR 159; Case 6/64, *Costa* v. *ENEL* [1964] ECR 585, [1964] CMLR 425.

12. Case 13/68, *Salgoil* v. *Italian Ministry of Foreign Trade* [1968] ECR 453, [1969] CMLR 181; Case 127/73, *Belgische Radio en Televisie* v. *SABAM* [1974] ECR 51 and 313, [1974] 2 CMLR 238. See also Case 13/61, *Bosch* v. *De Geus* (*supra*), and Case 31/68, *Chanel* v. *Cepeha* [1970] ECR 403, [1971] CMLR 403. For discussion of the wide sense in which the phrase "court or tribunal of a member state" (as used in A. 177) should be understood, see Jacobs and Durand, *op. cit.*, at pp. 156–57, and 163; Kapteyn and VerLoren van Themaat, *op. cit.* at pp. 177–82; Wyatt and Dashwood, *op. cit.* at pp. 57–58; Brown and Jacobs, *op. cit.* at pp. 142–45; Lipstein, The Law of the EEC (London, 1974) at pp. 328–30; Collins, *op. cit.* at pp. 85–90. In the last resort, any forum or tribunal which is in doubt whether the terms of A. 177 apply to it should pursue an exploratory reference with a view to elucidating this very point, i.e. effectively seeking a ruling upon the interpretation of A. 177 itself: *cf.* Case 61/65, *Vaassen-Göbbels* v. *Beambtenfonds Mijnbedrijf* [1966] ECR 261 at pp. 272–73, [1966] CMLR 508 at pp. 518–519; Case 166/73, *Rheinmühlen Düsseldorf* v. *EVst.* (*supra* n. 8); Case 107/76, *Hoffman-La Roche* v. *Centrafarm* [1977] ECR 957, at p. 973, [1977] 2 CMLR 334, at p. 354.

13. *cf.* P. Kapteyn and P. VerLoren van Themaat, *op. cit. supra* n. 10, at p. 176.

14. See A. 5 ECT, and see Case 33/76, *Rewe-Zentralfinanz and Rewe-Zentral* v. *Landwirtschaftskammer für das Saarland* [1976] ECR 1989, at p. 1997, [1977] 1 CMLR 533, at p. 550; Case 45/76, *Comet* v. *Produktschap voor Siergewassen* [1976] ECR 2043, at p. 2053, [1977] 1 CMLR 533, at p. 553.

15. A. 155 ECT. See also A. 169. Other Member States may also indict a fellow-Member which they consider to have failed to fulfil a Treaty obligation (A. 170), but this procedure has been little used to date.

16. *cf.* Case 16/65, *Firma C. Schwarze* v. *EVst. für Getreide und Futtermittel* [1965] ECR 877, at p. 886, [1966] CMLR 172, at p. 186: the judgment of the Court speaks of "The special field of judicial co-operation under A. 177 which requires the national court and the Court of Justice, both keeping within their respective jurisdiction, and with the aim of ensuring that Community law is applied in a unified manner, to make direct and complementary contributions to the working out of a decision". *cf.* also the submissions of A-G. Lagrange in Case 13/61, *Bosch* v. *De Geus supra* n. 11, at p. 56: "Applied judiciously — one is tempted to say loyally — the provisions of A. 177 must lead to a real and fruitful collaboration between the municipal courts and the Court of Justice of the Communities with mutual regard for their respective jurisdictions."

17. Between 1958 and 31 December 1979, out of a grand total of 1205 cases brought under the ECT, 714 were brought under A. 177. During the same period, out of 7 cases brought under the EAET, 3 were brought under A. 150. None of the 297 cases brought under the CST has to date been based upon A. 41. (See: Synopsis of the Work of the Court of Justice, Luxembourg, 1980.)

18. Case 26/62, [1963] ECR 1, [1963] CMLR 105.

19. There is an extensive literature regarding the doctrine of direct effect. See, for example, Bebr (1970) 19 ICLQ 257; Winter (1972) 9 CMLRev. 425; Dashwood (1978) 16 JCMS 229; Easson (1979) 28 ICLQ 319; Wyatt and Dashwood, *op. cit.* ch. 3.

20. *supra* n. 18.

21. [1963] ECR at p. 12, [1963] CMLR at p. 129. *cf.* The submissions of A-G. Roemer at [1963] ECR, pp. 19—26, [1963] CMLR at pp. 113—22.

22. [1963] ECR at p. 13, [1963] CMLR at p. 130.

23. *ibid.* at pp. 13—15 and p. 130, respectively. The Court implies the supremacy of Community law by its insistence that any increase in customs duties or charges having equivalent effect, contrary to the prohibition contained in A. 12 ECT, would be "illegal", and that the said Article confers upon individuals (parties upon whom such illegal charges are imposed) "rights" (i.e. the right *not* to have such charges imposed) which national courts "must protect".

24. Case 6/64, [1964] ECR 585, [1964] CMLR 425. *cf.* also the comments of Ld. Denning, M.R., in referring to what he called the "twin pillars on which Community law rests", in his judgment in *Shields* v. *E. Coomes (Holdings) Ltd.* [1979] 1 All E.R. 456, at pp. 460—62.

25. [1964] ECR at pp. 593—94, [1964] CMLR at p. 455.

26. [1964] ECR at p. 594, [1964] CMLR at p. 456.

27. *cf.* the Court's formulaic expression employed in ruling that Arts. 53 and 37(2) ECT are directly effective: "Such a ... prohibition which came into force with the Treaty throughout the Community, and thus became an integral part of the legal system of the Member States, forms part of the law of those states and directly concerns their nationals, in whose favour it has created individual rights which national courts must protect": [1964] ECR at pp. 596 and 597, respectively, [1964] CMLR at pp. 458 and 459.

28. Opinion of A-G. Lagrange [1964] ECR at p. 602, [1964] CMLR at p. 439.

29. *ibid.* at pp. 602—603 and 439, respectively (emphasis in original).

30. *cf.* the judgment of the German Bundesfinanzhof in response to the ruling of the Court of Justice in Case 28/67, *Molkerei-Zentrale* v. *HzA Paderborn* (cited *infra* n. 32). In its judgment of 11 July 1968, the German court stated: "If a rate of taxation contravenes A. 95, the relevant provision of the national law is *not void* in the sense that no tax may be levied under it at all. That view is contradicted by the fact that such a rate of taxation

contravenes a legal rule only in relation to Member States of the Community and not in relation to third countries. In the case of imports from Member States, therefore, a rate of taxation is inapplicable only to the extent that it contravenes A. 95": [1969] CMLR 300, at p. 312 (emphasis added).

31. [1964] ECR at pp. 602–603, [1964] CMLR at p. 439. The Advocate-General also went on to speak of "the co-existence within each Member State of *two systems of law*, domestic and Community, each operating in its own sphere of competence" (at p. 603 and p. 440, respectively).

32. The principal cases in this sequence are, in order of decision: Cases 28–30/62, *Da Costa en Schaake* v. *Nederlandse Belastingsadministratie* (*supra* n. 11); Case 57/65, *Lütticke* v. *Hauptzollamt Saarlouis* [1966] ECR 205, [1971] CMLR 674; Case 28/67, *Molkerei Zentrale* v. *HzA Paderborn* [1968] ECR 143, [1968] CMLR 187; Case 27/67, *Firma Fink-Frucht* v. *HzA München-Landsbergerstrasse* [1968] ECR 223, [1968] CMLR 228; Case 13/68, *Salgoil* v. *Italian Ministry for Foreign Trade* [1968] ECR 453, [1969] CMLR 181; Case 14/68, *Wilhelm* v. *Bundeskartellamt* [1969] ECR 1, [1969] CMLR 100; Case 33/70, *SACE* v. *Italian Ministry of Finance* [1970] ECR 1213, [1971] CMLR 123; Case 18/71, *Eunomia di Porro* v. *Italian Ministry of Education* [1971] ECR 811, [1972] CMLR 4; Case 127/73, *Belgische Radio en Televisie* v. *SABAM* (*supra*, n. 12); Case 106/77, *Amministrazione delle Finanze* v. *Simmenthal* [1978] ECR 629, [1978] 3 CMLR 263. All of the foregoing were principally concerned with Articles of the Treaty; with regard to secondary legislation of the Community, see also: Case 43/71, *Politi* v. *Italian Ministry of Finance* [1971] ECR 1039, [1973] CMLR 60; Case 93/71, *Leonesio* v. *Italian Ministry of Agriculture and Forestry* [1972] ECR 287, [1973] CMLR 343; Case 50/76, *Amsterdam Bulb B.V.* v. *Produktschap voor Siergewassen* [1977] ECR 137, [1977] 2 CMLR 218 (all concerning Regulations); Case 9/70, *Franz Grad* v. *Finanzamt Traunstein* [1970] ECR 825, [1971] CMLR 1 (decided together with Case 20/70, *Transports Lesage et Cie* v. *Hauptzollamt Freiburg* [1970] ECR 861, [1971] CMLR 1; and Case 23/70, *Haselhorst* v. *Finanzamt Düsseldorf* [1970] ECR 881, [1971] CMLR 1); Case 33/70, *SACE* v. *Italian Ministry of Finance* [1970] ECR 1213, [1971] CMLR 123; Case 41/74, *Van Duyn* v. *Home Office* [1974] ECR 1337, [1975] 1 CMLR 1; Case 36/75, *Rutili* v. *Minister of the Interior* [1975] ECR 1219, [1976] 1 CMLR 140; Case 51/76, *Verbond van Nederlandse Ondernemingen* v. *Inspecteur der Invoerrechten en Accijnzen* [1977] ECR 113, [1977] 1 CMLR 413 (concerning questions of the direct effectiveness of Directives and Decisions). For a convenient summary of the primary Treaty provisions which have been held to be directly effective, see Collins, *op. cit. supra* n. 10, at pp. 73–76.

33. Case 11/70, *Internationale Handelsgesellschaft* v. *EVst für Getreide und Futtermittel* [1970] ECR 1125, [1972] CMLR 255. For a survey of the various degrees of responsiveness displayed over the years by the national courts of the different Member States, see Bebr (1971) 34 MLR 481 and (1974) 11 CMLRev. 3; Simon (1974) 90 LQR 467 and (1976) 92 LQR 85; Simon and Dowrick (1976) 92 LQR 357 and (1979) 95 LQR 376; Bermann (1979) 28 ICLQ 458. For discussion of the theoretical considerations underlying the relationship between Community and national law, see Ipsen (1965) 2 CMLRev. 379, esp. at 394 *et seq.*; Van Dijk (1969) 6 CMLRev. 283; Mitchell (1967–68) 5 CMLRev. 112 and (1972) 9 CMLRev. 141; de Smith (1971) 34 MLR 597; Trindade (1972) 35 MLR 375; Winterton (1976) 92 LQR 591.

34. (1977) 93 LQR 349 at p. 351.

35. Case 13/61, *Bosch* v. *De Geus* [1962] ECR 45, at pp. 49–50, [1962] CMLR 1, at p. 26.

36. Case 14/68, *Wilhelm* v. *Bundeskartellamt* [1969] ECR 1, at p. 14, [1969] CMLR 100, at p. 119.

37. Case 18/71, *Eunomia di Porro* v. *Italian Ministry of Education* [1971] ECR 811, at p. 816, [1972] CMLR 4, at pp. 10–11.

38. Case 93/71, *Leonesio* v. *Italian Ministry of Agriculture and Forestry* [1972] ECR 287, at pp. 295—96, [1973] CMLR 343, at p. 354.

39. Case 36/75, *Rutili* v. *Minister of the Interior* [1975] ECR 1219, at p. 1229, [1976] 1 CMLR 140, at pp. 153-54.

40. Case 50/76, *Amsterdam Bulb B.V.* v. *Produktschap voor Siergewassen* [1977] 2 CMLR 218, at pp. 240 and 243.

41. Case 106/77, *Amministrazione delle Finanze* v. *Simmenthal* [1978] ECR 629, at pp. 643 and 645—46, [1978] 3 CMLR 263, at pp. 283 and 284.

42. *supra* n. 35.

43. *cf.* also the subsequent case-law involving the application of the *Bosch* v. *De Geus* decision in proceedings between private parties: e.g. *FIVA* v. *Mertens* [1963] CMLR 141; *SARIE* v. *UNEF* [1963] CMLR 185; *Re "Agfa-Optima"* [1963] CMLR 268.

44. [1974] Ch. 381, [1974] 3 All E.R. 51 (C.A.). The appeal was an interlocutory one, and the proceedings subsequently shed their "Community law" aspects. For another early case in which similar arguments were advanced (unsuccessfully, in the circumstances), at first instance, see *Esso Petroleum Co. Ltd.* v. *Kingswood Motors (Addlestone) Ltd.* [1973] 3 All E.R. 1057.

45. *cf.* also the acknowledgement by both the C.A. and the H.L. in relation to the effect of A. 85 ECT upon English law, in *Rio Tinto Zinc Corpn.* v. *Westinghouse Electric Corpn.* [1978] A.C. 547 (a case involving issues of privilege against self-incrimination).

46. [1974] Ch. 401, [1974] 2 All E.R. 1226 (C.A.). The provisions of Community Law invoked were A. 30 of Regulation 816/70, and Arts. 12 and 13 of Regulation 817/70.

47. [1974] CMLR 1. The provision of Community law invoked was A. 36 ECT.

48. [1975] Q.B. 416, [1975] 1 All E.R. 152 (C.A.), invoking A. 106 ECT. Although certain aspects of this decision have given rise to criticism, especially with regard to the omission by the C.A. to refer the interpretation of A. 106 to the Court of Justice, the actual ruling in the case, to the effect that English courts may henceforth award judgment expressed in a foreign currency, was subsequently confirmed by the H.L. in *Miliangos* v. *George Frank (Textiles) Ltd.* [1976] A.C. 443, [1975] 3 All E.R. 801 (discussed *infra* at p. 59).

49. This expression is employed as a term of art in s. 2(1) of the European Communities Act, 1972.

50. There is controversy at present on the question whether Directives and Decisions may also affect the rights of individuals *inter se* by virtue of the doctrine of direct effect. It is now generally accepted that directly effective provisions in Directives and Decisions certainly have consequences for the rights of individuals *vis-à-vis* the state. See literature cited *supra* n. 19, and especially Wyatt and Dashwood, *op. cit.* at pp. 36—42, and Easson, *loc. cit.* at pp. 342—44.

51. [1974] ECR 51, [1974] 2 CMLR 238.

52. [1974] ECR 1405, [1975] 1 CMLR 320, applying principles formulated in case 167/73, *Commission* v. *French Republic, Re French Merchant Seamen* [1974] ECR 359, [1974] 2 CMLR 216 (an infraction case in which the relevant conditions of employment in the sector of merchant shipping, which were the subject of specific statutory provisions under French law, were held to be in violation of A. 48 ECT, and of A. 4 of Regulation 1612/68, in so far as they maintained a discriminatory policy towards the employment of nationals of other Member States. See also Case 33/74, *Van Binsbergen* v. *Bestuur van de Bedrijfsvereniging voor de Metaalnijverheid* [1974] ECR 1299, [1975] 1 CMLR 298, and Case 39/75, *Coenen* v. *Sociaal-Economische Raad* [1975] ECR 1547, [1976] 1 CMLR 30, both concerning issues of the compatibility of restrictions based on a residential requirement with the freedom to provide services secured by Arts. 59—66 ECT.

53. Freedom of establishment, governed by Arts. 52–58 ECT inclusive, was first held to be an enforceable Community right in Case 2/74, *Reyners* v. *Belgian State* [1974] ECR 631, [1974] 2 CMLR 305.

54. See Case 2/74, *Reyners* v. *Belgian State* (*supra*), and also Case 71/76, *Thieffry* v. *Conseil de l'Ordre des Avocats à la Cour de Paris* [1977] ECR 765, [1977] 2 CMLR 373· and Case 11/77, *Patrick* v. *Ministre des Affaires Culturelles* [1977] ECR 1199, [1977] 2 CMLR 523.

55. [1976] ECR 455, [1976] 2 CMLR 98. See also Case 80/70, *Defrenne* v. *Belgian State* [1971] ECR 445, [1974] 1 CMLR 494, and Case 149/77, *Defrenne* v. *SABENA* [1978] ECR 1365, [1978] 3 CMLR 312. For comment on this litigation see, especially, Wyatt (1975–76) 1 E.L. Rev. 399–402, and 414–20, and (1978) 3 E.L. Rev. 483–88; Crisham (1977) 14 CMLRev. 102; Allott [1977] C.L.J. 7. See also Case 129/79, *Macarthys* v. *Smith* [1980] ECR 1275, [1979] 3 CMLR 44.

56. The Court of Justice imposed a special restriction upon the temporal effect of its ruling so as to restrict claims for arrears of pay and other benefits in respect of periods prior to the actual date of the judgment itself (8 April 1976): only those cases where legal proceedings had actually been commenced or some equivalent claim had actually been lodged before that date could actually benefit retrospectively: see [1976] ECR at 480–81, [1976] 2 CMLR at 128.

57. *cf.* the inchoate doctrine of the extraterritorial effectiveness of the Community law concerning competition: it has been hinted (though not yet actually held) that parties established outside the Community, or agreements concluded outside the Community, may alike be caught by the provisions of Arts. 85 and 86 ECT if *effects* are produced *inside* the Community: see Case 48/69, *I.C.I. Ltd.* v. *Commission* [1972] ECR 619, [1972] CMLR 557.

58. This point was emphasised by the Court of Justice in the "Third Defrenne" Case, Case 149/77, *Defrenne* v. *SABENA* (*supra* n. 55).

59. For a thorough discussion of these rights, and of the provisions of Community primary and secondary law by which they are secured, see, for example, Wyatt and Dashwood, *op. cit.* chs. 13–15; F.G. Jacobs (Ed.) European Law and the Individual (North-Holland, 1976), *passim*.

60. See Case 6/64, *Costa* v. *ENEL* [1964] ECR 585, [1964] CMLR 425, quoted *supra*, p. 31.

61. See, for example, A. Ehrenzweig, Specific Principles of Transnational Law (1968, III) 124 Hague Recueil des Cours, especially at pp. 182 and 219–54.

62. *cf.* A.E. Anton, Private International Law (Edinburgh, 1967) at p. 32.

63. *cf.* European Communities Act 1972, s. 3.

64. *cf.* Warner, *loc. cit. supra* n. 34, at p. 351.

65. *cf.* the impact of A. 119 ECT, discussed in relation to the *Defrenne* case, *supra* p. 37.

66. *cf.* D. Lasok, The Law of the Economy in the European Communities (1980), p. 418 *et seq.*

67. See Part II of this book.

68. *supra*, pp. 13 and 30.

69. For notable exceptions to this general assertion, see esp. Savatier (1959) 48 Rev. Crit. D.I.P. 237 (also printed in Les Problèmes Juridiques et Economiques du Marché Commun (Lille, 1960), p. 55); Hallstein (1964) 28 Rabels Z. 211; Zweigert, in Probleme des Europäischen Rechts (Festschrift Hallstein) (1966), 555; Drobnig (1967) 15 AJCL 204; Jähr (1972) 36 Rabels Z. 620; Graveson, in Liber Amicorum Ernst J. Cohn (1975), p. 61; Hauschild (1975) Rev. Trim. dr. Eur. 4.

70. *supra*, pp. 9–12.

71. For fuller discussion of these benefits, see Wyatt and Dashwood, *op. cit.* chs. 13, 14; Lasok, *op. cit. supra* n. 66, ch. 5; F. Jacobs (Ed.) European Law and the Individual, esp. chs. 2, 3 and 4.

72. See, for example, Regulation 1612/68 (J.O. 1968, L.257/2; O.J. Sp. Ed. 1968 (II), p. 475) Arts. 10–12; Directive 68/360 (J.O. 1968, L. 257/12; O.J. Sp. Ed. 1968 (II), p. 485); and Regulation 1251/70 (J.O. 1970, L. 142/24; O.J. Sp. Ed. 1970 (II) p. 402). See also annotations to the foregoing legislation in Encyclopaedia of European Community Law, vol. C IV.

73. See Regulation 1408/71 (J.O. 1971, L 149/2; O.J. Sp. Ed. 1971 (II), p. 416), A. 1(f), (g). See also Case 24/71, *Meinhardt* v. *Commission* [1972] ECR 269; [1973] CMLR 136 (question of the legal effects of a divorce granted by a German court to husband and wife both of German nationality, held to be governed by German law).

74. *cf.* Zweigert, *loc. cit. supra* n. 69.

75. *cf.* the widely-differing consequences which still result under the laws of different Member States from any finding that a given person is illegitimate. Whereas some States have reformed their laws with a view to eradicating all practical distinctions between legitimate and illegitimate persons, elsewhere within the Community these two categories are made the subject of profoundly discriminatory legal treatment, which in one instance at least has attracted the condemnation of the European Commission and Court of Human Rights: see Application no. 6833/74, *P. and A. Marckx* v. *Belgium*, Report of the Commission adopted 10 December 1977 and Judgment of the Court of 13 June 1979.

76. H.C. Ficker, *loc. cit. supra* p. 13, n. 39 (emphasis added).

77. Chapter 1 *ante* at pp. 12–16.

78. See Chapters 4 and 6 *post* at pp. 104 and 188, respectively, in relation to the Judgments and Bankruptcy Conventions.

79. See Chapter 5 *post*.

80. This, it is submitted, should have been the course adopted by the English Court of Appeal in *Schorsch Meier GmbH* v. *Hennin* [1975] Q.B. 416, mentioned *supra* on p. 36 and discussed *infra* at p. 58. *cf.* the *dictum* of Lord Denning M.R. in *Shields* v. *E. Coomes (Holdings) Ltd.* [1979] 1 All E.R. 456, at p. 462. See also Drobnig, (1967) 15 AJCL 204, at pp. 225–26.

81. These problems are further considered in Chapter 3, *post*.

82. *cf.* remarks in Chapter 1, *ante* at p. 16.

83. See Chapter 3, *post*, for some concessions to the possibility that, on pragmatic grounds at least, parallelisms may have to be maintained in exceptional cases, for the time being at least.

84. See the arguments presented *supra*, especially at pp. 13–14, to the effect that the eradication of such distortion constitutes one of the fundamental principles established by the Treaties.

85. Such a discrepancy might, for example, have a considerable bearing upon the question of the true commercial risk being assumed in practice by enterprises based in different Member States which compete with one another for business in the same overseas country.

86. This proposal has already borne fruit in the form of the Contracts Convention: see Chapter 5 *post*.

87. E.C. Commission Doc. 4.365/XIV/69. See, especially, pp. 3–4.

88. [1974] Ch. 401, refd. to *supra*, p. 36. (The decision of the Court of Appeal was a unanimous one, Stamp and Stephenson LJJ. concurring with the decision of the Master of the Rolls.)

89. [1974] Ch. at p. 418.

90. [1974] Ch. 381, refd. to *supra*, p. 36. (The decision of the Court of Appeal was

again a unanimous one, Stamp and Roskill LJJ. this time concurring.)

91. [1974] Ch. at p. 394. A little further on in the judgment (at p. 396) the following statement is to be found: "I should think that in equity if a person comes from abroad to the English courts seeking to enforce his strict rights in English law, he will not be allowed to enforce them, if by so doing he himself is unduly restricting competition within the Common Market or is abusing a dominant position within it."

92. See section 1, *supra*, pp. 23–43.

93. See, for example, *Manners* v. *Pearson and Son* [1898] 1 Ch. 581 (C.A.); *Owners of S.S. Celia* v. *Owners of S.S. Volturno* [1921] A.C. 544 (H.L.); *Re United Railways of the Havana and Regla Warehouses Ltd.* [1961] A.C. 1007 (H.L.).

94. [1975] Q.B. at p. 416.

95. [1975] Q.B. at p. 426.

96. *supra* n. 93.

97. [1975] Q.B. at p. 430.

98. *ibid.* at pp. 430–31.

99. See *supra* pp. 29–35 for explanation of the expression "directly effective".

100. *cf.* the criticism voiced by Lord Wilberforce in his speech in *Miliangos* v. *George Frank (Textiles) Ltd.* [1976] A.C. 443 at p. 465, and contrast the remarks of Lord Denning M.R. himself in *Shields* v. *E. Coomes (Holdings) Ltd., loc. cit. supra* n. 80, See also the decision of the Court of Justice itself concerning the interpretation of A. 106 ECT in Case 22/80, *Boussac* v. *Gerstenmeier* [1981] ECR 3427, [1982] 1 CMLR 202.

101. The defendant did not appear in the C.A. proceedings and was not legally represented.

102. [1976] A.C. 443 (H.L.); [1975] Q.B. 487 (C.A.). The "outside" contact in the case was with Switzerland.

103. This time consisting of Lord Denning M.R. and Stephenson and Geoffrey Lane L.JJ.

104. It follows of course that the C.A. were reaffirming the interpretation which had been applied to A. 106 in the former case by the same (differently constituted) court.

105. *supra* n. 94.

106. See [1976] A.C. at p. 459, *per* Lord Wilberforce, at pp. 472–73, *per* Lord Simon, and at p. 496, *per* Lord Cross.

107. See [1976] A.C. at p. 465, *per* Lord Wilberforce, at p. 477, *per* Lord Simon, and at p. 498, *per* Lord Cross.

108. See cases cited and discussed *supra* at pp. 29–35, esp. Case 106/77, *Amministrazione delle Finanze* v. *Simmenthal* [1978] ECR 629, [1978] 3 CMLR 263.

109. See [1976] A.C. at pp. 467–70, *per* Lord Wilberforce (with whose reasoning Lords Cross, Edmund Davies and Fraser all concurred). *cf. ibid.* at pp. 479–90, *per* Lord Simon.

110. [1979] A.C. 210.

111. Named after the case originally associated with the innovation of this species of remedy under English law, *Mareva Compania Naviera S.A.* v. *International Bulkcarriers Ltd.* [1975] 2 Ll. Rep. 509 (C.A.). Thus, the remedy was still in a somewhat formative phase of its development at the time of the proceedings in *The Siskina*, and it is perhaps noteworthy that several subsequent cases have contributed to its expanded use in several important ways: see *Allen* v. *Jambo Holdings Ltd.* [1980] 1 WLR 1252; *Barclay-Johnson* v. *Yuill* [1980] 1 WLR 1259; *Rahman (Prince Abdul) bin Turki* v. *Abu Taha* [1980] 1 WLR 1268 (C.A.).

112. R.S.C. Ord. 11, r. 1(1)(i), together with Supreme Court of Judicature (Consolidation) Act 1925, s. 45(1).

113. [1979] A.C. at p. 215.

114. [1979] A.C. at p. 225.
115. Lord Denning M.R. and Lawton LJ., Bridge LJ. dissenting.
116. [1979] A.C. at p. 243.
117. See [1979] A.C. at pp. 225–36, esp. at pp. 233–35.
118. See [1979] A.C. at pp. 258–59, and 262–63, respectively.
119. [1977] Q.B. at p. 529.
120. [1977] Q.B. at pp. 557–58.
121. [1977] Q.B. at pp. 570–71: The key passage of the judgment of Stephenson LJ. on this point contains the following statements: "We should also keep in step with the courts of the other countries who have signed the Treaty of Rome. A. 3(h) is primarily directed to such economic questions as distortion by competition, as Arts. 100–102 show. But it lays down a general idea of approximation or 'rapprochement' or 'Anglei-chung'; that is, 'harmonisation' to be undertaken by the Member States of the Council of Europe (*sic*) in the legal field ... which ought to result in the courts of all the European Economic Community countries coming as close to each other as possible in their decisions, the law which they apply, and their application of it".
122. [1979] A.C. 210, at p. 225.
123. [1979] A.C. at pp. 233–35.
124. [1979] A.C. at pp. 242–43. It has already been suggested (*supra* p. 58) that the appropriate way forward in such cases lies by way of a reference to the Court of Justice, using A. 177 ECT.
125. [1979] A.C. 210.
126. [1979] A.C. at p. 252. Lords Simon, Russell and Keith concurred without delivering separate speeches; Lord Hailsham delivered a speech concurring with that of Lord Diplock on all essential points.
127. [1979] A.C. at p. 259. See also the speech of Ld. Hailsham, *ibid.* at pp. 262–63.
128. In a passage of his speech immediately following that quoted in the text above, Lord Diplock observed that A. 220 required the Member States to make provision for recognition of the jurisdiction of each other's courts by means not of a Directive, but of a Convention. However, he laid emphasis on the fact that the United Kingdom had not, at the time of the proceedings, become a party to the Convention of 27 September 1968, and he declined to draw inspiration even from the terms of A. 24 of that Convention (discussed in Chapter 4 *post*) as furnishing any basis for amending current English legal practices: see [1979] A.C. at p. 259.
129. The outstanding examples of such initiatives by the Court of Justice include Case 2/74, *Reyners* v. *Belgian State* [1974] ECR 631, [1974] 2 CMLR 305; and Case 43/75, *Defrenne* v. *SABENA* [1976] ECR 455, [1976] 2 CMLR 98, both discussed *supra* at pp. 37–38.
130. [1977] ECR 765, [1977] 2 CMLR 373.
131. [1977] ECR at p. 777, [1977] 2 CMLR at p. 403. Here, it is submitted, although the Court was not specifically addressing its attention to the potential role to be played by the courts of Member States in collaborating to procure the realisation of the overall aims of the Treaty, such a notion is surely implicit, and follows logically from all that has been said in the first section of the present chapter about the nature and operation of the Community legal order.
132. See the publications cited *supra*, n. 69.
133. Hauschild (1975) RTDE 4, alluding in particular to the cogent force of the rules contained in conventions concluded under A. 220 ECT.
134. For discussion of this proposal and its consequences, see *supra* pp. 55–56.
135. Namely, *Miliangos* v. *George Frank (Textiles) Ltd.* [1976] AC 443; and *The Siskina* [1979] AC 210.

136. *supra* pp. 23—43.

137. *supra* pp. 43—56.

138. See Chapters 4—7 *post*.

139. See concluding remarks in Chapter 8 *post*.

140. *cf*. Drobnig (1967) 15 AJCL 204, together with literature cited therein in footnotes 1, 2 and 3 pp. 204—206.

141. The rule would thus seem to be applicable in any intra-Community conflicts case in which any question arises of the Community's competence in terms of national law.

142. *cf*. the opinion of A-G. Lagrange in Case 14/61, *Hoogovens* v. *H.A.* [1962] ECR 253, at pp. 283—284, [1963] CMLR 73, at p. 85.

143. *cf*. Judgments Convention (Chapter 4 *post*) A. 16(1).

144. *cf*. Draft Bankruptcy Convention (Chapter 6 *post*), A. 28.

145. *cf*. Draft Bankruptcy Convention, A. 19.

146. See the discussion *infra* of A. 215(1) on the question of the allocation of the "applicable law".

147. *cf*. the Contracts Convention (of 19 June 1980, discussed *post* in Chapter 5), A. 8.

148. *cf*. the Contracts Convention, A. 2.

149. *cf*. Drobnig, *loc. cit. supra* n. 140, at p. 212; Lorenz (1964) 13 AJCL 1, at p. 6. It has apparently become standard practice for contracts entered into by the Community to contain a choice of law clause: *cf*. Case 23/76, *Pellegrini* v. *Commission* [1976] ECR 1807, [1977] 2 CMLR 77.

150. Discussed *post* in Chapter 5. See esp. pp. 161—65 on the question of the determination of the proper law of the contract in the absence of express choice.

151. *cf*. Drobnig, *loc. cit. supra* n. 140, at p. 213, urging that the Court should develop the best and most progressive choice of law rules possible whether or not they happen to be derived from the existing laws of the Member States.

152. Taking account, in the case of the courts of any Member State, of the relevant jurisdictional principles established by the Judgments Convention, discussed in Chapter 4 *post*.

153. Discussed *post* in Chapter 5. See, especially Arts. 28 and 29.

154. *cf*. Dumon (1969) CDE 3; Lagrange (1965—66) 3 CMLRev. 10; D. Valentine, Court of Justice of the European Communities (1965), vol. 1, at pp. 327—28; A. Campbell, Common Market Law, vol. 3 (1973) at 6.237—6.255.

155. For example, it may be imagined that under some conditions the Community might seek to plead a defence based upon contract in response to an action for liability in tort. Should the proceedings be classified as contractual or non-contractual? *cf*. North (1977) 26 ICLQ 914.

156. Of the abundant literature concerning classification, see, for example, Kahn (1891) 30 Jhering's Jahrbücher 1; Bartin (1897) Clunet 225, 466, 720; Lorenzen (1920) 20 Col. L. Rev. 247; Beckett (1934) 15 BYBIL 46; A. Robertson, Characterisation in the Conflict of Laws (1940); Bland (1957) 6 ICLQ 10; Lederman (1951) 29 Can. Bar Rev. 3, 168; Nussbaum (1940) 40 Col. L. Rev. 1470; M. Wolff, Private International Law (2nd edn. 1950) pp. 146—67 (ss. 138—157); W.W. Cook, Logical and Legal Bases of the Conflict of Laws (1942), ch. 8; Kahn-Freund (1974, III) 143 Rec. des Cours 147, at pp. 369—82, also published as General Problems of Private International Law (1976), ch. IX; Dicey and Morris, Conflict of Laws (10th edn. 1980), ch. 2; E. Rabel, Das Problem der Qualifikation (Darmstadt 1962); J. Falconbridge, Conflict of Laws (2nd edn. 1954), chs. 3 and 4.

157. *supra* pp. 53—56.

158. One obvious problem for which a uniform approach is highly desirable is the classification of limitation as a matter of substantive or procedural law. *cf.* English Law Commission Working Paper no. 75 (February 1980).

159. For a full discussion of the subject, see G. Lysen, Non-Contractual Liability of the European Community (1976); Mackenzie Stuart, The Non-Contractual Liability of the EEC (1975 Maccabaean Lecture in Jurisprudence) (1975) 12 C.M.L.Rev. 493; Collins, *op. cit. supra* p. 77, n. 10, at pp. 184—86; Brown and Jacobs, *op. cit. supra* p. 77, n. 10, at pp. 107—23; Dumon, *loc. cit. supra* n. 154; Lagrange, *loc. cit. supra* n. 55.

160. See, for example, *supra* pp. 9—12, and also *infra* pp. 96—97.

161. *cf.* Lagrange, *loc. cit. supra* n. 55, at p. 32; Kapteyn and VerLoren van Themaat, *op. cit. supra* p.   , n. 10 at p. 94.

162. The influence of French administrative law is often discernible, e.g. in the adoption of the basic distinction between *faute de service* and *faute personnelle*, *cf.* Case 4/69, *Lütticke* v. *Commission* [1971] ECR 325.

163. But see Mackenzie Stewart, *loc. cit. supra* n. 159, at p. 20/506, *et seq.* for intimations of a potential trend in favour of the development of a principle of liability without fault and without illegality. *cf.* Cases 9 and 11/71, *Compagnie d'Approvisionnement* v. *Commission* [1972] ECR 391, [1973] CMLR 529; and Case 169/73, *Compagnie Continentale France* v. *Council* [1975] ECR 117, [1975] CMLR 578 (neither case is decisive on this point, however).

164. Cases 5, 7, 13-24/66, *Kampffmeyer* v. *Commission* [1976] ECR 245; Case 30/66, *Becher* v. *Commission* [1967] ECR 285, [1968] CMLR 169.

165. Cases 56—60/70, Kampffmeyer v. Commission [1976] ECR 711.

166. Case 4/69, *Lütticke* v. *Commission* (*supra* n. 162); Case 74/74, *CNTA* v. *Commission* [1975] ECR 533, [1977] 1 CMLR 171.

167. Examples of such "superior rules of law" are: the principle of respect for justifiable and reasonable expectations; the principle of legal certainty — Case 74/74, *CNTA* v. *Commission* (*supra*); the prohibition against discrimination — Case 97/76, *Merkur* v. *Commission* [1977] ECR 1063; Cases 44—51/77, *Union Malt* v. *Commission* [1978] ECR 57, [1978] 3 CMLR 703.

168. Cases 5, 7, 13—24/66, *Kampffmeyer* v. *Commission* (*supra* n. 164); Case 96/71, *Haegeman* v. *Commission* [1972] ECR 1015, [1973] CMLR 365.

169. As in Case 96/71, *Haegeman* v. *Commission* (*supra*).

170. *cf.* Hartley (1976) 1 ELR 299—304; 396—99; (1977) 2 ELR 249; Harding (1979) CMLRev. 389.

171. In the case of legal persons, the connecting factors are establishment under the law of one of the Member States, or the maintenance of a centre of operations within at least one of them.

172. Namely Arts. 85—90 ECT inclusive.

173. Emphasis added in each case.

174. *cf.* Case 48/69, *I.C.I. Ltd.* v. *Commission* ("*The Dyestuffs Case*") [1972] ECR 619, [1972] CMLR 557.

175. See Arts. 187 and 192 ECT; Arts. 18, 159 and 164 EAET; Arts. 44 and 92 CST.

176. See A. 192(2) ECT; A. 164(1) EAET: A. 92(2) CST.

177. In England and Wales, the designated authority is the High Court: European Communities (Enforcement of Community Judgments) Order 1972 (S.I. 1972 No. 1590), A. 3.

178. Specific rules for the enforcement of Community judgments in England and Wales have been introduced into Ord. 71 R.S.C. by means of the R.S.C. (Amendment No. 3) Order 1972 (S.I. 1972 No. 1898 (L 27)).

179.   See the Judgments Convention, Title III (*post*, Chapter 4). Special note should be taken of the provisions of Arts. 27 and 37 of the Convention.

180.   *cf.* A. 192(2), (3) ECT; A. 164(1), (2) EAET; A. 92(2) CST.

181.   A. 192(4) ECT; A. 164(3) EAET; A. 92(3) CST.

182.   On the possibility of an application for interpretation of a judgment, see Statute of the Court of the EEC, A. 40; on the possibility of revision of judgments, see *ibid*, Arts, 39 and 41.

183.   A. 27, which establishes five grounds for non-recognition of a judgment, is discussed in Chapter 4 *post* at pp. 134—36.

CHAPTER 3

Hydra Liberata: The Problem of Parallel Rules in Private International Law

1. Introduction

In the majority of cases it is possible to claim that the modifications, introduced into private international law in consequence of the programmes and initiatives being conducted on the international plane, have had the effect of rendering the operation of this notoriously controversial area of law more certain, more simple and more just. This is not altogether a matter for surprise since, after all, the pursuit of these beneficial objectives represents a major part of the very motivation underlying such ventures in international collaboration. But at the same time, it has begun to be apparent that these positive gains are frequently accompanied by a significant new phenomenon, more negative in character, occurring in an incidental manner as a result of the very attainment of the major purposes in view. This phenomenon is the effect herein termed "parallelism", by which is meant a development whereby a plurality of different sets of rules of private international law comes to be operated by the courts of one and the same country, the sphere of operation of each set of rules being determined by the number and identities of the States parties to each of the international agreements in question, and by the criteria of reference incorporated into the new rules embodied therein. Since, in actuality, international treaties and conventions in the field of private international law are concluded between relatively small numbers of states — often as few as two, and seldom amounting to even as many as thirty[1] — the issue inevitably arises whether the modifications which are being made to the laws of the participating States as they proceed to accommodate to provisions of the convention they have lately concluded, shall be made to apply *erga omnes*, or shall be limited in their effects to the cases specifically provided for in the convention itself, and to the instances of such cases in which the parties involved, or the jurisdictions concerned, belong to one or more of the high contracting parties to the convention. This issue presents itself to every one of the high contracting parties in turn, and unless the terms of the convention itself contain a provision which has the effect of determining the matter unequivocally,[2] is unlikely to be resolved in an identical way by all of those concerned. Since most of the rules established by international conventions are the result of either the wholesale renunciation by many, or even all, of the participating states of some long-established rule or principle, or (at best) of a degree of compromise thereon, much weight is likely to be accorded to arguments to the effect that the benefits and advantages of the new rules and procedures should not be lightly or freely extended to benefit the subjects of those States which have not themselves entered into the arena of negotiations and surrendered up their own contributions to the communal sacrifice offered in the interests of reciprocal advantage. Occasionally, the more liberal counsel is seen to prevail, with regard to some of the contracting States, and the new legal rules are there enabled to take effect in all cases falling within the material scope of the convention, regardless of the connections involved.[3] But in relation to every convention, in the case of each one of the contracting States which rejects the latter approach and gives effect to the former,[4] the net effect resembles that which ensued from any onslaught upon the monster of classical mythology: before the courts of that State, two legal rules henceforth operate in parallel where formerly there grew but one. Usually, the original rule is left intact, and continues to be applied in those cases which are held to fall outside the ambit of the changes brought about by the convention, while the new rule is perforce operative in those cases for which the convention was designed to provide. Possibly, according to circumstances, a third category of cases will be seen to exist in a species of "twilight zone" between the old rule and the new, by virtue of their containing elements which render it difficult to allocate them neatly and unequivocally to one main category or the other. Thus, unless some forceful — and hence possibly arbitrary — decision is taken to assimilate these "hybrid" cases into one category or the other, it is possible to envisage a third category of parallel rules of private international law undergoing development within the same jurisdiction.

We have encountered the phenomenon of parallelism in the preceding chapter, wherein attention was drawn to the consequences which appear to flow from the proposition that membership of the European Communities entails for each State the necessity to adjust its private international law so as to conform to a "Community norm", at least in relation to "internal" cases, whose elements are contained within the boundaries of the Community as a whole while simultaneously engaging the jurisdictions of at least two different Member States. It was also foreseen that in consequence of this proposition the further problems associated with "external" and "hybrid" conflicts cases would need to be reviewed, and it was suggested that the *optimum* solution, both in terms of uniformity and simplicity, as well as in terms of the logic inherent in the Community system of law, would be for the Member States and the Community to adopt and apply the same rule for all cases belonging to the same functional type.[5] Such an approach, if adopted, would eliminate the problem of parallelism, which would otherwise continue to be encountered indefinitely by all courts throughout the EEC. The foregoing comments have been devised in the attempt to find a pragmatic solution to the problem of parallelism, which will be encountered whether or not the arguments already presented in favour of the complete harmonisation of private international law within the Community prove acceptable in the immediate future. However, if it should transpire that the solution which is herein advocated fails to command wholesale acceptance throughout the Community for some time to come, it would seem to be both realistic and appropriate to call attention in the meanwhile to the consequences which will ensue from a failure to secure a uniform approach on the part of all courts within the Community to the basic questions of principle posed by the phenomenon of parallelism whose incidence is surely destined to proliferate as more and more developments take place bringing about direct changes in the rules of private international law to be applied within the Community. The problems which are destined to arise in this area are further complicated by two special factors, namely, first, the lack of precise delineation within the provisions of the basic Treaties themselves of the scope and effects which are required to be accorded to such developments in private international law as are therein at all mentioned, and secondly, the even more elusive character of Community law itself, as expounded and administered principally by the European Court of Justice,[6] which has been shown to be capable of making concrete advances whose full significance and purport may only be perceptible after much subsequent reflection and analysis. In the case of "external" conflicts, it might be supposed that the apparent silence of the founding Treaties with regard to such matters has perforce left the Member States free to maintain their established, individual approaches towards the solution of such problems, and indeed to apply their domestic law, where appropriate, in a form unmodified by the impact of Community law *per se*. Such a proceeding has, as we have seen,[7] been rendered improper in relation to any case upon which Community law may properly assert some influence (mainly, but not exclusively, cases in which the parties have a forensic connection with one or more Member State of the Community) but it has also been stressed that the impact of Community law upon national law does not go so far as to invalidate the latter *erga omnes*, even where it is rendered inapplicable against Community nationals. In effect, therefore, each Member State is already currently developing two parallel systems of private international law, the one to be applied to "Community", and in certain instances to "intra-Community" cases, in response to the influence asserted by Community law over national law, and the other to be applied to cases where at least one of the parties is unassociated with the European Communities so that rules of Community law may be regarded as having no bearing upon the case, or where the ingredients of the case *ratione loci* or *ratione materiae* fall outside what are considered by the court in question to constitute the limits of application of Community law. From the aspect of legal certainty, as well as for the purpose of ensuring that the development of the law is kept continuously and fully under review to avert the perpetration of needless complexities or inconsistencies, it is desirable that the emergence of this species of parallelism be acknowledged, and its progress monitored, and that the boundaries and relationships between the two be continuously surveyed and publicised, lest obscurity and uncertainty furnish the cause of needless hardship or injustice. Given the distinction which has now been created between the Member States of the Community and the outer world, the maintenance of disparate rules and procedures for dealing with legal issues which are respectively internal and external to the Community is probably inevitable for the foreseeable future. But at the very least, the foundations and principles on which the Community itself is conceived would necessitate the elaboration of a unified practice among the courts and legal systems of the Member States with regard to the exact delineation of the boundaries between "external" and "intra-Community" and "Community" conflict cases,[8] so as to avoid unevenness of treatment being accorded by the courts of different Member States to cases which are in principle identical, *mutatis mutandis*.

Although the Member States, and the judiciary therein, may perhaps be pardoned for at times giving the appearance of offering resistance to the claims advanced on behalf of Community law,[9] since its precise significance may well have escaped proper detection or general appreciation by the date in question, this latter aspect also renders it highly probable that the implications for private international law of many future developments taking place under Community law would remain undetected for a considerable length of time, until an appropriate case arises in which it is found necessary to assess their collateral impact. It is for this reason that it is highly imperative for the rules of private international law to be kept under constant review in every

Member State, so that every development taking place at Community level, whether in the form of secondary legislation or as part of the jurisprudence of the Court of Justice, may be assessed in terms of its effect upon existing, local rules and practices relating to conflict of laws. Only by monitoring developments in this way can the Member States avert the repetition of further unfortunate lapses of the kind encountered in *The Siskina,* [10] in which the English House of Lords' insistence upon a strict adherence to existing procedural and jurisdictional rules until such time as they might undergo amendment in the light of the eventual decision of the Rule Committee, [11] had the effect of making the plaintiffs in the action in question serve in a self-sacrificial capacity in the cause of legal reform.

2. Other Sources of Parallelism

Apart from the potential for giving rise to parallel sets of rules of private international law which is inherent in the very nature and working of the Community legal system, there are several other examples of international legal co-operation which are simultaneously capable of producing the same effect. Thus, any bilateral or multilateral treaty whereby states negotiate special, reciprocal arrangements for the benefit of their respective subjects before each other's courts has the invariable consequence of creating distinctions of the kind here under consideration. [12] The extensive programmes of legal co-operation promoted under the auspices of the Council of Europe (of which all ten current members of the EEC also are members) are not only capable of giving rise to developments overlapping those taking place as part of the working processes of the EEC, but on certain occasions have actually done so. [13] However, the possibility that these developments might give rise to problems of parallelism in the realm of private international law has in general been avoided by the Council of Europe's self-imposed policy of confining its approach mainly to questions of substantive law. [14] In some instances, however, the subject-matter of conventions concluded within the Council of Europe has carried inescapable connotations for cases involving an aspect of conflict of laws, as in the case of the European Convention on Establishment of Companies, [15] and those concerned with the Place of Payment of Money Liabilities [16] and on the Calculation of Time Limits. [17]

Nevertheless, it is mainly true to say that the Council of Europe has preferred wherever possible to leave questions of private international law to the specialised attentions of the Hague Conference on Private International Law. This organisation, [18] since its modern reconstitution in 1951, has pro-

ceeded to elaborate a series of conventions [19] dealing with matters pertaining
to virtually every aspect of private international law, with the result that
overlap has inevitably occurred between the work of the Hague Conference
(to which all Member States of the EEC also belong) and that of the EEC
itself in the same field. Hence, over and above the possibility that parallel
rules may be developed as a result of more than one international convention
dealing with the same subject, the spectre is raised of further possible conflicts between the conventions themselves, giving rise at times to inextricable
difficulties for those states unfortunate enough to discover that they have
committed themselves to separate international treaties capable of regulating
the same case. [20] Such a prospect indeed threatened for a time to become an
embarrassing reality during the period when the Hague Conference and the
EEC were simultaneously but independently at work producing conventions
in the field of the recognition and enforcement of foreign judgments in civil
and commercial matters. [21] The possibility that the work of other, different-
ly-composed international organisations such as UNIDROIT and UNCITRAL
may also produce effects in the field of private international law further
compounds the possibilities for overlap between conventions, as well as for
the multiplication of the parallel rules of private international law to which
each new development is likely to give rise. So complex has the situation
become already that for those states which are members of most, if not all,
of the organisations in question it has become a source of serious difficulty,
rendering every stage of negotiations, and the final decision on ratification,
an occasion for agonised circumspection in the effort to avoid assuming
mutually inconsistent commitments, or commitments which are irreconcilable with those previously undertaken as a result of earlier international
treaties which may have been entered into.

3. Competitive or Complementary Parallelism? – A Possible Way Forward

The problems adumbrated above did not altogether escape attention even at
the formative stages in the setting up of the organisations whose programmes
of legal activity were perforce destined to give rise to them. Thus, in A.230
ECT it was made incumbent upon the Community to establish all appropriate forms of co-operation with the Council of Europe, while A.229 similarly requires the maintenance of "all appropriate relations" with the organs
of the United Nations and its specialised agencies. For their part, the Committee of Ministers of the Council of Europe adopted Resolution (57) 27 in
December 1957, expressing the wish that "as soon as the institutions of the

European Economic Community and the European Atomic Energy Community are set up, close relations should be established between the Assemblies of the Council of Europe and the Communities of the Six and, in general, between the Council of Europe on the one hand and the EEC and the EAEC on the other". Pursuant to this resolution, steps were taken to formalise the processes of consultation and communication between the two organisations, [22] and at various subsequent times further efforts have been directed towards the improvement of collaboration in the legal field, with a view to avoiding the incidence of overlap between the activities of the two organisations.[23] In the same spirit, the Council of Europe has endeavoured to foster an attitude aimed at resolving the difficulties in a positive way through co-ordinated activities at national and organisational level which are so designed as to be complementary to each other. [24] This aspiration, aimed at replacing competitive parallelism with an orderly programme of complementary developments taking place in parallel, represents, it is submitted, a most sensible and practical response to the problem currently besetting, and threatening to frustrate, the legal programmes of the various international organisations concerned. A further, and highly promising, development which would, where it proves practicable, have the effect of eliminating all possibilities of competitive overlap between conventions, has been the creation of the facility whereby the European Community, in the exercise of the powers and capacities which it enjoys by virtue of its own founding Treaties, [25] may become an acceding party to the conventions of the Council of Europe. [26] A promising beginning has been made with the Community's accession to two Council of Europe Conventions in areas relatively free from controversy, [27] and more ambitious departures may be anticipated on the basis of these useful precedents. [28] It would indeed be highly satisfactory if a further development were to be undertaken along the same lines in relation to the Conventions of the Hague Conference on private international law. Despite the far more numerous and disparate membership of the Hague Conference as compared to that of the Council of Europe, the pursuit of complementary parallelism in the field of private international law is surely a sufficiently worthwhile goal to justify the expenditure of the considerable efforts which would be entailed thereby. Such collaborations would hold the promise of obvious advantages both in terms of the efficient consolidation of the resources devoted to the harmonisation of private international law, and also in terms of greatly reduced possibilities of separate sets of parallel rules of international law coming into existence as a result of such efforts. But in addition, it would be reasonable to expect that one further consequence would be that the rules of private international law actually adopted among the states making up the EEC would possess a more outward-looking and truly international character. This would do much to counter the unfortunate impression which the corporate behaviour of the EEC at times seems calculated to engender, namely that of an inward-looking and essentially xenophobic, "closed" community unwilling to meet the outside world on an equal footing, even in the more remote conceptual realms of private international law. Although it may be thought inappropriate that the Hague Conventions which have already been negotiated and concluded should be acceded to by the Community at this late stage, it would nevertheless be worth while for the Member States of the Community to approach future Sessions of the Hague Conference in the expectation that the Conventions to be concluded should be prepared in such a way as to admit of accession by the Community itself, as well as by the Member States in their own right. [29] In this way the new rules of private international law established by such Conventions would be clearly seen to operate at all levels within the legal systems of the Community, both as part of national law and as part of Community law, and thus any doubts concerning the unity of the rules of private international law to be applied both to internal and to external conflicts cases would be dispelled in a concrete and decisive manner. One other advantage of the adoption of this unified approach by the Community and its members towards negotiations taking place amongst representatives of the wider international community would be the furnishing of a further demonstration of the ability of the Community to function as a single unit in such a context.

A final method of bringing about parallel legal developments of a complementary, as opposed to a competitive, nature may possibly come about through the extended use by the Court of Justice of its occasional practice of making reference to treaties or conventions to which all the Member States happen to have become parties, as a source from which to discover principles or rules capable of being adopted as part of the Community legal order as "general principles of law". This practice has already been employed with skill allied to discretion in relation to the European Convention on Human Rights, which is unquestionably the most celebrated and successful of the Conventions hitherto produced by the Council of Europe, and whose provisions have on several occasions been declared by the European Court of Justice to express principles to which all Member States of the Community have signified their fidelity by virtue of their having ratified the Convention. [30] The same approach may eventually come to be employed by the Court of Justice in relation to other Council of Europe conventions such as the European Social Charter which, in the field of social and economic rights, represents a counterpart of the European Convention on Human Rights, whose provisions are concerned with civil and political rights and freedoms. [31] By a further extension of this process, it is at least foreseeable that, in due course, the European Court of Justice may come to regard the fact that all Member States of the Community have become ratifying parties to a particular Convention produced by the Hague Conference on private international law as a legitimate basis on which to assert that the provisions of the Convention in question must now be taken also to have been assimilated into the general principles of law of the Community itself. Subsequently, once again, there would arise the possibility of further harmonisation of private international law within the EEC as a consequence of the full working through of the processes of legal reasoning which, as has previously been explained, [32] have become established as part of the vital building material from which the Community has been constructed.

NOTES

1. This is true even of the more successful of the conventions produced by the Hague Conference on private international law: see examples quoted in Chapter 1 *ante* at pp. 5—6.

2. *cf.* the Contracts Convention of 19 June 1980, A.2, discussed in Chapter 5 *post*.

3. Such was the approach advocated by the Law Commission in its Report advising Her Majesty's Government on the appropriate measures to be taken in enacting the Hague Convention of 1 June 1970 on the Recognition of Divorces and Legal Separations: see Cmnd. 4542 (November 1970), esp. at para. 19, containing proposals on this point which were subsequently enacted in ss.2 and 3 of the Recognition of Divorces and Legal Separations Act, 1971.

4. This is the approach apparently favoured, on several grounds, by Graveson in his Conflict of Laws (7th edn. 1974) at p. 28.

5. See Chapter 2 *ante* at p. 52.

6. See, in particular, the evolution of certain key concepts of Community law, described in Chapter 2 *ante* at pp. 29—41.

7. Chapter 2 *ante*, section 1.

8. These terms are employed in the same sense as that explained in Chapter 2 *ante* at p. 44.

9. *cf.* the cases revealing uneven attitudes and approaches in operation at different levels of the English judicial hierarchy, discussed in Chapter 2 *ante* at pp. 56—64.

10. [1979] A.C. 210, discussed in Chapter 2 *ante* p. 60.

11. *cf.* the observations of Lord Denning M.R. at [1979] A.C. 235—236 with those of Bridge L.J., *ibid* at p. 242 (C.A.), and with those of Lord Diplock, *ibid* at p. 260, and of Lord Hailsham, *ibid* at p. 262.

12. For a historical survey of international treaties (bilateral and multilateral) in relation to bankruptcy, see Nadelmann (1944) 93 U. Pa. L. Rev. 58 (reprinted in Conflict

of Laws, International and Interstate (1972) at p. 299); in relation to recognition of foreign judgments, see M. Weser, Le Traité franco-belge du 8 Juillet 1899 (Paris 1951); also, by the same author, Convention Communautaire sur La Compétence judiciaire et l'exécution des décisions (Brussels, 1975) at pp. 145—95; Nadelmann (1967) 67 Colum. L.Rev. 995 (reprinted in Conflict of Laws (1972) at p. 238). In general: Rabel, The Conflict of Laws, a Comparative Study (2nd edn. 1964) vol. 1, p. 32 *et seq.*; Vitta (1969, I) 126 Hague Rec. des Cours, p. 137 *et seq.*; Kahn-Freund, General Problems of Private International Law (1976) at pp. 41—50 (also in (1974, III) 143 Hague Rec. des Cours.) *cf.* also the parallel sets of rules for enforcement of foreign judgments operated by English courts, depending upon whether the provisions of the Foreign Judgments (Reciprocal Enforcement) Act 1933 do or do not apply: see Dicey and Morris, Conflict of Laws (10th edn. 1980) ch. 33; Cheshire and North, Private International Law (10th edn. 1979) ch. 19.

    13.   See Dowrick (1978) 27 ICLQ 629 for examples. One celebrated instance occurred in relation to products liability: see Dowrick, *loc. cit.* at p. 636; Fleming (1975) 23 AJCL 729.

    14.   Details of a programme of activities planned in the legal field are contained in the annually-published Programme of Intergovernmental Activities, published by the Committee of Ministers of the Council of Europe.

    15.   Strasbourg Convention of 20 January 1966, E.T.S. No. 57.

    16.   Basle Convention of 16 May 1972, E.T.S. No. 75.

    17.   Basle Convention of 16 May 1972, E.T.S. No. 76. *cf.* also Resolution (72) 1 of the Committee of Ministers of the Council of Europe on the unification of the legal concepts of "domicile" and "residence".

    18.   Described in Chapter 1 *ante* pp. 5—7.

    19.   The Texts of the Conventions are collected and published as Recueil des Conventions (1951—1977) (The Hague 1977). See also M. Soumampouw, Les Nouvelles Conventions de la Haye (The Hague/Leiden 1976).

    20.   *cf.* Hauschild (1975) 11 RTDE 4, at pp. 5—6; M. Weser, Convention Communautaire (Brussels 1975) Part III.

    21.   See Hague Convention and Protocol of 1 Febraury 1971, and the Brussels Convention of 27 September 1968. For comments upon the period of rivalry ensuing from this overlap, see Nadelmann (1967—68) 5 CML Rev. 409, (1968) 16 AJCL at p. 601, and (1969) 82 Harv. L. Rev. 1282. See also Nadelmann and Von Mehren (1966—67) 15 AJCL 361, and (1966) 60 AJIL 803.

    22.   Commemorated in an exchange of letters on 18 August 1959 between Walter Hallstein, the President of the Commission of the EEC, and Lodovico Benvenuti, Secretary-General of the Council of Europe.

    23.   See, for example, the developments summarised by Dowrick, *loc. cit. supra* n. 13, at pp. 638—45, including the opening of the Council of Europe's liaison office in Brussels in 1975, and the established practice of admitting representatives of the European Commission to all meetings of the European Committee on Legal Co-operation.

    24.   *cf.* Report of the Secretariat on the legal activities of the Council of Europe, submitted to the Eleventh Conference of European Ministers of Justice at Copenhagen, 21—22 June 1978, at pp. 27—29, 42 and 64, together with the equivalent Report submitted to the Tenth Conference at Brussels on 3—4 June 1976, at pp. 5—7. See also Annual Programme of Intergovernmental Activities for 1978, Field of Activities VIII (Co-operation in the legal field) esp. pp. 201—49.

    25.   See ECT Arts. 210, 228, 235 and 238.

    26.   This development is discussed by Dowrick, *loc. cit. supra* n. 13, at pp. 641—45.

    27.   Namely, the European Agreement on the Exchange of Tissue-Typing Reagents

(E.T.S. No. 84) and the Convention on the Conservation of European Wildlife and National Habitats (E.T.S. No. 104), to which the European Community became a Contracting Party on 22 November 1977 and 19 September 1979, respectively.

28. For example, the Draft for a European Convention for the Protection of International Watercourses against Pollution is taking shape upon the integral assumption that the European Community will be a signatory from the outset.

29. It is probably too early to hope that the Member States would be content to allow the negotiations to be conducted exclusively by the Commission, as the Community's agent of execution, nor would it perhaps be realistic at this stage to expect the Member States to authorise the acceding signature of the Community to serve as the means whereby all ten Member States shall become parties to future Hague Conventions, but it is submitted that such should be the long-term objective in view.

30. See the following judgments of the Court of Justice: Case 29/69, *Stauder* v. *Ulm* [1969] ECR 419, [1970] CMLR 112; Case 11/70, *Internationale Handelsgesellschaft GmbH* v. *EVst [1970]* ECR 1125, [1972] CMLR 255; Case 4/73, *Nold* v. *Commission* [1974] ECR 491, [1974] 2 CMLR 338; Case 36/75 *Rutili* v. *Minister of the Interior* [1975] ECR 1219, [1976] 1 CMLR 140.

31. See the interesting arguments advanced by the late Professor Kahn-Freund on the potential role of the European Social Charter as a source of general principles of Community Law, in F. Jacobs (Ed.) European Law and the Individual (North-Holland, 1976) ch. 10, esp. at pp. 197—98.

32. See, in particular, Chapter 1 *ante* at p. 13, and Chapter 2 at pp. 29—35.

PART II

Special Part
The Community Conventions on Private International Law

The Convention of 27 September 1968 on Jurisdiction and the Enforcement of Judgments in Civil and Commercial Matters

1. Preliminary

The Convention on Jurisdiction and the Enforcement of Judgments in Civil and Commercial Matters (hereafter referred to as the "Judgments Convention") was signed at Brussels on behalf of the Six original Member States of the EEC on 27 September 1968.[1] It was destined to be the first of the Community Conventions in the field of private international law actually to enter into force, an event which occurred on 1 February 1973 following the completion of the process of ratification by all Six signatories, pursuant to Arts. 61 and 62. The subsequently-concluded Protocol on the Interpretation of the Convention by the Court of Justice, having been signed by the Six on 3 June 1971, similarly entered into force on 1 September 1975.[2] By this time, negotiations were under way to prepare for the accession to the Convention of the three new Member States of the Community. The Convention on the Accession of the Kingdom of Denmark, Ireland and the United Kingdom to the Judgments Convention, and to the Protocol on its Interpretation, was signed at Luxembourg on 9 October 1978 by all nine Member States of the EEC,[3] and constitutes the legal means by which the Judgments Convention will in due course enter into force in relation to the new Member States. The Accession Convention also effects numerous modifications to the principal Convention and to the 1971 Protocol thereto. A. 39 of the Accession Convention states that it will come into force, as between the States which have ratified it, on the first day of the third month following the deposit of the last instrument of ratification by the original Member States of the Community and one new Member State. At the time of writing, the United Kingdom is still in the process of fulfilling the requirements for ratification, but on the assumption that these will be completed in the near future, the following commentary has been written on the basis of the provisions contained in the Judgments Convention and in the 1971 Protocol as they will exist in force following ratification of the Accession Convention.[4]

2. Justification for the Convention

The legal justification for the Judgments Convention is contained in the fourth indent to A. 220 ECT, whereby the Member States of the EEC are committed "to enter into negotiations with each other with a view to securing for the benefit of their nationals ... the simplification of formalities governing the reciprocal recognition and enforcement of judgments of courts or tribunals, and of arbitration awards". Also of relevance are the more general terms of A. 220(1), which speaks of the attainment of "the protection of persons and the enjoyment and protection of rights under the same conditions as those accorded by each State to its own nationals", a provision which serves as a reminder of the basic principle contained in A. 7 ECT, namely that "within the scope of application of this Treaty ... any discrimination on grounds of nationality shall be prohibited". Despite the undoubted breadth of these enabling and motivating provisions of the Treaty, however, it cannot be denied that the subject of "Jurisdiction" is not expressly mentioned among the matters which the Member States pledged themselves to unify. Moreover, it could be argued that the requirements of A. 220(4) would have been adequately met by means of a "simple" or "indirect" type of Convention to establish common criteria which, if fulfilled in the case of any given judgment, would entitle that judgment to recognition and enforcement in the other Member States. Yet the fact remains that, as will shortly appear, the Convention as concluded is actually an example of a "double" or "direct" Convention, imposing mandatory rules for the assumption of jurisdiction which the courts of all Contracting States must obey, irrespective of whether the resultant judgment is or is not destined to require enforcement in other jurisdictions apart from that of the State which constitutes the *forum*.[5] Finally, it may be noted, A. 220 ECT actually speaks of the "nationals" of the Member States of the EEC as the intended beneficiaries of the Conventions contemplated by its provisions, yet, once again, the actual terms of the Judgments Convention have the effect of making its provisions operate for the benefit of persons "domiciled" in any of the Member States, whatever their nationality.[6] Paradoxically, therefore, some nationals of Member States of the EEC, who at the material time happen not to be "domiciled" in any of the Contracting States, may actually be excluded from the benefits which the Convention undeniably does confer, and may indeed experience some of the less admirable properties of the Convention which are capable of operating to the disadvantage of "non-Community-domiciled" persons.[7]

How may all of the above characteristics and properties of the Convention be reconciled with the enabling provisions of the Treaty, from which the Convention derives its authority? The answer is mainly to be sought, it is suggested, in the very nature of the conflicts process itself, and also in the more expansively-conceived notions of Community law and of the Community legal order which were discussed in Part I of this book. Properly understood, it is submitted, the entire theory and practice underlying the recognition and enforcement by courts in one jurisdiction of judgments originating from foreign jurisdictions are inexorably bound up with the complex, and often controversial, questions of the assumption and exercise of jurisdiction in cases containing a foreign element. No scheme for the mutual recognition and enforcement of judgments between countries can operate properly without there being some common agreement concerning the attributes which a judgment must possess if it is to be internationally exportable. Prominent among such considerations is the jurisdictional basis upon which the issuing court first came to entertain the proceedings from which its judgment has resulted. In conventions of the "simple" or "indirect" type, criteria are formulated which, if met in the circumstances of any given case, will provide the judgment with a "passport" enabling it to command full faith and credit in the other contracting states.[8] But the important aspect of the "indirect" type of convention is that it leaves all the High Contracting Parties free to retain and to apply their existing rules of jurisdiction, however exorbitant their character, against all parties *including* those who have any sort of legal connection with the other States Parties to the Convention. Hence, whenever the recognition provisions of such a Convention are invoked, it is always necessary for the recognising court to examine the circumstances in which the issuing court actually assumed jurisdiction, and to be able to form the conclusion that the criteria laid down in the Convention have been fully met thereby. Only then can recognition and enforcement be accorded. The situation which obtains under a "double" or "direct" type of convention is considerably different, because it imposes upon the High Contracting Parties mandatory rules of jurisdiction which they have no choice but to apply in every case falling within the ambit of the Convention, and in particular whenever the party who stands in the role of defendant in the proceedings is one who can properly claim to fall within the ambit of the Convention *ratione personae.* On the assumption that all courts of the States concerned will comply with this solemn obligation, the necessity disappears of scrutinising the original circumstances in which jurisdiction was assumed, and recognition can be accorded virtually automatically, and on the basis of the minimum of procedural formalities, to any judgment issuing from a court in any of the Contracting States, provided that the original proceedings properly fell to be regulated by the Convention *ratione materiae.*

The concluding of a Community Convention of the "direct" type thus fulfils in the most complete way possible both the command within A. 220(4) ECT to bring about the simplification of formalities governing reciprocal recognition and enforcement of judgments throughout the Community, and also that within A. 220(1), to ensure the conferment of equal legal protection upon all the denizens of the Community. Moreover, by taking the radical departure of employing the criterion of "domicile" (used in the sense of "habitual or substantial residence"), rather than that of "nationality" as the main connecting factor in the Convention, the Committee of Experts have demonstrated their awareness of the realities of economic and social existence in a manner which is particularly apposite in the context of the formulation of legal rules for use within an Economic Community. What is primarily of relevance is the *functional* nexus between the individual (whether legal or natural) and the socio-economic system of the Community, regarded as a single juridical entity, actually or potentially. While the factor of "nationality", of itself and without more, carries no such inevitable connotation of a functional link between the individual and the State of his or its "nationality", that of "habitual" or "substantial" residence generally does. In a subtle, but effective, way therefore, the Convention makes an important contribution to the conceptual development of the Community legal order, since it elevates the status of those who contribute to the functioning of the economy of the Community, or who fully participate within its social *milieu*, and correspondingly diminishes the status of those who, though associated with one of the Member States by the tie of nationality, choose (or happen) to be more closely associated at the time in question with some third State by virtue of the fact that they are mainly resident there, whether permanently or not.[9]

It is therefore submitted that the Convention is perfectly compatible with the remit conferred by the terms of the Treaty establishing the EEC. Moreover, the manner in which the task has been accomplished also goes a considerable way towards meeting the logical reasons for unifying rules of jurisdiction among the Member States, and for integrating them closely with the rules for recognition and enforcement of civil and commercial judgments. First among the logical justifications for such an undertaking, one may cite the fact that it is the planned destiny of the Community to function increasingly as a single, internal market within which judicial judgments should enjoy full freedom of circulation, in the same way as goods, persons, services and capital. [10] Indeed, since the existence of, and the capacity of individuals to exercise, the various privileges and rights (many of them directly effective) which together comprise the "four freedoms" of the Common Market, are both ultimately dependent upon the forthcomingness of the judicial process at every appropriate level, the creation of complementary arrangements for the exercise of jurisdiction and for the free circulation of judgments may be regarded as matters of Community necessity. In addition to these considerations, the crucial part played by the rules for assumption of jurisdiction in all cases with an international element cannot be too highly emphasised. Although much has already been done to harmonise the rules of choice of law among the Member States, [11] so that the *forum* of venue will increasingly cease to play a decisive role in determining the actual outcome of proceedings, much still remains to be done before this aspect of distortion, attributable to the variable features of the conflicts process, is altogether eradicated. [12] But even if such matters were to undergo total unification within the EEC, down to and including the final details of nuance inherent in such questions as characterisation and judicial technique in matters of private international law, there would still remain the large issue of principle concerning the appropriateness of making a given court the venue for proceedings in a given case. Here, the main questions to be considered are the relative degree of inconvenience caused to the respective parties by the fact that the proceedings are held in one place rather than another, and the overall, practical advantages inherent in allowing a given court to become the *forum*, such as the proximity to the court of the relevant property and documentation, and of the parties themselves and their witnesses, and the bearing all of this may have upon the ease with which the court may dispose of the case. As a general principle, the majority of authorities have come to regard the axiom *actor sequitur forum rei* as the appropriate notion from which to begin in matters of jurisdiction. Thus, it would normally be expected that the plaintiff should institute proceedings against the defendant in the *forum* which is most convenient from the latter's point of view — usually the court closest to the defendant's place of residence or establishment. [13] But considerations of both practicality and justice may require departure from this principle, especially where its observance would result in an economically weaker or less resourceful party being required to undertake litigation against a stronger party in a jurisdiction possibly far removed from the plaintiff's own country of residence. Actions by the consumer against the seller or supplier of goods or services furnish a ready example of this problem, since to require the consumer invariably to sue such a defendant at the latter's "local" *forum* might effectively lead to a denial of justice through the cost or inconvenience which the plaintiff would inevitably encounter. [14] Other grounds for departing from the general principle *actor sequitur forum rei* may also be readily conceded, as where the defendant voluntarily consents to be sued at some other place, [15] or where the nature of the subject-matter, and its close association with a particular jurisdiction, create such a strong, logical nexus between the proceedings and the jurisdiction in question as to outweigh (probably) the personal links of one or both of the parties with the jurisdiction of his residence, or else are sufficient to balance out these other factors. [16]

In the light of what has been stated above, it may be agreed that a properly-planned, uniform scheme for the exercise of jurisdiction would be the only satisfactory way to achieve a rationalisation of the levels of legal protection to be enjoyed by individuals throughout the territory of the EEC. At the same time, integration of such a scheme with standardised, community-wide arrangements for recognition and enforcement of judgments will provide a distortion-free legal environment in which rights may be enforced, and legitimate interests be protected, under uniform conditions everywhere within the Common Market.

One note of reservation must be registered, however, and must be related to a criterion for the evaluation of this Convention which is believed to follow inexorably from the arguments advanced in Part I of this book. This is that the Community Convention should serve to enhance, rather than to impede, the interplay of legal collaboration and mutual respect between the legal systems operating within the EEC and those of the various countries of the outer world. In this respect, unfortunately, the Judgments Convention displays a propensity to work in a sinister way towards those who do not reside somewhere within the borders of the EEC, by magnifying the exceptionable effects of any exercise of jurisdiction against such persons by the courts of Member States utilising rules of "exorbitant" jurisdiction. Such rules, though now proscribed from use against "Community-domiciled" defendants, are nevertheless permitted to be used against other persons. These rules, which hitherto would have given rise to judgments enjoying purely local effect, now possess Community-wide international effect by virtue of the fact that they fall within the ambit of the Convention. [17]

Regrettably, therefore, the Community's Judgments Convention in many respects fails to create the possibility for establishing a bridgehead from which to pursue the systematic enlargement of the sphere of international, legal co-operation between the Community and the outer world. On the contrary, it actually seems to have been designed to create an atmosphere of mutual suspicion poisoned by resentment, from outside the Community at least, at the almost perversely self-serving attitude betrayed by certain terms of the Convention. [18]

Apart from the one really serious blemish just referred to, however, the Convention undoubtedly constitutes an important, and indeed essential, step towards the realisation of the true juridical destiny of the Common Market. As the first, historically, of the Community Conventions in the field of private international law to enter into effect (and, at the time of writing, still the only one actually to have done so) it also has an enormous symbolic, as well as a practical, importance. Simultaneously, it signifies the magnitude of the task confronting the Member States of a supranational Community, who must sooner or later grasp the nettle posed by the state of diversity existing among them in matters of private international law, and it also offers the necessary proof that such problems can be successfully overcome, given the requisite energy and determination.

3. Evolution of the Convention

Work upon the Judgments Convention commenced in July 1960 as the result of a decision taken by the Committee of Permanent Representatives (COREPER) on 18 February of that year, to respond in a positive way to the invitation, issued to the Member States by the Commission on 22 October 1959, to begin negotiations for the purpose of fulfilling the requirements of A. 220 ECT. The Committee of Experts, to whom the task of drafting the Convention was entrusted, chose Professor A. Bülow and Mr. P. Jenard as its Chairman and Secretary, respectively. Following an intensive sequence of working sessions, a Preliminary Draft Convention was adopted in December 1964, [19] and after further consultation and revision a Draft Convention was adopted by the Experts in July 1966. Formal negotiations then took place between the Member States, and resulted in the Convention being signed in Brussels on 27 September 1968 by the Foreign Ministers of the Six, "meeting in the Council". This latter expression was intended to signify that the Convention was not in fact concluded as a formal act of the Community itself (for which purpose the Council of Ministers would repre-

sent the competent, law-enacting Institution of the Community). [20] A. 220
ECT itself did not expressly state which type of legal enactment was to be
employed for the purpose of giving effect to its provisions, although the
medium of the international Convention was suggested by the reference
therein to "negotiations" to be entered into between "the Member States".

The subtle distinction drawn between acts taken among the Governmental
representatives of the Six when meeting "as" the Council of the Community,
and acts taken among those same representatives meeting only "within" the
same, was (and is) a vital one, however. By rendering the Convention, technically speaking, a "non-Community act", it had the effect of preventing the
Convention and its provisions from being assimilated to other kinds of Community secondary legislation. Thus, for example, it became difficult, if not
impossible, to argue that any provision of the Convention could enjoy the
attribute of direct effectiveness or of direct applicability in the sense in
which these terms have come to be understood in relation to provisions of
the basic Community Treaties, or of Community secondary legislation enacted in the form of Regulations, Directives or Decisions. [21] Furthermore, it
was also impossible for any question of interpretation of the Convention to
be referred to the European Court of Justice by any national court using
A. 177 ECT, since that Article speaks explicitly of "acts *of* the Institutions of
the Community" (emphasis added). Nevertheless it was evident that the
consequence of leaving such questions as the interpretation of the Convention to rest with the courts of the Six alone, would ultimately defeat the
purpose of the Convention itself, since the traditional diversities of their
legal and judicial systems would gradually reassert themselves in practice. It
therefore became necessary to conclude an additional Protocol on the Interpretation of the Convention by the European Court of Justice, in order to
ensure the maintenance of an ultimate uniformity in such matters, and hence
it came about that the Protocol to this effect was signed in Luxembourg on
3 June 1971, this time by the Ministers of Justice of the Six, but meeting
once again "within the Council".

Upon completion of the requisite formalities for ratification, [22] the Convention itself entered into force on 1 February 1973, and the Protocol on
Interpretation did so subsequently on 1st September 1975. [23] In due course,
negotiations were completed with the three new Member States to enable
them to accede to the Convention and to the Protocol of Interpretation, and
a Convention on the Accession of these three States was signed by the
Ministers of Justice of all nine Member States of the EEC in Luxembourg on
9 October 1978. [24] Both the original Convention, and the Accession Convention, have been the subject of officially-published Reports prepared by Mr.

Jenard and by Professor P. Schlosser, respectively, each of whom played a prominent part in the various stages of the work of the Committee of Experts.[25] These Reports seem destined to assume the status of *travaux préparatoires* in the task of interpretation of the Convention by courts throughout the Community. Already during the period in which the Convention has been in force among the Six, it has given rise to a voluminous jurisprudence before the national courts of all the States involved, while with the coming into force of the Protocol on Interpretation by the Court of Justice in 1975, a steadily-growing *corpus* of interpretative rulings by the latter Court has developed in response to references submitted by the courts of the Member States.[26] This jurisprudential tableau, which even now is of somewhat daunting complexity, is destined soon to be augmented by the input from the jurisdictions of the three new Member States. The task of maintaining cohesion and uniformity in the application of the Judgments Convention is a most exacting one, and it provides a foretaste of what is likely to follow when, in due course, other Community Conventions enter into force and begin to give rise to interpretative problems. It is in such contingencies that the latent weaknesses and ambiguities in provisions whose drafting is the result of compromise, or of deliberate evasion of the real issue, become cruelly exposed, with consequences which can be unhappy and costly for the individual parties involved. A great burden of responsibility is in consequence thrust upon the shoulders of the judge, whether belonging to the Community or to the national Bench, who must exercise great ingenuity if the overall goal of Community legal integration is not to seem to have been won at the expense of justice in many individual cases. With such solemn reflections in mind, we will turn to a consideration of the Convention's substantive provisions.

4. Commentary: Scope of the Convention

The fourth paragraph of the Preamble to the Convention refers to the intention of the Contracting States to "determine the international jurisdiction of their courts". Thereby, the basic principle is established that the Convention is designed to apply only to such cases as raise some question of "international" jurisdiction.[27] Although the concept of "international jurisdiction" is nowhere defined within the Convention, interior evidence suggests that wherever the *forum* discovers that both parties to the impending proceedings are "domiciled"[28] within its own jurisdiction, the case may be considered to fall outside the scope of application of the Convention.

Ratione materiae the scope of the Convention is defined by A. 1, which declares that it shall apply "in civil and commercial matters whatever the nature of the court or tribunal". No definition of the expression "civil and commercial matters" is supplied, however, and so the first important question which arises is whether the phrase is to be understood as bearing such meaning as it may have under the law of any of the Member States, or whether some independently-derived meaning is to be attributed to it. Essentially, this is an issue of characterisation, since the same species of claim or remedy, factually speaking, may undergo different "labelling" according to the legal classifications adopted by the different systems of law operating within the Community. In principle, the Convention would rapidly experience a breakdown if the most fundamental of questions, namely that of its very scope of application, were to be allowed to receive a varying interpretation in accordance with the customary approaches adopted by the legal systems of Nine (and, soon, Ten) Member States. Accordingly, the Court of Justice, in Case 29/76, *L.T.U.* v. *Eurocontrol,* [29] one of its earliest interpretative rulings delivered under the Protocol to the Convention, sensibly took the opportunity to exclude such possibilities by insisting that in this context the expression "civil or commercial matters" bears an autonomous meaning, distinct from any meaning which the same word may have when used in the national legal system of any of the Member States. In the Court's judgment, the "Community" meaning of the expression under consideration "must be interpreted by reference, first, to the objectives and scheme of the Convention and, secondly, to the general principles which stem from the *corpus* of the national legal systems". [30] In this way, the Court was able to sidestep conflicts of characterisation which arose in the instant case between the laws of Belgium and of Germany, under the latter of which the proceedings in question would have been characterised as matters of public law falling outside the ambit of the Convention. However, in its final analysis, the Court declared that the application of the test which it had itself just formulated would produce the conclusion that proceedings between a public authority and a person governed by private law, in which the public authority is acting in the exercise of its public powers, are excluded from the area of application of the Convention. [31] It is submitted that this part of the judgment of the Court is regrettable, in that it creates a potentially very large exception to the application of the Convention on the basis of a distinction (namely, between actions under "public" law on the one hand and those done under "private or commercial" law on the other) which, in the context of the modern "mixed" economies of the Member States, may be neither valid nor useful.

Although A. 1 of the Convention does not of itself supply any positive indication of what types of proceedings constitute "civil and commercial matters", the four paragraphs of A. 1(2) indicate in a negative way several specific types of proceedings to which the Convention shall *not* apply. These are: (1) the status or legal capacity of natural persons, rights in property arising out of a matrimonial relationship, wills and succession;³² (2) bankruptcy, proceedings relating to the winding up of insolvent companies or other legal persons, judicial arrangements, compositions and analogous proceedings;³³ (3) social security; (4) arbitration. In addition, a final sentence has been added to A. 1(1) by virtue of A. 3 of the Accession Convention, to declare emphatically that the scope of the Convention shall not extend to revenue, customs or administrative matters. Despite the fairly specific language of these exclusionary provisions, it is evident that further questions of characterisation are destined to arise with regard to each of them, since the terminology employed therein does not carry the same meaning in all the Member States in relation to concrete litigious questions which arise before their courts. In such situations, the importance of making proper use of the Protocol, in order to enable the European Court of Justice to deliver a definitive interpretation of the matter, cannot be too highly stressed.

In three cases to date, the Court of Justice has been asked for rulings on the meaning of specific expressions employed in A. 1(2). In Case 143/78, *Cavel* v. *Cavel,* ³⁴ the Court interpreted the phrase "rights in property arising out of a matrimonial relationship" in A. 1(2)(1) in a broad sense so as to include not only property arrangements specifically and exclusively envisaged by certain national legal systems in the case of marriage but also any proprietary relationships resulting directly from the marriage or the dissolution thereof. The instant case was concerned with a judicial decision authorising provisional protective measures — namely the freezing of assets and the placing under seal of items of property belonging to the spouses — delivered during the course of proceedings for divorce. The Court of Justice declared that such matters will fall outside the scope of the Convention where the measures in question concern or are closely connected with either questions of status of the persons involved in the divorce proceedings or proprietary legal relations resulting directly from the matrimonial relationship or its dissolution. ³⁵ The test thus places great emphasis upon functional realities, although a hard and fast line may prove difficult to draw for all cases. A second reference to the Court of Justice arose out of the same divorce proceedings when, in Case 120/79, *Cavel* v. *Cavel,* ³⁶ a dispute between the parties concerning an interim maintenance award, made by a court in Paris, was considered to raise a further issue of the application of the Convention in principle. This time, the Court took the point that the Convention itself specifically included matters relating to maintenance among the special jurisdictional rules created in A. 5, and at the same time noted that maintenance obligations are not alluded to *eo nomine* in the exclusionary paragraph of A. 1(2). This particular aspect of the legal proceedings taking place between the spouses could therefore be characterised as "ancillary" to the divorce proceedings proper, and as such was not caught by the exclusionary provisions of the Convention despite the fact that the main proceedings themselves, being proceedings for divorce, were unquestionably concerned with the status of persons.

The Court of Justice also adopted a functional approach to the interpretation of the exclusionary provisions of A. 1(2)(2) in Case 133/78, *Gourdain* v. *Nadler*. [37] In that case, the question at issue was whether the terms of sub-paragraph (2), which exclude bankruptcy, winding up and analogous proceedings from the scope of the Convention, were to be understood as applying also to an order of a French court extending the liability for the debts of an insolvent company to an individual declared to be a *de facto* manager of the company. [38] While stressing yet again the need to accord an objective and independent meaning to the terms employed in A. 1(2), the Court concluded, in the light of a careful examination of the actual workings of French law in relation to the extension of liabilities of bankrupt companies, that such a close and direct connection exists in cases of this kind between the bankruptcy or liquidation proceedings themselves and the particular type of order in question that the latter must be considered to be excluded from the Convention alongside the main proceedings, which are undoubtedly comprehended within A. 1(2)(2).[39]

Ratione loci, A. 60 proclaims that the Convention applies to the European territories of the Contracting States, including Greenland, to the French overseas Départements and territories, and to Mayotte. However, several states are accorded the discretionary facilities of making detailed arrangements to suit their particular requirements in relation to certain territories for which they have responsibilities. [40] In the case of the United Kingdom, A. 60(3)(2) effectively provides that the Convention shall not apply to the Channel Islands, the Isle of Man or Gibraltar unless the United Kingdom makes a specific declaration to the contrary in respect of each of these territories. Such declarations are permitted to be made at any time by notifying the Secretary-General of the Council of the European Communities, and could therefore be lodged after the Convention has entered into force with regard to the United Kingdom itself. By A. 60(4) it is further provided that proceedings brought on appeal from courts in the Channel Islands, the

Isle of Man or Gibraltar shall be deemed to be proceedings taking place in those courts. Hence, the appellate stages of any proceedings originating from any of the territories in question will also fall outside the ambit of the Convention unless a declaration has been lodged with respect to that territory so as to cause the Convention to be applicable to it.

Ratione temporis, the Convention applies only to legal proceedings instituted, and to documents formally drawn up or registered as authentic instruments, after its entry into force. [41] In relation to the new Member States which acceded to it in 1978, the Convention's entry into force is regulated by the provisions of the Accession Convention which, as already stated, [42] will bring the Judgments Convention into force in relation to each of the new Member States upon completion of the provisions for ratification contained in Arts. 38 and 39 of the later Convention. For the new Member States, therefore, the Judgments Convention will apply *ratione temporis* only to legal proceedings instituted, and to authentic instruments drawn up or registered, after the Accession Convention has entered into force. [43] However, as between the Six original Contracting States to the 1968 Convention and the 1971 Protocol, Judgments given after the entry into force of the Accesion Convention in proceedings instituted before that date will be recognised and enforced in accordance with the provisions of the 1968 Convention as amended,[44] while, as between the original Six and the three new Member States, judgments in proceedings commenced before the entry into force of the Accession Convention will be recognised and enforced also in accordance with the provisions of the 1968 Convention if jurisdiction was founded upon rules which actually accorded with those of Title II of the Judgments Convention, as amended, or with provisions of a Convention which was in force between the two States concerned at the date when the proceedings were instituted. [45]

The scope of application of the Convention *ratione personae* is intimately bound up with the rules for the exercise of jurisdiction contained in Title II and will therefore be considered in the next section.

5. Jurisdiction: The Basic Rule

(a) *Actor Sequitur Forum Rei: Apotheosis of a Principle*

Title II of the Convention, comprising Arts. 2—24, bears the heading "Jurisdiction". Its purpose is to impose a uniform framework of rules governing the exercise of judicial jurisdiction by all domestic courts of the EEC. This it does, in the first instance, by establishing a primary rule for the attribution of jurisdictional competence by reference to a specific, personal attribute of the defendant party to civil or commercial proceedings, namely the place of that person's "domicile". A. 2 declares that, subject to the provisions of the Convention itself, persons "domiciled in a Contracting State" shall, whatever their nationality, be sued in the courts of that State. It is further provided that persons who are not nationals of the State in which they are domiciled shall be governed by the rules of jurisdiction applicable to nationals of that State. For those persons fortunate enough to be domiciled *somewhere* within the EEC at least, this simple form of words effectively achieves the realisation of a long-advocated ideal in matters of the exercise of jurisdiction in the conflict of laws, which is that proceedings should take place within the jurisdiction which most accords with the convenience of the defending party. This principle is often referred to by the Latin maxim, *actor sequitur forum rei.* There are many arguments in favour of allowing this principle to form the basis of a general rule. These range from considerations of the convenience of the party who is being made defendant, through to the realisation that to allow the plaintiff virtual *carte blanche* in determining the venue for litigation would create too many opportunities for *forum* shopping. Central to the thinking underlying the introduction of a rule which undeniably favours the defendant is the awareness of the need, in the modern world generally but within the Common Market in particular, to eliminate the distortions and injustices which can ensue from the exercise of jurisdiction by what are, in the circumstances of particular cases, jurisdictionally improper *fora.* [46] The majority of legal systems, including those of all the Member States of the EEC, have developed jurisdictional rules which are capable of such "long arm" operation, and which are nowadays usually referred to as rules of "exorbitant" jurisdiction. Thanks to A. 2, all persons domiciled within the territories to which the Judgments Convention applies will cease to be liable to become involuntary defendants in proceedings initiated outside the jurisdiction of their domicile before a court exercising jurisdiction on the basis of any such rule of an exorbitant character. Although A. 2 would suffice to establish this state of affairs, A. 3 serves to impart a still greater degree of certainty to the matter by emphasising that, in the case of any person to whom the Convention applies *ratione personae,* the only permissible exceptions to the operation of the principle *actor sequitur forum rei* are those contained within Arts. 5—18 of the present Convention. In particular, A. 3(2) specifies by name those jurisdictional rules currently to be found within the laws of the Member States, which are forbidden to be used against persons domiciled in a Contracting State of the

EEC. In the case of the United Kingdom, the proscribed rules are those which enable jurisdiction to be founded on the service of the writ of summons upon the defendant during his temporary presence in the United Kingdom, [47] or on the presence within the United Kingdom of property belonging to the defendant, or on the seizure by the plaintiff of property situated in the United Kingdom. [48]

Everything which has been described thus far represents, it is submitted, an admirable set of arrangements, fully in accord with the concepts and principles on which the Common Market is based. In particular, the solemn prohibition in A. 7 ECT against the maintenance of any distinction based upon nationality, at any rate in matters involving the citizens of the Member States, has been not merely honoured, but indeed transcended, so that the privileges and immunities of the Convention are extended to all persons "domiciled" anywhere within the EEC, regardless of their nationality. However, the provisions which are made applicable to persons who are *not* domiciled within the Community give rise to certain important objections.

(b) Community Non-Domiciliaries: Unprincipled Chauvinism

While the effects of the Convention are undoubtedly highly convenient and advantageous from the point of view of any defendant who is domiciled in the Community, the very reverse is true in the case of defendants domiciled somewhere in the outer world. This is because A. 4 provides that in relation to all such defendants, the jurisdiction of the courts of each Contracting State shall, subject to the provisions of A. 16, [49] be determined by the law of that State. It therefore becomes important to note that the Convention, although containing "direct" rules of jurisdiction to be applied by the courts of all Contracting States in cases falling within its scope, does not go to the length of requiring the actual repeal of any domestic jurisdictional rules which may be incompatible with these jurisdictional principles. Consequently, these domestic rules are enabled to remain in force, albeit Arts. 2 and 3 forbid their use against persons who are entitled to the immunities conferred by the Convention. In particular, the rules of exorbitant jurisdiction listed in A. 3(2) can be maintained in force and may, in accordance with A. 4(1), be used against any defendant not able to avail himself of the protections bestowed by the Convention upon Community domiciliaries.

An immediate paradox which emerges from the foregoing statement is that a person who is not domiciled within the Community may experience whatever disadvantages result from the application of jurisdictional licence conferred upon the Member States' courts by A. 4(1), even though that person may happen to be a citizen of one of the Member States. In this respect the Committee of Experts' deliberate rejection of nationality as a connecting factor results in privileges and immunities being enjoyed by persons who are not citizens of any Member State of the EEC, but who happen to be "domiciled" in one of them, whereas any person who is not so domiciled will be denied these privileges and immunities even though he may be a citizen of one of the Member States, and may indeed be a bearer of a "Community" passport. [50] To this extent, at least, the directions of A. 220 ECT, requiring the Member States to secure certain benefits "for their *citizens*", have been disregarded.

Worse is to follow, however, from the point of view of the "non-Community-domiciliary", whatever his or her nationality. In the first place, it is made clear by A. 4(2) that, against such persons as defendants, any person domiciled in a Contracting State may, whatever his nationality, avail himself in that State of the rules of jurisdiction there in force, and in particular those specified in A. 3(2), in the same way as the nationals of that State. This rule is clearly intended to respect the precepts of A. 7 ECT, imposing an absolute prohibition of the practice of discrimination on grounds of *nationality* within the EEC. By thus creating a "pooled" category of persons whom Community law looks upon with favour, a situation is created in which domestic jurisdictional rules, which may originally have been expressed so as to be invocable only by plaintiffs who are citizens of the State in question, [51] are now required to be invocable by all plaintiffs domiciled within that State. From this it follows that, in certain instances, A. 4(2) may produce the effect that a plaintiff who is not a citizen of any Member State of the EEC may, by virtue of his domiciliary contact with the jurisdiction of one of the Member States, be able there to found proceedings upon a rule of exorbitant jurisdiction contained in the law of that State, even where the defendant is a citizen of one of the States of the EEC.

The foregoing provisions, with their potential for producing somewhat paradoxical effects under certain circumstances, could perhaps have been dismissed as mere curiosities were it not for the further, most important fact that any judgment resulting from an exercise of jurisdiction under A. 4 will technically qualify for recognition and enforcement throughout the EEC in accordance with the provisions of Title III of the Convention. [52] This gives rise to a serious issue of principle, since the Convention is hereby openly condoning the violation of the basic philosophy upon which its own jurisdictional scheme is established (namely *actor sequitur forum rei*) in all cases where the defendant is, by definition, domiciled outside the EEC. Moreover, the operation of the Member States' rules of exorbitant jurisdiction is thereby given an augmented force far exceeding the limits of effectiveness which have hitherto been understood to apply to them. Traditionally, the use of such rules has been defended on the ground that it enables plaintiffs within the "jurisdictionally improper" *forum* to take legitimate steps to protect their interests where the defendant has withdrawn abroad and is personally out of reach. In this way, any assets left behind by the defendant might at least be made available to satisfy the claims of his creditors in that jurisdiction, but it would never be seriously contemplated that any judgment thereby obtained should enjoy international exportability since, *ex hypothesi*, the court at the *forum* had lacked jurisdiction in the international sense. The possibility now arises, however, that a judgment rooted in the rules of one particular jurisdiction within the EEC may enjoy full faith and credit in all the Member States, despite the fact that it belongs to the category of "exorbitant" judgments. Any pretence that such effects are a "natural counterpart" of the cancellation of traditional legal frontiers within the EEC must surely be seen to be spurious, since the selfsame "jurisdictional frontiers" are still very much maintained as an integral part of the Convention's own scheme of operation. Moreover, the rules of exorbitant jurisdiction listed in A. 3 are confined for use by the courts of the particular Member States by which they have been developed, and do not become available for use by litigants domiciled outside the national jurisdiction with which these rules have been historically associated. Thus, it is submitted, A. 4(1) in its present form constitutes an unprincipled aggression upon the legitimate legal interests of persons domiciled outside the EEC, and cannot be supported. [53]

It remains to be seen whether the above provisions will in time provoke any organised, retaliatory action on the part of the States belonging to the outside world. Certainly, at an early period when the Judgments Convention was in its formative stages, the implications of the proposed Arts. 3 and 4 threatened to create a severe crisis within the Hague Conference on Private International Law, which was simultaneously evolving its own Convention on the Recognition and Enforcement of Foreign Judgments in Civil and Commercial Matters. [54] Finally, after a somewhat acrimonious period of disagreement, [55] a compromise was adopted which resulted in the conclusion of a Supplementary Protocol to the Hague Convention, [56] and in the insertion of A. 59 in the Judgments Convention. This latter provision effectively permits each of the Contracting States to enter into separate obligations towards third States, to be undertaken in the form of conventions on the recognition and enforcement of judgments concluded bilaterally, in which they agree not to recognise judgments given in other Contracting States against defendants domiciled or habitually resident in the third State where, in cases provided for in A. 4, the judgment could only be founded on one of the "exorbitant" grounds of jurisdiction listed in A. 3(2). There is, however, a specific exception to this facility for "individualised contracting out" from the particular effects of the Convention which we are now considering. This is as a result of the provision in A. 59(2), which denies the Contracting States the right to undertake not to recognise judgments of courts in other Contracting States where jurisdiction has been based on the presence within that State of property belonging to the defendant, or the seizure by the plaintiff of property situated there, if either: (i) the action is brought to assert or declare proprietary or possessory rights in that property, seeks to obtain authority to dispose of it, or arises from another issue relating to such property; or (ii) if the property constitutes the security for a debt which is the subject-matter of the action.

Thus, in a somewhat cumbersome fashion, the Judgments Convention now enables the Contracting States individually to circumvent some of the worst excesses to which its own provisions could potentially give rise. [57] It is submitted, however, that a far superior example would have been set if the Convention had contained a simple provision enabling the Commission to negotiate on behalf of the Community as a whole with any third State wishing to enter into reciprocal arrangements for recognition and enforcement of judgments, based upon a mutual renunciation of the exercise of any rules of exorbitant jurisdiction against defendants domiciled or habitually resident in the other party's territory.

(c) Domicile

In view of the crucial role played by the concept of domicile in effectively determining the scope of the Convention *ratione personae*, much interest is inevitably focused upon the question of the meaning to be ascribed to this term within the framework of the Convention. This interest is now further heightened in view of the accession of the two States representing the Common Law tradition, since the meaning borne by the term "domicile", when employed within the legal systems of all parts of the United Kingdom, and also that of Ireland, is so different from that borne by the same term within the legal systems of the Member States belonging to the civilian tradition that it is necessary to admit that, in reality, the one term is being used to denote two completely distinct concepts. Disappointingly, the Convention contains no provision designed to supply a unified definition of "domicile" for present purposes, but instead the draftsmen have taken the less audacious course of incorporating a uniform conflicts rule to determine any question of domicile in relation to the working of the Convention. This rule is contained in A. 52, which contains the instruction that in order to determine whether a party is domiciled in the Contracting State whose courts are seized of a matter, the *forum* shall apply its own internal law. If a party is not domiciled in the State of the *forum* then, in order to determine whether the party is domiciled in another Contracting State, the court is directed to apply the law of the State which constitutes the alleged domicile. There is a subsidiary rule to cover the case of persons whose national law makes their domicile depend on that of another person or on the seat of an authority: A. 52(3) specifies that the domicile of such persons shall be determined in accordance with their national law.

The Convention applies to both natural and legal persons, and hence it is necessary to establish a further conflicts rule to enable courts to determine the domicile of the latter for the purposes of applying the Convention. A. 53 supplies such a rule, in the form of a provision which requires the "seat" of a company or other legal person to be treated as its domicile. However, in order to determine the whereabouts of that seat, the *forum* is to apply its own rules of private international law. [58] No definition is offered in this Convention of the term "seat" as employed in A. 53, but some reference by analogy could probably be made to A. 5 of the Convention of 29 February 1968 on Mutual Recognition of Companies, [59] which equates the notion of the "real registered office" of a company (the company's "real seat" or *"siège réel"*) with the place where its central administration is established. Nevertheless, the direction to apply the rules of private international law of the *forum* in order to determine the whereabouts of the company's seat (however conceived or defined) seems to signify the abandonment of all attempts to create a unified, independent approach to the fixing of a key factor in the exercise of judicial jurisdiction over legal persons under the terms of the Convention. One can but lament the failure of nerve or will on the part of those responsible for this provision.

It is submitted that, in order to reduce as far as possible the potential for serious confusion being caused by the terminological ambiguousness of "domicile" as a connecting factor, the Member States which belong to the Common Law tradition should seriously consider supplying a special definition of the term "domicile" for use in relation to the Judgments Convention. Taking inspiration from the internal evidence of the Convention itself, as expressed in the various languages in which it was originally enacted, it seems clear that something more closely resembling "habitual residence" was really intended to form the basis for the operation of the jurisdictional rules contained therein. [60] By introducing such a definition in place of the concept of "domicile" as it would be customarily understood by their courts, the United Kingdom and the Republic of Ireland would go some way towards avoiding the possibility that one and the same person might be held to be simultaneously "domiciled" in two different Contracting States by virtue of the application to his personal circumstances (perhaps in different proceedings) of the internal laws of two different Member States. Eventually, it is submitted, the Member States must grasp this particular nettle and agree upon uniform definitions of the primary connecting factors which are to serve for the purpose of this, and other, Community Conventions.

6. Jurisdiction: Exceptions to the Basic Rule

The general rule of jurisdiction, based upon the principle *actor sequitur forum rei* established by the terms of Arts. 2 and 3, could not possibly ensure satisfactory or just results in all situations. A number of special situations have therefore been made the subject of specific provisions within Sections 2—6 of Title II (comprising Arts. 5—18), whereby a variety of exceptions are created to the basic rule which has been described above. Some of these exceptions have the effect of creating an alternative jurisdictional competence, in addition to that of the courts in the defendant's State of domicile, in favour of the courts of some other Contracting State; other exceptions are of a more absolute character, and require the issue of jurisdictional competence to be referred to a completely different connecting factor, regardless of the domicile of the parties (see A. 16).

(a) Special Jurisdiction

A. 5 has the effect of establishing seven categories of proceedings in which a person domiciled in a Contracting State is also made liable to be sued in another Contracting State. It should be emphasised that under the provisions of this Article, the courts of the defendant's domicile also retain their competence, and hence it becomes open to the plaintiff to elect in which jurisdiction to initiate the proceedings, assuming that the defendant happens to be domiciled in a Contracting State other than the one whose courts enjoy jurisdiction by virtue of A. 5.

The seven categories of proceedings, together with the connecting factor determining jurisdiction, are as follows. Proceedings may take place:

(1) in matters relating to a contract, in the court for the place of performance of the obligation in question;

(2) in matters relating to maintenance, in the courts for the place where the maintenance creditor is domiciled or habitually resident, or, if the matter is ancillary to proceedings concerning the status of a person, in the court which, according to its own law, has jurisdiction to entertain those proceedings, unless that jurisdiction is based solely on the nationality of one of the parties; [61]

(3) in matters relating to tort, delict or quasi-delict, in the courts for the place where the harmful event occurred;

(4) as regards a civil claim for damages or restitution which is based on an act giving rise to criminal proceedings, in the court seized of those proceedings, to the extent that that court has jurisdiction under its own law to entertain civil proceedings;

(5) as regards a dispute arising out of the operations of a branch, agency or other establishment, in the courts for the place in which the branch, agency or other establishment is situated;

(6) as settlor, trustee or beneficiary of a trust created by the operation of a statute, or by a written instrument, or created orally and evidenced in writing, in the courts of the Contracting State in which the trust is domiciled;

(7) as regards a dispute concerning the payment of remuneration claimed in respect of the salvage of a cargo or freight, in the court under the authority of which the cargo or freight in question: (a) has been arrested to secure such payment, or (b) could have been so arrested, but bail or other security has been given, provided that this provision shall apply only if it is claimed that the defendant has an interest in the cargo or freight or had such an interest at the time of salvage.

It is submitted with respect that the above schedule of exceptions to the principle *actor sequitur forum rei* is acceptable, and should enable a reasonable balance of convenience to be achieved in many situations where a rigid adherence to the basic rule contained in Arts. 2 and 3 would otherwise give rise to substantial practical disadvantages for the plaintiff. Nevertheless, the want of precision and clarity in the wording of some of the paragraphs of A. 5 has already given rise to several references to the Court of Justice. Usually, the Court in its decisions has attempted to stress the independence of meaning of certain key terms when they appear in the provisions of the Convention, and has thereby helped to diminish the potential for conflicts of characterisation, and other interpretative variations, to occur when the Convention is being applied by national courts. However, somewhat disappointingly, in Case 12/76, *Tessili* v. *Dunlop*, [62] in which the Court was requested to interpret the expression "place of performance of the obligation in question" in A. 5(1), it was held that the meaning of this phrase is to be determined in accordance with the law which governs the obligation in question according to the rules of conflict of laws of the court before which the matter is brought. By taking refuge in the maxim that the *forum* should consult its own conflicts rule in order to discover which system of law shall supply the precise meaning of the key connecting term in each instant case, the Court of Justice unquestionably opened the way for some limited ventures into the realm of "*forum* shopping". Admittedly, it may have been anticipated that the coming into force of the Contracts Convention in due course would have the effect of unifying the conflicts rules to be applied by the courts of all Member States for this purpose, *inter alia*. But it is by no means certain that such complete unification will ensue from the operation of the Contracts Convention, at least in any cases where the parties to a contract have failed to exercise a valid and unequivocal choice of the law to govern it. [63] Therefore, the plaintiff's initiative in selecting the court in which to begin proceedings may result in that court upholding its own jurisdictional competence on the basis that the law which the conflicts rule of the *forum* selects as the proper law of the contract would, when applied substantively, produce the determination that the place of performance was to be within the jurisdiction of the *forum*. It is submitted that where any court arrives at such a conclusion on the basis of the application of its own conflicts rule for determining the proper law of a contract in the absence of a choice by the parties, the court should further consider whether the same law would have been chosen as proper law under the equivalent conflicts rule of the Contracting State which the defendant contends is the true "place of performance" of the contract. If such is not the case, the *forum* should give serious consideration to the possibility that the plaintiff may be seeking to gain an improper litigious advantage by *forum* shopping, and should, if necessary of its own motion, renounce jurisdiction by invoking the doctrine of *forum non conveniens* in the interests of the fair and orderly administration of justice within the Community. Mention may also be made of the special privilege extended to persons domiciled in Luxembourg who are sued in the court of another Contracting State pursuant to A. 5(1). A. I of the Protocol to the Convention permits the Letzeburger to refuse to submit to the jurisdiction of the foreign court, which is obliged in default of appearance by the defendant to renounce jurisdiction of its own motion. [63a]

A more straightforward ruling was supplied by the Court of Justice in Case 14/76, *DeBloos* v. *Bouyer*,[64] in which it was affirmed that the word "obligation" in A. 5(1) refers to the obligation forming the basis of the proceedings. Hence, it would be an insufficient ground for jurisdiction that certain of the obligations contained in a particular contract were to be performed at the place where the action is commenced, unless the action itself relates to at least one of the obligations which were to be performed in that jurisdiction. A further issue raised somewhat tangentially in the same case concerned the definition to be ascribed to the expression "branch, agency or establishment" in A. 5(5), a question to which the Court of Justice was subsequently required to address its attention in a direct fashion in Case 33/78, *Somafer* v. *Saar-Ferngas*.[65] In this latter decision, the Court resumed its more characteristic approach by insisting that, in the interests of legal certainty and equality of rights and obligations for all parties concerned, the concepts in A. 5(5) must necessarily receive an independent interpretation, common to all the Contracting States. Therefore, the meaning of the three terms in question should not be determined by reference to the law or laws of any particular Contracting States, but should be given a "Community law" meaning in the context of the present Convention. On this basis, the Court declared that, on the one hand, a "branch or agency" must be in fact subject to the direction and control of the parent body, and also that, on the other hand, the alleged branch or agency must be a place where business is carried on and which has the appearance of permanency, with a management and material equipment to enable it to negotiate business with third parties in such a way that the latter will not normally need to deal with the parent body abroad, but may transact their business entirely at the place constituting the extension.

It would appear that the phrase "the place where the harmful event occurred" which is employed in A. 5(3), was deliberately formulated by the Committee of Experts so as to have an ambiguous meaning.[66] This "compromise" was designed to overcome a fundamental disagreement whether jurisdictional competence in tort cases should be accorded to the courts of the place where the defendant "acted" or to those of the place where the plaintiff sustained injury (where these lie in separate countries). The Court of Justice has in fact contrived to make a virtue out of necessity in this instance by holding that where the "place of the defendant's acting" and the "place of impact" lie in different Contracting States, the plaintiff may elect which of the two jurisdictions shall be designated as "the place where the harmful event occurred" for the purpose of initiating proceedings against the party alleged to have wronged him tortiously.[67] In view of the diminished likelihood that the Member States' rules of private international law in matters of non-contractual liability will undergo unification in the near future,[68] this plaintiff-oriented ruling is of considerable significance, since under the most extreme of circumstances it will enable the plaintiff to select

between three possible *fora* for litigation, including that of the defendant's
state of domicile, assuming it to be separate from either the place of acting
or the place of impact.

A. 6 introduces three further bases of jurisdiction, each of which may
enable a person to be sued in a Contracting State other than that in which he
is domiciled. The first of these utilises the *forum connexitatis* principle, so
that in cases where there are multiple defendants the plaintiff shall not be
prejudiced by the possibility that these may be domiciled in different States.
A. 6(1) accordingly provides that in such cases, all of the defendants may be
sued in the courts for the place where any one of them is domiciled. Likewise, where the defendant occupies the role of third party in an action on a
warranty or guarantee or in any other third party proceedings, the court
seized of the original proceedings may exercise jurisdiction over him, provided these proceedings are genuine in character. A proviso to A. 6(2) indicates that jurisdiction may not be exercised over a third party if the original
proceedings were instituted solely with the object of removing him from the
jurisdiction of the court which would be competent in his case. Thirdly,
where a person, having sued as plaintiff in some jurisdiction other than that
of his domicile, is made defendant to a counter-claim arising from the same
contract or facts on which the original claim was based, A. 6(3) properly
enables the proceedings on the counter-claim to be heard by the court in
which the original claim is pending.

(b) Jurisdiction in Matters Relating to Insurance

Arts. 7—12A inclusive form a special section concerned with the exercise of
jurisdiction in matters relating to insurance. Their purpose is to enable the
policy-holder to enjoy a more favoured position, in cases where he wishes to
institute proceedings against his insurer, than would otherwise obtain by
virtue of the general or special jurisdictional rules so far discussed. Effectively,
the insurer is rendered amenable to be sued either in the State in which he is
domiciled, or (if he is a co-insurer) in the courts of the Contracting State in
which proceedings are brought against the leading insurer, or in the courts of
the Contracting State in which the policy-holder is domiciled. [69] In addition,
in the case of liability insurance or insurance of immovable property, the
insurer may be sued in the courts for "the place where the harmful event
occurred". [70] Conversely, the policy-holder, the insured or a beneficiary may
be sued by the insurer only in the courts of the Contracting State in which
the defendant is domiciled, subject to the proviso that where the insurer's
action takes the form of a counter-claim, the action may be brought in the

court in which the original claim is pending notwithstanding that this may not be at the domicile of the party against whom the counter-claim is maintained. [71]

There are additional provisions to forbid the modification of the foregoing rules by means of any express agreement between the parties to the contract of insurance, except under circumstances which remain basically favourable to the insured, the policy-holder or the beneficiary, as the case may be. [72] In derogation from the foregoing rules, the Convention, as amended by the Accession Convention, now provides through A. 12(5) together with A. 12A that the provisions relating to insurance may be departed from by an agreement on jurisdiction which relates to a contract of insurance insofar as it covers one or more of the risks set out in A. 12A, which are risks involving the commercial usage of sea-going ships, or aircraft or offshore installations, and risks involving goods in transit, but excepting in all cases any risks involving bodily injury to passengers or loss of or damage to their baggage.

(c) Jurisdiction over Consumer Contracts

The nowadays characteristic legal policy of favouring the consumer as against the seller or supplier of goods or services has been allowed to determine the content of the special rules contained within Arts. 13–15. Essentially, these provisions confer upon the consumer (herein defined as one who has concluded the contract "for a purpose which can be regarded as being outside his trade or profession"[73]) the privilege of being able to elect in which jurisdiction he will sue the party who has contracted to supply him with goods or services, or to furnish him with credit to finance the purchase of goods. In such proceedings, the consumer as plaintiff may sue in the courts of the Contracting State in which he himself is domiciled, or in the courts of the State in which the defendant is domiciled. [74] Conversely, the consumer as defendant retains the immunity from being sued against his will in the courts of any Contracting State other than that in which he is domiciled, unless this takes place by way of a counter-claim brought in a jurisdiction in which the consumer himself has elected to sue. There are additional safeguards, as in the case of insurance contracts, to inhibit the scope for derogation from the legal protections conferred by the Convention upon the consumer: A. 15 allows such departures to be accomplished only by means of agreements which are in substance favourable to the consumer, or which, being concluded after the dispute has arisen, should in theory be entered into by the consumer with full realisation of the implications for the specific dispute in which he is engaged. [75]

(d) Exclusive Jurisdiction

A. 16, which is the single Article comprising Section 5 of Title II, is one of
the most important in the Convention. It specifies five types of case in which
exclusive jurisdiction is conferred upon the court of one of the Contracting
States irrespective of the domicile of either of the parties to the litigation.
The courts which enjoy exclusive jurisdiction are identified as follows:

(1) in proceedings which have as their object rights *in rem* in, or tenancies of, immovable property, the courts of the Contracting State in which
the property is situated;

(2) in proceedings which have as their object the validity of the constitution, the nullity or dissolution of companies or other legal persons or associations of natural or legal persons, or the decisions of their organs, the courts
of the Contracting State in which the company, legal person or association
has its seat;

(3) in proceedings which have as their object the validity of entries in a
public register, the courts of the Contracting State in which the register is
kept;

(4) in proceedings concerned with the registration or validity of patents,
trade marks, designs, or other similar rights required to be deposited or
registered, the courts of the Contracting State in which the deposit or
registration has been applied for, has taken place or is under the terms of an
international convention deemed to have taken place;

(5) in proceedings concerned with the enforcement of judgments, the
courts of the Contracting State in which the judgment has been or is to be
enforced.

In each of the above instances, the conferment of exclusive jurisdiction is
felt to be justified in the circumstances by virtue of the close connections
which exist between the subject-matter of the proceedings and the territory
of the Contracting State on whose court a jurisdictional monopoly is thus
conferred. [78] This connection is considered to be so important as to outweigh the possible inconvenience which may be caused to either or both of
the parties by the necessity of maintaining the action in the *forum* so designated. Indeed, the provisions of A. 16 are given such a pre-eminent position
in the Convention's jurisdictional scheme that they even override the possible use of "exorbitant" rules of jurisdiction against defendants who are not
domiciled within the Community: A. 4(1) expressly states that the exercise
of jurisdiction over such defendants by the courts of the Contracting States
shall be subject to the provisions of A. 16.

Up to the time of writing, only one case has come before the Court of

Justice containing a request for interpretation of any of the provisions with-in A. 16. This was Case 73/77, *Sanders* v. *Van der Putte*, [77] in which the Dutch Supreme Court (the Hoge Raad) sought clarification of the meaning to be ascribed to A. 16(1). The proceedings in question arose out of a dispute regarding a contract containing an agreement to rent a retail florist's business carried on in a shop situated in Germany and rented from a third person by Van der Putte, the lessor. The point taken on behalf of the defendant Sanders before the Dutch courts was that, under the circumstances, exclusive jurisdiction was enjoyed by the courts of Germany. Unquestionably, the tenancy of the shop itself could be characterised as "a tenancy of immovable property" within the meaning of A. 16(1), but the Dutch courts formed the conclusion that in the agreement in question the emphasis fell less on the rent or lease of immovable property than on the business as such. The question referred to the Court of Justice was therefore whether the words "tenancies of immovable property" within A. 16(1) must be given a broad meaning so as to include also an agreement to rent under usufructuary lease a retail business carried on in immovable property rented from a third party by the lessor. This question was answered in the negative by the Court which, while conceding the validity of the rationale underlying A. 16(1) in respect of those cases where the dispute itself is concerned with the actual tenancy of the immovable property (as in the case of disputes between the lessor and the tenant concerning the existence or interpretation of the lease itself), concluded nevertheless that a proper distinction could be drawn in cases such as the instant one. The Court of Justice effectively endorsed the approach adopted by the Dutch court and accordingly ruled that, where the principal aim of the agreement is not the creation of a tenancy of immovable property as such, but is, for example, the creation of a contractual right to operate a business, A. 16(1) is not necessarily applicable, with the consequence that the courts of Contracting States apart from the one in which the immovable property is situated are in principle capable of exercising jurisdiction over a dispute arising out of the parties' agreement. Although this interpretation by the Court of Justice can claim the merits of flexibility and realism in its approach to the interpretation of a provision of the Convention which is of an especially restrictive character, it is submitted that the absence from the judgment of any firm guide-lines to assist national courts in future to decide for themselves on which side of the vital line a particular dispute belongs will, at best, give rise to a succession of further references to the Court of Justice to test the position once again on the basis of slightly varying facts. At the worst, on the other hand, this ruling could become responsible for an uneven and subjective jurisprudence emanating from the courts of different Member States which have responded in different ways to cases involving basically similar facts.

(e) Prorogation of Jurisdiction

The purpose of A. 17 is to enable parties by agreement to confer jurisdiction upon the courts of a Contracting State which would not otherwise enjoy competence to entertain proceedings between them. Such agreements, whereby parties replace the jurisdictional arrangements established by the Convention with an alternative attribution of jurisdiction of their own choice, are permitted to operate, subject to certain limits and safeguards. Thus, A. 17(1) requires that, to be effective, such an agreement must either be in writing or, if oral, be evidenced by writing, or, in international trade or commerce, be in a form which accords with practices of that trade or commerce of which the parties are, or ought to have been, aware. Where such an agreement is effective, the court or courts so designated enjoy exclusive jurisdiction. A. 17(4), however, provides that where an agreement of this kind is concluded for the benefit of only one of the parties, that party shall retain the right to bring proceedings in any other court which has jurisdiction by virtue of the Convention.

The special rules in A. 17(2) and (3) also make it possible for a trust instrument to confer exclusive jurisdiction upon the courts of a particular Member State, although such an agreement will be invalid if it contravenes the provisions of A. 12 or A. 15, or if its effect would be to exclude the jurisdiction of courts possessing an exclusive jurisdiction by virtue of A. 16 of the Convention.

Not entirely unexpectedly, A. 17 is providing the basis of a developing jurisprudence by the Court of Justice. Importantly, the Court has placed emphasis upon the need to construe this provision strictly, in view of the consequences which the upholding of a *forum* clause may entail for the parties who are held to be bound thereby. Accordingly, a party seeking to invoke the jurisdiction of a court on the basis of a *forum* clause must be able to prove conclusively to that court that the clause purporting to confer such jurisdiction was in fact the subject of a true consensus between the parties. Thus, it will not suffice if a clause conferring jurisdiction is included among the general conditions of business of one of the parties which are printed on the back of a contract: at the very least, the contract signed by both parties must contain an express reference to those general conditions. [78] In the case of an orally-concluded agreement, it has been held to be necessary for both parties subsequently to create written, commemorative documents in which they clearly indicate their consent to the terms of any *forum* clause allegedly incorporated therein, even though the remainder of the contract may exist in purely oral form. [79] An exception to this latter requirement may be tolerated, however, in cases where a continuous trade relationship exists between the parties which is based up on the general conditions of business of one of them: if one party issues a written confirmation of their oral agreement, to which the other party raises no objections, it may be possible under these circumstances to treat such licence as amounting to acceptance of any clause conferring jurisdiction which may be contained within the general conditions. [80]

It may be noted that, in contrast to the situation where the efficacy of an oral agreement is being scrutinised from the standpoint of A. 17, a relatively more relaxed policy prevails with regard to the admission of purely oral agreements for the purposes of certain other provisions in the Convention. Thus, if a plaintiff is effectively seeking to utilise A. 5(1) as a basis of jurisdiction to enable him to bring proceedings in the court for the place of performance of a contractual obligation, the strict requirements of A. 17 may be ignored as irrelevant in the circumstances, and a purely oral agreement to the effect that the jurisdiction in question should constitute "the place of performance" is capable of being effective, provided at least that this item of agreement is valid according to the law which constitutes the proper law of the contract itself. [81]

In a further ruling on the interpretation of A. 17(1) the Court of Justice has held that there is no objection in principle to the parties to a contract so devising their *forum* clause that it has the effect of conferring jurisdiction in the alternative on the courts of two Contracting States, according to the circumstances of the proceedings. The validity of a "reciprocal jurisdiction clause", whereby each party undertook to initiate any proceedings in the courts of the Member State which constituted the place of establishment of the defendant to those proceedings, was therefore upheld, but the Court further ruled that it must remain a matter for the national court before which any proceedings are initiated pursuant to such a clause to determine whether the clause in question shall be allowed to operate in such a way as to preclude the defendant from introducing a defence by way of a claim for set-off. [82] A certain degree of interest also surrounds the ruling of the European Court of Justice in Case 25/79, *Sanicentral v. Collin,* [83] since the Court, besides confirming that contracts of employment fall within the scope of the Convention, held that the effect of A. 17, together with A. 54, was such that, in proceedings commenced after the entry into force of the Convention, clauses conferring jurisdiction concluded prior to that entry into force may be held to be valid even in cases where they would have been regarded as void under the national law in force at the time when the contract was entered into. Once again, therefore, the supremacy of a rule belonging to Community law is asserted over a rule belonging to the legal order of one of the Member States.

In addition to the attribution of jurisdiction by prior consent between the parties, it is also considered to be permissible for jurisdictional competence to be conferred upon a court *ex post facto,* as it were, through the defendant's voluntary appearance before a court which would otherwise have lacked jurisdiction according to the rules of the Convention. A. 18 confirms this possibility of jurisdiction being enjoyed by consent of the defendant, but subject to two important qualifications. In the first place, as a necessary protection in the interests of the defendant, A. 18 provides that the defendant's appearance for the sole purpose of contesting jurisdiction shall not be treated as a voluntary appearance conferring jurisdiction upon the court in question.[84,84a]   Secondly, it is also expressly provided that this type of voluntary submission to the jurisdiction cannot confer competence upon a court where another court has exclusive jurisdiction by virtue of A. 16.

(f) Examination as to Jurisdiction and Admissibility, and Related Matters

It is an integral feature of a "direct" Convention such as the one presently under examination that the principal burden of ensuring that the Convention operates as intended is borne by the Court in which proceedings are commenced. This is in any case far preferable to any belated attempt at the enforcement stage to restrict the damage through an improper assumption of jurisdiction, which by then amounts to a *faite accompli.* Quite properly, A. 19 makes it incumbent upon any court at the inception of proceedings to ascertain whether the courts of another Contracting State have exclusive jurisdiction by virtue of A. 16, and if so it is required that the court shall of its own motion renounce jurisdiction. If a defendant fails to enter an appearance, A. 20 requires the court further to scrutinise its own jurisdictional competence, and to have a special regard to the question of the defendant's domicile within the meaning of the Convention. If, applying the rules already described for ascertaining the defendant's domicile,[85] the court discovers that the defendant is domiciled in another Contracting State, it is required to renounce jurisdiction, again *proprio motu*, unless it can discover a basis within the Convention itself for exercising jurisdiction in the circumstances. Moreover, in all cases in which the defendant fails to enter an appearance, A. 20(2) obliges the court to stay proceedings until it has proof of the timely service upon the defendant of the document instituting the proceedings, or of the taking of all necessary steps to achieve such service. [86], [86a]

A. 21 makes provision for cases where proceedings involving the same cause of action and between the same parties are brought in the courts of different Contracting States. Somewhat arbitrarily, the Convention accords supremacy to the court first seised of the matter, and requires other courts to decline jurisdiction of their own motion in favour of that court. It is regrettable that no more rational arrangement has been devised for ensuring that the proceedings are ultimately centred in the most appropriate *forum*. [87] Perhaps the way towards achieving this lies through an imaginative use of A. 21(2), which permits a court which would be required to decline jurisdiction to stay its proceedings if the jurisdiction of the other court is contested. In such cases, the latter court might be induced to relinquish jurisdiction in favour of a sister court of the EEC on the basis of the doctrine of *forum non conveniens*. Use may also be made of A. 22, which permits the consolidation of related actions which are originally brought in the courts of different Member States, provided that the court first seised has jurisdiction over both actions.

A. 24, which is potentially a most useful provision, has the effect of permitting application to be made to the courts of the Contracting State for such provisional, including protective, measures as may be available under the law of that State, even if the courts of some other Contracting State have jurisdiction over the main proceedings. Despite the fact that this provision merely refers to "such ... measures as may be available" under the law of the State to which application is made, it is urged that courts should build upon this provision with a view to making a positive contribution towards the realisation of the goal of a juridically-integrated Community, each of whose constituent jurisdictions operates in such a way as to complement the workings of the others. [88]

7. Recognition and Enforcement

The further characteristic of a "direct" or "double" convention is that, on the assumption that the courts of all Contracting States will properly understand and comply with the rules for the assumption of jurisdiction in matters falling within the Convention, the international recognition and enforcement of such judgments can be allowed to take place virtually automatically. The maxim: *omnia praesumuntur rite et solenniter esse acta*, is thus given full rein. It follows from this that any defendant party who believes that the exercise of jurisdiction over him by a particular court would contravene the requirements of the Convention should take steps at once to challenge the jurisdiction of the court before the matter proceeds to judgment. As we have seen, A. 18 ensures that the defendant does not thereby "throw away his shield", since an appearance of this kind cannot be treated as amounting to consent to the jurisdiction of the court. What is equally important to stress is that it is no longer safe for a defendant who believes, or suspects, that the court in question lacks proper jurisdictional competence, to allow that matter to pass unchallenged in the original proceedings. This is because, assuming that the court of original jurisdiction has complied with the precepts of A. 20 in the event of the defendant's failure to enter an appearance, the judgment must be given full faith and credit throughout the EEC, and in the majority of cases [89] it is not possible for the defendant to the original proceedings to resist such enforcement even by pleading the want of jurisdiction of the court in question. Hence, if the defendant's initial attempt to persuade the *forum* of its own lack of jurisdiction is unsuccessful at first instance, the most advisable step for him to take next is to challenge the court's finding on appeal within the national legal system of the State in which the *forum* is situated. No reliance should be placed upon the feasibility of introducing at the enforcement stage any defence based upon want of jurisdiction on the part of the court from which the judgment originates.

The foregoing remarks are immediately borne out by the combined effect of Arts. 25 and 26, which declare that any judgment given by a court or tribunal of a Contracting State shall be recognised in the other Contracting States as of right and without any special procedure being required, regardless of what that judgment may be called in its State of origin, including (for purposes of illustration) a decree, order, decision or writ of execution, as well as the determination of costs or expenses by an officer of the court. Moreover, A. 29 absolutely forbids any review of the substance of a foreign judgment by any court which is required to recognise it. This prohibition, somewhat unnecessarily, is reiterated *verbatim* in A. 34(3), perhaps in an effort to prevent any spurious points of distinction being taken as between the "recognition" and the "enforcement" of a foreign judgment for this particular purpose. By this provision, a major part of the previously-developed law governing the enforcement of foreign judgments in the Member States is made redundant in relation to any judgment falling within the scope of the Convention. [90]

The sole grounds upon which recognition may be refused are those specified in Arts. 27 and 28. Since it is axiomatic that the enforcement of a foreign judgment is dependent upon its commanding recognition within the State of enforcement, the grounds contained within these two Articles are effectively the key to all else which follows.

A. 27 provides that a judgment shall not be recognised:

(1) if such recognition is contrary to public policy in the State in which recognition is sought;

(2) where it was given in default of appearance, if the defendant was not duly served with the document which instituted the proceedings or with an equivalent document in sufficient time to enable him to arrange for his defence;[90a]

(3) if the judgment is irreconcilable with a judgment given in a dispute between the same parties in the State in which recognition is sought;

(4) if the court of the State in which the judgment was given, in order to arrive at its judgment, has decided a preliminary question concerning the status or legal capacity of natural persons, rights in property arising out of a matrimonial relationship, wills or succession in a way that conflicts with a rule of the private international law of the State in which the recognition is sought, unless the same result would have been reached by the application of the rules of private international law of that State;

(5) if the judgment is irreconcilable with an earlier judgment given in a non-Contracting State involving the same cause of action and between the same parties, provided that this latter judgment fulfils the conditions necessary for its recognition in the State addressed.

A. 28 contains the further provision that a judgment shall not be recognised if it conflicts with the provisions of Section 3, 4 or 5 of Title II, or in the case provided for in A. 59. The Sections referred to are those concerned with jurisdiction in matters relating to insurance and to consumer contracts, and the rules of exclusive jurisdiction contained in A. 16. The reference to A. 59 is designed to link up with any arrangements made pursuant to the latter Article whereby Member States may undertake not to enforce the judgments of sister States of the EEC where these result from the assumption of jurisdiction over defendants domiciled or habitually resident in third States, using rules of exorbitant jurisdiction.[91]

In these cases only does the Convention permit the recognition and enforcement of a foreign judgment to be refused on the ground that the court of origin lacked jurisdiction, and even in such cases, A. 28(2) insists that the court or authority applied to shall be bound by the findings of fact on which the court of the State in which the judgment was given based its jurisdiction. This may of course include a finding on the vital question of the facts relevant to any determination of the defendant's domicile in the eyes of the law of the *forum*, or, *semble*, even of some other Contracting State. It is further emphasised by A. 28(3) that, apart from the cases just mentioned in which refusal of recognition may be based upon a proven lack of jurisdiction, "the jurisdiction of the court of the State in which the judgment was given may not be reviewed", and moreover "the test of internal 'public policy' referred to in A. 27(1) *may not be applied to the rules relating to jurisdiction*" (emphasis added). This last provision ensures that the potentially elastic notion of public policy cannot be used as a "long stop" to enable recognition and enforcement to be resisted in cases where the proper course of action which the defendant ought to have pursued was to contest before the foreign court the propriety of its initial assumption of jurisdiction.

Enforcement of a foreign judgment is enabled to take place by means of a simple, standard procedure, the essence of which consists of the making of an *ex parte* application for an enforcement order to the court designated in A. 32 as the competent court for this purpose in the State of enforcement. [92] The issue of an order of enforcement by the court to which application is made has the effect of rendering the judgment enforceable in that Contracting State. [93] It is, however, a precondition to such exportability that the judgment which is to be enforced is legally enforceable in its State of origin. It should be noted that this requirement could be met in some cases despite the fact that, technically, the judgment is still amenable to appeal. However, in such cases Arts. 30 and 38 enable the party against whom enforcement is sought to apply for a stay of enforcement pending the outcome of any appeal against the judgment in the State in which it was given. If no appeal is actually pending, the court may specify a time within which such an appeal is to be lodged. [94]

A. 33(1) states that the procedure for making the application for an enforcement order shall be governed by the law of the State in which enforcement is sought. Nevertheless, Arts. 46—48 together create a set of common provisions governing the main essentials of such applications, including such matters as the documents which are to be produced to the court to establish the authenticity of the judgment together with its enforceable character in its State of origin, and also, in the case of a default judgment, to establish that the requirements for due service of notice of the proceedings upon the defendant were complied with. Translation of the relevant documents may be required at its discretion by the court to which they are produced. A. 34 requires the court to give its decision without delay, and emphasises that the application may be refused only for one of the grounds specified in Arts. 27 and 28, which have been set out above. Moreover, the court must necessarily discover for itself whether one of these grounds is applicable to the judgments under consideration, since A. 34(1) denies the party against whom enforcement is sought the right to make any submissions on the application at this stage.

Although the party who will be most affected by the order of enforcement is not allowed to make any submission at the initial hearing, if the order is made, A. 36 allows him to appeal against that decision within one month of being served with notice thereof, or within two months if the appellant is domiciled in a Contracting State different from that in which the order of enforcement was made. A further list is contained in A. 37 to indicate the appropriate court before which such an appeal should be lodged according to the State in which the proceedings take place. [95] Appeals against the judgment given on such appeals may be contested before the courts additionally listed in A. 37. Pending the outcome of any challenge to enforcement pursuant to A. 36, no measures of enforcement may be taken other than protective measures against the property of the party against whom enforcement is sought. [96]

In the event that the original *ex parte* application for an order of enforcement is unsuccessful, the applicant in turn may pursue an appeal. Such appeals are to be heard by the appropriate court from the list contained in A. 40, with further appeal to the courts listed in A. 41. [97] In all proceedings of this kind, an applicant who has received some measure of legal aid in the original proceedings is by virtue of A. 44 entitled to benefit from the most favourable legal aid or the most extensive exemption from costs or expenses provided for by the law of the State addressed. Furthermore, A. 45 forbids the imposition of any additional requirements as to security, bond or deposit upon the applicant for enforcement of a foreign judgment merely on the ground that he is a foreign national or is domiciled or resident abroad. This latter provision is a further instance of the systematic eradication of discrimination against the residents, or nationals, of sister States of the Common Market.

In most cases, the procedure for enforcement of foreign judgments established by the Convention should serve its intended purposes admirably, and furnish an expeditious and inexpensive method of satisfying a judgment throughout the EEC, according to need and circumstance. Occasionally, however, it may exceptionally transpire that the extant procedures under national law for the enforcement of foreign judgments may hold the promise of even greater savings in terms of time and expense. Despite this possibility, the Court of Justice held in Case 42/76, *DeWolf* v. *Cox* [98] that the regime for enforcement created by the Convention is now required to be followed in all cases without exception.

By arts. 50 and 51, the process of application for an order for the enforcement of a foreign judgment is extended to enable persons who so desire to obtain an order for the enforcement of official documents ("authentic instruments") which embody an undertaking to pay a certain sum of money and which are enforceable in their state of origin, and likewise to obtain an order for the enforcement of settlements approved by a court in the course of proceedings. In either case, enforcement of the document or settlement in question may be refused only if enforcement is contrary to public policy in the State in which the application is made.

8. Conflicts of Conventions

The possibility that a permanent and damaging conflict might have arisen between the present Convention and its near-contemporary "rival" produced under the auspices of the Hague Conference on Private International Law has already been alluded to. [99] As was also explained, that particular conflict was resolved, in a not altogether satisfactory manner, by means of the provision in A. 59. It is presently unclear whether the effort involved in concluding the arrangements capable of obviating the worst of the threatened excesses under the present Convention will be thought to outweigh the possible "advantages" which may be gained thereby. The writer suspects, however, that very few Conventions, if any, will be concluded to take advantage of the facility in A. 59.

A. 55 lists 13 bilateral Conventions and one trilateral Treaty to which some of the Contracting States are currently parties, and which are declared to be partially superseded and replaced by the provisions of the present Convention. A. 56 emphasises that these international Conventions shall continue to have effect in relation to matters falling outside the ambit of the Judgments Convention. A potential conflict arises by virtue of the fact that the determination of the respective scope of the Community Convention on the one hand, and any of the bilateral Conventions listed in A. 55 on the other, will be referred to different systems of law. Thus, one and the same judgment may be considered not to be a judgment in a "civil or commercial matter" according to the definition applied under the Judgments Convention, and yet it may be considered to belong to the identically-termed category for the separate purposes of one of the bilateral Conventions. The Court of Justice was confronted by this paradox in Cases 9 and 10/77, *Bavaria Fluggesellschaft Schwabe* v. *Eurocontrol,* [100] but found that the conceptual difficulties could be resolved, on the assumption that the provisions of the Community Convention must at all times be enabled to prevail. Effectively, the Court directed the national judge who may be confronted by such a problem to refer first to the question of the possible applicability of the Judgments Convention, using the interpretative apparatus established by the Convention itself, as elucidated by the Court of Justice. If the matter falls within its scope, the Judgments Convention must be applied, but if not, the judge is free to turn to any other Convention whose provisions may be relevant to the case. Applying the separate rules of definition and interpretation which are apposite to the bilateral Convention (which may entail accepting a classification made by the court first giving judgment in the proceedings) the judge may find it possible to recognise and enforce the foreign judgment in question and may validly do so, notwithstanding that he is utilising a category within that Convention (namely, its provisions regarding "civil and commercial matters") which has ostensibly been eclipsed and supplanted by the provisions of the Judgments Convention.

A final provision to avoid conflict between the Judgments Convention and other conventions to which the Contracting States are or may become parties is contained in A. 57. This Article first concedes priority of effect to other Conventions which govern jurisdiction or the recognition or enforcement of foreign judgments in relation to "particular matters" (an expression of somewhat uncertain meaning). Secondly, it similarly accords priority of effect to any provisions which, in relation to "particular matters", govern jurisdiction or the recognition or enforcement of judgments and which are or will be contained in acts of the Institutions of the European Communities, or in national laws harmonised in implementation of such acts. Thus, the maxim *generalibus specialia derogant* combines with the paramount principle of the supremacy of Community law to give rise to a rule whereby the provisions of the Judgments Convention may in future be overridden in the event of any conflict with particular provisions contained in Community secondary law.[101] A special case is made of the Franco-Swiss Convention of 15 June 1869, whose provisions are permitted to prevail over those of the present Convention by virtue of A. 58.

9. Interpretation by the Court of Justice

To ensure the proper and uniform application and interpretation of the Judgments Convention, as now modified by the provisions of the Accession Convention, the Protocol on Interpretation (as amended by the latter) confers upon the Court of Justice jurisdiction to give rulings on the interpreta-

tion of both of these Conventions and also of the Protocol itself. The terms
in which the Protocol has been formulated differ in several important respects from those of A. 177 ECT, whose basic substance nonetheless provides the model for the procedure established by the Protocol.[102] In particular, in consequence of A. 2, references to the Court of Justice may not be
made by national courts of first instance sitting as such, but only by the
supreme courts of the Contracting States, or by other courts of those States
when sitting in an appellate capacity. References may also be submitted by
courts hearing appeals in accordance with A. 37 of the Convention against
decisions authorising the enforcement of judgments. Thus, courts of first
instance, being denied the right to refer questions of interpretation of the
Convention, must arrive at an initial decision on any question governed by
the Convention without the benefit of such assistance. For this reason, it will
be incumbent upon any party aggrieved by the ruling thus given to have
recourse to an appeal, whereupon the possibility of a reference to the Court
of Justice will arise if, in the words of A. 3(2), the court in question "considers that a decision on the question is necessary to enable it to give judgment". The making of a reference in such circumstances is a matter of
discretion for all courts except any of the supreme courts listed in A. 2(1) of
the Protocol. In the case of these courts, A. 3(1) establishes a mandatory
obligation to refer any question on which the court considers a decision on
interpretation to be necessary in order to enable it to give judgment.

A. 4 of the Protocol makes additional provision for special references to
be made to the Court of Justice by the judicial authorities in any Contracting State in cases where judgments given by the courts of that State conflict
with an interpretation given either by the Court of Justice itself or in a
judgment of one of the appellate or supreme courts of another Contracting
State. This special procedure offers a means of curing inconsistencies of
interpretation which emerge in practice, and it will be for the United Kingdom to designate the appropriate legal officer or officers in whom shall be
vested this power to request the Court of Justice to give rulings "in the
interest of the law".

While it would have been preferable, it is submitted, for the facility of
making references to the Court of Justice to have been extended to courts of
first instance, the authorities in the Member States, by carefully monitoring
the way in which the Convention is being interpreted in the State to which
they belong, could employ the procedure created by A. 4 to seek to rectify
for the future any serious aberrations perpetrated either by the national
courts or by those of sister States. Unfortunately, A. 4(2) unblushingly ensures that any such requests for interpretation submitted "in the interest of
the law" shall not affect the judgments which inspired the request for inter-

pretation, and therefore the immediate "victims" of any local misapplications of the Convention will fail to secure any redress, assuming that there remains no possibility of pursuing an internal appeal in their case.

NOTES

1. For the text of the Convention as originally signed, see E.C. Bull. Supp. 2/1969 at pp. 17—45; also printed (together with the Protocol of 3 June 1971) as Appendix B in K. Lipstein (ed.) Harmonisation of Private International Law by the EEC (1978) (hereinafter referred to as "Harmonisation"); as annex 1 to ch. 9 of A. Campbell (ed.) Common Market Law, vol. 3 (1973) at p. 506. The text is also published in M. Weser, Convention Communautaire sur la Compétence Judiciaire et Effets des Jugements dans le Marché Commun (1975) at pp. 485—503; in G.A.L. Droz, Compétence Judiciaire et Effets des Jugements dans le Marché Commun (1972), annex I, at p. 485; and in the Council of Europe, Practical Guide to the Recognition and Enforcement of Foreign Judicial Decisions in Civil and Commercial Law (1975), part II, at p. 105. The English and French texts are published together in J.H. Dalhuisen, International Insolvency and Bankruptcy (1980), vol. 2, appendix 4.

2. For the text of this Protocol in its original form, see E.C. Bull. Supp. 4/1971, and also in the treatises cited in n. 1 *supra*.

3. For the text, see O.J. 1978 L 304/1; Encyclopaedia of European Community Law, vol. BII, Section B11-191; Dalhuisen, *op. cit. supra* n. 1, vol. 2, appendix A (English and French texts).

4. The Convention of 1968 and the Protocol of 1971, both as amended by the Accession Convention of 1978, are contained in Appendix A, *post*. The same texts are also published in O.J. 1978 L 304/77, and L 304/97, respectively, and in Encyclopaedia of European Community Law, vol. BII, at Sections B11-194 and B11-222, respectively. Implementation of the Convention in the United Kingdom will be achieved with the coming into force of the Civil Jurisdiction and Judgments Act, 1982.

5. See generally Title II of the Convention, Arts. 2—24 inclusive, discussed *infra*.

6. See, especially, commentary on Arts. 2 and 3 *infra*, where the expression "domiciled" is also discussed.

7. See, especially, Arts. 3 and 4 of the Convention, in conjunction with Title III (Arts. 25—49 inclusive), discussed *infra*.

8. The Hague Convention of 1 February 1971 on Recognition and Enforcement of Foreign Judgments is a convention of this type: see, especially, Arts. 10—12 thereof. (The Convention is not yet in force, however.)

9. *cf.* the Jenard Report on the Judgments Convention, E.C. Bull. Supp. 12/1972, at p. 25 *et seq.*, O.J. 1979 C59/1, at p. 13 *et seq.* (subsequent references to this Report will furnish the alternative page references to its two published versions).

10. *cf.* ECT Part 2 (Arts. 9—84).

11. See the Contracts Convention (*post*, Chapter 5) and the Bankruptcy Conve ition (*post*, Chapter 6). These Conventions, in their respective ways, effectively complement the provisions of the Judgments Convention.

12. On the question of such distortion, see the arguments in Chapters 1 and 2 *ante*, especially at pp. 13 and 53.

13. *cf.* Arts. 2 and 3 *infra*.

14. *cf.* Arts. 13—15 *infra*; see also Arts 7—12A.

15. *cf.* Arts 17 and 18 *infra*.

16. *cf.* A. 16, and also A. 5 *infra*.

17. See A. 4, together with the provisions of Title III of the Convention. See also A. 59 thereof, together with the Supplementary Protocol to the Hague Convention on Recognition and Enforcement of Foreign Judgments in Civil and Commercial Matters, concluded on 1 February 1971. All are further considered *infra*.

18. See especially the sustained invective by Nadelmann (1964) 58 AJIL 724, (1967) 67 Colum. L. Rev. 995 (also printed in Conflict of Laws (1972) at p. 238), (1967—68) 5 CML Rev. 409, (1968) 16 AJCL 601, (1969) 82 Harv. L. Rev. 1282. See also Nadelmann and Von Mehren (1960) 60 AJIL 803, (1966—67) 15 AJCL 361.

19. Doc. 1437/IV/64; Report thereon, Doc. 2449/IV/65.

20. See Arts. 100, 189 and 235 ECT.

21. See the account of this aspect of development of Community Law given in Chapter 2 *ante* at pp. 29—35.

22. Prescribed by Arts. 61 and 62 of the Convention (original version) and by Arts. 7 and 8 of the Protocol on Interpretation.

23. For the text of the Convention and of the Protocol in this form, see references given *supra* notes 1 and 2, respectively. For comment thereon, see: Droz, *op. cit. supra* n. 1; Weser, *op. cit. supra* n. 1; D. Holleaux Compétence du juge étranger et reconnaissance des jugements (1970); K. Lipstein, The Law of the European Economic Community (1974), pp. 270—80; B. Goldman, European Commercial Law (1973), ch. 30; D. Lasok, Law of the Economy in the European Communities (1980), pp. 419—29; Arnold (1965) 15 BBAWD 321, (1969) 19 BBAWD 89, (1972) 22 BBAWD 389, (1972) N.J.W. 997; Bellet (1977) RTDE 32, (1965) 92 Clunet 833; Bülow (1965) 29 Rabels Z 473; Collins, in Harmonisation (Ed. Lipstein), p. 91; Fragistas (1968) Riv. Dir. Int. priv. e process. 745; Giardina (1978) ICLQ 263; Goldman (1971) RTDE 1; Gothot and Holleaux (1971) 98 Clunet 747; Hartley in Harmonisation (Ed. Lipstein), p. 103; Hauschild (1975) RTDE at pp. 4—13; Hay (1968) 16 AJCL 149; Herzog (1977) 17 Virg. J. Int. L. 417; Homburger (1970) 18 AJCL 367; Jenard (1975) RTDE 14; Jeantet (1972) CDE 375; Leleux (1977) CDE 144; McLellan (1978) 15 CML Rev. 228, (1979) 16 CML Rev. 268; Mok (1971) 8 CML Rev. 485; Mercier (1967) CDE 367, 513; Nadelmann, references given *supra* n. 18; Newman, in Legal Aspects of an Enlarged Community (Ed. M.E. Bathurst) (1972), p. 58; Padis (1974) 94 Gaz. Pal., Doctrine 278; Pointon (1975) 2 Leg. Iss. Eur. Int. 1; Pocar (1978) 42 Rabels Z. 405; Rasmussen (1978) CML Rev. 249; Weser (1959) Rev. Crit. D.I.P. 613, (1960) *id.* 21, 151, 313, 533, (1961) *id.* 105, (1961) 10 AJCL 323, (1964) 13 AJCL 45, (1965) Univ. Ill. L. Forum 771, (1969) Trav. Com. Fr. D.I.P. 1016, (1975) RTDE 24; Zaphiriou [1969] JBL 74. See also G.A.L. Droz, in The Influence of the European Communities upon Private International Law of the Member States, ed. by P. Bourel and others (Brussels, 19F) at pp. 49—76.

24. For the text of this Convention, see references given *supra* n. 3. The signing of the Accession Convention was also expressed as taking place *"within* the Council".

25. For the Jenard Report, see E.C. Bull. Supp. 12/1972; revised version in O.J. 1979 C59/1. For the Schlosser Report, see O.J. 1979 C59/71.

26. The judgments of the Court of Justice, together with important decisions by national courts interpreting or applying the Convention, are conveniently collected by the Documentation Branch of the Court of Justice, Luxembourg and published as a series entitled: Synopsis of Case Law: the EEC Convention of 27 September 1968 (1977—   ). Periodical surveys of national jurisprudence relating to the Convention appear in the European Law Review, in the Revue Critique de droit international privé, and in the Netherlands International Law Review.

27. *cf.* Jenard Report, references *supra* n. 25, at pp. 16/C59/8.

28. The meaning of this expression is explored *infra* in relation to Arts. 2—4 and 52.
29. [1976] ECR 1541, [1977] 1 CMLR 88.
30. [1976] ECR at p. 1551, [1977] 1 CMLR at pp. 100—101.
31. *Ibid.* at pp. 1552—53, and 102, respectively. See also Case 814/79, *Netherlands State* v. *Ruffer* [1980] ECR 3807, [1981] 3 CMLR 293.
32. *cf.* Contracts Convention (*post*, Chapter 5) A. 1(2)(a), (b).
33. *cf.* Draft Bankruptcy Convention, (*post*, Chapter 6) A. 1 together with A. 1(a) and (b) of the Protocol thereto.
34. [1979] ECR 1055, [1979] 2 CMLR 547. See Hartley (1979) ELR 222.
35. [1979] ECR at p. 1067, [1979] 2 CMLR at p. 560.
36. [1980] ECR 731 [1980] 3 CMLR 1.
37. [1979] ECR 733, [1979] 3 CMLR 180. See Hartley (1979) ELR 482.
38. Pursuant to French Law No. 67—563 of 13 July 1967, A. 99.
39. This ruling accords nicely with the provisions incorporated into the Draft Bankruptcy Convention (*post*, Chapter 6), A. 11 of which allocates jurisdiction in such matters to the courts of the State in which the bankruptcy of the company or firm has been opened. A. 67 of that Convention now provides, however, that the recognition and enforcement of any judgment awarded against a manager or director in such circumstances shall take place under the Judgments Convention: see *post* p. 238.
40. See A. 60(2), (3) and (5) for provisions relating to the Netherlands Antilles and the Faroe Islands. For the counterpart provisions of A. 60 in the other Community Conventions, see Contracts Convention, A. 27; Draft Bankruptcy Convention A. 79, and *cf.* Convention on Mutual Recognition of Companies A. 12.
41. A. 54(1). See, however, Case 25/79, *Sanicentral* v. *Collin* [1979] ECR 3423, [1980] 2 CMLR 164, on the interaction between the Convention and national law concerning the validity of agreements concluded before the Convention entered into force.
42. *supra* p. 103.
43. Accession Convention, A. 34(1).
44. *Ibid.* A. 34(2).
45. *Ibid.* A. 34(3).
46. From the expanding literature upon this topic, see Nadelmann (1967) 67 Colum. L. Rev. 995 (also published in Conflict of Laws (1972) at p. 238), and the same author in Twentieth Century Comparative and Conflicts of Law, Essays in Honour of H. Yntema (1961) at p. 321 (also published in Conflict of Laws (1972) at p. 222); de Winter (1968) 17 ICLQ 705; Siegal (1971) 20 ICLQ 99; Smit (1972) 21 ICLQ 335; Collins (1972) 21 ICLQ 656; Kahn-Freund in General Problems of Conflicts of Law (1976) at p. 34 (also in (1974, III) 143 Hague Rec. des Cours 147 at p. 180); A. Ehrenzweig, Private International Law, Vol. 2, Special Part (1973) at pp. 4—49.
47. For recent examples of such practices serving to establish the jurisdiction of the English courts, see, for example, *Colt Industries* v. *Sarlie* [1966] 1 All E.R. 673; *Maharanee of Baroda* v. *Wildenstein* [1972] 2 Q.B. 283.
48. On the Scots law jurisdictional device of arrestment *ad fundandam jurisdictionem*, see A.E. Anton, Private International Law (1967) at pp. 106—17.
49. A. 16 is discussed *infra*.
50. There is currently a proposal that all citizens of the Member States should become the bearers of a standardised "Community Passport".
51. Examples of such "nationality-based" rules mentioned within the provisions of A. 3(2) are A. 15 of the Code Civil of Belgium, Arts. 14 and 15 of the Code Civil of France, and Arts. 14 and 15 of the Code Civil of Luxembourg.
52. Discussed *infra*. See especially the words of A. 25, which define the term "judgment" for the purposes of the Convention as meaning "any judgment given by a court or

tribunal of a Contracting State ...".

53. Among the many criticisms of this aspect of the Convention, see, especially, Nadelmann, *loc. cit. supra* n. 46 (first citation), (1967–68) 5 CML Rev. 409, (1968) 82 Harv. L. Rev. 1282; Hay (1968) 16 AJCL 149, esp. at pp. 160–62.

54. See the Hague Convention of 1 February 1971 (now in force, but so far ratified by only the Netherlands and Cyprus).

55. See Nadelmann and Von Mehren (1966) 60 AJIL 803, (1966–67) 15 AJCL 361; Nadelmann (1968) 16 AJCL 601; Newman (1969) 18 ICLQ 652.

56. See the Supplementary Protocol to the Hague Convention on the Recognition and Enforcement of Foreign Judgments in Civil and Commercial Matters, concluded on 1 February 1971 (now in force but with only the minimum two ratifications so far effected, as with the main Convention; see n. 54 *supra*).

57. At one time it seemed likely that a Judgments Convention would be adopted between the United Kingdom and the United States of America to take advantage of the facility created by A. 59. See the text of a Draft Judgments Convention, initialled on 26 October 1976 (Cmnd. 6771) and comment by Hay and Walker (1978) 18 Virg. Jnl. Int. L. 753. However, this Convention has subsequently been abandoned.

58. A. 53(2) also directs the *forum* to apply its own rules of private international law in order to determine whether a trust is "domiciled" within the Contracting State in which it sits. The notion of the "domicile" of a trust is a somewhat novel one for Common lawyers, but will probably not cause too much difficulty in actual practice.

59. See Chapter 7 *post*.

60. The key expressions in the French and German versions of the Convention are: "*domiciliés*" and "*die ihren Wohnsitz ... haben*". *cf.* Graveson in Liber Amicorum, Ernst J. Cohn (1975) at p. 66.

It is also worth noting that A. 10(1) of the Hague Convention on Recognition and Enforcement of Foreign Judgments, *supra* n. 54, allocated jurisdiction to the court of the State of origin of a judgment if the defendant had, at the time when the proceedings were instituted, his habitual residence in the State of origin. If the defendant is a legal person, jurisdiction may be founded upon the presence of the seat, place of incorporation *or* principal place of business within the State of origin of the judgment (*ibid.*).

61. *cf.* the issues raised in the second of the *Cavel* Cases, Case 120/79 (*supra* n. 36).

62. [1976] ECR 1473, [1977] 1 CMLR 60. *cf.* Case 56/79, *Zelger* v. *Salinitri* [1980] ECR 89, [1980] 2 CMLR 635.

63. See Chapter 5 *post*, especially in relation to Arts. 3 and 4 of the Contracts Convention.

63a. See Case 784/79, *Porta Leasing GmbH, Trier* v. *Prestige International S.A.* [1980] ECR 1517, [1981] CMLR 135.

64. [1976] ECR 1497, [1977] 1 CMLR 26.

65. [1978] ECR 2183, [1979] 1 CMLR 490. See Hartley (1979) 2 ELR 127. See also Case 139/80, *Blankaert and Willems* v. *Trost* [1981] ECR 819.

66. See the Jenard Report *supra* n. 25, at pp. 44–45/C59/25–26.

67. Case 21/76, *Bier B.V.* v. *Mines de Potasse* [1976] ECR 1735, [1977] 1 CMLR 284. See Hartley (1977) 2 ELR 143. *cf.* also Case 814/79, *Netherlands State* v. *Ruffer, supra* n. 31.

68. See *post* Chapter 5, p. 150 and Chapter 8, p. 273 on the severance of non-contractual liability from the Convention on Choice of Law in the field of Obligations.

69. A. 8.

70. A. 9. *cf.* the interpretation placed upon the expression "place where the harmful event occurred" in Case 21/76, *Bier B.V.* v. *Mines de Potasse, supra* n. 67.

71. A. 11.

72. A. 12.
73. A. 13(1). See also Case 150/77, *Société Bertrand* v. *Paul Ott K.G.* [1978] ECR 1431, [1978] 3 CMLR 499, in which the Court of Justice gave an "independent" interpretation to the words "instalment credit sale" in A. 13.
74. Arts. 13, 14.
75. See A. 15(1).
76. See Jenard Report *supra* in 25, at pp. 60 CO/CEO/81 2C.
77. [1977] ECR 2383, [1978] 1 CMLR 331. See Hartley (1978) ELR 164.
78. Case 24/76, *Colzani* v. *RÜWA* [1976] ECR 1831, [1977] 1 CMLR 345. See Hartley (1977) 2 ELR 148. For the effects of the even more stringent requirements in favour of parties domiciled in Luxembourg, imported into A. 17 by A. I of the Protocol, see Case 784/79, *Porta Leasing* v. *Prestige International* [1980] E.C.R. 1517, [1981] C.M.L.R., 35.
79. Case 25/76, *Segoura* v. *Bonakdarian* [1976] ECR 1851, [1977] 1 CMLR 361. See Hartley, *loc. cit. supra* n. 78.
80. Case 25/76, *Segoura* v. *Bonakdarian supra.*
81. Case 56/79, *Zelger* v. *Salinitri* [1980] ECR 89, [1980] 2 CMLR 635.
82. Case 23/78, *Meeth* v. *Glacetal* [1978] ECR 2133, [1979] 1 CMLR 520.
83. [1979] ECR 3423, [1980] 2 CMLR 164.
84. *cf.* the recent, unhappy decision of the English C.A. in *Henry* v. *Geoprosco International Ltd.* [1976] Q.B. 726, effectively reviving the much-criticised decision in *Harris* v. *Taylor* [1915] 2 K.B. 580. See Collins (1976) 92 LQR 268; Solomons (1976) 25 ICLQ 665. It is submitted that these decisions must cease to be regarded as authoritative, at least with respect to any cases falling within the ambit of the Judgments Convention.
84a. See also Case 150/80 *Elefanten Schuh* v. *Jacqmain* [1981] ECR 1671 in which the Court ruled that the unity conferred by A. 18 upon defendants whose appearance is made solely for the purpose of challenging the jurisdiction of the Court may be lost if the defendant makes additional submissions in the substance of the action itself. In order to retain the immunity provided by A. 18, the defendant must ensure that in the pleading which, under the National procedural law of the Court seised, constitutes the defendant's first defence, formal notice is given to the plaintiff and to the Court that the defence is to be understood as contesting the Court's jurisdiction.
85. See Arts. 52 and 53, discussed *supra* p. 121.
86. A. 20(3) provides for the replacement of the requirements of A. 20(2) by the provisions of A. 15 of the Hague Convention of 15 November 1965 on the service abroad of judicial and extrajudicial documents, where the document in question is one to which that Convention applies. (All of the Member States of the EEC have ratified this Convention, apart from Ireland, Greece and Italy. Italy has signed the Convention, but has not yet ratified it.)
86a. The need for the original proceedings to afford the opportunity to the defendant to appear and participate effectively was emphasised in Case 125/79, *Denilauler* v. *Couchet Frères* [1980] ECR 1553, [1981] CMLR 62.
87. *cf.* criticisms, *post*, Chapter 6, of the similarly arbitrary results which may arise under Arts. 13 and 58 of the Bankruptcy Convention.
88. See, however, the regrettable failure of the English House of Lords to adopt the approach advocated in the text, in *The Siskina* [1979] A.C. 210, discussed in Chapter 2 *ante* at pp. 60–63. Note however, the requirements that proceedings for interim relief in which the defendant is afforded no opportunity to appear or to be heard will not command international full faith and credit under the Convention: Case 125/79, *Denilauler* v. *Couchet Frères supra* n. 86a.
89. See A. 28(1), which states that a judgment shall not be recognised if it conflicts

with the provisions of Section 3, 4 or 5 of Title II (effectively, Arts. 7—16 inclusive) or in the case provided for in A. 59. (These provisions have been considered *supra*.)

90.   For the traditional rules governing enforcement of foreign judgments, see, for example, Dicey and Morris. *op. cit.* (10th edn. 1980), ch. 33; J.H.C. Morris, The Conflict of Laws (2nd edn. 1980), ch. 27; Cheshire and North, Private International Law (10th edn. 1979), ch. 19; Graveson, Conflicts of Laws (7th edn. 1974), ch. 21. On the erstwhile practice, under French private international law, of reviewing the substance of foreign judgments, see Nadelmann (1964) 13 AJCL 72; Hay (1968) 16 AJCL 149, at pp. 167—68.

90a.   For an important ruling upon the effects of A. 27(2), see Case 166/80, *Klomps* v. *Michel* [1981] ECR 1593 in which the Court of Justice held that, even though the mode of notification of the defendant may be valid according to the law of the State in which the proceedings have originated, it is incumbent upon the Court of the State in which enforcement is sought to examine independently whether the defendant was in fact afforded sufficient time to arrange his defence and to take measures ensuring that a decision enforceable under the Convention would not be given against him in default. See also Case 125/79, *Denilauler* v. *Couchet Frères, supra* n. 86a.

91.   This provision has already been discussed *supra* at pp. 119—20.

92.   In the United Kingdom, the courts so designated are: in England and Wales, the High Court of Justice or, in maintenance matters, the Magistrates' Court on transmission by the Secretary of State; in Scotland, the Court of Session or, in maintenance matters, the Sheriff Court on transmission as above; and in Northern Ireland, the High Court of Justice or, in maintenance matters, the Magistrates' Court on transmission.

93.   A. 31(1).

94.   See Case 43/77, *Industrial Diamond Supplies* v. *Riva* [1977] ECR 2175, [1978] 1 CMLR 349, in which the Court of Justice supplied an independent, but broad, definition of the expression "ordinary appeal" as used in Arts. 30 and 38.

95.   The list of courts in A. 37 differs in several respects from that contained in A. 32. However, in the case of the United Kingdom, the courts are identical in each instance.

96.   A. 39. It is submitted that, in the United Kingdom, protective measures such as the *Mareva* injunctions (discussed in Chapter 2 *ante* at pp. 60—61) should be made readily available under relatively liberal conditions.

97.   As with the lists contained in Arts. 32 and 37, there are some differences in the case of other Member States, but for the United Kingdom the relevant courts are the same as those designated in Arts. 32 and 37 (see *supra* n. 92 and 94).

98.   [1976] ECR 1759, [1979] 2 CMLR 43. See Hartley (1977) 2 ELR 146.

99.   *Supra* p. 119.

100.   [1977] ECR 1417, [1980] 1 CMLR 566.

101.   For criticism of the deficiencies of A. 57, see Bellet (1965) 92 Clunet 833, at p. 868. See also Pocar (1978) 42 Rabels Z. 405, at pp. 428—30. For commentary on, and explanation of, the provisions contained in Title VII (Arts. 55—59), see Jenard Report, *supra* n. 25, at pp. 102—107/C59/58—62.

102.   On these differences of drafting and substance, see Mok (1971) 8 CML Rev. 485; Rasmussen (1978) 15 CMLR Rev. 249.

CHAPTER 5

The Convention of 19 June 1980 on the Law Applicable to Contractual Obligations

1. Preliminary

On 19 June 1980 the representatives of seven of the Member States signed the Community Convention on the law applicable to contractual obligations.[1] Although the United Kingdom and Denmark did not at once become signatories to this Convention, it is likely, and is indeed greatly to be hoped, that both will in due course do so following a further period of contemplation of its overall implications.[1a] It is therefore probable that, after enacting the requisite enabling legislation, the United Kingdom along with the other Member States will eventually incorporate the provisions of the Contracts Convention into its rules of private international law, and on this assumption the following commentary will attempt to describe the legal provisions which will thereafter obtain in matters of contract involving international characteristics.

2. Justification for the Convention

The legal justification for the Contracts Convention is to be found, not in the provisions of A. 220 ECT directly, but is rather derived indirectly from the conclusions, already referred to in Chapter 2 above,[2] which have been deduced from an appraisal of the overall requirements predicated by Community law, and which regard the full unification of private international law as the "natural sequel" to the fulfilment of the specific obligations engendered by A. 220 itself. This general framework of reasoning underlay the proposal, initiated by the Benelux countries and formally submitted on their behalf to the Commission on 8 September 1967, to the effect that a programme for the systematic unification of the private international law of the Member States should be agreed and embarked upon.[3] It may therefore be argued that, by responding in a positive way to this proposal, and in particular by establishing a standing working party of governmental experts to act upon it, the original Six Member States objectively manifested their acquiescence in the gloss upon the Treaty's purport and requirements which formed the fundamental premise upon which the proposal itself was based. It is furthermore encouraging to note that, despite the absence of any express requirement in the Treaty and Act of Accession to oblige the new Member States to accede to any Conventions apart from those actually provided for in A. 220 ECT,[4] all three of them duly responded to the invitation to join in the deliberations of the Brussels Working Group on private international law from which the Contracts Convention ultimately emerged. Thereby, if perhaps only tacitly, the new Member States may be said to have acknowledged the legal legitimacy of what was being undertaken under the auspices of the Community, while, in the case of the Republic of Ireland, an even more significant manifestation of assent has been forthcoming from the fact that that country became one of the seven original signatories to the Convention along with all of the original Member States of the EEC.

The logical justifications for this Convention arise from several distinct, but related, considerations. In the first place, it is a widely-held view among writers upon the subject of private international law that the ideals of justice and the practical needs of commerce would be simultaneously fulfilled by means of a standardised approach to questions of choice of law in the realm of obligations. In reality, however, the quest for this particular "holy grail" has proved to be a characteristically elusive one, although in relation to certain specific types of contract – such as the international sale of goods – a degree of progress has been achieved within the programme of activities of the Hague Conference on Private International Law,[5] and also under the auspices of UNCITRAL.[6] Hence, the possibility that the area of contracts might be comprehensively governed by means of a single Convention is in principle an attractive one, albeit one whose realisation would seem destined to be both an arduous and a controversial undertaking. However, quite apart from the general desirability of a Convention to regulate this aspect of private international law, it may be said that the Community Contracts Convention is logically essential to serve as the natural complement to the Convention on Jurisdiction and Enforcement of Judgments.[7] For, just as the introduction of schematic provisions to regulate the question of the venue of proceedings containing an international character gains powerful justification from the fact that *forum* shopping will thereby be largely eliminated, so too in matters of the choice of law rules to be applied by the court which exercises jurisdiction (a matter on which the Judgments Convention itself is silent) the substitution of agreed, uniform conflicts rules in place of the individually-developed rules formerly employed by each State's courts holds forth the prospect of a further, significant reduction of the extent to which, whether by chance or by choice, the factor of the venue of proceedings is capable of exerting a material effect upon the actual outcome in any given case. Thus, although it may be a matter for speculation to what extent exploitative use is made of choice-of-law facilities available to either or both of the parties who enter into a contract,[8] a properly constructed Convention would have the decided attraction of placing such matters altogether outside the realms of doubt, and would accordingly enhance still further the level of legal protection and legal certainty obtaining within the Community. An additional consideration, and one much in accord with the arguments expressed in Part I of this book, is that the creation of unified conflicts rules for the EEC in contractual matters will eliminate a further aspect of legal and competitive distortion from the Community's sphere of application. Nevertheless, the very fact that contracts are employed in so many diverse kinds of situation, and therefore touch upon many diverse interests simultaneously, at once gives rise to an acute practical difficulty inherent in any attempt to cover the subject comprehensively within a single international Convention. Almost any solution which might be agreed upon would in all likelihood remain susceptible to criticism on one or more grounds, and such has indeed proved to be the case.

3. The Evolution of the Convention

The labours of the Working Group commenced in February 1970 under the chairmanship of Mr. P. Jenard, and were originally directed at the elaboration of a convention to cover both contractual and non-contractual obligations. By June 1972, a Preliminary Draft Convention on the law applicable to contractual and non-contractual obligations, together with an explanatory Report, was completed and submitted to the governments of the Member States.[9] This first version of the Draft consisted of 36 Articles together with an Annexe containing possible variants for some of the Articles, and a Joint Declaration. At this stage, the contents of the Draft became available for critical appraisal and comment and, almost simultaneously, the Working Group was augmented by the inclusion of representatives from the three new Member States, the heterogeneousness of whose traditions in matters of private international law was in any event destined to require a thorough reappraisal of the contents of the Preliminary Draft. This second phase of activity did not actually begin until the end of 1975, by which time the original version of the Draft had been subjected to no small degree of critical censure, both in and out of print.[10] After the resumption of its deliberations, the Working Group took the important decision, in March 1978, to limit its immediate concern to the preparation of a Convention dealing with contractual obligations alone, thus leaving the negotiation of a further convention on non-contractual obligations to be pursued at a later date. Thereafter, the Convention was put into a finalised version for submission to the Council of Ministers in June 1979. In its revised version, the Draft Contracts Convention consisted of 31 Articles, together with a Joint Declaration,[11] and was accompanied by a revised explanatory Report prepared by Professors Giuliano and Lagarde.[12] Subsequently, inter-governmental negotiations took place which had the effect of producing numerous changes in points of detail, and also of expanding the length of the Convention to 33 Articles, together with a Protocol and two Joint Declarations. In this form, the Convention was opened for signature in Rome on 19 June 1980, following its formal acceptance by a meeting of the Ministers of Justice of the Member States of the European Communities.[13]

4. Commentary

(a) Criteria for Evaluation

In an area of law which is at once so vital, so diversified and so controversial as that of the private international law relating to contracts, it is intrinsically improbable that any negotiated solution to its notoriously complex practical and conceptual problems will enjoy universal acclaim and acceptance. Hence, the chorus of critical denunciations which greeted both the first and the final versions of the Contracts Convention was not altogether unexpected, nor does it in itself amount to conclusive proof that the Convention is a failure. After all, if seven (and, eventually one hopes, nine and later ten) States can unify their private international law in accordance with the rules worked out by their negotiators, that in itself is a highly significant and useful development, even though it may be true that the rules upon which they have settled are the result of diplomatic or juridical compromises, and may in many respects fall short of some "absolute" ideal. It is therefore proposed to apply the following, pragmatic criteria in evaluating the rules contained in the Convention.

(i) Are the rules themselves sufficiently flexible to enable the courts of the Member States to escape from the necessity of perpetrating insensitive and mechanical decisions which in many cases will fail to accord with generally-accepted notions of justice and good sense?

(ii) On the other hand, do the rules give clear expression to firm and sound principles which will enable parties to arrange their affairs in full confidence of the legal effects which will ensue from a particular form of agreement or course of action?

(iii) Finally, does the Convention succeed in complementing the other Conventions and Community legislative provisions with which it is supposed to be functionally integrated (in particular, the Judgments Convention), and does it maintain an overall consistency with the basic principles and concepts upon which Community law itself is established?

Here, one is mindful in particular of the concern of Community law to procure a basic uniformity in the levels of legal protection obtaining throughout the Member States of the EEC, and also to furnish a means of redressing the characteristic imbalances in such contractual relationships as those between the consumer and the supplier of goods or services; those between insured persons (or policy-holders) and their insurers; and those between employees and their employers. While much can be done to remedy these notorious problems by means of harmonisation of internal laws, and by means of specially restrictive rules pertaining to the exercise of judicial jurisdiction,[14] there is further scope for the utilisation of *dirigiste* legislative policies in the field of choice of law, so as to inhibit the opportunities for the socially and economically strong to dominate those who are relatively weak.

(b) Scope the Convention

The most immediately striking aspect of the Convention's scheme of application is that the negotiators have succeeded in transcending such purely parochial considerations as the personal attachment of parties to at least one of the Member States or its system of laws, or the not infrequently fortuitous factor that the law governing a particular contract turns out to be that of one of the Contracting States. Instead, the bolder, but infinitely more satisfactory, step has been taken of conferring a fully universal sphere of application upon the choice of law rules embodied in the Convention, with the consequence that they will be applied to all contracts which fall within the scope of the Convention *ratione materiae*, irrespective of the nationality, or country of residence or domicile of the parties to them, irrespective furthermore of whether the law to be applied is or is not that of any of the Contracting States,[15] and finally without any requirement of reciprocity. Thus, upon ratifying, all the Contracting States will be obliged to substitute the rules of the Convention for those which they currently apply in matters of private international law relating to contracts, and to apply them to all cases over which they exercise jurisdiction.[16] This greatly minimises the possibilities for the spawning of new "parallelisms" as a result of the adoption of the Convention, since effectively a single, "common" body of rules of law will be employed by the courts of all Contracting States in all cases. A certain danger remains of the creation of conflicting bodies of "common" rules by means of different international conventions, but in this respect A. 21 endeavours to avert the threat of total *impasse* which would result, since it expressly provides that the present Convention shall not prejudice the application of other international conventions to which a Contracting State is, or becomes, a party. Accordingly, special areas of contract law — such as sale of goods[17] — may validly be made the subject of more detailed international provisions embodied in separate conventions which, in the event that their provisions give rise to any possible overlap with those of the Contracts Convention in given situations, shall be allowed to prevail over the latter. Furthermore, A. 20 of the Contracts Convention specifies that the Convention shall not affect the application of provisions which, in relation to particular matters, lay down choice of law rules relating to contractual obligations which are, or which will be, contained in acts of the Institutions of the Community or in national laws harmonised in implementation of such acts.[18] Here again, a convenient solution is offered for cases of conflict between legal provisions belonging to different legal norms, namely the Community legal order and the international legal order, with precedence here being accorded to the former by means of an inbuilt provision actually contained within an instrument belonging to the latter. It should not be too readily assumed, however, that the provisions contained in Arts. 20 and 21 will yield satisfactory or easily-workable results in practice,[19] and it would be as well if those who, whether within the Community or the international sphere, are engaged upon future ventures which will touch upon the realm of contract law, were to give constant and careful thought to the possibilities of overlap between the projects upon which they are working and the Contracts Convention already concluded. Where necessary, specific provisions should be devised to give a clear indication of how any unavoidable conflicts between conventions, or between Directives or Regulations or national legislation on the one hand and the Contracts Convention on the other, are to be dealt with in practice.[20] In this context, the significance of Arts. 23 and 24 may also be emphasised, for these two Articles establish a formal, consultative procedure to be followed henceforth whenever any Contracting State either wishes to adopt a new choice of law rule with regard to any particular category of contract falling within the scope of the Convention, or to become a party to a multilateral convention whose sphere of application would overlap with that of the Convention.[21] It is noteworthy that the regime thus imposed upon Member States has the effect of leaving them finally free to elect to follow an individualised legal policy once more, and hence the unity achieved initially upon the coming into force of the Contracts Convention will not necessarily endure indefinitely. However, the consultative procedure which is required to be pursued should have the virtue of enabling the Member State in question to explain its position to its EEC partners, while they in turn will be enabled to bring to bear whatever moral and persuasive influences lie within their command, with a view to mitigating or even totally avoiding any adverse and disharmonious consequences which may be threatened by the course of action in contemplation. However, it must be conceded that, at the end of the day, the individual Member State is left free to follow its own predilections in the matter. It should also be observed that A. 23 does not authorise Member States to create new *general* rules in matters of contract to replace those embodied in the Convention: what is permitted is the creation of a choice of law rule in relation to a *particular category* of contract.

The scope of the Convention *ratione materiae* is delineated by means of the provisions in A. 1. In the first place, A. 1(1) indicates the scope of the Convention by means of positive language in the widest possible terms: it is to apply to contractual obligations in *any* situation involving a choice between the laws of different countries.[22] Consequently, whenever the Court can discern no question of choice of law whatsoever within the case before it, the Convention is not applicable and the Court may proceed to apply the internal law of the *forum* without more ado. Where, however, the presence of a question of choice of law is detected, the Court must proceed to refer to the Convention and to apply its rules to the case before it, even though it may transpire that the "choice" in question will be (or, even, has been) in favour of the *lex fori*. The fact that the Convention is so expressed as to be applicable to any situation in which a question of choice of law arises would have the consequence that its provisions would be applicable in principle to any case whose elements, though confined within the United Kingdom as a whole, nevertheless raised the question of choice of law as between the laws of different countries of the United Kingdom. However, A. 19(2) provides that a State, within which different territorial units have their own rules of law in respect of contractual obligations, shall not be bound to apply the

Convention to conflicts solely between the laws of such units. Thus, the United Kingdom is at liberty to decide upon its own policy and practice with regard to such matters. It is submitted, however, that the better approach to adopt, and one which would have the virtue of maintaining consistency with the overall principles advocated herein, would be for the rules of the Convention to be applied also in cases otherwise confined within the boundaries of the United Kingdom. This would also complement in the most appropriate way the provision contained in A. 19(1) to the effect that where any State is so sub-divided into different "law districts", each of them shall be considered as a country for the purposes of identifying the law applicable under the Convention.

In the second paragraph of A. 1, the material scope of the Convention is limited by means of a list of specific cases to which it is declared not to be applicable.[23] These are:

(a) questions involving the status or legal capacity of natural persons;[24]

(b) contractual obligations relating to wills and succession, rights in property arising out of a matrimonial relationship, and rights and duties arising out of a family relationship, parentage, marriage or affinity, including maintenance obligations in respect of children who are not legitimate;[25]

(c) obligations arising under bills of exchange, cheques and promissory notes and other negotiable instruments to the extent that the obligations under such other negotiable instruments arise out of their negotiable character;

(d) arbitration agreements and agreements on choice of court;[26]

(e) questions governed by the law of companies and other bodies corporate or unincorporate such as the creation, by registration or otherwise, legal capacity, internal organisation or winding-up of companies and other bodies corporate or unincorporate and the personal liability of officers and members as such for the obligations of the company or body;[27]

(f) the question whether an agent is able to bind a principal, or an organ to bind a company or body corporate or unincorporate to a third party;[28]

(g) the constitution of trusts and the relationship between settlors, trustees and beneficiaries;[29]

(h) evidence and procedure.[30]

A. 1(3) contains the further, specific exclusion from the scope of the Convention of contracts of insurance which cover risks situated in the territories of Member States, with the rider that a Court which encounters the necessity of determining whether a risk is situated within the EEC is to apply its internal law to settle the question. By A. 1(4), however, it is effectively provided that contracts of re-insurance are not excluded from the scope of the Convention, irrespective of the *situs* of the risk to which they relate. Despite the formal exclusion from the scope of the Convention of direct insurance contracts covering risks situated *within* the EEC, it is naturally open to the Member States to apply rules based on those in the Convention to contracts of this kind, at least in so far as they are left free to do so following the enactment of the Community Directives which are being produced in the area of insurance.[31] It is submitted that it is highly desirable that all Member States should adopt the common practice of applying to contracts of insurance where the risk happens to be situated within the EEC the same rules of choice of law as are required by the Convention to be applied in cases where the *situs* of the risk is elsewhere. Quite apart from the fact that the use of the *situs* of the risk as a choice of law connecting factor in this context may well be inappropriate,[32] the differentiation between intra- and extra-Community situated risks is objectionable in principle, both on account of its threatened arbitrariness in many instances and also on account of its function of giving rise to two parallel sets of legal rules whose respective application is made dependent upon this very point of distinction. Since it is now too late to eliminate this instance of *gaucherie* from the text of the Convention itself, at least until such time as the Convention comes to undergo a revision, the most sensible way of minimising its more unfortunate consequences lies through the Member States' refusal to perpetrate further examples of parallelism wherever it is in their power to avoid doing so.

The scope of the Convention *ratione temporis* is governed by A. 17 together with Arts. 28–30. A. 17 provides that the Convention shall apply in a Contracting State to contracts made after the date on which the Convention has entered into force with respect to that State. Retrospective effect is thus denied, but in addition it is important to note that a contract may become subject to the provisions of the Convention within some of the Member States before such time (if ever) as the Convention enters into force with respect to each and every one of the Member States of the EEC. This is because the procedure for ratification laid down by Arts. 28 and 29 is so arranged that the Convention will come into force on the first day of the third month following the deposit of the fifth instrument of ratification, acceptance or approval by the Signatory States.[33] Thereafter the Convention will enter into force with respect to each State which becomes a ratifying party at a subsequent date on the first day of the third month following the deposit of that State's instrument of ratification.[34] This "accelerated" bringing into force, facilitated by A. 29, is to be welcomed as a practical solution to the unfortunate difficulties which have arisen in the past as a result of the tardiness of some Member States in completing the processes of ratification.[35] The duration in force of the Convention is regulated by means of A. 30 which provides that it is to remain in force for 10 years from the date when it first enters into force. This 10-year duration is absolute, and hence for any States which ratify the Convention after it comes into force, the initial period of duration will be reduced *pro tanto*. However, by A. 30(2), if the Convention has not been denounced by any of the parties, it shall be renewed tacitly every five years. Denunciation, in accordance with the provisions of A. 30(3), may be accomplished by any Contracting State by means of notice communicated to the Secretary-General of the Council of the European Communities not less than six months before the expiration of the period of ten or five years, as the case may be.[36] However A. 30(4) makes it clear that the act of any State in denouncing the Convention merely cancels its effectiveness in relation to the denouncing State: as between all the other Contracting States, the Convention will remain in force.

The scope of the Convention *ratione loci* is determined by A. 27, which declares that it shall apply to the European territories of the Contracting States, including Greenland, and to the entire territory of the French Republic. In the usual way, special arrangements are created in the case of those overseas territories over which certain of the Member States exercise some control or responsibility.[37] In the case of the United Kingdom, A. 27(2) (b) provides that the Convention shall not apply to any European territory situated outside the United Kingdom for the external relations of which the United Kingdom is responsible, unless this country makes a declaration to the contrary in respect of any such territory. A. 27(4) further provides that proceedings brought in the United Kingdom on appeal from Courts in one of these territories shall be deemed to be proceedings taking place in those Courts. Thus, the Convention will not apply at all to any non-European territories over which the United Kingdom exercises responsibilities, while in the case of those European territories outside of the United Kingdom itself over which such responsibilities exist (i.e. the Channel Islands, the Isle of Man, and Gibraltar) the Convention will only be applicable if the United Kingdom makes a declaration to that effect.

5. The Rules Governing Choice of Law

Title II of the Convention (Arts. 3—22 inclusive) contains the uniform rules which are to be applied to all questions of choice of law.

(a) Where there is a Choice by the Parties

A. 3 embodies the basic principle of party autonomy in relation to the choice of law in matters of contract. This principle is already generally accepted and applied in the private international law of all the Member States, and by the majority of other developed systems of private international law.[38] Thus, although the term "proper law" is nowhere actually employed in the Convention, it can fairly be stated that, where the parties expressly choose a law to govern their contract, or where the terms of the contract or the circumstances of the case make it possible to demonstrate with reasonable certainty that the parties have chosen a particular law, that law will constitute the proper law of the contract,[39] and as such will be applied by the Courts of whichever Contracting State becomes the *forum* for litigation. A. 3(1) further accepts the operation of *dépeçage* by enabling the parties to select the law applicable to the whole, or to only a part, of the contract, while A. 3(4) makes a cross reference to the further provisions of Arts. 8, 9 and 11 for the purpose of determining any questions of the existence and validity of the consent of the parties as to the choice of the applicable law.

(b) Validity of the Choice

The Convention contains a special provision designed to resolve the logical conundrum regarding the law which is to be referred to in order to determine the validity of a contract containing an express choice of law. By means of a species of "bootstrap" rule contained in A. 8(1), any questions of the existence and validity of a contract, or of any term thereof, are to be referred to the law which would govern it under the Convention if the contract or term were valid. Hence, the "putative proper law" is sensibly made the object of a reference to determine the validity of the parties' exercise of their freedom of choice in this matter. Where, however, a party is seeking to base his argument upon his own lack of consent to an alleged choice of law, it would be most unjust if he were to be prejudiced on account of a material difference between the putative proper law and the law of the country in which he has his habitual residence, and whose provisions would be most likely to have influenced his behaviour in relation to such matters as the formation of any contract, and the choice of the law to govern it. Accordingly, A. 8(2) contains the necessary proviso to the effect that a party may rely upon the law of the country of his habitual residence to establish that he did not consent, if it appears from the circumstances that it would not be reasonable to determine the effect of his conduct in accordance with the putative proper law of the contract. This will occasionally mean that a contract, or a clause therein, which would have been valid by virtue of the operation of the rule in A. 8(1), will be rendered invalid through the invocation of the rule in A. 8(2) by one of the parties. However, the converse does not hold true, and so a contract which would not be held valid by virtue of a reference to its putative proper law cannot be "saved" and rendered valid through the invocation of the law of the habitual residence of one or both of the parties to it.[40]

Further aspects of the validity of the formation of a contract are governed by Arts. 9 and 11, which are concerned with matters of formal validity and of contractual incapacity, respectively. In relation to the former, where the parties concluding the contract are in the same country, the principle *locus regit actum* is introduced, so that the contract is formally valid if it satisfies the formal requirements either of the law of the country where it is concluded or of the law which constitutes the proper law of the contract.[41] Where the contract is concluded between parties who are in different countries, its formal validity may be established by reference to the law of one of the countries concerned, or again, in the alternative, by reference to the proper law of the contract.[42] The possibility that the parties, or one of them, may contract via an agent is met by means of the provision in A. 9(3) to the effect that the country in which the agent acts shall constitute the "relevant country" for the purpose of testing the formal validity of the contract. With regard to questions of contractual incapacity, wherever a contract is concluded between persons who are in the same country, A. 11 imposes a restriction upon the ability of a person to invoke an incapacity resulting from a law other than that of the place of contracting. Where that person would have capacity under the law of the country in which the contract was concluded, he may only invoke his incapacity resulting from another law (typically, the law of his domicile or nationality, or just possibly that of his habitual residence) if the other party to the contract was aware of this incapacity at the time of the conclusion of the contract, or if his lack of awareness thereof was as a result of negligence. It is not stated, but is presumably to be understood, that the "negligence" in question must be on the part of the party against whom the plea of incapacity is being invoked: it would scarcely be consistent with principle if a person were allowed to plead his own want of capacity where negligence on his part has been responsible for the other party's lack of awareness of it.[43] It should in any case be noted that A. 11 applies only to cases of incapacity of natural persons, and therefore has no bearing upon situations where a legal person may seek to invoke a want of legal capacity on its part.

(c)   Time of Exercise of the Choice

Assuming that the validity of the parties' attempt to exercise a choice of law to govern their contract can be established on the basis of the foregoing tests directed at controlling questions of formal and essential validity, the further question arises of the time at which such acts of choice may be exercised. In the majority of cases, the parties who are intent upon exercising a choice at all will doubtless do so at some stage during the course of formation of the contract. However, two other possibilities require to be considered. The first is where the parties have not originally exercised any choice of law, but subsequently seek to do so, while the second possibility arises where parties, having originally chosen one law at the time of concluding their contract, subsequently wish to substitute some alternative law as the proper law of the contract. The first difficulty attending such situations is one of policy: shall parties be allowed, at some time subsequent to the formation of their contract, to elect to change the law by which their contract is governed, whether that law is one which the parties themselves actively chose as the proper law, or whether it is the law which, in the absence of any act of choice by the parties, is the one which the private international law of the *forum* would hold to constitute the proper law of the contract? The second attendant difficulty is essentially a question of principle in relation to choice of law: assuming that the possibility of changing the proper law of the contract is admitted, the question remains of which law ought to be considered as governing the act of change itself: should it be the *lex fori*, the "original" proper law or the "substitute" proper law?[44] A. 3(2) answers the question of policy in an affirmative way, by providing that the parties may at any time agree to subject the contract to a law other than that which previously governed it, whether as a result of an earlier choice under A. 3 itself or as a result of other provisions of the Convention.[45] However, the way in which A. 3(2) has been drafted is such that the law which will govern the actual change of proper law in each given case will be the *lex fori*. This is because the Convention has the function of creating rules of the *lex fori*, so that any Court encountering this particular question will find itself directed by the terms of A. 3(2) itself to accept the validity of what the parties have done, and to apply as the proper law of the contract the law which the parties have chosen by means of their *latest* act of choice. However, as a choice of law rule to employ in such cases, the provision is open to serious logical and practical objections.[46] A contract is, by definition, a species of agreement which affects the legal relationship of the parties thereto. As such, a contract is itself dependent for its effects and for its effectiveness upon the provisions of that system of law by which it is, in principle, regulated from its inception. A contract is only a contract because it is formed under a legal system of some kind: it cannot be born in a vacuum.[46a] Once the contract is *"in esse"*, therefore, it is surely axiomatic that any question of the legal effect of an attempt to alter the identity of the proper law must be referred in the first instance to the law which, for the time being, constitutes the very *fons et origo* of the contract as a legally operative agreement. Thus, if the original proper law of the contract would refuse to recognise the effectiveness of the parties' attempt to modify their contract, it cannot but be an act of aggression by the *lex fori* to interpose its own preference for accepting the validity of what the parties have purported to accomplish. In practice, perhaps, no great harm will be done in cases where the parties have merely sought to substitute the law of one Member State for that of another as the proper law of their contract, since the uniform rule insinuated by A. 3(2) into the laws of all the Member States would produce the result that the parties' new choice of a proper law would be held valid, whether the question were referred to the *lex fori*, or the original proper law, or (even) to the "substitute" proper law. If, however, the process of change involves the law of any non-Member State, the Community is surely behaving in a high-handed and "aggressive" way by refusing to require its Courts to pay any regard to the compatibility of the alleged change of law with the provisions and requirements of the other system or systems of law concerned. It is submitted that the Convention has adopted an over-simplified, and logically indefensible, approach to what is in fact a highly complex matter, at least whenever the contract in question falls to be governed by the law of a non-Member State whose relevant provisions it is incompetent for the EEC to presume to alter by means of rules adopted in common among its own Member States. To conform with basic principles, the validity of any purported change in the proper law of a contract should be referred to two different laws successively: first, to the law which constitutes the original proper law of the contract, in order to determine whether it accepts the efficacy of the parties' attempt to modify their contract; and secondly, to the "substitute" proper law in order to confirm the very same question. Only if both of the systems of law concerned would concur in finding that the parties' actions have had the effect of substituting the one for the other as the proper law of the contract should the *forum* proceed henceforth to deal with the contract on that footing.[47] Thus, it is submitted, A. 3(2) is an infelicitous aberration, and ought at some future date to be reviewed with the intention of according the legal systems of non-Member States the consideration and respect which they are currently denied by this provision of the Convention in its present form.[48]

In view of the adverse comments which have just been made about the main thrust of the provision contained in A. 3(2), it is necessary to remark that the proviso to A. 3(2), whose function is to safeguard the position of third parties in the event of a variation of the proper law of the contract, is fully acceptable, and is indeed essential if the facility for changing the law which governs a contract is to be prevented from giving rise to injustice, whether unintended or otherwise. In addition to preserving the rights acquired by third parties previous to the alteration of the proper law, the proviso to A. 3(2) also insists that such alteration shall not prejudice the formal validity of the contract under A. 9.

6. Applicable Law in the Absence of Choice

A. 4 contains the crucial provision whereby the Convention endeavours to furnish an answer to the question posed whenever the parties to a contract have not availed themselves of the opportunity to choose the law by which their contract is to be governed. In the absence of an active choice made by the parties, the rules of private international law of the *forum* will generally contain some kind of formula whose application will produce a conclusion of some sort as to the law by which the contract is to be governed. Naturally, since the precise content of the formula will vary from one system of private international law to another, the actual conclusion in terms of the law selected as the proper law of any given contract is capable of varying according to the *forum* of litigation.[49] In an attempt to obviate all possibilities for such variations to occur before the Courts of the EEC, A. 4(1) introduces the uniform rule that, to the extent that the law applicable to the contract has not been chosen in accordance with A. 3, the contract shall be governed by the law of the country with which it is most closely connected. A rider is added, however, to the effect that a severable part of the contract which has a closer connection with another country may exceptionally be held to be governed by the law of that other country — a provision which effectively mirrors the toleration of *dépeçage* or scission expressed in the final sentence of A. 3(1).

The opening provision in A. 4(1) is in itself incapable of furnishing any uniform rules for the decision of actual cases, because it fails to indicate the criteria by which, or the analytical processes by which, the Court is to determine the country with which any particular contract is "most closely connected". The answers to these vital questions, or some of them, are to be found in the next three succeeding paragraphs of A. 4, which express a number of presumptions and rules whereby the search for the proper law may be narrowed down, if not decisively resolved. It is important to observe, however, that A. 4(5) concludes with the assertion that the presumptions contained in paragraphs (2), (3) and (4) "shall be disregarded if it appears from the circumstances as a whole that the contract is more closely connected with another country". This does appear to accord considerable freedom to each *forum* within the Community to reintroduce its individual predilections in this field of choice of law in situations where it is unhappy with the results which would flow from the application of the other provisions of A. 4. Effectively, the Court in question could return to the open-worded proposition in A. 4(1) and proceed to supply its own interpretation of what constitutes the country with which the particular contract before it is most closely connected.[50] It therefore remains to be seen whether A. 4 will succeed in giving rise to any kind of uniformity of approach by the Courts of the different Member States towards the task of supplying the proper law of a contract in the absence of any choice made by the parties.

Perhaps the least familiar, and hence most controversial, of the presumptions implanted in A. 4 is that contained within A. 4(2) which declares that, subject to the provisions of paragraph (5), "it shall be presumed that the contract is most closely connected with the country where the party who is to effect the performance which is characteristic of the contract has, at the time of conclusion of the contract, his habitual residence, or, in the case of a body corporate or unincorporate, its central administration". However, it is further provided that if the contract is entered into in the course of that party's trade or profession, the relevant country shall be the country in which the principal place of business is situated or, where under the terms of the contract the performance is to be effected through a place of business other than the principal place of business, the relevant country shall be the one in which that other place of business is situated. With these words, the Convention thus proclaims its adoption of the so-called "characteristic performance" doctrine as the preferred means of attributing the proper law of the contract. The doctrine, which is largely of Swiss origin,[51] has not hitherto become adopted as a choice of law rule by the legal systems of any of the Member States, but that fact of itself certainly furnishes no ground for resenting its incorporation into the present Convention. The unfamiliarity of the doctrine is however likely to prove a severe impediment to its easy operation by Courts within the EEC, at least during the early years of the Convention's life, and it seems highly probable that some unevenness of approach, as between different jurisdictions, will manifest itself over time. But the real source of objection to the doctrine of characteristic performance lies not in these difficulties — which are, after all, curable through time and experience — but with the inherent vagaries and imprecisions of the doctrine itself, and above all with its highly questionable, if not totally spurious, attempt to attribute a functional significance to the law of the country of habitual residence of one of the parties to the contract (or to the country where the centre of administration is situated, in the case of a legal person), without any regard whatsoever to the material content of the contract itself, much less to any other surrounding circumstances. Thus, it is highly mystifying, to say the least, to be informed that every contract "properly belongs" to the "social-economic environment", not of the country in which the characteristic performance is to take place, but of the country in which the characteristic *performer* has his habitual residence. Indeed, the doctrine appears to the present author to threaten to give rise to highly artificial, not to say arbitrary, results in practice, particularly where the grouping of significant contacts bearing upon a given contract and its performance can be seen to have nothing at all to do with the country of habitual residence of that party who happens to be identified — in accordance with the sibylline rubric which seems integral to the entire theory — as the "characteristic performer". Moreover, even the doctrine of characteristic performance itself — which Professor Jessurun D'Oliveira has damagingly stigmatised as a latter-day manifestation of that *Begriffsjurisprudenz* in which the scholars of former generations were accustomed to indulge themselves[52] — seems upon closer acquaintance to have such elastic and intangible properties as to render the task of identifying the party whose performance is to be regarded as characteristic in any given situation far less of an exact science than is surely desirable in such situations. At the very least, an agreed list of enumerated examples of the doctrine's application in concrete cases should have been included in, or attached to, the provisions of the Convention. Preferably, however, the Convention should have espoused the approach of the Second American Restatement of Conflict of Laws,[53] whose approach to the problem in hand is, it is submitted, a far more satisfactory one than that offered in A. 4(2), and is moreover one whose results are logically and intellectually defensible without the need to resort to the dubious and pretentious assertions which seem to commend themselves to advocates of the doctrine of characteristic performance.[54] Given, however, that the Convention as adopted does embody the doctrine, the best that can be said is that the more unsatisfactory consequences of its application in practice may perhaps be obviated through the judicious invocation of the provision in A. 4(5), whereby it is made permissible to disregard paragraph (2) altogether if the characteristic performance cannot be determined, or if it appears "from the circumstances as a whole" that the contract is more closely connected with another country. Furthermore, it should be remembered that, by its own admission, paragraph (2) merely establishes a *presumption*, and hence Courts should hold themselves in readiness to examine whether the presumption may be rebutted by reason of the presence of overwhelmingly strong connections with the law of some other country.

Far less controversial in substance and purport is the second presumption, contained in A. 4(3), to the effect that, notwithstanding the provisions of paragraph (2), "to the extent that the subject matter of the contract is a right in immovable property or a right to use immovable property it shall be presumed that the contract is most closely connected with the country where the immovable property is situated". This provision reflects, once again, the traditional deference to the claims of the *lex situs* of immovable property to play a pre-eminent role in all questions of legal relationships which are in any way connected with that property. Perhaps the key phrase in this provision is that containing the words "to the extent that", which seem to provide a basis for a further scission or *dépeçage* in the process of determination of the proper law, so that it would be open to a court to create a discrete sub-compartment of the contract, wherein the question of rights in immovable property or its use were held to be subject to the provisions of the *lex situs*, while at the same time other aspects of the same contract could be held to be properly regulated by some other system of law. Moreover, it is worth stressing once again that A. 4(3) merely establishes a *presumption*, and not a mandatory rule of choice of law, so that it would be equally open to a Court, in some circumstances, to conclude that the particular features of the contract in question were such as to overwhelm the claims of the *lex situs* to supply the proper law of the contract, even in relation to those parts of it which involve rights in immovable property.[55]

A. 4(4) creates a further exception to the initial presumption established by paragraph (2) in favour of the law of the habitual residence of the "characteristic performer". By A. 4(4), contracts for the carriage of goods are excluded altogether from the effects of paragraph (2), and it is instead provided that if the country in which, at the time the contract is concluded, the carrier has his principal place of business is also the country in which the place of loading or the place of discharge or the principal place of business of the consignor is situated, it shall be presumed that the contract is most closely connected with that country. It is further stated that single voyage charterparties and other contracts whose main purpose is the carriage of goods shall be treated as contracts for the carriage of goods for the purposes of applying A. 4(4). Therefore, where any such contract is visited by one of the concurrences of contacts enumerated in paragraph (4), the presumption in favour of the law of the country in which the carrier[56] has his principal place of business will operate. It will no doubt be tempting for Courts to argue by analogy that other instances of "paired" contacts — such as a coincidence between the place of loading and the country of residence of the consignee — might be persuasive pointers towards the country with which the contract of carriage is most closely connected, on the supposition that all other relevant contacts are distributed singly elsewhere. But it is more probable that the effects of A 4(4) will in practice be confined to the specific cases actually mentioned therein, so that Courts will tend to follow a homeward trend when dealing with other cases involving contracts of carriage, and employ more familiar and traditional methods for ascertaining the country with which the contract is most closely connected. Consequently, the existing, divergent practices in this matter of choice of law are likely to remain in a non-unified state, apart from those cases where there is a "pairing" of contacts corresponding to one of the types instanced in A. 4(4) itself. The same general conclusion may require to be drawn for A 4 taken as a whole: the open texture of its various provisions may leave such a degree of freedom to the Courts of the Member States that, in practice, the degree of uniformity which is attained may well prove to be very small indeed.[57] It must therefore be submitted that, although A. 4 may possess sufficiently flexible characteristics such that mechanical and unjust decisions may be averted through the exercise of a modicum of judicial *nous*, it is in other respects to be considered a failure, since it will give rise neither to fully uniform practices in this area of choice of law, nor even to precise and predictable consequences which parties can readily determine for themselves in order to decide how to order their affairs for the best.[58]

7. Special Cases

Arts. 5 and 6 have the function of supplying special rules for choice of law to be applied in two types of cases, namely certain consumer contracts and individual employment contracts. Both of these types of contract are nowadays considered to require special treatment by the law, for the purpose of redressing the imbalance between the relative strengths of the respective parties, whether envisaged in social or economic terms. A similar overall approach is adopted in both A. 5 and A. 6, namely that specific rules are established to select the proper law of the contract in the absence of choice, while additional provisions are included with a view to assuring a certain level of legal protection for the "weaker" party even where a choice of law is exercised by the provisions of the contract. However, in their substantive provisions the two Articles are considerably different from each other.

With regard to consumer contracts, A. 5 has the effect of ensuring that certain forms of protection secured to the consumer under the law of the state in which he has his habitual residence are not withheld from him by virtue of the fact that he enters into a contract containing cross-frontier elements. It is important at the outset to identify the type of consumer contract to which A. 5 relates. This is dependent upon the definition supplied by A. 5(1), which makes the Article applicable to a contract the object of which is the supply of goods or services to a person ("the consumer") for a purpose which can be regarded as being outside his trade or profession, or a contract for the provision of credit for that object. Although the absence of any reference to the status of the other party, or the capacity in which the latter contracts, may appear to give rise to an exceedingly wide notion of what constitutes a "consumer contract" for this purpose, the fact that, as will be seen, A. 5 serves merely as a "lead-in" to the national rules of law for the protection of consumers means that in practice any additional, restrictive definitions which are used for the purpose of identifying "consumer contracts" within any given national law,[59] will have a bearing upon the application of the provisions of that law pursuant to A. 5. Moreover, a further restriction upon the scope of A. 5 is introduced by A. 5(4), which altogether excludes its provisions from applying to a contract of carriage of any kind,[60] or to a contract for the supply of services where the services are to be supplied to the consumer exclusively in a country other than that in which he has his habitual residence.[61]

The main thrust of the protective provisions of A. 5 is contained in paragraphs (2) and (3). The first of these contemplates the possibility that a consumer contract may contain an express choice of law clause which would otherwise be accorded full efficacy by virtue of A. 3. A. 5(2) declares that such an express choice of law shall not have the result of depriving the consumer of the protection afforded to him by the mandatory rules[62] of the law of the country in which he has his habitual residence, provided that at least one of the following three conditions is satisfied: either (i) the conclusion of the contract must have been preceded by advertising or by a specific invitation addressed to the consumer in the country of his habitual residence, and he must have taken in that country all the steps necessary on his part[63] for the conclusion of the contract; or (ii) the other party or his agent must have received the consumer's order in the country of the latter's habitual residence; or (iii) if the contract is for the sale of goods and the consumer travelled from the country of his habitual residence and gave his order in some other country, the consumer's journey must have been arranged by the seller for the purpose of inducing the consumer to buy.

The preservation of the force of mandatory rules for the protection of the consumer under the law of the latter's habitual residence is thus made conditional upon the presence of a relatively substantial connection with the jurisdiction in question when the contract is in its formative stages. These same connecting elements are again incorporated by reference into the even more forceful provisions of A. 5(3) which is designed to be operative under the alternative circumstance that the consumer contract contains no express choice of law clause, but rather that it is concluded in such a manner that the application of the provisions of A. 4 would lead to the selection as proper law of the contract of the law of some country other than that where the consumer is habitually resident. This time, the scope of the protection conferred upon the consumer is in fact more extensive than that afforded by paragraph (2), because it is provided that, if any of the three alternative conditions described in paragraph (2) is satisfied in the case of a consumer contract, the law which shall apply in the absence of any choice shall be the law of the country in which the consumer has his habitual residence. Thus, A. 5(3) does not content itself with merely preserving the force of the mandatory rules of the consumer's "own" law, but indeed goes to the full limit of making that law in its entirety serve as the proper law of the contract. Moreover, the words employed by paragraph (3) are absolute ("shall ... be governed ..."), so that, unlike those cases in which, as we have seen above, A. 4 effectively gives the Court a fairly free hand in determining the law which is to apply in the absence of an express choice, in any case which falls to be governed by the provisions of A. 5(3) the proper law of the contract will invariably be that of the consumer's country of habitual residence.

It should finally be noted that A. 9(5) creates a specific exception in the case of consumer contracts with regard to the rules governing formal validity of the contract: it is expressly declared that any contract to which A. 5 applies, and which is concluded in the circumstances described in A. 5(2), shall have its formal validity determined by the law of the country in which the consumer has his habitual residence.

A. 6 introduces special rules for determining the law applicable to individual employment contracts. In the absence of any choice of law, and unless there are any special circumstances, such contracts are declared to be governed by either (a) the law of the country in which the employee carries out his work in performance of the contract, or (b) the law of the country in which the place of business through which he was engaged is situated. The factor which determines which of these alternative choice of law rules shall apply in

any given case is one which is perhaps amenable to some flexibility of interpretation: if the employee habitually carries out his work in one country,
the law of that country will be the proper law of the contract of employment even if he is temporarily employed in another country. On the other
hand, if the employee does not habitually carry out his work in any one
country, the contract will be governed by the law of the country in which is
situated the place of business through which he was engaged. Further flexibility is imparted by the proviso to A. 6(2), which is to the effect that neither
of the foregoing, alternative rules need be decisive where it appears from the
circumstances as a whole that the contract is more closely connected with
another country. By concluding with the words that, in such cases, "the contract shall be governed by the law of that country", A. 6(2) effectively leaves
it open to the Court to discover a sufficiently substantial connection between
the contract and another country, in which case the law of that country will
constitute the proper law of the contract.

In cases where a contract of employment contains an express choice of
law which would otherwise take effect in accordance with A. 3, the provisions of A. 6(1) ensure that any such choice of law shall not have the result
of depriving the employee of the protection afforded to him by the mandatory rules[64] of the law which would be applicable under A. 6(2) in the absence of choice. Thus, even where a choice of law has been made, the Court
must nevertheless undertake the task of determining that law which, in the
circumstances, would have constituted the proper law of the contract if there
had been no such express choice. Having done so, the Court must further
consider whether the law thus ascertained, assuming it to be different from
the one expressly selected under the contract, contains mandatory rules conferring a protection upon the employee which he would not enjoy under the
chosen proper law. If such rules are found to exist, the Court must proceed
to ensure that the employee continues to enjoy the benefit of whatever protection they confer. By this somewhat elaborate — even labyrinthine — procedure, A. 6 aspires to fulfil the objective of securing an enhanced level of
legal protection to the employee *vis-à-vis* his employer in view of the former's
relatively weaker position in their contractual relationship. In the majority
of cases this purpose will be achieved, but the mechanisms implanted in A. 6
are far from being fail-safe ones. Thus, a multinational corporation whose
places of business are scattered in many different countries both inside and
outside the Common Market would have little difficulty, should it so desire,
in arranging matters so that "inconvenient" mandatory rules are excluded
from applying to a given contract of employment on any basis whatever.
This could be accomplished, for example, by contriving to engage an em-

ployee through a place of business situated in a country where the law affords minimal protection to the employee, and by thereafter arranging that the employee's performance of his duties under the contract will result in the law of that country becoming the hypothetical proper law of the contract of employment by virtue of the operation of A. 6(2) (b), so that the "mandatory rules" alluded to in A. 6(1) would in reality confer no appreciable degree of protection upon the employee at all. It would surely have been far preferable if A. 6 had ensured that any mandatory rules under the law of the *actual* place of work would invariably apply to the contract of employment in relation to matters arising out of any duties performed there.[65]

8. Mandatory Rules

In addition to the protection conferred upon parties to certain specific types of contract by the provisions of Arts. 5 and 6, more generalised forms of protection are secured by the provisions in A. 3(3) and A. 7. Each of these provisions makes reference to what are termed "mandatory rules", an expression which also recurs in Arts. 5(2) and 6(1),[66] and in A. 9(6). From the terms of A. 3(3) — and also from those of A. 9(6) — it is possible to infer that the expression "mandatory rules", in relation to the law of any given country, is intended to denote such rules of law as, by the law of that country, cannot be derogated from by contract.[67] The notion of mandatory rules is thus closely associated with that of public policy, and it is by no means historically unusual for Courts to insist upon applying certain principles of public policy of the *lex fori* even when dealing with cases otherwise governed entirely by some foreign law. But the increasingly common judicial practice of according effect to such rules even in cases where they belong neither to the *lex fori* nor to the *lex contractus* is a remarkable example of the extent to which in recent times the previously sacrosanct principle of party autonomy in matters of contract has been eroded in response to a more activist view of the "appropriate" function of the Court, which may be summarised as being to ensure the prevalence of an idealised concept of "justice", if necessary by *dirigiste* means rather than by adhering to the traditional role of "neutral umpire".[68] Recently-elaborated theories regarding the necessity for accommodating provisions of mandatory rules of law which, if more traditional conflicts approaches were adhered to, would play no part in regulating the parties' relationship, may thus be seen as a logical counterpart of the increasing trend towards interventionism within the domestic legal sphere for the purpose of redressing social and economic imbalances by means of rules

inhibiting freedom of contract. The redactors of the Contracts Convention
have sought to enable such theories to be applied in practice within the EEC.

Of the two respective provisions dealing with mandatory rules, that contained in A. 7 is broader in scope but discretionary in character, while that
contained in A. 3(3), though narrower in scope, is of an obligatory character.
A. 7(1) states that, when the Court of the *forum* is applying the law of a
country in accordance with the provisions of the Convention, effect *may* be
given to the mandatory rules of another country with which the *situation*
has a *close connection*, if and in so far as, under the law of the latter country,
those rules must be applied whatever the law applicable to the contract.[69] It
is further stated that, in considering whether to give effect to these mandatory rules, regard shall be had to their nature and purpose and to the consequence of their application or non-application. This provision has been justly
criticised at all stages of its evolution,[70] on account of its vagueness and im-
precision, although some writers have been willing to defend it in principle,
and even in detail.[71] It remains to be seen whether any semblance of a uniform approach will emerge on the part of national Courts with regard to the
effect to be accorded to A. 7(1). It would seem highly probable that the vagueness and elasticity of such key terms as "close connection" and "situation",
and the extent to which it may prove to be a matter of uncertainty whether,
and if so, how far, the law from which they emanate requires the application
of any given rules "whatever the law applicable to the contract",[72] would
combine to give rise to a varied and uneven jurisprudence coloured by impression and circumstance. Further judicial subjectivity is encouraged by the
direction to have regard to the nature and purpose of the rules in question,
and to the consequences of their application or otherwise. What is beyond
question is that no party can henceforth be fully confident that he has properly calculated all the legal consequences of a particular contractual agreement, since it will be necessary to foresee not only the potential "close connections" which will arise under every conceivable "situation", but also the
way in which the Court before which any dispute may come to be litigated
would ultimately decide to exercise the discretion conferred upon it to give
effect to any mandatory rules which have thereby been brought into consideration. It may be added that there will also be considerable scope for inconsistency in the crucial task of identifying, and properly classifying, the alleged
"mandatory rules" themselves, and that the way would seem to have been
opened to allow Courts which are so minded to embark upon exercises in
"governmental interest" and "policy evaluation" analysis which are bound
to prove highly controversial, albeit they may, in skilled hands, be employed
for the purpose of promoting uniformity of decisions throughout the EEC.[73]

It may further be noted that A. 22(1) enables any Contracting State at the time of signature, ratification, acceptance or approval of the Convention, to reserve the right not to apply the provisions of A. 7(1).

Contrastingly, A. 7(2) contains a perfectly unexceptionable, and almost tautologous, provision to the effect that no restriction is intended to be imposed upon the power of the *forum* to apply the rules of the *lex fori* in a situation where they are mandatory irrespective of the law otherwise applicable to the contract. On the premiss that the *forum* is well able to interpret the force and character of provisions forming part of its own law, this paragraph should give rise to few problems in practice.

The provision contained in A. 3(3) is specifically addressed to the hypothetical situation where the parties have chosen a foreign law as the proper law of their contract (whether or not they have additionally incorporated a choice of *forum* clause therein), but where all the other elements relevant to the situation at the time of the choice are connected with one country only. In such a situation, it is declared that the parties' choice of some foreign law *shall not* prejudice the application of the mandatory rules of the law of the country with which the contract is in all other relevant respects exclusively connected. This further limitation upon the exercise of total freedom of choice by the parties to a contract has at least the virtue that, where its inbuilt conditions are properly met, the court is not accorded any discretion in the matter but must give effect to those rules of law of the country in question whose "mandatory" character can be established. A certain residue of flexibility remains however by virtue of the presence of the word "relevant", which leaves some scope for subjective evaluation on the part of the court acting as the *forum*. Moreover, since it is required that *all* the other elements relevant to the situation at the material time must be connected with a *single* country only, the requirement to give effect to the mandatory rules of the law of that country may seldom actually arise in practice.

A more restricted reference to mandatory rules is to be found in A. 9(6), amongst the provisions of the Convention concerned with the formal validity of contracts.[74] It is there provided that the preceding paragraphs of A. 9 shall not affect the principle that a contract whose subject matter is a right in immovable property or a right to use immovable property shall be subject to the mandatory requirements of form of the country in which the property is situated, provided that by the law in question those requirements are imposed irrespective of the country where the contract is concluded and irrespective of the law governing the contract. Assuming that the word "mandatory" here bears the same meaning as that ascribed to it in the other provisions of the Convention, the terms of the proviso to A. 9(6) appear somewhat tautologous. However, they do serve as a reminder that the *forum* must engage in the task of properly characterising the relevant rules of the *lex situs* in order to discover whether they are designed to have a bearing upon the circumstances of the instant case. In practice, such cases are probably destined to arise but seldom.

To complement the foregoing provisions, each of which is capable of giving rise to the application by the *forum* of foreign rules of law[75] whose character and force are derived from some principle of public policy pertaining to the foreign system in question, A. 16 contains a succinct provision whose purpose is to inhibit the capacity of the court at the *forum* to decline to apply any rule of foreign law on the grounds of its incompatibility with the public policy (*ordre public*) of the *forum*. Although A. 16 is expressed in general terms, so as to be applicable whenever any rule belonging to a foreign system of law is specified by the provisions of the Convention, it is perhaps of particular relevance in cases where the courts of one country are called upon to defer to the so-called "mandatory" rules belonging to the system of law of another. In the abstract, it may easily be envisaged that the court of the *forum* would inevitably be inclined to give priority of effect to its own domestic public policy in the event that any aspect of foreign public policy were found to be in irreconcilable conflict therewith. A. 16, while not seeking altogether to abrogate that ultimate reserve power of the *forum*, nevertheless establishes a degree of control over its utilisation by means of a requirement that, if the application of any rule of foreign law is to be refused on the ground of public policy, it must be the case that such application is *manifestly* incompatible with the *ordre public* of the *forum*. It is to be noted that it is the *application* of the foreign rule (and hence the results of such application) which are required to constitute an affront to the public policy of the *forum*, and not merely the foreign law itself *in abstracto*. It may also be affirmed that the notion of public policy within any Member State of the EEC must now be considered to include Community public policy (*ordre public Communautaire*), since this is now an integral part of the legal order of every Member State.[76] Having asserted this much, however, it must be conceded that the *forum* retains the final initiative in these matters, and therefore the term "manifestly" may be found to possess a certain convenient elasticity. It is to be hoped, nevertheless, that the courts of Member States will exercise a policy of restraint in the employment of arguments based upon the notion of public policy, and that they will remain mindful of the fact that they now form part of a wider legal order, namely that of the Community itself, whose overall standards and objectives it is their solemn duty to uphold and to further.

9. Scope of the Applicable Law

The remaining provisions of Title II include several which are of considerable importance, and which effectively complement and "round out" the provisions contained in the main Articles concerned with choice of law. Thus, A. 10, which bears the heading "scope of the applicable law", has the function of clarifying the actual extent to which the contract will be governed by the law whose application is required in accordance with Arts. 3-6 and 12 of the Convention. Although the list is non-exhaustive (as is indicated by the use of the prefatory words "in particular"), paragraphs (a)-(e) inclusive of A. 10(1) identify five particular matters which are to be unquestionably held to be regulated by the proper law of the contract, namely: (a) interpretation; (b) performance (including such questions as the degree of care or skill to be exercised, conditions concerning time and place of performance, and conditions relating to the discharge of the performing party);[77] (c) (within the limits of the powers conferred on the court by its procedural law) the consequences of breach, including the assessment of damages in so far as it is governed by rules of law;[78] (d) the various ways of extinguishing obligations, and prescription and limitation of actions:[79] and (e) the consequences of nullity of the contract. In relation to this last matter, A. 22(1) (b) affords to Contracting States the opportunity, by means of express reservation, not to apply the provision contained in A. 10(1) (e). It may further be observed that the provisions of A. 10(1) contain nothing to disturb the continued operation of the customary practice in private international law that all matters of a procedural character are controlled by the *lex fori*, and hence, in view of the non-exhaustive manner in which the scope of the proper law is delineated in A. 10(1), it is necessary to re-emphasise the extreme desirability of the development of uniform practices towards questions of characterisation in law as between (here) matters of substance and matters of procedure. In the absence of such uniformity of approach, opportunities will still remain for uneven and distorted applications of the Convention to occur as a consequence of the differences between the approaches to this key aspect of the conflicts process which are maintained within the legal traditions of the different Member States.[80]

A further attenuation of the scope to be accorded to the proper law of the contract arises by virtue of A. 10(2), which requires that in relation to the manner of performance and the steps to be taken in the event of defective performance, regard *shall be had* to the law of the country in which performance takes place. This provision appears to owe its vagueness and lack of precision to the almost wilful determination of the Working Group to avoid giving it any clear meaning.[81] Thus, the concept of "manner of performance" is intentionally left without any unifying definition, with the consequence that the current diversity of approaches among the various laws of the Member States is apparently to be allowed to continue. Accordingly, the precise meaning of the words "manner of performance" in each instant case will be supplied by the *lex fori*.[82] Moreover, since the court at the *forum* is merely required to "have regard" to the provisions of the *lex loci solutionis* in this particular matter (conceived, as we have seen, in terms of the approach adopted by the *lex fori*), the concrete results of the operation of this provision of the Convention are likely to be highly individualised and subjective. It would, however, appear to furnish the basis for an exercise by the forum in the melding or blending of the requirements of two different laws, namely the *lex contractus* and the *lex loci solutionis*, a process which may or may not yield just and satisfactory results, depending upon the degree of skill and sensitivity which the court can bring to bear upon the task.

10. Burden and Mode of Proof

The first paragraph of A. 14, which is concerned with the burden of proof in litigation arising from contracts governed by the Convention, establishes the basic proposition that the proper law of the contract shall apply to the extent that it contains, in the law of contract, rules which raise presumptions of law or determine the burden of proof.[83] This provision does threaten to encroach upon the principle that questions of evidence and procedure are subject to the *lex fori*, and hence its scope and effect must be strictly construed and applied. The reference in A. 14(1) is exclusively to those rules of the *lex contractus* which raise presumptions of law or determine the burden of proof. The decision to treat such rules as being essentially rules of substantive law is based upon the conclusion that these rules effectively help to define and clarify the obligations of the respective parties, and hence ought not to be severed from the corpus of rules with which they functionally belong.[84] However, to avoid the solecism of purporting to treat as rules of substantive law provisions which, within the system to which they actually belong, are properly considered to be of a procedural character only, A. 14(1) includes the requirement that the rules in question must be contained "in the law of contract" of the system in question, and hence any rules whose true function and character can be shown not to pertain to the substantive law of contract in the context in which they operate will fall outside the scope of A. 14(1).

A. 14(2) deals with the further question of the mode of proof by which a contract or an act intended to have legal effect may be proved. It is declared that such matters may be proved by any mode of proof recognised by the law of the forum or by any of the laws referred to in A. 9 under which the contract or act in question is formally valid,[85] provided that such mode of proof can be administered by the *forum*. This further incursion into the monopoly hitherto enjoyed by the *lex fori* in matters of evidence and proof is justified by the need to ensure the fullest respect for the legitimate expectations of the parties, which are at least as likely to have been derived from the provisions of the law (or laws) controlling the formation of their contract as from the provisions of the law of the country in which their contractual dispute eventually comes to be litigated. Thus, if the law controlling the formal validity of the contract were to allow an oral agreement to be enforceable without the need for written evidence, it would impose a considerable disadvantage upon any party whose actions had been framed in reliance upon this fact if the *forum* were to insist upon the application of more rigorous standards of proof required under the provisions of the *lex fori*. The cross reference to A. 9 contains the precondition that the law thus referred to must regard the contract as formally valid. If in fact the relevant provision of A. 9 invokes the application of two different laws,[86] by each of which the validity of the contract is upheld, the parties are effectively free to elect which of the two systems of law shall be referred to in order to establish the appropriate mode of proof (assuming that the two systems differ from each other in this particular). However, it would seem better to accord with principle if each party were to be required to establish that the system of law, whose provisions respecting mode of proof he seeks to invoke, can reasonably be regarded as having played some part in the formation of his original expectations.

11. Renvoi

It is commonly accepted amongst exponents of private international law that the doctrine of *renvoi*, where it operates at all, is not an appropriate doctrine to apply to questions of choice of law concerning contracts.[87] In practice, therefore, courts which, having applied the rules of private international law of the *forum*, arrive at a finding that the proper law of the contract with which they are concerned is the law of some other country, invariably take it for granted that this finding comtemplates the application of the internal (or municipal) law of the country in question.[88] Although such a practice would in all probability be adhered to by every court within the EEC before which there arose any question of the application of foreign law in accordance with the Convention, A. 15 seeks to make assurance doubly sure by expressly and unequivocally excluding *renvoi* from the Convention and its operation. Hence, all courts are to interpret any reference to the law of some other country than that in which they sit as being a reference to "the rules of law in force in that country *other than* its rules of private international law" (emphasis added).

12. Voluntary Assignments

The provisions of A. 12 are designed to resolve problems of conflicts of law with regard to the voluntary assignment of contractual rights. The assignment of choses in action is a particularly fraught and controversial area of private international law, and a variety of theories have been propounded for the purpose of identifying the proper law to govern the assignment itself, and the subsequent relations between assignor and assignee, and between both these parties and the original debtor.[89] The approach chosen in the Convention is to sever these problems into two functional parts, and to subject any questions concerning the mutual obligations of the assignor and assignee to the law which, according to the standard rules established by the Convention itself, constitutes the proper law of the contract between the assignor and the assignee.[90] On the other hand, the more general questions, such as the very assignability of the right in question, the relationship between the assignee and the debtor, the conditions under which the assignment can be invoked against the debtor, and any question whether the latter's obligations have been discharged, are all declared to be governed by the law governing the right to which the assignment relates.[91] This will usually connote a reference to the proper law of the contract between the debtor and the assignor, but the expression actually used in the Convention allows for the possibility that different parts of the contract may be governed by different laws, thus necessitating a more specific indication of the relevant law. It is submitted that both these provisions are sound, and that they should work well in practice. From the point of view of English private international law they will have the welcome effect of replacing a highly unsatisfactory and retrograde jurisprudence with rules which are at once both logically and practically defensible.

13. Subrogation

The concept of subrogation, or the substitution of one creditor for another, is made the subject of particular provisions in A. 13. Subrogation is encountered typically in cases where an insurer has fulfilled his duty to indemnify his insured under the terms of the contract of insurance, or where, under a contract of guarantee or surety, the guarantor has discharged the obligation owed by the primary obligor towards the creditor or obligee, or where one of a number of persons who are jointly and severally liable to the same creditor has satisfied the creditor. In such situations it is frequently the case that the party thus paying becomes invested with the rights of the creditor under the obligation in question, so that the insurer acquires such rights as his insured may have enjoyed against the party responsible for the loss incurred, while the guarantor acquires such rights as the creditor may have enjoyed against the debtor whose liability the guarantor has discharged. Subrogation is thus a species of assignment which takes place by operation of law, and one which moreover has a wide application within the law of obligations. A. 13(1) has been devised in such a way as to restrict its application to cases in which the right which undergoes assignment through subrogation is of a contractual nature only. This immediately excludes cases where an insurer has indemnified his insured against loss arising from tortious behaviour (although it would seem that this exclusion would not be operative in cases where the insured has been indemnified against loss sustained through some breach of contract). To fall within the ambit of A. 13(1), therefore, a situation must exist in which a contractual claim subsists between creditor and debtor, and a third person either has a duty to satisfy the creditor or has in fact satisfied the creditor in discharge of that duty. Under such circumstances, the choice of law rule supplied by the Convention is to the effect that the question whether, and if so to what extent, the third person is subrogated to the creditor's right against the debtor under the law governing their relationship shall be determined by the law which governs the third person's duty to satisfy the creditor. Effectively, therefore, questions of subrogation are made to be governed by the proper law of the contract of guarantee, rather than by the proper law of the contract guaranteed, or indeed any other law. Suffice it to add that, as with all other contracts to which the Convention applies, the proper law of the contract of guarantee is to be discovered by applying the relevant provisions of the Convention itself.

Where several persons are subject to the same contractual claim and one of them has satisfied the creditor, A. 13(2) merely provides that the same rule shall apply as is contained in A. 13(1).

14. Uniform Interpretation of the Convention

At the time of writing, the Contracts Convention differs from the other
Community Conventions which have so far reached the stage of undergoing
signature by the Member States,[92] in that no binding commitment has been
undertaken by the Contracting States to enable the European Court of Justice to exercise an interpretative jurisdiction over the Convention when it
enters into force.[93] As concluded and opened for signature, the Contracts
Convention contains two Joint Declarations, the first of which commemo-
rates the anxiety of the Contracting States to avoid the proliferation of diverse choice of law rules, and of diverse instruments containing choice of law
rules. To this end the wish is expressed that the Institutions of the Communities, acting under the Treaties, will, where the need arises, endeavour to
adopt choice of law rules which are as far as possible consistent with those
of the present Convention. The first Joint Declaration further expresses the
view that the Convention should be acceded to by any State which in future
becomes a Member of the European Communities. By the second Joint Declaration, the Contracting States, voicing the desire to ensure that the Convention is applied as effectively as possible, and that its unifying effect is not
impaired through differences of interpretation, declare themselves ready to
examine the *possibility* of conferring jurisdiction in *certain matters* on the
Court of Justice and, if necessary, to negotiate an agreement to this effect,
and also to arrange regular meetings between their representatives.[94] This latter Declaration closely resembles that which originally accompanied the Judgments Convention in the form in which it was first signed by the Six on 27
September 1968, and which in due course led to the conclusion of the Protocol on Interpretation by the Court of Justice, signed on 3 June 1971 and
now in effect in relation to that Convention.[95] It is submitted that it is most
important that the Contracts Convention be complemented by a similar Protocol containing provisions *at least* as extensive as those concluded in relation to the other private international law Conventions. Indeed, one would
go further and urge that the Member States should adopt a more liberal policy
towards conferring jurisdiction on the European Court of Justice by enabling
Courts of first instance to refer questions of interpretation of the Contracts
Convention, since otherwise the elucidation of its by no means exiguous
number of points of obscurity or ambiguity may become dependent upon
the appearance upon the litigious scene of parties wealthy enough — or per-
verse enough — to pursue points of interpretation on appeal.

Pending the negotiation of a Protocol to the Convention, and even thereafter, it is submitted that much emphasis should be placed upon the provision

concerning interpretation which is already contained in A. 18. This somewhat exhortatory provision simply declares that "in the interpretation and application of the preceding uniform rules [i.e. in Title II] *regard shall be had to their international character and to the desirability of achieving uniformity in their interpretation and application*" (emphasis added). Although the formal commitment imposed by this Article may not seem to possess the virtues of concreteness or exactness, it does at the same time provide a basis upon which a Court, if so minded, could adopt an enlightened and positive approach to the task of achieving legal integration within the Community, thereby contributing to the fulfilment of the overall purposes for which the Community exists.[96] Needless to say, such an approach would accord very fully with the views embraced by the present writer. At the very least, A. 18 could supply the basis for the development of a practice among the Courts of the Contracting States of freely accepting the citation of each other's decisions in which the Convention has undergone interpretation, and wherever possible treating such decisions as authoritative in the instant case.

NOTES

1. For the full text, see Appendix B, *post*. The text is published in the *Official Journal of the European Communities* for 9 October 1980: O.J. 1980 L. 266/1.
    1a. Denmark subsequently signed the Convention on 10 March 1981: O.J. 1980 C 80/1.
2. See Chapter 2 *ante*, especially at pp. 55—56.
3. *ibid*.
4. *cf.* Act of Accession, A. 3(2).
5. See the Convention of 15 June 1955 on the Law Applicable to International Sale of Goods (in force since 1 September 1964, currently ratified by eight States with one further adhesion, and signed by three others. Of the EEC Member States, Belgium, Denmark, France and Italy have ratified the Convention, and Luxembourg and the Netherlands have so far signed it). Conversely, neither the Hague Convention of 15 April 1958 on the Law Applicable to the Transfer of Title in International Sales of Goods, nor the Convention, of the same date, on Choice of Court in International Sales of Goods, have yet attracted sufficient signatures to enable them to enter into force (one ratification with one further signature, and four signatures, respectively).
6. See the two Conventions signed at the Hague on 1 July 1964, relating to a Uniform Law on International Sale of Goods and to a Uniform Law on Formation of Contracts for International Sale of Goods, published with commentary in R.H. Graveson, E.J. Cohn and D. Graveson, The Uniform Laws on International Sales Act 1967 (London, 1968). See *ibid*. at pp. 18—19 for observations on the interaction and potential conflicts between these conventions and those referred to in the previous note.
7. For elaboration of the arguments based on principle, see Bredin (1963) 90 Clunet 938—63; Zweigert in Probleme des europäischen Rechts (Festschrift Hallstein) (1965) 555, at p. 562 *et seq.*; Houin, in Etudes offertes a J. de la Morandière (1964) at p. 223; Nadel-

mann, in Conflict of Laws, International and Interstate (1972) at pp. 85—165; Savatier, in Proceedings of Colloquium, Lille 1960, at p. 55, and in (1959) 48 Rev. Crit. D.I.P. 237; Hallstein (1964) 28 Rabels Z. 211.

8. See for example, the assertions of Haak (1975) 22 NILR 183, at pp. 189—90; Lipstein, in Harmonisation of Private International Law by the EEC (1978) (hereinafter cited as "Harmonisation") at p. 4.

9. Docs. E. Com. XIV/398/72 (Text of Convention); and XIV/408/72 and XIV/579/72 (Explanatory Report by M. Giuliano et al.). The Text of the Convention may be found published in (1973) 21 AJCL, at pp. 587—93; (1972) 19 NILR, at pp. 220—27; (1973) 62 Rev. Crit. D.I.P. 209—16 (French); (1974) 38 Rabels Z. 211—19 (German); O. Lando (Ed.) European Private International Law of Obligations (1975) (hereinafter referred to as EPILO) at pp. 230—40 (English) and at pp. 220—29 (French); K. Lipstein (Ed.) Harmonisation, Appendix "A", at pp. 139—47; and in the Consultative Document (379-12-02, L61/ 258) circulated in August 1974 by the English and Scottish Law Commissions. The Report may be found published in (1973) 9 Riv.Int.Priv. & Process. 198—260 (French) and in EPILO 241—314 (French).

10. For comment upon the first Preliminary Draft, see Lando (Ed.) EPILO, *passim*; Lipstein (Ed.) Harmonisation, chs. 1—8 inclusive; Nadelmann (1976) 24 AJCL 1; Collins (1976) 25 ICLQ 35; Lando (1974) 38 Rabels Z. 6; Haak (1975) 22 NILR 183; Jessurun d'Oliveira (1975) 22 NILR 194; Batiffol (1975) RTDE 181; Vander Elst (1975) RTDE 187; Von Overbeck and Volken (1974) 38 Rabels Z. 56; Cavers (1975) South. Calif. L. Rev. 626.

11. Published as Doc. III/120/79E, and also published in English by the Lord Chancellor's Department under the title Private International Law: Text of a Draft EEC Convention on the Law Applicable to Contractual Obligations (London, HMSO, 1979), and also in [1979] 2 CMLR 776.

12. Published as E. Com. CTIII/862/79-E, Private International Law Doc. No. 173 (hereinafter referred to as "Giuliano Report"), also published in the Official Journal of the European Communities for 31 October 1980: O.J. 1980 C 282.

13. For the full text, see Appendix B *post*. This represents the definitive text of the Convention, and is the one referred to henceforth unless the contrary is stated. For comment upon this version of the text, see Diamond (1979) CLP 166; Bennett (1980) CML Rev. 269; Hartley (1979) ELR 236; North [1980] J.B.L. 382; Williams [1981] Ll. Mar. Q. 177.

14. See Judgments Convention (*ante*, Chapter 4), Arts. 7—15.

15. Arts. 1(1), 2. *cf.* Giuliano Report at pp. 12 and 25.

16. One incidental paradox which arises is that, while the Judgments Convention leaves the courts of Member States free to retain their rules of "exorbitant" jurisdiction for use against parties not "domiciled" anywhere within the EEC (see Arts. 3 and 4 of that Convention, *ante*, Chapter 4), the rules of private international law which must be applied to the case, assuming it to be one concerned with the law of contract, will be no different from those to be applied in cases between parties domiciled within the EEC.

17. See refs. *supra* notes 5 and 6.

18. See Giuliano Report at p. 97. This provision corresponds to A. 57(2) of the Judgments Convention.

19. For example, supposing that some other international Convention were to embody a provision identical to that contained in A. 21 of the Contracts Convention, the result would be a conceptual "hall of mirrors" which could not be resolved without recourse to some extrinsic — and possibly arbitrary and variable — factor or rule.

20. See the expression of intent to this general effect contained in the Joint Declaration to the Convention itself.

21. For background to these provisions, see Giuliano Report at pp. 100—103 (where the Articles are referred to under their pre-final numbering as Arts. 22 and 23). See also the warning uttered by Nadelmann in (1976) 24 AJCL 1, at p. 20.

22. This final formulation replaces the less felicitous, and arguably unworkable, expression "situations of an international character", which appeared in the original Preliminary Draft.

23. The Giuliano Report at p. 10 also contains the observation that it is implicit in the use of the term "contractual obligations" that the Convention does not apply to cases involving property rights or intellectual property *per se*. See the Report, further at pp. 17—18, for expression of the general intention to match the provisions of the Judgments Convention in the important provisions delineating the scope of the Contracts Convention.

24. Save for questions governed by A. 11, *q.v. infra.*

25. This elaborate formulation is intended to effect the exclusion of all matters of family law: Giuliano Report at pp. 16—17.

26. On agreements on choice of court, see Judgments Convention (Chapter 4 *ante*) A. 17. There is a possibility that arbitration agreements may eventually become the subject of a further Convention. See also Giuliano Report at pp. 18—20: "Where an arbitration clause forms an integral part of a contract, the exclusion relates only to the clause itself and not to the contract as a whole."

27. See Giuliano Report at pp. 20—22. Note that acts or preliminary contracts whose sole purpose is to create obligations between interested parties (promoters) with a view to forming a company or firm are *not* covered by this exclusion, which is intended to affect only those acts which are *necessary* to the creation of a company or firm and to the regulation of its internal organisation and winding-up.

28. Only this aspect of the law of agency is excluded from the Convention: e.g. the relationship between principal and agent, and that between agent and third party, are capable of being regulated by the Convention in so far as they raise questions of a contractual nature.

29. Only "trusts" as understood within the English "Common-law" tradition are covered by this exclusion: continental analogues to the trust, which tend to be essentially of a contractual nature, therefore fall within the scope of the Convention: Giuliano Report, p. 23.

30. This exclusion is expressed to be without prejudice to A. 14, *q.v. infra.*

31. For an excellent analysis and summary of the potential interaction between the proposed Directives relating to Insurance and the rules of the Contracts Convention, see the Report of the English and Scottish Law Commissions, 11 April 1979, on the Choice of Law Rules in the Draft Non-Life Insurance Services Directive (HMSO).

32. See the Law Commission's Report (previous note) esp. at paras. 35—39, 54, 59, and 61—80 for cogent criticisms.

33. A. 29(1).

34. A. 20(2). Instruments of ratification, acceptance or approval are to be deposited with the Secretary-General of the Council of the European Communities, and are to be notified by him to the other States Parties: Arts. 28(2) and 31.

35. As in the case of the Convention on Mutual Recognition of Companies (*post*, Chapter 7), which has still not entered into force for want of the necessary, sixth ratification on the part of the Netherlands. The Convention on Jurisdiction and Enforcement of Judgments (*ante*, Chapter 4), signed on 27 September 1968, did not enter in force until 1 February 1973, following completion of the ratification requirements of A. 62 of that Convention.

36. There is no counterpart to this provision in the Conventions concluded under A. 220 ECT proper, since none of them countenance the possibility that any State would

denounce a Convention entered into as part of its solemn commitments under the ECT.
37. A. 27(2). *cf.* comparable arrangements contained in the Judgments Convention
(Chapter 4 *ante*), A. 60; and in the Bankruptcy Convention (Chapter 6 *post*), A. 79.
38. *cf.* Giuliano Report at pp. 26—31.
39. See A. 3(1), and also Giuliano Report at pp. 31—32.
40. *cf.* Giuliano Report at p. 64.
41. A. 9(1): see Giuliano Report at pp. 65—73. A. 9(4) makes the same "alternative
reference" to the place of acting or the proper law in the case of acts intended to have
legal effect relating to an existing or contemplated contract — e.g. offers, acceptances,
notices of termination of contract, repudiation, etc.
42. A. 9(2).
43. *cf.* Giuliano Report at pp. 78—79, which explains that A. 11 has been deliberately
drafted in such a way as to leave open the question on whom the burden of proving good
or bad faith and the presence or absence of negligence is to be imposed. This remains a
matter for the national law applied by the *forum*.
44. English law on this point is certainly unclear, as suggested in the Giuliano Report
at p. 35. See Dicey and Morris, The Conflict of Laws (10th edn., 1980), rule 145 and
comments thereto; Kahn-Freund, General Problems of Private International Law (1974,
III) 143 Hague Rec. des Cours, at p. 402 (arguing in favour of reference to the *lex fori*).
cf. M. Wolff, Private International Law (2nd. edn., 1950), p. 426; F.A. Mann (1954) 31
B.Y.B.I.L. 217, 222 (arguing in favour of reference to the original proper law of the contract); Diamond, *loc. cit. supra* n. 13, at pp. 162—65 (also favouring reference to the original proper law).
45. See principally A. 4, *infra*, and also Arts. 5, 6 and 7.
46. See the views of Wolff, Mann, Diamond and Kahn-Freund, refs. *supra* n. 44.
46a. *cf. Armar Shipping Co. Ltd.* v. *Caisse Algérienne d'Assurance et de Réassurance
— The Armar* [1981] 1 All E.R. 498 at p. 504, *per* Megaw LJ.
47. *cf.* Diamond, *loc. cit. supra* n. 13, at p. 165, where it is suggested that the question should simply be referred to the (original) proper law.
48. A. 26 enables any Contracting State to request the revision of the Convention by
means of a special revision conference.
49. For a survey of the various approaches found among the laws of the Member
States, see Giuliano Report at pp. 38—42. These approaches vary from one of seeking to
identify the *probable* wish of the parties, or their presumed wish, to a more objective, or
activist, approach based upon a consideration of various significant factors, or "pointers",
which are regarded as indicative of the country with which the contract is most closely
connected. For a more detailed review of English Law, see Dicey and Morris, *op. cit.* (10th
edn. 1980), rule 145, sub-rules 2 and 3, with comments thereto; Cheshire and North,
Private International Law (10th edn. 1979), ch. 8, esp. at pp. 206—12; J.H.C. Morris, The
Conflict of Laws (2dn. edn. 1980), ch. 13, esp. at pp. 219—26; R.H. Graveson, Conflict
of Laws (7th edn. 1974), ch. 12 esp. at pp. 405—39.
50. *cf.* Diamond, *loc. cit. supra* n. 13, at pp. 165—67.
51. *cf.* Vischer, Internationales Vertragsrecht (Bern, 1962), and the same author's
contribution to Harmonisation (Ed. Lipstein) at pp. 25—30; Giuliano Report at pp. 42—45;
Diamond, *loc. cit. supra* n. 13, at pp. 168—70. See also Von Hoffman in EPILO (Ed. Lando) at pp. 7—11; Lando, *ibid.* at pp. 136—39; Jessurun d'Oliveira in Bulletin No. 71 (1975)
of the Netherlands International Law Association, ch. V, also published in revised form in
(1977) 25 AJCL 303; Batiffol (1975) RTDE 181; Nadelmann (1976) 24 AJCL 1, at pp.
9—12; Haak (1975) 22 NILR 183, at pp. 190—92; Jessurun d'Oliveira, *ibid.* at p. 196; Collins (1976) 25 ICLQ 35, at pp. 44—49; English and Scottish Law Commissions, Consultative Document, refs. *supra* n. 9, at paras, 4.1.1—4.2.9.

52. See (1975) 22 NILR at p. 196.
53. See American Law Institute, Restatement of the Law, Conflict of Laws (Second) (1969) §§186—188, together with §6.
54. See, for example, Vischer in Harmonisation (Ed. Lipstein) at p. 27: "The principle requires an examination of the function of a contract with special regard to its social purpose. The question: Which is the State in whose social-legal sphere the contract is embedded? Is sought to be answered by concentrating on those rights and duties in a contract which characterise its social function. This social function is normally characterised by the non-pecuniary performance." *cf.* also Giuliano Report at p. 43: "The concept of characteristic performance essentially links the contract to the social and economic environment of which it will form a part." It is respectfully submitted that neither of these contentions is tenable in relation to the doctrine of characteristic performance as it is actually formulated and applied.
55. *cf.* Giuliano Report at pp. 45—46.
56. See *ibid.* pp. 46—47 for the important information that "the carrier" here means "the party to the contract who undertakes to carry the goods, whether or not he performs the carriage himself". Thus, if A contracts to carry goods for B, but in fact A arranges for C actually to carry the goods, A is nevertheless "the carrier" for the purpose of the contract between A and B, albeit that in any subsidiary contract between A and C, the latter will be the carrier.
57. *cf.* Diamond, *loc. cit. supra* n. 13, at pp. 170—71.
58. See the three criteria for evaluation proposed *supra* at pp. 150—51.
59. *cf.* the definition of "dealing as a consumer" in s. 12 of the Unfair Contract Terms Act 1977. A. 5(1) concentrates exclusively upon the capacity in which the "consumer" contracts, and the purpose for which the goods or services are supplied to him, whereas s. 12 of the Act additionally has regard to the capacity in which the other party contracts. (The latter must "make the contract in the course of a business": s. 12(1) (b). Moreover, in the case of the sale or hire purchase of goods, the goods must be "of a type ordinarily supplied for private use or consumption": s. 12(1) (c).)
60. i.e. not merely to contracts for the carriage of goods, to which, for example, A. 4(4) is exclusively applicable.
61. A. 5(5) specifically provides, however, that A. 5 is not excluded by para. (4) from applying to a contract which, for an inclusive price, provides for a combination of travel and accommodation. The "package holiday" contract is therefore subject to the protective rules contained in A. 5, even in cases where the services contracted for by the holidaymaker are to be supplied to him or her entirely abroad.
62. The meaning of the expression "mandatory rules" is discussed *infra*.
63. The use of the words "all the steps necessary on his part" avoids the difficulties which would arise if the provisions were to refer to "the place where the contract was concluded", which may often prove to be in a different country from that in which the consumer's acts towards conclusion of his contract were performed.
64. The meaning of the expression "mandatory rules" is discussed *infra*.
65. See also Hepple in Harmonisation (Ed. Lipstein) at pp. 39—49. There would still remain the difficulty of ensuring adequate levels of protection in relation to such specialised situations as contracts for employment aboard ocean-going vessels, and aboard off-shore drilling installations. *cf. Sayers* v. *International Drilling Co. N.V.* [1971] 3 All E.R. 163, in which the English C.A., on varying grounds, upheld the application of Dutch law as the law regulating the relationship between the parties, and declined to treat the provisions of s. 1(3) of the Law Reform (Personal Injuries) Act 1948 as possessing the force and character of "mandatory rules": see Collins (1972) 21 ICLQ 320, esp. at pp. 329—32; North (1977) 26 ICLQ 914, esp. at pp. 923—27.

66. See previous section of this chapter *supra*.

67. According to the context, "mandatory rules" are also referred to as "*lois impératives*"; "*lois d'application immédiate*"; "*lois de police et de sûreté*"; "*leggi di applicazione necessaria*"; or "*Eingriffsnormen*".

68. cf. *The Alnati* (Netherlands Hoge Raad, 13 May 1966), (1967) 56 Rev. Crit. D.I.P. 522, (1967) Nederlandse Jurisprudentie No. 3, (1968) 15 NILR 82. See also *Ralli Bros.* v. *Compania Naviera Sota y Aznar* [1920] 2 K.B. 287; *Regazzoni* v. *K.C. Sethia (1944) Ltd.* [1956] 2 Q.B. 490. Contrast *Kleinwort, Sons & Co.* v. *Ungarische Baumwolle Industrie A.G.* [1939] 2 K.B. 678.

69. Emphasis added in all three instances.

70. See Drobnig, in EPILO (Ed. Lando) at pp. 82—86 (coolly favourable, though suggesting several improvements to the 1972 version of the Draft); Diamond (1979) CLP 155, at pp. 171—74 (expressing acceptance of the final version of the Draft, but with reservations regarding its lack of certainty); Collins (1976) 25 ICLQ 35, at pp. 49-51; Mann in Harmonisation (Ed. Lipstein) at pp. 31—37 (unreservedly critical). See also Hartley (1979) 4 ELR 236.

71. cf. the arguments advanced by Drobnig and by Diamond, *loc. cit.* n. 70, and see also Giuliano Report at pp. 58—62, which is however disappointing and unconvincing in its reasoning on this point.

72. cf. Unfair Contract Terms Act 1977, ss. 26 and 27, and see Mann (1978) 27 ICLQ 661.

73. So advocated by Drobnig, *loc. cit. supra* n. 70, at pp. 84—85.

74. The other provisions of A. 9 are discussed *supra* at p. 158.

75, With the obvious exception of A. 7(2), discussed *supra*.

76. See Chapter 2 *ante*, esp. at pp. 23—35.

77. See Giuliano Report at p. 75.

78. *ibid.* pp. 75—76, where it is admitted that this provision is the result of a compromise between the views of different delegations, some of which felt that quantification of damages should not be covered by the Convention at all. As worded, A. 10(1) (c) has the effect that questions of fact (such as proof of actual amounts of loss) will remain matters for the *lex fori*.

79. This necessitates a uniform classification of rules of limitation and prescription as belonging to substantive law, rather than as matters of procedure falling under the control of the *lex fori*. cf. Law Commission Working Paper No. 75 (1980), recommending that English private international law be changed in favour of the same approach as that adopted in A. 10(1) (d).

80. See references cited in n. 156 in Chapter 2 *ante* p. 85.

81. See Giuliano Report at pp. 76—77.

82. cf. A. 4 of the Hague Convention of 15 June 1955 on the Law Applicable to International Sales of Corporeal Moveables.

83. A. 14(1). See also A. 1(2) (h), discussed *supra* p. 154 which excludes evidence and procedure from the scope of the Convention, but with the exception of the provisions of A. 14 in relation to such matters.

84. cf. Giuliano Report at pp. 85—86, referring by way of example to Arts. 1147 and 1731 of the French *Code Civil*.

85. A. 9 is discussed *supra* p. 158.

86. For such possibilities, see A. 9(1) (2), discussed *supra*.

87. cf. Dicey and Morris, *op. cit.* (10th edn. 1980), rule 1 (commentary pp. 64—82) and rule 145 (commentary at p. 750); Cheshire and North *op. cit.* (10th edn. 1979) at pp. 60—76 and 198; Graveson, Conflict of Laws (7th edn. 1974) at pp. 64—77; Batiffol and Lagarde, Traité de droit international privé (6th edn. 1974), vol. 1, pp. 380—97. See also the

"modern generation" of Hague Conventions on private international law, including A. 2 of the Hague Convention of 15 June 1955 on the Law Applicable to International Sales of Corporeal Moveables, and A. 5 of the Convention of 14 March 1978 on the Law Applicable to Agency. See also A. 6 of the Draft Hague Convention on the Law Applicable to Certain Consumer Sales, incorporated among the Decisions in the Final Act of the 14th Session of the Hague Conference, 25 October 1980.

88.   *Re United Railways of Havana and Regla Warehouses Ltd.* |1960| Ch. 52, at pp. 96–97 and 115 (C.A.), affd. *sub. nom. Tomkinson* v. *First Pennsylvania Banking and Trust Co.* [1961] A.C. 1007.

89.   See Cheshire and North, *op. cit.* at pp. 536 and 549; Dicey and Morris, *op. cit.*, rules 81–83 inclusive (commentary at pp. 569–77); Graveson, *op. cit.* at pp. 469–81.

90.   A. 12(1). See the Giuliano Report at p. 80 for an explanation of the somewhat tortuous drafting employed in this provision.

91.   A. 12(2).

92.   Namely, the Judgments Convention and the Convention on Mutual Recognition of Companies, discussed in Chapter 4 *ante* and in Chapter 7 *post*, respectively.

93.   The Draft Bankruptcy Convention also makes provision for interpretation by the Court of Justice: see Chapter 6 *post*.

94.   Both emphases have been added.

95.   See Chapter 4 *ante*.

96.   See the arguments advanced in Part I of this book *ante*, Chapters 1–3.

The Draft Convention on Bankruptcy and Related Matters

1. Preliminary

The EEC Convention on Bankruptcy, Winding-up, Arrangements, Compositions and similar proceedings (hereafter referred to as "the Bankruptcy Convention") has undergone a protracted gestation, and at the time of writing still exists only in Draft form. However, in view of the probability that the current text is, for the most part, that which will eventually be adopted, if at all, by the Member States, it has been thought expedient to devote this chapter to a consideration of the Draft Convention and its implications. The version of the Draft which has been employed for present purposes is the latest to which the author has had access, and represents the state of the text as at April 1980.[1]

For ease of reference, the term "bankruptcy" will be employed generally in this chapter to indicate proceedings of the type falling within the scope of the Convention: it must be borne in mind that the full scope of the Convention includes all the types of proceeding mentioned at the outset of the preceding paragraph. At certain points in the discussion which follows, specific types of proceedings will be discussed by name wherever appropriate.

2. Justification for the Convention

The legal basis upon which the elaboration of this Convention has taken place is the express provision in A. 220 ECT, the fourth indent of which commits the Member States to securing, for the benefit of their nationals, "the simplification of formalities governing the reciprocal recognition and enforcement of judgments of courts or tribunals ...". This provision, which has already provided the basis for the Convention of 27 September 1968 on Jurisdiction and the Enforcement of Judgments in Civil and Commercial matters,[2] also naturally embraces the field of insolvency proceedings which, in view of their highly specialised and intricate character, were nevertheless felt to merit separate but parallel attention. Accordingly, at an early stage, the Committee of Experts which from July 1960 onwards[3] was at work in response to the challenge posed by A. 220 ECT, took an important decision whereby proceedings concerned with insolvency were deliberately separated from the subject-matter of the main project for the Judgments Convention. It was understood, however, that wherever possible common principles were to be employed in the two Conventions, and that their provisions should ultimately be so devised as to be mutually complementary.

It may be remarked at once that, as with the Judgments Convention, the Committee of Experts have clearly adopted a liberal interpretation of the remit contained in A. 220 itself, which actually mentions the issues of recognition and enforcement only, and says nothing about questions of jurisdiction or choice of law as such. Likewise, the opening words of A. 220 allude merely to the advantages to be afforded to *nationals* of the Member States. The degree to which the scope and effects of the concluded text actually transcend the somewhat modest requirements of A. 220 is not difficult to defend, however, and it will suffice here to recall the arguments on these same points advanced in Chapter 4 in relation to the Judgments Convention.[4]

The logical justification for the production of a convention to simplify, and also to harmonise, the formalities and procedures associated with international insolvency lies in the demonstrable benefits which would ensue for both creditors and debtors alike whenever they experience the onset of an insolvency in which the laws of more than one state are capable of becoming applicable. While this general proposition is true for any species of civil or commercial proceeding, the very character and comprehensiveness of insolvency proceedings give rise to complexities of a far greater intensity than that normally associated with cases of "single" actions which are litigated *inter partes* in relation to a single obligation or item of property. Insolvency proceedings invariably affect the legal relationships of a number of different parties, all of whom have had some sort of dealings with the debtor, while in the case of the latter any adjudication of bankruptcy (or winding-up order in the case of a legal person under United Kingdom or Irish law) will affect the total patrimony of the debtor and will moreover have a not inconsiderable effect upon his status until such time, if ever, as he obtains his discharge, and possibly even beyond that date.[5] Thus, it may at once be perceived that there exists a great potential for the discovery of conflicts of laws issues in relation to insolvency cases, whether by virtue of the relative whereabouts of personal legal connections of the debtor and some or all of the creditors or by virtue of the locations of the various assets involved, or by reason of the fact that certain aspects of the debtor's transactions and liabilities are found to be governed by "foreign" law. It so happens that in relation to virtually every significant issue associated with insolvency the laws of at least some of the Member States exhibit material differences from one another.[6] Typical areas of disharmony include the very requirements prescribed for the opening of insolvency proceedings;[7] the proprietary and personal effects of adjudication; the extent to which those effects may extend retrospectively to a point in time anterior to the moment of adjudication; the extent to which after-acquired property may also become available for distribution to creditors; the powers and duties of the trustee or liquidator; the question of priority of payments of different types of debts; the position of creditors who enjoy some species of security for their debts;[8] and the conditions attaching to discharge from bankruptcy, including the question of release of liabilities. Since so many vital matters are made the subject of variable provisions under the substantive laws of the Member States, the role of private international law in any case of international insolvency is a more-than-usually crucial one. Here again, however, the Member States' laws have attained to such a profusion of differing, and often irreconcilable, approaches that all semblance of fidelity to the ideal of a unified and distortion-free internal market is presently absent.[9] Diversity exists in relation to such key questions as the exercise of jurisdiction over non-residents;[10] the international effects which are claimed by the laws of each Member State in respect of the adjudications of its own courts, and conversely, the effects accorded by the same States to the adjudications pronounced by one another's courts; the relative legal positions accorded to domestic and foreign creditors,[11] and the international effects enjoyed by any order of discharge issued by the courts of any Member State.

Despite the present lack of statistical evidence to indicate the frequency of occurrence of international insolvencies within the Community, it is reasonable to suppose that their rate of incidence will progressively increase as the transformation of the EEC into a single internal market becomes fully realised, and is reflected in the manner in which individuals and enterprises manage their affairs with a diminishing regard for traditional legal "frontiers". Hence, in view of the manifold problems discernible within the tableau of disarray which emerges from any investigation into the substantive or conflicts laws of the Member States in matters of insolvency, the logical need for a collaborative approach to the solution of at least the most serious of the difficulties likely to be encountered in practice is surely obvious. Although any thoroughgoing programme of harmonisation of substantive insolvency law would necessarily be a slow-moving one, on account of the numerous, interconnected issues of legal and social policy raised by almost any question of insolvency law, it would not be unrealistic in the meanwhile to seek ways in which to minimise the adverse effects of the existing disparities between the Member States' domestic laws by means of an agreed rationalisation of the conflicts rules to be employed in those cases which possess international characteristics. It was to this task that the Committee of Experts addressed their labours over a period of almost twenty years.

3. The Evolution and Principal Outlines of the Convention

As compared with other species of Conventions regulating questions of private international law, examples of bankruptcy treaties have hitherto been relatively scarce.[12] Although the majority of such treaties as have hitherto incorporated provisions relating to insolvency have been bilateral in character, some encouragement to those seeking for a multilateral solution was offered by the success associated with certain developments in other regions of the world, such as the Scandinavian Bankruptcy Convention of 1933, the Montevideo Treaties of 1889–1939, and the Havana Treaty (Code Bustamante) of 1928.[13] By contrast, the most ambitious recent attempt amongst (at the time) a mainly European grouping of States, aimed at regulating insolvency matters, namely the Model Treaty on Bankruptcy adopted by the 5th Session of the Hague Conference on Private International Law in 1925,[14] was never ratified by any State, while the Benelux Convention on Private International Law, in which there are provisions relating to bankruptcy, has not yet come into effect. The extended labours of the Committee of Experts of the EEC may be divided into two broad stages, during the first of which the Committee's work was undertaken on behalf of the original six Member States in the presence of observers from the Hague Conference on Private International Law, the Benelux Commission for the unification of law, and the Commission of the European Communities. Since, technically, the Committee was composed of governmental delegates from the six countries destined to become parties to the Convention, the role and status of the Commission was, at least ostensibly, restricted to that of an observer, albeit one both able and willing to offer expert, informed assistance as and when required to do so. This first phase of work culminated in 1970 with the publication of a Preliminary Draft Convention,[15] together with a Report thereon written by two of the members of the Committee of Experts, M. Jean Noël (who had for much of the time served as Chairman of the Committee), and M. Jacques Lemontey.[16] This

Draft, consisting of 82 Articles, 2 Annexes and a Protocol of 15 Articles together with a Joint Declaration, was the subject of an increasingly wide circle of critical comment, much of it adverse, at least in relation to matters of detail.[17] At the date upon which the entry of Denmark, Ireland and the United Kingdom into the Community became effective on 1 January 1973, the pro ject for a Bankruptcy Convention remained still in a fluid and unconcluded state,[18] and in consequence the labours of the Committee of Experts, augmented now by representatives of the three new Member States, re-commenced in an atmosphere of some uncertainty as to the prospects for reaching any settled conclusion.[19] However, by the summer of 1980 the terms of a revised Draft, differing in many respects from the version of 1970, had assumed a comparatively settled form and were submitted to the Member States for study and eventual comment.[20] The Draft in its present version consists of 87 Articles, 2 Annexes and a Protocol of 14 Articles, together with a Joint Declaration. Although the final versions of some of the provisions have yet to be agreed, the way appears to be clear at last for formal negotiations to take place within the Council of Ministers during the early 1980s. A further interval of time will inevitably elapse following the signing of the Convention, while the Member States undertake the steps necessary to enable them to ratify it, but there is at least a reasonable prospect that this major landmark on the journey towards eventual harmonization of the law of insolvency within the EEC will be reached sometime in the mid 1980s.

In the most recent version of the text, the main outline and basic conception of the Draft Convention remains essentially that which was achieved at the end of the first phase of the preparatory process which has been described above. However, the rigorous revisions made during the second phase of the work have resulted in the incorporation of numerous modifications and refinements in detail, and some transformations on matters of principle, which render it appropriate to essay a new critical appraisal of what now appears to represent something close to the final version of the Convention. As a preliminary to any detailed commentary upon the contents of the Draft in its current version, it is as well to describe its structure in general terms.

The Committee of Experts appear to have formed the conclusion at an early stage of their deliberations, that the comprehensiveness and complexity of insolvency and also the intimacy of its relationship to matters belonging to the realm of public policy (*ordre public*) in each Member State, combined to render it unrealistic to aspire to the full harmonisation of the insolvency laws of the Member States, whereby a single "European" type of bankruptcy would be substituted for all the varieties presently known to the laws of the different Member States.[21] The Committee therefore set themselves the primary objective of ensuring that the Convention would secure the twin characteristics of unity and universality, which would mean that in every given case there should be but one "proper" forum for the opening of bankruptcy proceedings, and that proceedings commenced in that forum would enjoy Europewide effects. Arts. 2 and 34 of the Draft embody these two related principles, which are, regrettably but perhaps inevitably for the time being, subject to certain specific exceptions which mainly reflect continuing and fundamental differences between the bankruptcy laws of the Member States.[22] The extent to which these goals of unity and universality have however been realised is the direct result of what is, in reality, the most remarkable characteristic of the Draft Bankruptcy Convention, namely that, like the Judgments Convention with which it was jointly conceived,[23] it has been developed as a "double" or "direct" type of multilateral convention. That is to say, it does not merely establish criteria which, if satisfied, will render a Bankruptcy Judgment eligible to be recognised and enforced in every Member State, but instead introduces positive provisions affecting the jurisdictional competence of all courts with regard to cases falling within the provisions of the Convention. These mandatory rules of jurisdiction are contained in Title II (Arts. 3-16 inclusive) and have the purpose of greatly circumscribing the freedom of national courts to assume jurisdiction in any of the types of insolvency proceedings which are listed by name in A. 1 of the Protocol to the Convention. A. 1 of the Convention itself indicates that the exclusive criterion for fixing the scope of the Convention is to be the fact that the proceedings in question are among those listed in A. 1 of the Protocol: the nationality of the persons concerned is expressly declared to be irrelevant.[24] Title III (Arts. 17—19) contains provisions to determine the law to be applied by any court which assumes jurisdiction in accordance with the Convention, so far as concerns the requirements for the opening of a bankruptcy, the procedure to be followed thereafter, the legal effects of the bankruptcy (subject to exceptions contained in Title IV), and the characterisation of property. More detailed provisions to regulate the general effects of bankruptcy are contained in Title IV (Arts. 20—54 inclusive). The recognition and enforcement of Bankruptcy Judgments is thereafter governed by the provisions of Title V (Arts. 55—69 inclusive), which incorporates the features, typical of "double" conventions, of expeditiousness and near-total automaticity. This is possible because, on the assumption that any court within the EEC which issues a Bankruptcy Judgment will necessarily have complied meticulously with the regime imposed by the Convention in matters of jurisdiction and choice of law, it is considered to follow that the resultant judgment or order of the court must be accorded full faith and credit everywhere within the Community without any special procedure being required. The basic principles which are thus established are that both recognition and enforcement will occur as of right, with the possibility of challenge being strictly limited to only two, specified grounds,[25] and being moreover confined to a prescribed procedure for challenge which may be brought only in a specifically-designated court in each Member State.[26] The type of Convention which has been devised thus fulfils in the most complete way possible the rubric contained in A. 220 ECT, which requires the "simplification of formalities governing reciprocal recognition and enforcement",[27] since it has been rendered unnecessary for a Community Bankruptcy judgment to undergo any material scrutiny by courts or officials in any other Member State, unless some interested party takes positive steps to challenge the judgment. In this respect, the arrangements for recognition and enforcement of Bankruptcy Judgments have been designed to match as closely as possible those established under the Judgments Convention.[28] In particular A. 67 of the Bankruptcy Convention utilises the close interrelationship between the two Conventions by providing that many of the types of judgment issued in the course of bankruptcy proceedings shall actually be enforced under the Judgments Convention.

The interlocking assumptions upon which the proper working of a "double" Convention depends, make it essential that the Convention be everywhere interpreted and applied in a uniform manner, and in full accordance with its underlying spirit and purpose. Therefore, quite properly, provision has been incorporated in Title VI (Arts. 70—74) for the Court of Justice to play its now familiar role in supervising and co-ordinating the interpretation of the Conventions. The subsequent titles of the Convention (Titles VII—XI, Arts. 75—87) are designed to regulate the Convention's territorial scope and time for commencement, its relationship to other Conventions, and such matters as the necessity for any state which becomes a Member of the Community at some future date to undertake to negotiate on the basis of the Convention with a view to becoming a party thereto (A. 82). It is also made incumbent upon States which become Contracting Parties to the Convention to incorporate into their own bankruptcy legislation provisions in conformity with the "Uniform Law" contained in Annexe I to the Convention. This latter adjunct to the Convention, containing but three Articles, has now become a pale shadow of what was, already in the 1970 version of the Draft Convention,[29] only a modest schedule of six provisions designed to harmonise the laws of the Member States on certain aspects of internal law which have a significant bearing upon cases of insolvency. This further retreat from the challenge of a more thorough and immediate harmonisation is to be regretted, but may be regarded as a politic and tactical expedient forced upon the Committee by the realisation that to attempt too much may be to achieve nothing.

Having thus summarised the provisions of the Draft Bankruptcy Convention in a very general way, we shall now proceed to a closer examination and critical appraisal of this project in its present form.

4. Commentary

(a) Criteria for Evaluation

It seems appropriate to begin by setting down the evaluative criteria which are to be applied in the following, critical examination of the Draft Convention. Broadly speaking, these are: (i) internal and external consistency; (ii) overall compatibility with accepted standards of fairness, stability and predictability in the administration of justice; and (iii) practical suitability with respect to the maintenance of the legitimate interests of both creditors and debtors. There is a considerable interplay between these three broad categories of criteria.

(i) Internal and External Consistency

It must be capable of demonstration that the Convention achieves internal consistency in the application of the main principles, namely those of unity and universality of bankruptcy, on which it is claimed to be based. In themselves, these basic principles are certainly those to which the majority of modern doctrinal scholarship subscribes as constituting the ideal foundation for international bankruptcy law,[30] but in the absence of a complete harmonisation of the insolvency laws of the Member States (especially in relation to their field of application *ratione personae*), difficulties have inevitably confronted the Committee of Experts in their attempts to maintain fidelity to these principles at every stage of the Convention. The result, as will become apparent, has been a retreat from principle in some exceptional cases where, in deference to the special requirements of some of the Member States, bankruptcies opened in certain jurisdictions against certain types of debtor will not enjoy universal full faith and credit throughout the Community, nor do so exclusively.[31]

It is equally important that the Convention achieve external consistency, in the sense of ensuring not only that it fulfils the requirements of A. 220 ECT from which it derives its level motivation, but also that it does so in a way which harmonises with, and is complementary to, other developments in Community law including the other Conventions which have been or are being developed. Strenuous efforts have clearly been devoted to the attainment of this objective, but it remains to be seen whether the courts which will be required to apply the Convention will find its provisions easy to understand and apply in practice. It is therefore necessary to consider whether the Convention contains its own inbuilt mechanisms for ensuring that any such doubts, and possible inconsistencies, which are experienced or discovered in practice can be properly resolved by means of an efficient and authoritative interpretative procedure. Here, the limitations upon the facility of seeking a ruling from the Court of Justice[32] may give rise to difficulties which will, in turn, involve a transgression of the next main criterion to be considered.

(ii) *Overall Compatibility with Accepted Standards of Fairness, Stability and Predictability*

It is most undesirable that an international Convention should give rise to any possibility that persons may become the victims of miscarriages of elementary principles of justice and fairness which there is no readily accessible way of putting right. A certain degree of peril is therefore inherent in any system of international recognition and enforcement of judgments which incorporates a high degree of automaticity, coupled with a greatly restricted scope for challenge on the part of any individual who may be concerned.[33] It has been well said that, while certainty is one of the key ingredients in a system of justice, certainty of injustice is an infinitely worse thing than uncertainty of a just outcome, in any given case.[34] Thus, it is vital that the Convention should be free from obscurities in expression which will inevitably give rise in due course to inconsistent interpretations, and hence to irremediable injustices which are likely to be repeated on account of the inability of those who are adversely affected to afford the cost of obtaining a corrective ruling on the point. For these reasons, it is necessary to indicate that some apprehension is engendered by the realisation that the rules for allocation of jurisdiction may not work with faultless precision,[35] that the Convention specifically prohibits at the stage of recognition and enforcement any challenge to the jurisdictional competence of the court which opened the bankruptcy,[36] and that the possibility of making a reference to the Court of Justice for interpretation of such questions as the jurisdictional provisions of the Convention is denied to courts of first instance,[37] before which the vast majority of insolvency proceedings are perforce heard and disposed of on account of the natural reluctance of the majority of interested parties to undertake the additional financial risks inherent in the pursuit of any appeal. Insolvency is, after all, a situation where, *ex hypothesi*, the financial position of the debtor is such that there must be a real danger that any protracted litigation with one or perhaps several appellate stages will severely reduce the amount of money available to be distributed to creditors. Hence, ominous possibilities are presented for miscarriages of justice to be left unredressed for want of any party able or willing to afford the expense of putting matters right while, even in those instances where this is achieved, the expense inevitably entailed may have the effect of rendering the victory a Pyrrhic one for the parties concerned.

The related characteristics of stability and predictability assume a special importance in the context of a "double" Convention utilising the concepts of unity and universality, since the act of assuming jurisdiction on the part of a court in any contracting state can have such profound and far-reaching consequences for the debtor and creditors alike. Hence, it becomes absolutely imperative that the provisions of the Convention which regulate the key issue of the exercise of exclusive or co-ordinate jurisdiction[38] should be clear and unambiguous, and should utilise connecting factors which are properly defined and commonly understood, so that it is possible to anticipate with precision the jurisdiction which will constitute the *forum concursus* of any given debtor. This is not merely for the sake of enabling creditors, dealing with a debtor during the period of his (or its) manifest solvency and creditworthiness, to calculate precisely the legal incidents of any transaction, including the potential impact of the law which would be applied in the event of any subsequent insolvency of the debtor, but it is also for the sake of ensuring that legal uncertainty does not operate as an exacerbating factor during the critical period when a debtor has, to the creditor's knowledge, become financially embarrassed. In this latter phase, creditors are frequently confronted by the necessity of making difficult decisions regarding the granting of further credit to the debtor, or at least of extending the period of time in which the debtor must honour existing liabilities. These decisions invariably involve the making of nice calculations by creditors who may appreciate that the rate of return on their debts is likely to be meagre in the event of the debtor's undergoing bankruptcy, and may be correspondingly greater if the debtor is given a reasonable opportunity to retrieve his position. If, however, they are simultaneously aware of the possibility that a bankruptcy may meanwhile be opened in some other jurisdiction, and moreover that such a bankruptcy would thereafter preclude any possibility of an insolvent administration of the debtor taking place within, and under the law of, their "local" jurisdiction, creditors who must perforce consult their own interest first and foremost, will be disinclined to risk injecting further credit when this might, in the event, merely pass almost at once into the hands of some foreign trustee in bankruptcy. If anything, the natural course of action of creditors under such circumstances will be to yield to the promptings of their more nervous instincts and act pre-emptively by opening bankruptcy proceedings under local law sooner per-haps than they otherwise might have done. Thus, the consequence of any state of uncertainty regarding the "proper" whereabouts of the *forum con-* *cursus, or any state of nervousness engendered by the realisation that this un-* certainty will be resolved by the simple expedient of ensuring that one is the first to act, will be that bankruptcies will tend to be provoked into taking place when they might have been averted or avoided. As a rule, this is un-likely to be an advantageous situation, either for debtors or for the majority of creditors. It is generally true of bankruptcy, as of so many other of life's more unpleasant vicissitudes, that prevention is better than cure, but one thing which is certain above all else is that creditors cannot be induced to par-ticipate in a "rescue" operation designed to prevent a bankruptcy from taking place unless they can be thoroughly assured in advance that their overall legal position will continue unimpaired, should the worst come to the worst.

(iii) *Practical Suitability with Respect to the Maintenance of the Legitimate Interests both of Creditors and Debtors, and of other Interested Parties*
Modern notions of the proper purpose of insolvency law lay stress upon the need to balance the plurality of interests which are seen to be at stake. The law exists to protect and, if possible, to facilitate the rehabilitation of the debtor, and achieves this by imposing a controlled regime under which credi-tors' powers of individual resort to private acts of diligence are suspended and, in the majority of cases, superseded. The law also exists to protect the interests of creditors, treated collectively, by securing the equalisation of the position of all creditors of comparable degree, irrespective of the time at which they originally became creditors. Thus, in application of the maxim that "equality is Equity", a rateable distribution of dividends serves as the means of ensuring equitable treatment for all creditors when there exists no possibility of their all receiving payment in full. The law further secures pro-tection of the general interest of those who from time to time extend credit to others, by means of a variety of investigative procedures and sanctions cal-culated to discover and to punish, and hence generally to deter, irresponsible or fraudulent conduct on the part of debtors who so conduct themselves as to expose their creditors to an enhanced risk of failing to be repaid in full. Finally, the striking of an apposite balance between the legitimate interests of debtors and creditors is seen as being conducive to a general public in-terest through the maintenance of high standards of probity and responsibility in association with the giving and receiving of credit.

It is necessary to consider to what extent the above triadic arrangement of interacting interests will be well served by the working system for which the Convention provides. In those cases in which unity and universality are achieved, it will obviously be beneficial from every point of view to have the assured prospect that a single insolvent administration will enjoy universal effects throughout the EEC, if not in the world beyond. In such cases, the confidence of creditors is likely to be enhanced, since they can accurately appraise the merits of any proposed course of action, taking account of the legal principles which are destined to have a bearing upon their interests. The savings in costs and administrative expense which will accrue from the facility of resorting to a single set of proceedings are also a considerable advantage from the creditors' point of view. Correspondingly, the debtor's legitimate interest is likely to be well served by arrangements which effectively restrict the possibilities of his (or its) being subjected to the drastic remedy of bankruptcy within a jurisdiction with which relatively little substantial "contact" has been established: as a natural counterpart to the attainment of predictability concerning the *forum concursus*, it should be possible for any negotiations with creditors aimed at averting the need for the opening of bankruptcy proceedings to be conducted in a more stable and calculated atmosphere. By the same token, the general public interest that there should be a controlled and stable regime affecting the law of credit and security should become realised on a Community-wide basis.

Conversely, however, any demonstrable defects in the arrangements for which the Convention makes provision will be capable of operating to the detriment of all three of the interests referred to above. If circumstances exist in which the *forum concursus* cannot be accurately predicted, creditor confindence will be diminished, and the interests of the debtor will be correspondingly affected in an adverse way. If it transpires that — by reason either of the openness or of the ambiguousness of the relevant provisions of the Convention — victory in a race to open proceedings will hold forth the promise (whether genuine or not) of significant material advantages, bankruptcies will actually be precipitated, sometimes needlessly, and will moreover be accompanied by a wastage of legal costs for those creditors who fail to win the race, coupled perhaps with a less specific array of consequences from the aspect of their anticipated legal position, by virtue of the fact that the bankruptcy will be administered largely in accordance with the law of the *forum concursus*. Still worse would be a situation where loopholes were left available for exploitation by the unscrupulous, whether debtors or creditors. It should therefore be a major test of the quality of the Convention to ascertain whether, under certain conditions, it is capable of bringing about the defeat of legitimate interests of creditors or debtors, by confounding the expectations of parties who have themselves acted in a reasonable way. To the extent that such adverse effects are capable of being experienced, there is correspondingly a deficiency in the level of legal protection which is being afforded within the Community to the parties concerned.[39]

Finally, it must be affirmed that the interests of all parties are in principle best served by rules which, especially in relation to the exercise of jurisdiction from which, in a Convention of this type, so much else flows automatically, are above all devised with a view to producing results which accord with the natural promptings of common sense. It cannot but be a source of mischief, not to say of outright injustice on occasions, if an international Convention is seen to be capable of subjecting parties to a regime of insolvent administration which, on any objective view, is clearly the *least* appropriate one in the circumstances.[40]

(b) Scope of the Convention

The formal title of the Convention, which has the function of simultaneously indicating in general terms the intended scope which the Convention shall enjoy, has been deliberately formulated so as to correspond to the group of proceedings specifically excluded from the scope of the Judgments Convention.[41] With regard to the detailed delineation of the scope of the Bankruptcy Convention, however, A. 1 contains several, key propositions. In the first place, it is made clear that the scope of the Convention, *ratione materiae*, is to be determined in a restrictive manner by reference to the schedule of proceedings contained in A. I of the Protocol. In this latter provision, proceedings are listed according to the name under which they are known to the legal systems of the respective Member States, so that a court in any given Member State may be aware at once whether the Convention is, at least theoretically, applicable to the proceedings in front of it by simply having regard to the question whether the type of proceeding which is pending, or in progress, is one of those listed in A. I of the Protocol. Consequently, if the proceeding in question is not among those specifically mentioned by name in A. I, the Bankruptcy Convention does not apply and the procedure will fall to be regulated, if at all, by the provisions of the Judgments Convention. Thus, in the case of the United Kingdom, the following proceedings *only* will fall within the scope of the Bankruptcy Convention:[42] compulsory winding-up, winding-up under the supervision of the court, and bankruptcy (England, Wales and Northern Ireland); sequestration (Scotland); administration in bankruptcy of the estate of persons dying insolvent (England, Wales and Northern Ireland). Also, the following arrangements, compositions and other proceedings will come within the scope of the Convention and be regulated by its provisions unless it is otherwise specifically provided:[43] creditors' voluntary winding-up, compositions and schemes of arrangement (England and Wales); compositions (Northern Ireland); arrangements under the control of the court (Northern Ireland); deeds of arrangement approved by the court (Northern Ireland); and judicial compositions (Scotland). Conversely, non-judicial procedures such as deeds of arrangement in England and Wales, and also the judicial procedure for the making of administration orders by the County Court, are alike excluded from the scope of the Convention by virtue of the fact that neither of them is mentioned in the relevant sections of A. I (a) or (b) of the Protocol.

In view of the special features of English company law, an exception has been made to the original conception of the Convention, which was intended to apply to judicial procedures only. In the case of creditors' voluntary winding-up, of which frequent use is made in practice, logic and common sense required that the procedure be included. As the Convention is founded on the basic concept of insolvency proceedings, it was equally logical to exclude from its scope the voluntary winding-up of a company by its members, since in such proceedings the company is by definition in a state of solvency at the time of winding-up. However, it is to be noted that no additional refinement has been incorporated in relation to the inclusion of the compulsory winding-up of companies,[44] which can take place in cases where the company is either solvent or insolvent. Hence, all cases of compulsory winding-up in the United Kingdom will henceforth be regulated by the provisions of the Convention, irrespective of the grounds on which the petition is presented.

After the Convention is brought into effect, if it is sought to initiate any of the types of proceeding which are listed in A. I of the Protocol before any court sitting within any part of the United Kingdom, the court in question will be obliged to have regard to, and comply with, the requirements of the Convention, first in relation to whether it may properly assume jurisdiction to open the proceedings, and thereafter with regard to the approach to be adopted at each successive stage in the administration of the bankruptcy, winding-up or composition, as the case may be.

One further, and most important, group of provisions bearing upon the scope of the Convention are those contained in A. 15, concerning "Actions arising from the bankruptcy". This Article effectively provides that, once a bankruptcy has been opened in one Member State, the courts of that State shall enjoy exclusive jurisdiction to entertain proceedings concerning any of a series of specified matters which are regarded as arising from the bankruptcy in the context in which they are brought. By virtue of this connection, the proceedings in question are made to fall within the scope of the Bankruptcy Convention, when otherwise it might have been expected that they would be regulated by the Judgments Convention.[45]

It is expressly provided in A. I (1) that the Convention is to apply *irrespective of the nationality of the persons concerned.* Thereby one important, potential limitation upon the scope of operation of the Convention *ratione personae* is altogether renounced. It is not even required that it be demonstrable, or even reasonably foreseeable, at the inception of proceedings that the insolvency will have repercussions in other countries besides the one in which proceedings are to open. In view of the uniquely comprehensive quality of insolvency, it will in any case seldom be practicable to calculate the territorial localisation of every relevant interest or issue, and it is moreover apparent that the Committee of Experts was averse to the creation of two sets of material rules for insolvency within the EEC.[46] One apparent obstacle to be surmounted in formulating this provision was the express reference in A. 220 ECT to the creation of arrangements by the Member States "for the benefit of their nationals". The Committee was clearly able to respond to the same persuasive arguments as had previously induced the redactors of the Judgments Convention to eschew any limitation of the effects of that Convention to persons who happen to be nationals of the Member States.[47] Indeed, it is clear that the considerations which commended themselves in relation to cases of proceedings to enforce singular obligations are applicable *a fortiori* to bankruptcy matters which are concerned with functional activities and transactions between debtors and creditors in which considerations of nationality are of negligible account.[48] Consequently, A. I (1) is so worded as to make it apparent that the Convention is to be applied by the courts of all Member States without making any discrimination between those who are nationals of *some* Member State and those who are nationals of none. Thus, an American citizen who has his centre of administration in London should be regarded as being subject to the bankruptcy law of England exclusively, in accordance with the provisions of the Convention,[49] while, conversely, a British citizen who has neither his centre of administration nor any establishment within any Member State of the Community should be regarded as, in principle, liable to undergo a local bankruptcy within any Member State whose law of bankruptcy permits the courts there to open proceedings against him.[50]

Although the primary definition of the scope of the Convention is expressed *ratione materiae*, a major exception to its scope is created *ratione personae* by A. I (3), which limits the application of the Convention in the case of direct insurance undertakings. These undertakings will become subject to the scope of the Convention only when the Directive dealing with co-ordination of national laws in this respect has been brought into force, and only in so far as the Directive itself does not otherwise provide.[51] A further exception is created under certain conditions in the case of undertakings which are engaged only in re-insurance: while these are, as a general rule, to be immediately subject to the Convention as it stands, a special exception is created for mutual re-insurance companies which have entered into agreements with mutual insurance companies involving the complete re-insurance of the insurance contracts of these latter companies, or the complete assignment of their obligations arising under such contracts.[52]

The Convention applies, *ratione personae*, to both natural and legal persons, but in view of the fact that A. I (1) alludes to the quality of legal personality ("irrespective of the nationality of the persons concerned"), it is logical to infer that the provisions of the Convention are inapplicable in cases where the entity in question has no recognised legal personality. Thus, in the case of partnerships under the law of England and Wales (and Northern Ireland), it would appear that the provisions of the Convention do not apply in relation to any proceedings against them, because the law at present denies that such partnerships enjoy a legal identity distinct from that of the members, and moreover it is impossible for a partnership *per se* to be made bankrupt.[53]

The scope of application of the Convention *ratione loci* is regulated by A. 79, which has the effect of rendering the Convention applicable in the European territories of the contracting states, plus Greenland, the French overseas departments, and Mayotte. Special optional arrangements are incorporated to allow the Netherlands and Denmark to retain a degree of flexibility in relation to the Netherlands Antilles and the Faroe Islands, respectively, while in the case of the United Kingdom a similar flexibility is accorded by A. 79 (3) so that at the time of ratification or subsequently the Convention may be made applicable to any of its dependent territories by means of a declaration lodged with the Council of the Communities. In the absence of any such declaration, proceedings brought in the United Kingdom from courts in those dependent territories will be deemed to be proceedings taking place in those courts, and hence outside the sphere of application of the Convention. To make assurance doubly sure, it is further provided by A. 79 (4) that any European territory situated outside the United Kingdom, for the international relations of which the United Kingdom is responsible, shall not be regarded as falling within the ambit of the Convention unless the United Kingdom makes a declaration to the contrary in respect of the territory in question.[54]

(c) Universality and Unity of Bankruptcy

The twin pillars around which the scheme of the Convention is built are expressed in A. 2, which proclaims that proceedings regulated by the provisions of the Convention shall, when opened[55] in any of the Contracting States, take effect as of right in the other Contracting States and, so long as they have not been closed, shall preclude the opening of any other proceedings in those other States. The aspect of universality of bankruptcy is further emphasised by the provisions of A. 34(1) which declares that such bankruptcies shall take effect in relation to the whole of the debtor's assets situated within the Contracting States. In fact, as will be seen, in certain special instances the possibility remains for a plurality of bankruptcies to take place upon a territorial basis,[56] but it is generally true that the Convention succeeds in establishing the two, much-acclaimed characteristics of universality and unity of bankruptcy as the basis upon which, henceforth, the insolvency law of the Common Market shall operate.

No overt attempt is made to assert that a bankruptcy opened within the Community shall enjoy the attributes of unity and universality upon a global basis,[57] although indirectly the Convention seems to hint at such an attitude by means of provisions, at times verging upon the chauvinistic, which appear effectively to accord less respect to the legal systems of non-Member States than is accorded to those of Member States.[58] While it would be unrealistic for the Convention to pretend that the Community enjoys a capacity to create legislative provisions which enjoy world-wide validity *proprio vigore*,[59] it would perhaps have been a more accommodating position from which to encourage an enhanced level of respect both by the Common Market and by the outer world for the judicial determinations emanating from each side, if the Convention had expressly incorporated a mechanism for the development of mutual recognition of each other's bankruptcy adjudications between the Common Market collectively and such individual members of the world community as may be desirous of bringing about a more rational and convenient regime of international bankruptcy. To render such a *rapprochement* genuinely likely, however, it would have been necessary to attenuate (or at least to insert provisions able to procure the attenuation of) those provisions in the Convention which create the most blatant distinctions between debtors within and outside the realm of "Community privilege", namely the rules of jurisdiction and (in some respects) choice of law. Here, quite clearly, the Convention creates possibilities for debtors primarily established outside the EEC to undergo adjudication which, under certain conditions, will enjoy Community-wide effect, whereas a logical extension to such debtors of the jurisdictional principle which is made applicable to debtors primarily established within the Community would necessarily entail the conclusion that such extensive effects ought to be accorded only to a bankruptcy which is opened in the state which represents the debtor's "centre of administration."[60] Again, in various ways which will be described in due course, the choice of law rules implanted in the Convention have the unfortunate effect of creating a privileged category of "Community-based creditors", with the remaining creditors from outside the Community occupying a decidedly inferior legal position. Thus, as with the Judgments Convention,[61] it becomes possible to allege that the Convention is capable of giving rise to the impression that the EEC functions as a sort of "regional conspiracy" against outsiders, by failing to accord to them, and to the foreign legal systems with which they are mainly associated, a level of basic legal protection equal to that accorded to those who are considered to be "Community subjects". It is submitted that the spirit of legal internationalism would be better served if the Community were to display at least a *prima facie* willingness to extend the jurisdictional and other juridical principles which it apparently regards as consonant with the sound and fair administration of justice, to situations in which it may be not inappropriate to have regard to the legitimate claims of the law of some outside State to regulate the affairs, and status, of the party or parties in question. While, as ever, reserving one's position with regard to foreign systems of law whose legal rules and standards are grossly incompatible with those prevalent within the Community, it is urged that a more magnanimous and outward-looking policy would, in the circumstances, be the right one.[62]

(d) Jurisdiction

Title II of the Convention contains the rules which are to determine the exercise of jurisdiction to open bankruptcy and analogous proceedings. The vital importance of these rules would be difficult to exaggerate in view of the many, related consequences which flow from the initial act of opening proceedings in accordance with the provisions of the Convention, including numerous choice of law provisions, and of course the qualities of unity and universality which have already been described. All this serves to render the jurisdictional rules of more than ordinary interest, and simultaneously makes it essential that the rules themselves should be capable of working smoothly and predictably in practice.

The essential feature of jurisdictional rules is that they establish a three-tier, hierarchical structure of jurisdictional competence, the third (i.e. lowest) tier of which is now deprived of the Community-wide effects which are accorded to the first two.[63] As between the two tiers which serve to confer competence to open proceedings enjoying universal and exclusive effectiveness throughout the EEC, the first rank is accorded to the courts of the Member State in which is situated the "centre of administration" of the debtor (A. 3), while the second embraces the situation where the debtor lacks a "centre of administration" within the Community, but has "an establishment" in one or more of the Member States. A. 4 provides that in such circumstances the courts of *any* Contracting State in which the debtor has an establishment shall have jurisdiction to open bankruptcy proceedings. Thus, while the existence of a "centre of administration" serves to confer *exclusive* jurisdiction upon the courts of the State in question, it is foreseen that, where jurisdiction is exercised on the basis of the presence of an establishment, this will give rise to the existence of concurrent jurisdictional competence in favour of as many states as have become host to an "establishment" belonging to the debtor.[64]

The key expressions for jurisdictional purposes are thus "centre of administration" and "establishment". Any court which is contemplating opening any proceedings which fall within the ambit of the Convention will henceforth be obliged to inquire first, and if necessary of its own motion, into the question of the whereabouts of the debtor's centre of administration. If this is found to be situated within the Member State in which the court sits, the court may exercise jurisdiction under A. 3, but if no such finding is possible, the court must proceed to inquire whether the debtor's centre of administration is situated in any other Member State, and if this proves to be the case, must renounce jurisdiction in favour of the courts of the latter State.[65] Only if it is found that the debtor's centre of administration is not situated in any Member State of the EEC may the court proceed to consider whether it may exercise jurisdiction under A. 4 by virtue of the presence of an establishment belonging to the debtor. In the absence of any establishment within the State in question, the court must investigate whether the debtor has an establishment in one or more of the other Member States, for if so this fact precludes the court in question from exercising jurisdiction. If however no establishment exists anywhere within the EEC, A. 5 permits the court to proceed to exercise jurisdiction in accordance with any provisions of its local law which enable it to do so, with the important proviso that a bankruptcy thus declared is now excluded from the scope of the Convention, and hence will enjoy merely local effect within the State in which it is opened.

For the Convention to work smoothly, it is essential that all courts in every Member State should adopt an identical approach to the interpretation of the basic rules contained in Arts. 3 and 4, and in this respect it is necessary to voice some apprehensions that the correct identification of the location of a debtor's "centre of administration" or, failing that, of any "establishment", may not in all cases be so straightforward as to produce total unanimity amongst the courts concerned. Thus, the definition of "centre of administration" contained in A. 3 (2), to the effect that it means "the place where the debtor usually administers his main interests" begs certain questions with regard to the precise evaluation of those interests which are "main", and those which are to be considered as secondary, and with regard to the exact meaning of the term "usually".[66] While clearly scope exists for persons who are engaged in trade so to disperse their activities as to render it difficult to pinpoint their "centre of administration", it must be contended that this criterion seems even less well suited for employment in the exercise of jurisdiction over non-traders, the details of whose private conduct of their affairs it may in some cases be virtually impossible for their creditors to discover. There may be some inclination, in the case of non-traders, for courts to equate "centre of administration" with "legal domicile", but in view of the variations in the meaning borne by the term "domicile" in the different legal systems of the Member States, this could well give rise to "positive" conflicts of jurisdiction which, as described below, could prove virtually irresolvable in practice.[67]

Only slightly clearer indications of the location of the centre of administration are likely to be available in relation to firms, companies or other legal persons, of whom A. 3 (2) declares that the place of its location shall be presumed to be their registered office, if any, until the contrary be proved. This still leaves interested parties much scope for argument concerning the true whereabouts of the "centre of gravity" in a complex business organisation which may have been incorporated (perhaps for convenience) under the law of one Member State, but whose affairs and administration may be widely distributed both within and outside the Community. Only in the case of legal persons which are authorised to carry on business as insurance or credit institutions is the place of their registered office made to serve as the invariable location of their centre of administration for the purposes of the Convention.[68] It is submitted that the Convention would work with greater precision if more use could have been made of such irrebuttable presumptions, coupled with the requirement that persons (legal and natural) who engage in a trade or business should give adequate publicity to the whereabouts of their registered "centre of administration" (or "principal place of business") so that there could be no doubts as to the proper *forum* in which to seek to open bankruptcy proceedings concerning them. In the case of non-traders, the inescapable conclusion would seem to be that some more reliable indicator should have been chosen as the connecting factor on which to base the exercise of jurisdiction. Perhaps the point of principal registration for the purposes of liability to personal taxation would furnish the most appropriate centre in which to locate bankruptcy proceedings involving a non-trader.

With regard to jurisdiction based upon the presence of an "establishment", A. 4 (2) of the Convention now[69] essays a definition, to the effect that an establishment exists in a place where an activity of the debtor comprising a series of transactions is carried on by or on his behalf". Here again, the definition is a less than felicitous one, and leaves open such questions as how many transactions suffice to comprise a "series", and how frequently or continuously the activity must be practised in order for it to be "carried on" within the meaning of the definition. It is true, besides, that this definition also suffers from the defect that it has been conceived with "traders" in mind, and is less than appropriate to regulate the case of the non-trading debtor. In relation to the latter, if "establishment" is merely equated with "a private residence" of some kind, the owner (or perhaps, even the lessee) of, say, a holiday cottage within an EEC country may find that he thereby becomes liable to undergo a bankruptcy enjoying Community-wide effect, even though he may be habitually resident outside the Community and makes use of the cottage for only a few days each year. Yet, conversely, if the definition is construed as having application only in relation to persons or entities which carry on a business activity, many non-traders whose main residence is outside the Community will escape the application of A. 4 altogether, even though they may maintain substantial private interests within the EEC. At the most, their creditors may be able to secure the opening of a "territorial" bankruptcy under A. 5.

(e) Concurrent Jurisdiction

Where a debtor lacks any centre of administration within the EEC, but has establishments in more than one Member State, the courts of each of those States possess concurrent jurisdiction. The same is also true where a debtor transfers his centre of administration from one Contracting State to another: A. (6)(1) provides that for a period of six months from the date of such transfer the courts of both Member States shall enjoy concurrent jurisdiction to declare the debtor bankrupt. Following the expiry of the six months' period, the courts of the new centre of administration will acquire exclusive competence under A. 3.[70] This rule is not matched exactly in the case of a transfer of the centre of administration to a non-Contracting State: A. 7 provides that in such cases the courts of the Contracting State in which the debtor's centre of administration was previously situated are to retain competence for a full twelve months after the date of transfer. It is submitted that this provision is a further, unhappy example of the Community openly applying an aggressive policy towards non-Member States and their legal systems, here exemplified by the application of a doubled period of time, as compared with intra-Community transfers, during which a Community-wide bankruptcy may be opened in the state from which the debtor's centre of administration has been moved.

A further instance of concurrent jurisdiction arises in the case where, jurisdiction of the courts of a Contracting State being founded on the existence of an establishment, that establishment is transferred to another Member State: A. 8 (1) provides that a six-month period of concurrent jurisdiction shall ensue in the case where the transfer takes place to another Contracting State, while the extended period of twelve months, prescribed by A. 7, is to apply in the case of transfer to a non-Contracting State. Comparable, and again discriminatory, provisions are made in A. 8 (2) in the case of the closure of an establishment in one Contracting State, on the alternative hypotheses either that there remains another establishment within the Community, or that there does not.

Wherever, for any of the above reasons, the courts of different Contracting States are found to enjoy concurrent jurisdiction at the moment when the question of the opening of bankruptcy proceedings first arises, the solution adopted in A. 13 (2), and reiterated in A. 58 (1) with regard to recognition, is to treat the court which is the first actually to open a bankruptcy in respect of the debtor as the one which shall constitute the *forum concursus* for the purposes of the Convention. Accordingly, all courts in other Member States are required to stay proceedings for so long as the judgment opening the bankruptcy can be the subject of internal appeal within the legal system in which it has been given,[71] and thereafter, so long as the original proceedings have not been closed, the courts of all other States are precluded from opening any other such proceedings against the same debtor.[72] In the event that, through inadvertence or for any other reason, bankruptcies are opened against the same debtor by the courts of different States which enjoy concurrent jurisdiction, the Convention requires that recognition throughout the Community be accorded only to the judgment of the court which gave judgment first, even in the States where the other judgments may have been given.[73] We have elsewhere subjected this rule to criticism[74] on account of its insensitivity to the possibility that, of the various courts enjoying co-ordinate jurisdiction, practical convenience may best be served by enabling the bankruptcy to be conducted in that State in which, for example, the majority of the creditors, or perhaps the greater bulk of the assets, are to be found. This "most appropriate" *forum* may not always happen to be the one in which a judgment opening bankruptcy is first obtained. Indeed, there is no small probability that some creditors (or even the debtor personally) may take precipitate steps to initiate proceedings in a State in which it will be most convenient from their personal point of view that the bankruptcy should be centred. Such steps may be taken simply to suit the convenience of the parties concerned, but may besides be resorted to in view of certain legal advantages which will ensue by virtue of the fact that the *lex fori* will be applied in the bankruptcy. For whatever reasons such steps are taken, it is submitted that it is unsatisfactory that the legitimate interests of creditors in other Member States (and indeed, the interest of the debtor under some circumstances) cannot be taken into account in the process of determining which jurisdiction shall become the *forum concursus*. The consequence of the present rule is likely to be that creditors in each Member State will be tempted — even driven, out of regard for their personal interests — to strike at the earliest available moment, lest creditors elsewhere (known, or even merely suspected, to enjoy a concurrent competence to initiate the debtor's bankruptcy abroad) should "win the race", together with its numerous, if dubious, prizes. This is a formula for the precipitation of sometimes needless bankruptcies, and for the wastage of much effort and expense in many quarters.

To make matters worse, a further, utterly mechanical rule is contained in A. 58 (2) in an attempt to meet the case where, acting with an uncanny sense of timing, the courts in two different States are found to have given judgment on the same day. The arbitrary — and frankly absurd — solution offered is to give precedence to the judgment of that court which sits in a place whose place-name is first alphabetically.[75] Thus, if a debtor has establishments in Dundee and Bari, but the preponderance of the assets, and creditors, happen to be situated in Scotland, the only way in which the Scottish creditors (and the debtor also) can be spared the ludicrous expense and inconvenience of having their claims dealt with in a Southern Italian administration of the debtor's entire estate is to ensure that a sequestration is opened in Dundee at least a day ahead of any proceedings which may be opened by the creditors in Bari: if the two sets of proceedings happen to take place simultaneously, the entire administration will have to be centred in Bari, regardless of the wishes of the majority of creditors, or even of the debtor himself. Surely, to avoid the possibility of such absurdities, it would have been sensible to include a provision for liaison to take place between the authorities in different courts in which proceedings were pending or contemplated, with a view to ensuring that maximum convenience could be secured by means of cross-Community co-operation. This could be achieved either by means of the application of an agreed set of common-sense criteria to enable the "weighing" of interests to take place, or, where the balance is extremely fine and it can be demonstrated that positive injustices will ensue from the arbitrary allocation of sole jurisdiction to one court or the other, it should be permitted for two local bankruptcies to be declared in the "rival" jurisdictions, with a duty imposed upon each trustee or syndic to co-operate with the other, and with the aggregate of any assets which are situated anywhere outside the jurisdiction of the two "bankruptcy centres" being divided between them, in the first instance, in proportions corresponding to the relative sizes of the aggregated amounts of indebtedness disclosed in each set of proceedings (all creditors being obliged to elect between one or other of the administrations for the purpose of lodging proof for any particular debt).

(f)   Conflicts of Jurisdiction

Arts. 13 and 14 have as their respective purposes the prevention of "positive" and "negative" conflicts of jurisdiction. In the case of the former, it is required of any court when considering whether to open bankruptcy proceedings, to scrutinise its own jurisdictional competence in the light of the regime created by the Convention. It is then expected that any court which perceives that, under the circumstances, the jurisdiction of some other State's courts is prevalent, will duly renounce jurisdiction, or at any rate stay proceedings for so long as the theoretical precedence enjoyed by any other court is sustained.[76] What remains unprovided for is the situation where one court (or, just possibly, more than one court) fails to acknowledge that the proper application of the rules of the Convention leads to the conclusion that the jurisdiction of some other court prevails. This may arise either through lack of a uniform understanding of the meaning of the relevant provisions of the Convention — especially in relation to the definitions of "centre of administration" and "establishment" — or through confusion attributable to differences between the facts about the debtor which are adduced and evaluated before the different courts concerned. Several possibilities suggest themselves. For example, each of two courts, respectively sitting in States A and B, might conclude that the debtor's centre of administration was located within the court's own jurisdiction, thus conferring exclusive jurisdiction upon it. Alternatively, a court in State A might conclude that the debtor's centre of administration lies outside the EEC altogether, and, having been the first in time to open proceedings on the basis of a finding that the debtor has an establishment within its jurisdiction, may be confronted by a decision of a court in State B to the effect that the debtor's centre of administration is actually within State B, whereupon the latter court would claim absolute priority for its own adjudication of bankruptcy, even if in fact it was not chronologically the first to open. In the event of such discordant opinions being formed by the courts of two different Member States the Convention appears to offer no obvious means of resolving the positive conflict of jurisdictions which thereby arises: both A. 13, and Arts. 57 and 58 (which attempt to establish the principles of recognition by the courts of other Contracting States in cases of conflict between non-co-ordinate and between co-ordinate jurisdictions, respectively) are alike formulated on the presupposition that the existence of a basis of jurisdiction, and its proper quality, will be readily discoverable in such a way that all courts throughout the Community will invariably arrive at the same conclusions. Moreover, the fact that A. 62 (2) (b) specifically prohibits any party from challenging the bankruptcy in other jurisdictions of the Community on the ground that the court which opened the bankruptcy had no jurisdiction, means that no ready way lies open to the courts of the other Member States to discover whether their proper "allegiance" lies to the one school of interpretation or the other. In a case such as that described, it would appear that, unless one of the issuing courts withdraws its own order, the two mutually inconsistent orders are to be accorded full faith and credit in every jurisdiction of the Community, including in each instance the Member State whose court has issued the "rival" order: *quod est absurdum*. One way out of the deadlock would appear to lie through an appeal to the European Court of Justice in the hope that its interpretative ruling will determine which court is to regard itself as lacking in jurisdictional competence. But in view of the terms of A. 71, this would require some interested party (presumably the creditors in the rival bankruptcy or the trustee in that bankruptcy) to become involved in challenging one of the adjudications upon its native heath, and to sustain the expense of carrying an appeal before one of the courts empowered to make a reference to the European Court of Justice.[77] Even then, if the jurisdictional conflict is attributable to inconsistent findings of fact on the part of the two national courts, rather than to a disagreement on the question of construction or interpretation of the Convention, not even the Court of Justice may be able to resolve the *impasse*. Perhaps the most expeditious means of severing this particular Gordian knot would be furnished if the Convention were to be modified so as to enable a court of original jurisdiction to seek guidance from the Court of Justice when it became aware that such a positive conflict either had arisen, or would arise by virtue of the ruling it was minded to make regarding its own jurisdictional competence. Otherwise, it is perhaps asking too much of those creditors who have succeeded in persuading their local court that it can properly exercise jurisdiction that they should be so altruistic as to appeal against this ruling in order to place the question in the hands of an appellate court from which a reference may be submitted to the Court of Justice. Indeed, it is still asking a great deal of the creditors who, in their turn, have succeeded in procuring the opening of proceedings in some other Member State that they should now enter the fray in the "rival" *forum*, and champion the cause of "their" bankruptcy by challenges and appeals directed to the same end. At any rate, it is submitted that this *lacuna* in the logical structure of the Convention is a serious one which should receive further attention.

A. 14 is aimed at resolving cases of "negative" conflicts of jurisdiction — that is to say conflicting disclaimers of jurisdiction by the courts of two different States in the belief that it is properly vested in a court elsewhere. After A. 14 (1) has reiterated the basic duty of every court actively to disclaim jurisdiction where it recognises the existence of a superior jurisdictional competence in the courts of another Contracting State, A. 14 (2) attempts to avert the particular sort of denial of justice that might arise if a sequence of mutually-conflicting disclaimers were pronounced. The resolution of this problem is accomplished, in theory at least, by enacting that, after a court has declined jurisdiction by a judgment which is no longer appealable, the courts of the other Contracting States may not decline jurisdiction on the ground that the State which originally renounced jurisdiction was mistaken in its failure to perceive the pre-eminence of its own jurisdictional competence. Certainly, this provision enables a way forward to be found in some cases, as where a debtor has establishments in one or more of the Member States apart from the State in which the centre of administration is situated. The courts of any of those States could thus proceed to open Community-wide proceedings on the basis of A. 4. But if no establishment can be held to exist outside the State which, in the eyes of every other Member State apart from itself, contains the debtor's centre of administration, it would appear that no Community-wide bankruptcy can be opened anywhere, since there appears to be no warrant within A. 14 (2) of the Convention as presently drafted for any court purporting to act under that provision fictitiously to *deem* the debtor to possess an establishment (or, even, his centre of administration) within its own jurisdiction when such is not genuinely the case. Consequently, the courts in other States would be constrained to act under A. 5 of the Convention which, as has been explained, expressly denies Community-wide effect to a bankruptcy opened in any Member State in which there is not to be found at least an establishment, if not the centre of administration, of the debtor. This would further entail the opening of local bankruptcies within as many Member States as proved to contain some assets belonging to the debtor — including, chiefly, the State in which the latter's centre of administration is in reality located, and whose courts' previous erroneous determination has led to a breakdown of the main schedule of arrangements intended by the Convention. The expense and inconvenience of such circuitous, and duplicated, proceedings — which indeed represent the very type of *débâcle* which the Convention was expected to put an end to — may be considerable, and would in themselves furnish justification for efforts designed to improve the technical operation of the Convention, for example by imparting greater clarity to the key definitions, and by creating proper arrangements which would effectively establish objectively in relation to every debtor whose centre of administration lies within the EEC, the whereabouts of its precise location.

(g) Special Cases

A. 10 contains one of the limited number of exceptions to the principle of universality which have been admitted in the present version of the Convention. Effectively, where the law of any Member State excludes one or more categories of persons from the operation of its laws of insolvency, that State is to be permitted to maintain its existing practices. Such practices are established, for example, in the cases of France, Belgium, Luxembourg and Italy, by each of whose laws non-traders (*non-commerçants*) cannot undergo bankruptcy, and in the further case of Italy, where the same exemption is also applied to small traders (*piccoli imprenditori*).[78] Likewise in the United Kingdom, in the case of infant debtors, it is possible to invoke the remedy of bankruptcy only in cases where the debts were incurred in respect of "necessaries". By virtue of A. 10, any persons who belong to one of these special categories, and who are in principle subject exclusively to the law of one of those Member States according to the jurisdictional scheme of the Convention, continue to be immune from the possibility of any bankruptcy being opened against them in that jurisdiction which will, effectively, constitute a bankruptcy "haven" from the point of view of those able to construe this particular immunity in such terms.[79] However, if such a debtor has an establishment in any other Member State, the courts of that State may open a bankruptcy in accordance with the provisions of their local law, and such a bankruptcy will enjoy Community-wide effect in every Member State except that in which the debtor's centre of administration is situated.[80] Paradoxically, therefore, such a bankruptcy may command recognition and enforcement in several Member States, each of whom would accord the "privilege" of exemption from bankruptcy to the same debtor if his centre of administration were located within their jurisdiction. The legal position of the debtor's assets situated in the State of his centre of administration is not explained in A. 10, but presumably, since the courts of that State are absolved from the duty to recognise any bankruptcy pronounced against that debtor, his trustee in bankruptcy will not be accorded any special entitlement to such assets under the local law of their *situs*. These assets will accordingly become the objects of a characteristic "race of diligence" in which, as a rule, local creditors tend to enjoy obvious advantages as against others, including the foreign trustee in bankruptcy, who simultaneously lay claim to them from outside the jurisdiction. Another unexplained problem concerns the question of the eligibility of creditors, who are themselves resident or established in the Member State which happens to constitute a "bankruptcy haven" for their debtor, to lodge proof in any bankruptcy which he may undergo elsewhere in the EEC.[81] Although it may be argued that these creditors should, in principle, be excluded from the bankruptcy altogether, it is probably more likely that the principle of *par condicio creditorum* will be adhered to, with the consequence that these creditors will be permitted to lodge proof in the foreign bankruptcy, or even indeed to initiate the proceedings. However, equitable principles would require any such creditors who lodge proof to surrender into hotchpot the fruits of any acts of diligence which they have carried out against the debtor's assets situated within his "bankruptcy haven".[82]

(h)   Actions Arising from or Connected with a Bankruptcy: Vis Attractiva Concursus

When bankruptcy has been opened in a Contracting State in accordance with the provisions of the Convention, so that the court in question thereby becomes the *forum concursus*, certain further jurisdictional capacities become vested exclusively in that *forum* by virtue of provisions whose purpose is to ensure that proceedings which are very closely connected with the bankruptcy are concentrated in the same *forum* as the bankruptcy proceedings proper. In the absence of such provisions, the actions in question might frequently be expected to fall within the ambit of the Judgments Convention, and hence competence might be regarded as belonging to the courts of one or more other Member States, in accordance with the jurisdictional scheme of that Convention as applied to the subject-matter of the proceedings, or to the personal circumstances of the party or parties involved.[83] By A. 11 of the Bankruptcy Convention it is first provided that, in the case of the bankruptcy (or winding-up) of a company or firm or other legal person, the courts of the State in which the bankruptcy has been opened shall enjoy exclusive jurisdiction to determine actions concerning the consequential liabilities incurred by persons who have directed or managed the affairs of the company or firm in question. Such proceedings may include questions of liability to pay compensation for loss or damage suffered by the general body of creditors,[84] or even for loss or damage sustained by the company.[85] Secondly, where the members of a bankrupt firm or company have undertaken or incurred unlimited liability for its debts, the court of the bankruptcy is to be exclusively competent to determine actions concerning the extent of that liability. The recognition and enforcement of judgments resulting from either of these two types of proceedings will however be governed by the Judgments Convention,[86] while any proceedings undertaken with a view to bringing about the personal bankruptcy of any persons whose liability is established by such proceedings will now have to be brought in the courts of that Member State (or those Member States) whose jurisdiction to adjudicate is determined afresh by applying the principles of Arts. 3 and 4 in relation to the individual circumstances of each person involved.[87]

Further jurisdictional provisions are contained in A. 15, which embodies the principle of *vis attractiva concursus* to confer upon the court which has opened bankruptcy proceedings exclusive competence to entertain any of the nine types of actions specified in the Article itself.[88] Once again, there is ample logical justification for concentrating these actions in the hands of the court in which the bankruptcy has been declared, even at the expense of creating significant exceptions to the observance of such other jurisdictional principles as *actor sequitur forum rei*, or that which accords jurisdiction over questions concerning immovable property to the courts of the *situs*.[89] However, since A. 15 supplies a rule of merely jurisdictional purport, it is left to the court on which competence is thereby conferred to proceed to apply its own legal rules, including its rules of private international law, in actually determining the questions thus falling under its control. This surely provides a powerful illustration in support of the thesis which has been argued in Part I of this book, namely that it is imperative that the rules of private international law of the Member States be progressively harmonised, for otherwise material variations in both the quality and the extent of any liabilities arising under A. 15 will in practice be attributable to differences in the conflicts rules which may come to be applied to factually identical examples of behaviour. Thus, most of the objections to permitting the *forum concursus* to hear realted actions involving immovable property would be deprived of any substance if it could be ensured that, by a uniform rule of private international law, any court which happened to constitute the *forum concursus* would invariably refer to the *lex situs* whenever it became necessary to apply a substantive rule of law; but if no such uniformity of approach were to obtain, the results could be most unhappy.[90] The further significance of A. 15 is that it lends even greater weight to the arguments previously advanced concerning the crucial need to devise jurisdictional rules which are both sensible and workable with regard to the original opening of bankruptcy proceedings: the principle of *vis attractiva concursus* is primarily calculated to serve the convenience of the trustee or liquidator, and of those creditors (and generally also the debtor) who reside or are established in the State which is the *forum concursus*. But as the liquidator is a creature whose identity is formed *after* the adjudication has commenced, the really vital question is whether the centring of the proceedings within that particular jurisdiction will best serve the interests and convenience of the majority of creditors, and also of the debtor. It should now be apparent, moreover, that any arguments based upon these parties' best interests must be coloured by the fact that the eventual whereabouts of the *forum concursus* in combination with the rules established by A. 15, may have serious implications in terms of the defeat of some parties' reasonable legal expectations by reason of the fact that their rights come to be dependent upon rules of law whose application was previously unanticipated.

Of the actual rules contained in A. 15 the majority are sufficiently clearly expressed and require no special discussion. Special mention will be made of three cases, however, on account of the important exceptions which they contain. First, under paragraph (2), claims for payment or recovery of property founded upon the premiss that the transaction whereby the debtor made the payment or disposed of the property in question was void as against the general body of creditors, may only be maintained exclusively in the *forum concursus* when they are made directly against the party who transacted with the debtor: if the property has been further disposed of to a third party, any action for its recovery must be brought in the courts of the Member States which would have jurisdiction in ordinary circumstances. Here, once again, the jurisdictional rules of the Judgments Convention will reassert their authority. Secondly, while paragraph (7) provides that actions relating to the admission of debts *per se* shall be exclusively brought at the *forum concursus*, this rule is expressly stated not to cover either actions to determine whether a fiscal or social security debt, or one arising under a contract of employment, actually *exists* as a debt and, if so, its amount and its character as a preferential debt or otherwise, or actions to determine the existence of secured rights, or general or special preferential rights, in relation to property which is subject to registration. In each instance, these functions are to be retained by the courts which are competent in the ordinary way, but it should be noted that A. 16 has been inserted in the Convention in order to make it clear that questions whether any of these types of debt are to be admitted to proof remain within the jurisdiction of the Court of Bankruptcy. Thirdly, although paragraph (8) indicates that actions for the purpose of terminating current contracts under a provision of bankruptcy law[91] are to be heard in the *forum concursus*, a specific exception is created in relation to contracts of employment and contracts relating to immovable property, which in consequence will remain within the jurisdictional purview of the courts to which they would normally belong.[92]

(i) Choice of Law

A. 17 contains an important general rule in relation to the requirements for the opening of bankruptcy proceedings: the court which has jurisdiction according to the present Convention is to apply the internal law of the Contracting State in which it sits. Thus, *lex fori* is to be applied not merely with regard to procedural matters, but also with regard to matters of substantive law. Since, at present, the relevant laws of the Member States remain unharmonised — to an extent which will be apparent even upon a perusal of the different lists of the relevant proceedings under the law of each Member State which are contained in A. I of the Protocol — the rule established by A. 17 is of far-reaching significance. A detailed, parallel study[93] of the conditions contained in the laws of all Member States with regard to the requirements for opening each of the different types of proceedings falling within the Convention indicates the near-infinite variety of the discrepancies which remain extant within this vital area of the law. There can be no doubt but that, at present, a state of inequality exists between debtors (and creditors also) whose factual circumstances are totally identical but for the fact that, under the Convention, the courts of different States will constitute the *forum concursus*: in some cases, more exacting requirements are imposed in order for proceedings to open than would be imposed in other jurisdictions, while in certain instances, on the same given facts bankruptcy could be opened under the laws of some States but not under those of others. A considerable amount of time and resources will doubtless have to be devoted to the rectification of this "distorted" state of affairs, but it is to be hoped that an early beginning will be made upon this as the next, logical step towards the necessary creation of a "European" bankruptcy law.[94] Further general rules concerning choice of law are contained in A. 18, which specifies, first, that the internal law of the *forum concursus* shall determine the procedure to be followed (a perfectly usual and unexceptionable provision) and secondly that, except where there is a specific provision to the contrary contained in Title IV of the Convention (comprising Arts. 20–54), the law of the *forum concursus, including where appropriate its rules of private international law*, shall determine the effects of the bankruptcy and also the conditions under which the bankruptcy is effective against third parties. The notable, additional dimension which is hereby bestowed upon those provisions of the *lex concursus* is of course that, by virtue of the principle of universality with which the Convention is imbued, the effects which are thus generated will obtain on a Community-wide basis.[95] However, precisely because of this, the special rules contained in Title IV demand careful attention, not least because of the numerous ways in which they utilise uniform conflicts rules which effectively create exceptions to the prevalence of the *lex concursus*.

The first Section of Title IV concerns the effects of the bankruptcy independently of advertisement, and by A. 20 it is declared that such effects as are made applicable to the debtor under the law of the *forum concursus*, including in particular the cessation of his power to deal with his property, shall automatically apply in all the other Contracting States independently of the provisions for advertisement.[96] Thus, no uniform rule is introduced to regulate the effects of bankruptcy against the debtor, but instead it is provided that the effects accorded to any given bankruptcy *vis-à-vis* the debtor shall be co-extensive with the effects taking place within the Contracting State which constitutes the *forum concursus*. This rule may give rise to difficulties in relation to certain species of proceedings within the United Kingdom, since in company liquidations the property of the company is not normally divested unless the liquidator specially applies for a divesting order,[97] so that the company may normally continue to deal with its property, albeit in reality all such dealings are controlled by the liquidator. It is also notable that in a Scottish sequestration, divestiture of the debtor does not take place immediately upon the award of sequestration but when, after some interval of time, the trustee obtains his act and warrant of confirmation.[98] In view of the length of time which will inevitably elapse between the moment when a bankruptcy acquires universal effect against the debtor by virtue of A. 20, and the moment when the bankruptcy becomes adequately publicised by means of gazetting, there is a clear need for the laws of all Member States to incorporate some provision to protect persons who, during that interval, have dealings with the bankrupt in good faith without notice.[99]

With regard to the effect of the opening of bankruptcy proceedings upon the rights of creditors to initiate new proceedings, including enforcement measures, against the bankrupt's property A. 21 again makes the law of the *forum concursus* the metewand for determining the date upon which, in each instant case, this prohibition shall become operative even in the absence of advertisement. In the same way, A. 22 makes provision for the bankruptcy to operate automatically to stay all actions affecting the debtor's assets which were already commenced before the opening of bankruptcy. Provision is made for the continuation of such proceedings to be sanctioned by leave granted by the court of bankruptcy, and upon conditions to be determined by the law of the State wherein the court sits. In the latter event, the court which originally assumed jurisdiction may retain its competence if it has already made an order of some kind in the course of the proceedings, apart from an order merely relating to jurisdiction.[100] A further exception to the general rule concerning the staying of actions is comprised in A. 22 (2), which effectively excludes from such a staying effect any proceedings which have already passed "the point of no return" within the jurisdiction in which they are taking place, in the sense that, under the law of the Contracting State where they were commenced, a bankruptcy opened in that State would no longer have had any staying effect in relation to them. A saving provision is contained in A. 23, however, to reverse the rights of national authorities to collect fiscal and similar debts within their own territory, irrespective of the provisions of Arts. 21 and 22. This again creates a not insignificant exception to the principle of universality, because any assets of the debtor situated in each respective Member State will remain accessible to the national authorities despite the opening of a bankruptcy somewhere in the Community, provided the national laws of the *situs* of the assets allow for such continued enforcement to take place. Correspondingly, the assets available for distribution to the "private" creditors throughout the Community may be seriously depleted as a result of the exercise locally of such exorbitantly privileged powers by the authorities of any of the Member States, and hence it is submitted that this provision in the Convention is objectionable in principle in that it violates the basic nature and spirit of the Common Market.

One further exception to the general rules established by Arts. 21 and 22 is contained in A. 24, which preserves the position of third parties who will lose certain rights against the debtor unless they perform a particular act within a specified time limit.[101] If the bankruptcy of the debtor is opened before the expiry of that time limit, the third parties in question are to be permitted to proceed to perform the requisite acts at any time up until the bankruptcy becomes effective against them in accordance with A. 27,[102] and will thereby prevent the period of limitation from expiring, even as against the general body of creditors.

The gazetting of bankruptcy proceedings, and its consequential effects,

are regulated by Section II of Title IV. The provisions of A. 26 are designed
to ensure that the liquidator (or some other person or authority, if the *lex
concursus* so permits) is required to effect the advertisement of the bankruptcy by a variety of means, ranging from entry in the trade or company
registers in which the bankrupt is registered to the insertion of entries in the
Official Gazettes of the Contracting States besides that of the *forum concursus*.[103] In addition, it is specially provided by A. 26 (1) that, where an establishment of the bankrupt is situated in a Contracting State other than that
in which bankruptcy has opened, or whenever the court of bankruptcy so
orders, the liquidator must insert an advertisement of the bankruptcy in
the *Official Journal of the European Communities*, and also that in other
cases he may insert the same advertisement of his own initiative if he thinks
fit. A further number of judgments, acts and notices which are required to
undergo advertisement in the *Official Journal* under the same conditions as
any judgment opening a bankruptcy are listed in A. IV of the Protocol,
while Arts. III and VI thereof indicate what are to constitute the standard
form and contents of such advertisements.[104]

A. 27 of the Convention stipulates that in Contracting States other than
that in which bankruptcy has been opened, the bankruptcy shall take effect
in full as against third parties from the eighth day following its advertisement
in the *Official Journal*, and that acts done after the expiry of that period
shall be void as against the general body of creditors if they cause detriment
to the latter. It is further provided that acts done before advertisement, or
within the seven-day period thereafter, are also voidable as against the general body of creditors if they were done by a third party who, at the time,
either knew or ought reasonably to have known of the opening of the bankruptcy.[105] This provision effects a full harmonisation of the laws of the
Member States with regard to the effectiveness of bankruptcy against third
persons, and may be contrasted with the non-uniform provisions of Arts.
20–22, which are specifically sundered from the provisions for advertisement
contained in A. 26. However, A. 27 (3) permits an extension of any rules of
the State in which bankruptcy has been opened which relate to the invalidity
of acts done by the debtor before the bankruptcy was opened, so that these
may be applied to acts done by the debtor between the opening of the bankruptcy and the eighth day following its advertisement in the *Official Journal*.
By means of this provision, certain acts which would not be deprived of their
validity by virtue of the rules contained in either paragraph (1) or paragraph
(2) of A. 27, may be declared invalid as against the general body of creditors
through the application of some rule contained within the *lex concursus*.

A special choice of law rule creating a general exception to the foregoing rules relating to the effects of bankruptcy is introduced by A. 28, which is concerned exclusively with rights relating to property which is subject to public registration, and with rights and securities which are similarly registered. It is provided that the effects of bankruptcy with regard to the creation, modification, transfer or termination of such rights shall be determined by the law of the Contracting State in which the register is kept as if the bankruptcy had been opened in that State. Thus, the effect of bankruptcy upon the interests of third parties who are affected by such rights is properly to be referred to the bankruptcy law of the State of registration, which would be the law which such parties may reasonably be expected to have consulted in planning their affairs.

(j) *Powers and Functions of the Trustee or Liquidator*

An important, and necessary, counterpart to the declaration of principle concerning the universal effects which shall be enjoyed by bankruptcies governed by the Convention, is the securing of uniform recognition of the powers and status of the trustee or liquidator, both *de iure* and *de facto*, within all the Contracting States. Thus, A. 29 declares that in each case the *lex concursus* shall determine the nature and extent of the powers which shall be exercisable by the trustee throughout the EEC, and A. 33 further requires the trustee, acting within the scope of those powers, to take protective measures and effect disposals of property of the debtor wherever this may be situated. Moreover, A. 32 refers to the appropriate authority within the State of the *forum concursus* the question of any authorisation to empower the trustee to continue to manage the bankrupt's business in any other Contracting State. Despite the present lack of full uniformity between the Member States' laws on the vital matter of the powers of the trustee or liquidator, it is perhaps foreseeable that practical experience of the comparative merits of the various laws, which will be engendered within each State through a gradual exposure to the operations of the laws of sister States, may furnish an incentive towards a gradual assimilation by all of them of any specially useful or convenient provisions of the laws of the individual members of the Community.

To balance the rule which enables the powers of the trustee to be determined substantively by the *lex concursus*, Arts. 29 (1) and 33 (1) and (2) further provide that in the exercise of these respective powers in the Contracting States the trustee shall operate in conformity with the procedural provisions of the State in which the exercise of his powers produces its effects, or of the State in which the property in question is situated.[106] There

is also a sensible, subsidiary provision to the effect that, where the appointment of more than one trustee, or the delegation of certain of his powers to
other persons, is permitted by the *lex concursus*, this may be effected in
such a way that the joint trustees, or delegated persons, are chosen from
qualified persons from the territories of different Member States so as to
maximise the convenience of a multistate administration. A uniform certificate of appointment has been devised to facilitate the trustee's establishing
his status and credentials within Contracting States outside the *forum concursus*.[107] The specific power to order the redirection of the bankrupt's mail
so that it is transmitted by the postal authorities to the trustee in the first instance, is enabled henceforth to operate upon a Community-wide basis, subject to certain safeguards to ensure a degree of due process of law in relation
to the making of orders of this kind.[108] The convenience of creditors known
to be resident outside the State of the *forum concursus* is served by means
of a provision to require individual notification to be sent to them of any
need to lodge proof in the bankruptcy, and by the sanctioning of a comparatively informal mode of lodging proof by means of a letter which may be
written in any of the official languages of the Contracting States,[109] containing the essential, minimum information concerning the amount and nature (whether preferential or secured) of the debt, and accompanied by copies
of any supporting documents which may exist.[110] These letters are to be sent
to the bankruptcy authorities of the State where the bankruptcy is being administered, as specified in A. X of the Protocol, and it shall be for the authorities concerned to make provision for translation, where necessary.

(k) Proprietary Effects of Adjudication

By A. 34 (1), the principle of universality is reaffirmed in relation to the effects of bankruptcy upon the whole of the debtor's assets situated anywhere
within the Contracting States. Thus, as a general principle, the destiny of
both movable and immovable property will in this instance be determined
by the *lex concursus*. In derogation from this general rule, besides the special cases, already described,[111] where the Convention exceptionally permits
a bankruptcy to be denied full faith and credit in certain jurisdictions only,
a further exception is created in relation to property which the bankrupt
holds on trust. Property in this latter category is declared to be excluded
from the debtor's assets for the purposes of bankruptcy.[112] In the case of
property to which the bankrupt becomes entitled only after the opening of
bankruptcy ("after-acquired property"), A. 34 (2) permits the *lex concursus*
to determine whether such property shall be included within the effects of

the bankruptcy. In this instance, therefore, the law of bankruptcy rather than the law of the *situs* will determine whether after-acquired property is to be comprised within the assets available for distribution to creditors.[113] However, in relation to property which is excluded from the bankruptcy for other reasons, A. 34 (3) stipulates that the law of the *situs* shall regulate the question of its exclusion from the effects of bankruptcy. Hence, items which are traditionally exempt from passing to the trustee in bankruptcy — such as bedding, personal clothing, and tools of the bankrupt's trade[114] — will continue to enjoy that exemption, irrespective of the requirements of the *lex concursus*, provided that they are so exempted under the law of the Contracting State in which they are situated at the opening of bankruptcy. Thus, a further species of exception to the principle of universality is admitted, albeit one whose practical consequences are unlikely to be of very great moment, since the aggregate value of excluded property is never likely to be very large in proportion to the total amounts of debts and assets involved in any insolvency occurring in a Community-wide context.[115]

Although A. 34 furnishes rules for application to the debtor's assets situated within the EEC, it fails to make provision for any cases where assets are situated outside the Community at the opening of bankruptcy. It could be argued that the Community should aspire to claim universality in the full global sense for bankruptcy adjudications issuing from courts within the EEC, but the attainment of this reality would admittedly be dependent upon the co-operation of the courts of independent States in the outer world. However, as a statement of principle it would clarify matters from the point of view of courts sitting in third States which may otherwise be persuaded that such bankruptcies are purposely confined in their effects to the territory of the EEC itself, thus leaving the way open for courts in non-Member States to open local bankruptcies in parallel, or to permit other species of diligence to be carried out within their jurisdiction. However, the present writer feels strongly that the assertion of such world-wide effects on behalf of a Community bankruptcy would make it incumbent upon all Member States to engage in a genuine *quid pro quo* by extending an equal measure of co-operation, and acknowledgement of effects, to bankruptcies pronounced by courts sitting in third States where jurisdiction was assumed on the basis of rules identical, or comparable, to those established by the present Convention.

One further conflict rule is created in relation to the effects of bankruptcy upon property. This is the provision in A. 35 whereby the attempt is made to accommodate the various approaches adopted under the laws of the different Contracting States to the possibility that property which at the instant of bankruptcy may be owned by the spouse of the bankrupt, may originally have been acquired with the help of the latter's funds. In particular, the laws of some States have the effect of conferring a basic advantage upon the creditors by means of a presumption (the so-called Mucian presumption) that property acquired for valuable consideration by the bankrupt's spouse[116] since the date of marriage has been acquired with the bankrupt's money. Consequently, it is made incumbent upon the spouse to adduce positive proof to show that each item of patrimony which was acquired in the specified circumstances was in fact acquired with independently-owned funds. Under the Convention, where bankruptcy is opened in a Contracting State whose law applies a presumption of this kind, A. 35 (1) refers to the *lex situs* of any property belonging to the bankrupt's spouse to determine whether or not such a presumption shall attach to it, subject to a proviso that property which would thereby escape from the application of the presumption may nevertheless be held to be subject to it if the law governing the spouses' matrimonial property rights includes such a presumption.[117] Conversely, however, where both the *lex concursus* and the *lex situs* apply such a presumption, A. 35 (1) will require its application despite the fact that it would be excluded under the law governing the spouses' matrimonial property rights. There is an accompanying rule to the effect that, where the presumption is applied, all modes of proof shall be admissible to enable the spouse to attempt to rebut it.[118] Despite this ameliorating provision, the main thrust of A. 35 is seriously objectionable, in that it creates an unwarranted intrusion upon the settled, reasonable expectations of a spouse whose matrimonial property rights are regulated by a system under which no such presumption would be applied. Hence, the spouse may omit to keep the sort of detailed records and documentation which would enable the presumption to be rebutted in the event of the bankruptcy of the husband or wife, as the case may be. While one is not unmindful of the opportunities for fraud which arise from the maintenance of a distinction between the legal identities of husband and wife, it would appear that this "aggressive" rule, which in any case runs counter to the basic principle that innocence is generally presumed, has been accorded an undue predominance within A. 35 at a time when it forms part of the laws of only a minority of the Member States, and even then in a less than uniform manner. It is submitted that the better solution would be to permit the presumption to be applied in relation to all property, irrespective of its situation, provided that the presumption is applied under both the *lex concursus and* the law governing matrimonial rights, but not otherwise.

Further exception may be taken to the provision within A. 35 (2) to the effect that the *lex concursus* alone shall determine the extent to which gratuitous disposals of property by the bankrupt in favour of his or her spouse, and *"les avantages matrimoniaux"* (benefits under marriage property agreements, express or implied) may be held valid as against the general body of creditors. Here again, the settled rights and expectations of parties, conferred by the law which regulates their matrimonial property rights, are made capable of being overturned by the chance that one of the spouses becomes liable to undergo bankruptcy in a different jurisdiction, whose legal system applies different rules and standards to the questions of matrimonial property rights.[119] It is therefore submitted that, as in the case of A. 35 (1), this again violates two of the primary criteria which were previously specified for the purpose of testing the soundness of the provisions of the Convention,[120] and accordingly ought to be reconsidered. If it is felt that the existing disparities between the laws of the Member States in relation to these matters are capable of giving rise to serious impediments to the fair administration of insolvencies occurring within the EEC, the solution should undoubtedly be sought by means of measures to harmonise the relevant provisions of internal law so that they are uniformly in accord with one another. In the meantime, an imperfect solution may be achieved by means of a uniform conflicts rule supplied by A. 35, but in that case it is absolutely essential that the rule which is most suitable, and which is generally the most fair to all interests concerned, should be the one to be employed.

(l) Past Acts and Current Contracts

The right of creditors of the bankrupt to set off liabilities which they themselves owe to the bankrupt's estate against the debts for which they would ordinarily be obliged to lodge proof, is of considerable importance in view of the self-evident fact that, in any instance of genuine insolvency, the dividends payable to creditors in respect of the debts owing to them will amount to considerably less than 100% of the sums involved. A. 36 therefore establishes the basic entitlement to set-off by prescribing that the laws of all the Contracting States must allow it at least to the minimum extent specified in A. 2 of the Uniform Law contained in Annexe I to the Convention.[121]

With regard to recovery actions whereby past acts of the debtor, which have perpetrated fraud against his creditors, may be set aside and property which had passed thereunder be recovered on behalf of the general body of creditors, the former version of the Draft Convention contained ambitious proposals to harmonise the laws of the Member States by means of the Uniform Law.[122] The present version of the Draft presents a radically scaled-down proposal in A. 37, to the effect that where such recovery actions are, under the law of the *forum concursus*, provided for only by provisions of law rather than that State's law of bankruptcy,[123] the conditions regulating the setting aside of any transaction shall be those of the law of the State which governs the transaction, which will therefore be applicable as though the bankruptcy had been opened in that State. Once again, in the face of disagreement between the representatives of the negotiating States, the attempt to create a Uniform Law has had to be abandoned in favour of a uniform conflicts rule which, in this instance, is supportable as being designed to operate in a way which respects legitimate expectations derived from the law by which the original transaction was properly regulated.

Arts. 38–41 inclusive regulate the effects of bankruptcy upon different sorts of current contracts to which the bankrupt is a party. In relation to contracts of employment, A. 38 declares that where the law governing the contract is that of one of the Contracting States, the effects of bankruptcy upon the contract shall be determined by the law of that State. On the other hand, if the contract is governed by the law of a non-Contracting State, it is stated that the *lex concursus* shall apply in this matter. Thus, once again, a deplorably parochial, and discriminatory, attitude is demonstrated: if it is considered apposite that the law of the contract should be applied, in order to avoid overturning the settled expectations of the parties to it, it is surely right that such a principle should be applied uniformly in relation to all contracts of employment to which persons undergoing bankruptcy anywhere within the EEC happen to be parties. Certainly, a subsidiary rule could and should be incorporated to cope with the possibility that the law of some non-Contracting State may have been selected as the law of the contract with a view to avoiding its being regulated by the law of any Member State of the EEC, or even by the law of some other third State by which it would more "naturally" fall to be governed. But in view of the more open-minded approach now exhibited by the provisions of the Contracts Convention itself,[124] A. 2 of which disclaims any intention to discriminate between the laws of the Contracting States and those of other States with regard to the key question of the "proper" law of the contract, the purport of A. 38 of the Bankruptcy Convention now seems distinctly anomalous, and surely requires reconsideration.[125]

A uniform choice of law rule to be employed in determining the effects of bankruptcy upon any lease or tenancy of immovable property, or to any lease or tenancy comprising both movable and immovable property, is established by A. 39 which refers all such questions to the *lex situs*. It may be noted that no reference is made to the possibility that the *situs* of the property may lie outside the EEC, and hence it is submitted that this provision should be understood as authorising reference to the law of *any* State, whether or not it is a party to the Convention. It may further be observed that, since the Convention now contains no express provision regarding contracts for the leasing of movable property, any questions of the effects of bankruptcy upon such contracts are, by virtue of A. 18 (2), to be referred to the law of the *forum concursus*, including where appropriate its rules of private international law. This diversity of conflicts rules, related to the basic division of property into movable and immovable, serves to illustrate the particular importance of the process of characterisation in private international law, and it may be as well to recall that A. 19 of the Convention expressly requires that the characterisation of property shall itself be determined by reference to the character which the property in question is considered to bear according to the law of the place where it is situated.[126]

With regard to sale contracts, the distinction between movable and immovable property forming the subject-matter of the contract again proves to be fundamental. A. 40 selects the *lex situs* (again, without any words of reservation to confine this rule to cases of property situated in one of the Member States) for the determination of the effects of bankruptcy upon contracts for the sale, lease-sale, hire-purchase or leasing of immovable property, and also upon contracts for the sale of movable and immovable property in combination. Once again, therefore, the provisions of A. 18 (2) will ensure that any similar questions arising in relation to contracts for the sale, lease-sale, hire-purchase, or leasing of *purely* movable property shall be referred to the *lex concursus*. Here, as also with regard to contracts for the hiring of movable property, it is a little startling to find that no attempt is made to respect the obvious claims of the proper law of the contract to be determinative of the parties' rights in the event of the bankruptcy of either of them. Considerations based upon the previous lack of unanimity between the Member States in relation to the identification of the proper law of a contract *ought* now to be rendered obsolete by virtue of the uniform rules embodied within the Contracts Convention.[127]

In relation to the special problems associated with contracts of sale in which a reservation of title clause[128] has been inserted, no final version of the relevant provision of the Convention exists at the time of writing. Several variants have been produced for the eventual text of A. 41, and would have the various effects of referring the "validity of the sale" (and hence, the particular question of the validity of the reservation of title clause) either to the private international law of the *forum concursus*,[129] or to the proper law of the contract,[130] or, by means of an omission from the Convention of any express provision covering the point, to leave the matter to the internal law of the *forum concursus* through the operation of the rule contained in A. 18 (which could again give rise to the application of certain of that State's rules of private international law in accordance with the provision contained in A. 18 (2)). While each of these three variants has its own special difficulties, it is submitted that the solution which would most accord with principle would be that which would require the question of the validity of a reservation of title clause, as against the general body of creditors, to be referred to the law which, following the application of the rules contained in the Contracts Convention, is found to constitute the proper law of that contract. While it would be additionally desirable to procure a unanimity of approach to this somewhat vexed matter on the part of all the Member States' laws, it would need to be borne in mind that a faithful application of the rules for determining the proper law of a contract may well lead to the law of some non-Contracting State being referred to. Thus, full uniformity of effect could never be achieved until such time as reservation of title clauses themselves come to enjoy uniform treatment under the laws of all legal systems. In the meantime, however, it is surely preferable to submit any question of their validity in the aftermath of a bankruptcy to the law with reference to which the reasonable expectations of the parties, but particularly those of the non-bankrupt party, have been formed.

(m) Preferential and Secured Creditors

While all modern systems of bankruptcy are based upon the initial principle of equality of distribution of the available assets, distinctions are invariably drawn between different categories of creditors, so that the claims of some are discharged ahead of those of others. Further distinctions are made in relation to secured creditors, who may be permitted to realise their security and thus recover full or partial repayment of their debts, without being considered thereby to violate the general rule that the opening of bankruptcy suspends the rights of creditors to exercise individual acts of diligence against their debtor's property. In an international bankruptcy, the main source of difficulty is derived from the variety of approaches which may be adopted by the bankruptcy laws of the different countries which are potentially involved, to questions concerning the rights of preferential or secured creditors. Having concluded that it was currently not possible to achieve the harmonisation of the Member States' internal rules in this area,[131] the draughtsmen have in Arts. 43–52 of the Convention attempted, so far as concerns bankruptcies opened within the Community, to regulate these problems by means of uniform conflicts rules.[132]

A. 43 establishes a basic rule of "localisation of assets", so that in each of the Contracting States in which assets of the debtor are situated[133] at the opening of bankruptcy, a separate, sub-estate ("local asset pool") is considered as being established for purposes of accounting and distribution. By a less happily-conceived rule, once more redolent of the regional chauvinism from which the Convention suffers at numerous points, A. 43 (2) specifies that assets recovered or realised in non-Contracting States shall be aggregated with the sub-estate situated in the State of the *forum concursus*. As a corollary to this provision, it will transpire that the schedule of distribution of property recovered in non-Contracting States will be that of the *forum concursus*. Effectively therefore the principle of universality of effect is totally respected only in relation to assets found either within the jurisdiction of the *forum concursus* itself or outside the Community altogether: in all other cases the facility is created whereby special predilections of the laws of the other Member States may be accorded scope for application. Bystanders, disinterested or otherwise, who survey the resultant scene from outside the Community could be pardoned for inferring that the Community was herein aspiring to function as an aggressive and xenophobic mutual protection society, offering no hand of friendship towards the outside world.

The first application of a system of "local asset pools" occurs under the provisions of A. 44. First, in relation to creditors whose debts were incurred after the opening of the bankruptcy on behalf of the general body of creditors, it is provided that they shall be satisfied by means of contributions out of the assets situated in each of the Contracting States where they are considered to be liabilities of the general body of creditors, the contributions being made from each sub-estate according to the ranking laid down in the Contracting State concerned, and in proportion to the assets available for this purpose.[134] Secondly, creditors for civil or commercial debts incurred prior to the opening of bankruptcy are to be accorded the benefits of the principle of unity and universality by means of a provision enabling them to invoke their preferential rights, or rights against the general body of creditors, in every State in which assets are situated, but are there to be accorded only such standing as the local law attaches to the debts in question. The possibility that one and the same debt may be so differently regarded under the laws of different Member States that in some of them it enjoys a general right of preference, while elsewhere it is deemed to be a debt incurred by the general body of creditors, is met by a provision to the effect that all the relevant sub-estates shall be required to contribute towards satisfaction of the debt, in accordance with the elaborate scheme laid down in A. 50.[135] Thirdly, however, the principle of unity and universality is renounced in relation to debts which are not of a civil or commercial character — primarily taxes, social security contributions, rates and similar liabilities incurred before or after[136] the opening of bankruptcy. The authorities to whom these liabilities are owed will be confined in the exercise of their preferential rights, or in recovering payment of a debt incurred on behalf of the general body of creditors, and will be allowed to accomplish this only in relation to assets situated within their own jurisdiction. However, they are to be allowed to lodge proof in respect of any unsatisfied balance, provided that the debt would have been admitted to proof in a bankruptcy opened in their own State, and shall be ranked alongside the ordinary unsecured creditors for the purpose of receiving any dividends distributed out of assets recovered in other jurisdictions. This latter proposition has aroused some controversy because it runs counter to the long-established rule of English law, based upon considerations of public policy, whereby courts in the United Kingdom have refused to enforce foreign penal or revenue claims, even when they emanate from the authorities in States which are members of the Commonwealth.[137] While recognising the force of those arguments which have led some to conclude that, until the Member States' laws in this regard are properly harmonised, this radical enhancement of the already over-extensive privileges of governmental and local authorities constitutes an unacceptable encroachment upon the interests of ordinary creditors, the present writer still believes that, on balance, it is necessary here to maintain fidelity to the logic inherent in the concept of a Common Market, and to regard internal fiscal and administrative frontiers as archaic entities to be transcended wherever possible. It is necessary to add, however, that the more progressive approaches to insolvency questions nowadays display a tendency to favour the position of the ordinary creditors as against the claims of the State or its subsidiary authorities, and hence one would strongly advocate a concerted approach at Community level to the rescheduling of all such liabilities so that, in the majority of cases, they rank alongside the claims of ordinary creditors.[138]

When the various sub-estates have been compiled, the problem arises of administering the distribution of claims constituting general rights of preference which, as stated in A. 44 (2), may be asserted by those creditors who enjoy such rights against the assets situated in each of the Contracting States by whose law such a preference attaches to their debts.[139] A. 50 therefore attempts to regulate the procedure to be followed where it transpires that a given debt enjoys preferential status under the laws of more than one State in which sub-estates exist. First, if the debt is actually accorded the same ranking under the laws of the different sub-estates, and if moreover the amounts accorded are the same under the respective laws, the debt will be borne in equal shares by the sub-estates concerned. If, however, one of the sub-estates is insufficiently large to provide the full amount of the equal share it has been allotted to bear, this "unsatisfied balance" will be represented for a second time to receive a second distribution out of the funds remaining in the other sub-estates which still have funds available. On this second round, assuming there are two or more sub-estates still participating, the amount of the unsatisfied balance will once again be divided equally between them.[140]

Where the general right of preference attaches to the same debt in two or more States, but for different amounts because the extent of the preference is not the same in all the States concerned, the debt is to be borne by each sub-estate up to the amount of the most extensive right of preference in proportion to the sums to which the general right of preference attaches in each State and up to the amount of those sums. Thus, if maximum sums of £800 and £400 are specified under the laws of two different Member States, the creditor will be allowed a maximum recovery of £800, to be borne by the two sub-estates in the proportions of two-thirds and one-third, respectively.[141] Again, if the debt is not wholly discharged upon a first round of distribution, either because of insufficiency of funds in some of the sub-estates, or because of the operation of a "ceiling" imposed by the law of one or more of them, then a second and subsequent distributions are to be made from the assets remaining available in any of the sub-estates which are participating, subject to the proviso that no sub-estate may be called upon to make further contributions beyond the point where the total of the contributions derived from the sub-estate in question equals the maximum amount of preferential payment allowed to be made to such a debt under the law of the State in which the sub-estate is constituted.[142]

A. 50 (2) endeavours to meet the further possibility that one and the same type of debt may be regarded as preferential according to the laws of different Member States but may yet be accorded at differing rank of preference within some of them, so that in those States the debt will be ranked equally with other debts of a preferential character. The chosen formula for solution is that, in those States in which a number of debts rank equally, the local sub-estate shall be distributed in proportion to the amounts of those debts, and the contributions from each of the sub-estates towards the discharge of any one debt shall not exceed the amount of the share available for such distribution. On the other hand, if any given debt is differently ranked within the different sub-estates, to the extent that it will be impossible simultaneously to satisfy a general preference from the different sub-estates, A. 50 (3) specifies that the debt shall be first borne by the sub-estate in which it enjoys the highest ranking, and if after this assets are found to be simultaneously available from more than one sub-estate, those estates shall come in, if need be, and furnish contributions in accordance with the principles established in paragraphs (1) and (2) of A. 50.

In relation to each sub-estate generally, A. 45 specifies that the law of the Contracting State in which any group of assets were situated at the date of opening the bankruptcy [143] shall control the distribution of that particular pool of assets by determining the order of priority, and the amounts of any preferential debts towards whose satisfaction that sub-estate will furnish contribution. Thus, the amount and priority of any preference to be paid out of assets recovered and realised within the United Kingdom in a bankruptcy opened anywhere in the EEC will be determined in accordance with the law of the United Kingdom. A similar reference to the provisions of the *lex situs* is ordained with regard to secured rights and special rights of preference, A. 46 providing that the subject-matter, extent and ranking of such rights shall be determined by the law of the Contracting State in which the property charged with such a right was situated at the opening of the bankruptcy. To avoid any possibility of doubt, it has been expressly provided by A. 48 that the right to a lien on property shall be governed by the law of the Contracting State in which the property is held, and hence rights of this kind are treated in the same way as secured rights governed by A. 46. Where any question arises of the relative precedence to be accorded to the different species of rights governed by A. 45 and A. 46, respectively, A. 49 once again has the effect of making the *lex situs* determinative so far as concerns assets making up each of the separate asset-pools. Special directions for determination of the *situs* of property for the purposes of Arts. 43—46 inclusive, together with A. 49, are provided for in A. 51, which declares that tangible movable property (apart from that referred to in A. 47) [144] shall be deemed to be situated in any Contracting State in which it is registered, inscribed or recorded in a national public register; whilst incorporeal property generally which is registered, inscribed or recorded only in an international public register shall be deemed to be situated in the State of the *forum concursus*. This provision, where applicable, may thus have the effect of removing the property thereby affected out of the asset-pool formed in the Contracting State in which it was *actually* situated at the opening of bankruptcy, and of inserting it into the asset-pool of the State of registration, or into that of the *forum concursus*, as the case may be.

An elaborately-constructed provision, parts of which remain unsettled at the time of writing, seeks to make special provision for rights secured upon ships, boats and aircraft, assets which of their very nature are freely mobile so that chance alone may frequently determine the jurisdiction in which they happen to be located in the opening of bankruptcy.[145] By derogation from the principle established in A. 46, A. 47 (1) declares that in the distribution of the proceeds on realisation of assets of this kind, the law which shall determine the priority to be accorded to unregisterable special rights of preference shall be that of the Contracting State in which the aircraft or vessel is situated, not at the date of bankruptcy, but at the date when it is sold. Where, however, it transpires that at the time of the sale the ship or aircraft is located in a non-Contracting State, a subsidiary rule requires the application of the law of the State of its registration. So, too, in the case of registered secured rights over assets of this type, A. 47 (2) specifies that the priority of mortgagees' interests shall be determined by the law of the State in which the ship or aircraft is registered. These rules, although justifiable on the principle of securing parties' expectations based upon such a formal act as the registration of a secured interest, could result in some bizarre references being made to the bankruptcy laws of various foreign States which constitute the state of registration for vessels or aircraft operating under flags of convenience. In view of the dubiousness of the practice of operating under flags of convenience, it is surprising, to say the least, to find an EEC Convention actually conferring an indirect blessing upon their use by persons and entities whose "proper" centre of operations lies within the EEC.[146] Perhaps some modification should be inserted to reserve the right of the official administering the Community bankruptcy to declare in favour of some more appropriately-applicable law (even, here, that of the *forum concursus* itself) when the application of the law of the State of registration would be manifestly unjust or absurd in the circumstances. A. 47 (5) seeks to fix the notional situation of property referred to in A. 47, primarily for the purpose of allocating to the appropriate sub-estate any surplus proceeds of the realisation of ships, boats or aircraft after all special rights of preference and registered secured rights have been discharged.[147] A. 47 (5) has the effect that, where the law which is to be applied in determining any special or secured rights over the item in question is that of a Contracting State, the surplus will be credited to the asset-pool belonging to that State, whereas, in any case where the other provisions of A. 47 will require this preliminary issue to be determined by the law of a non-Contracting State, any surplus proceeds derived from that item of property will be credited to the asset-pool formed in the *forum concursus*, in accordance with the requirements of A. 43 (2).[148]

One further, general comment which requires to be made in respect of all the rules in the Convention which concern the distribution of assets in settlement of creditors' claims is that the principles of unity and universality have at this stage receded almost to vanishing point. Rules of fiendish complexity

have had to be resorted to in order to accommodate the reluctance of the negotiators to relinquish particularly cherished provisions of their local laws
concerning preferential and secured rights. Paradoxically, the attempt to
achieve a compromise solution, in which "universality" is allowed to rejoin
the banquet after the more voracious guests have consumed a first sitting, has
given rise to a situation which is even more inordinately favourable to preferential claimants than might usually be the case since, before the ordinary
creditors may enjoy their first bite, any morsels remaining within the sub-
estates are still reserved to be devoured first by the preferential gormandisers
who have failed to achieve satiety from consuming the viands upon their own
plates. To make matters worse, the characteristic duality of standards applied
towards the denizens of the Community on the one hand, and those of the
outer world on the other, will generally reduce the latter to the unenviable
metaphorical role of an Oliver Twist, in that no effort is made to respect
preferential rights arising under the laws of non-Member States, in whose
jurisdiction assets may be recovered, since it is in relation to precisely these
assets that the appetite for universality finds its belated gratification through
the assertion of the dominant role of the *lex concursus*. Finally, it is noteworthy that it has proved impossible to accord universality of effect to the
provisions of the *lex concursus* even in relation to the personal effects upon
a debtor of undergoing bankruptcy within the Community. By A. 53 it is left
to the laws of the various Contracting States to determine whether, and to
what extent, disabilities, disqualifications and restrictions of rights will be
entailed within their respective jurisdictions in consequence of a bankruptcy
opened in any Contracting State. The spectre thus arises of "limping" inca-
pacities inflicted upon a bankrupt under the laws of some Member States,
but not under the laws of all, an uneven state of affairs which may give rise
to no small amount of confusion in practice.

(n) Recognition and Enforcement

Although, as we have seen, the Convention contains extensive concessions in
the direction of territorial localisation with regard to the administration of
bankruptcies, Title V (Arts. 55—69 inclusive) reaffirms the basic notions of
unity and universality of bankruptcy in the distinct, but related, fields of
recognition and enforcement. Thus, A. 56 proclaims that, with the exception of bankruptcies covered by the provisions of Arts. 5, 10 (2) or 66,[149] and
with the further exception of any judgments concerning the liberty of the
individual,[150] judgments concerning the opening and procedure of any of the
forms of proceedings listed in A. I of the Protocol, including judgments under

A. 15 (3) of the Convention and arrangements and compositions approved by a court, shall, if made in one of the Contracting States, be recognised in all of them as of right and without any special procedure being required.[151] The definition of the term "judgment" for the purposes in hand is supplied by A. 55, and means "any judgment given by a court, tribunal or authority of a Contracting State, whatever the judgment may be called, including a decree, decision, order or writ of execution, as well as the determination of costs or expenses by an officer of the court". The definition also expressly includes the decisions listed in A. V of the Protocol, which, in the case of the United Kingdom, means that company resolutions for voluntary winding-up in a "creditors' voluntary winding-up", and a resolution by the meeting of creditors for the appointment of a "liquidator" in a "creditors' voluntary winding-up" are both assimilated to the notion of a judgment for the purposes of the Convention.

The effects of Arts. 57 and 58, which are concerned with the resolution of conflicts of jurisdiction, have already been considered above in relation to the rules for the exercise of jurisdiction under the Convention.[152] Let it suffice here to note that A. 59 has the further effect of preserving the validity of acts performed in accordance with any judgment which is subsequently rendered ineffective through the operation of the rules contained in either of the aforesaid Articles. This provision is essential in order to enable prompt and effective action to be taken by the relevant parties, including chiefly the trustee or liquidator, pursuant to any judgment which, to all local appearances, is perfectly regular and valid when made.

While no special procedure is required for a bankruptcy to enjoy Community-wide recognition in principle, it is necessary to create additional arrangements to provide for those situations in which any kind of enforcement is required. Here, typically, a defendant party or parties may wish to raise some point of objection to the enforcement against them of a judgment or order in bankruptcy emanating from a court or official administering the bankruptcy from some State other than that to which the defendant belongs. In the first instance, however, the Convention is exceedingly faithful to the logic inherent in the framework of a "double" Convention, and provides in A. 60 that judgments (and also judicially-approved arrangements and compositions) which are recognised under the provisions of Arts. 56—59 shall also take effect as of right and be enforced in the other Contracting States. Thus, the "automatic" effects at the enforcement stage, consequential upon the implementation of a mandatory regime for the exercise of jurisdiction in bankruptcy matters, are even more impelling under the Bankruptcy Convention than under the Judgments Convention where, at least, a formal act of registration of the judgment, plus the issue of an order for its enforcement, are essential prerequisites to its actual enforcement within any jurisdiction of the Community.[153] By contrast, judgments concerning the opening and procedure of bankruptcy are made enforceable without any need for registration or the issue of an enforcement order by the courts of the State in which enforcement is to take place. However, a restricted facility to resist recognition and enforcement in any State other than that which constitutes the *forum concursus* is made available to any party who is concerned to oppose it within that jurisdiction alone, and consists of the latter's undertaking the relatively drastic step of bringing an action to challenge the judgment opening the bankruptcy itself, in accordance with the provisions of Arts. 61–66. In the majority of cases it would be appropriate for any challenge to the bankruptcy to be maintained before the courts of the *forum concursus* itself, and hence, not surprisingly, the grounds on which it is made permissible to challenge the bankruptcy before the courts of any other State are rigorously circumscribed. Indeed, A. 62 (1) allows only two grounds to serve as the basis of an action to challenge the bankruptcy outside the *forum concursus*. These are: (a) that, as a result of circumstances for which he cannot be held responsible, the debtor did not have knowledge of the proceedings in sufficient time either to prepare his defence, or to avail himself of any legal remedy against the judgment opening bankruptcy; or (b) if recognition of the judgment opening the bankruptcy is contrary to the public policy of the State in which the action to challenge the bankruptcy is brought. However, A. 62 (2) mentions five specific grounds which may not be considered to furnish a valid basis for the invocation of the public policy exception admitted in A. 62 (1) (b).[154] Chiefly notable among these five excluded grounds are the allegations that the court which opened the bankruptcy had no jurisdiction,[155] or that the judgment has been given against a person or entity which could not have been declared bankrupt in the jurisdiction in which the action to challenge is brought, provided that the bankrupt does not have, or no longer has, his or its centre of administration in that State.[156]

In each of the Contracting States, actions to challenge the bankruptcy outside the *forum concursus* may only be brought in a court designated for this purpose in A. XI of the Protocol.[157] The defendant in such proceedings will be the person or persons having the powers of trustee or liquidator in the bankruptcy according to A. 29 (2) of the Convention, and the party bringing them may be either the *"ministère public"*, the debtor or any other interested party, with the exception of the person who brought the original bankruptcy proceedings in the *forum concursus*.[158] A relatively brief time limit is specified in A. 64 (2), which declares that the action may not be brought after the expiration of a period of three months from the date of advertisement[159] of the bankruptcy judgment in the *Official Journal of the European Communities* or, in the absence of such advertisement, from the date when the person bringing the action had knowledge of the judgment. An absolute limit of six months from the date on which the bankruptcy is opened is furthermore imposed, together with a prohibition barring the action from being brought at all after the bankruptcy has been closed, however early this may be.

It is important to contrast the effect of an action to challenge the bankruptcy under A. 61 *et seq.*, with those which would ensue from a successful appeal against the judgment opening the bankruptcy pursued in the jurisdiction from which the judgment originates. The latter proceeding will have the effect that the bankruptcy will cease to exist in the eyes of all the jurisdictions of the Member States, whereas the former, even if successful, will be confined in its effectiveness to the jurisdiction of the Member State in which the action was pursued: in that jurisdiction alone the bankruptcy will cease to be recognised or to command effect under the Convention (subject to the usual saving provisions to preserve the validity of any acts performed prior to the declaration of invalidity).[160] Even the step of bringing an action to challenge the bankruptcy does not, at that moment and of itself, operate to stay enforcement of the judgment opening the bankruptcy, although provision is made for the court seized of the action to decide at its discretion to stay enforcement, albeit only within the jurisdiction of the Member State in which it is sitting, pending the outcome of its consideration of the case. The court may also order interim protective measures to preserve the estate situated within that jurisdiction.[161] If the court's judgment is that the bankruptcy is invalid, upon the judgment acquiring the force of *res judicata* it takes effect *erga omnes* within the jurisdiction in which it was rendered (but nowhere else), and is required to be advertised in the *Official Journal of the European Communities* by the authority which advertised the bankruptcy judgment.[162] Finally, A. 66 provides that where an action to challenge the opening of a bankruptcy is successfully brought in any of the Member States, a separate bankruptcy, of purely territorial effect, may be opened in that State. This therefore constitutes a further, permitted exception to the principles of unity and universality of bankruptcy,[163] since it is plainly in contemplation that two simultaneous bankruptcies will ensue from such situations. Indeed, it is not unforeseeable that one successful action to challenge a bankruptcy may be followed by others elsewhere, with a consequent plurality of bankruptcies resulting. Despite the obvious defeat for the Convention's larger purposes entailed by such developments, it is clearly preferable to deny the debtor any opportunity to create an *ad hoc* "bankruptcy-haven" by means of the action of challenge.

The foregoing provisions concerning recognition and enforcement have related exclusively to judgments or compositions referred to in A. 56 of the Convention.[164] A. 67 now expressly stipulates that the recognition and enforcement of all other types of judgment which are delivered in the course of bankruptcy proceedings, including settlements approved by a court or made before a judge, shall be governed by the Judgments Convention of 27 September 1968, as amended.[165] This principle is also to apply in the case of instruments for enforcement delivered to creditors in bankruptcy proceedings in accordance with the law of the State in which the proceedings have been opened, but a specific exception is once again made in relation to judgments concerning the liberty of the individual. By virtue of A. 67, a neat interconnection is established between the two Conventions whose provisions are purposely designed to be complementary to each other.[166] The particular consequence is that judgments to which A. 67 applies will require to be registered in any Member State in which it is sought to enforce them, and an order for enforcement will have to be obtained by means of the established procedure which enables the party against whom enforcement will take place to lodge a specific appeal against the making of the enforcement order.[167]

(o) Interpretation by the Court of Justice

Title VI of the Convention confers upon the Court of Justice of the European Communities jurisdiction to give rulings on the interpretation of the Convention together with its Protocol and Annexe I.[168] Apart from the important and symbolic fact that Title VI stands within the body of the Convention itself, the substance of the provisions contained in Title VI largely corresponds with that of the Protocol to the Judgments Convention,[169] and it will suffice here to note only those matters on which the Bankruptcy Convention differs from its forerunner in this sphere. Thus, A. 71 (which lists by name the courts of the Member States which are alone competent to submit requests for preliminary rulings) is notable because it has the consequence that in the case of the United Kingdom not only the House of Lords but also the Court of Appeal (and in Scotland, the Inner House of the Court of Session, and in Northern Ireland, the Court of Appeal in Northern Ireland) will be obliged to submit references where they consider that a decision on a question of interpretation of the Convention is necessary to enable them to give judgment. This extended provision is made necessary because under certain circumstances the intermediate appellate courts may constitute courts of final appeal in bankruptcy matters, and indeed their competence under A. 71 (a) is restricted to those cases in which they occupy the position of courts of last resort. However, by virtue of A. 71 (b) a discretionary competence to make references is also conferred upon any of the courts of the Contracting States when they are sitting in an appellate capacity.[170]

(p) Final Provisions

A. 76 delineates the extent to which existing Conventions between some of the Member States of the Community shall become superseded when the Bankruptcy Convention comes into force, while A. 77 endeavours to avert any irreconcilable conflict between the present Convention and any existing Conventions which have previously been concluded between any of the Contracting States with any non-Contracting State. In the latter contingency it is provided that the Community Convention shall be precluded from applying, and hence it must be remarked, with respect, that in this instance the Community deserves to be commended for its self-restraint. Since it is expected of all Member States of the EEC that they shall become signatories to this Convention the provision in A. 80 is especially significant in that it effectively prevents the Convention from coming into force until all Member States have ratified, it being stated that the moment of entry into force shall be on the first day of the sixth month following the deposit of the instrument of ratification of the last State to take this step. It is further indicated that States which become Members of the EEC in the future will be required to accept the present Convention "as a basis for negotiations" in the course of fulfilling their obligations under A. 220 ECT.[171]

Although A. 81 retains the commitment, previously contained in A. 76 of the earlier version of the Draft Convention,[172] whereby Member States are required to amend their own legislation so as to achieve conformity with the Uniform Law laid down in Annexe I, this obligation, which was scarcely of overwhelming magnitude even as originally proposed, now amounts to very little indeed since, as has already been observed,[173] Annexe I now contains but three Articles, of which one still remains subject to final agreement.[174]

By A. 85 it is provided that the Convention is concluded for an unlimited period, while A. 86 creates a mechanism for the revision of the Convention to take place by means of a conference between the parties to be convened by the President of the Council of the European Communities at the request of any Contracting State.

5. Concluding Remarks

The 1980 version of the Bankruptcy Convention is still a long way short of being an ideal example of an international Convention concluded between closely-aligned States. But, given the highly sensitive and specialised character of insolvency law, it is perhaps not really surprising that the draftsmen and negotiators have encountered such gargantuan problems at every stage of their labours. It will be a long time, indeed, before the processes of harmonisation of the domestic laws of the Member States will arrive at a point which will resolve all of the questions of fundamental disagreement which have led to the Convention being assembled in its present, uneven form. The resort to an agreed, uniform conflicts rule as the way around difficulties arising from a failure to agree upon a uniform substantive rule of law has enabled some kind of progress to be achieved. But the resulting conflicts rules, considered as a set, are remarkably uneven and frequently appear inconsistent when considered against the framework of evaluative criteria proposed at the outset of this chapter. Thus, it is clear that a truly "European" law of insolvency, faithful to principle and satisfactory in all its concrete applications, is still a long way off. Nevertheless, flawed though it is and though it may remain even after the final stages of negotiation have been concluded, it is hoped that this Convention will be adopted and put into effect within the Community. Only then can its sounder elements be demonstrated by means of the practical benefits which they will yield, and only then, too, can the empirical data be properly assembled to reveal in which sectors it would be desirable to concentrate the follow-up efforts in the field of legal harmonisation, and eventual revision of the Convention itself.

NOTES

1. Text published in English by the Department of Trade as Text of the EEC Draft Bankruptcy Convention, with explanatory notes, April 1980, and reproduced in Appendix C. *post.*
2. Discussed in Chapter 4 *ante.*
3. The Committee of Experts was convened as the result of a decision taken by COREPER on 8 February 1960 in response to a Note from the Commission to the Member States, dated 22 October 1959, inviting the latter to undertake the negotiations necessary to fulfil the requirements of A. 220 ECT.
4. See Chapter 4 *ante* at p. 106. *cf.* also Hunter (1976) 25 ICLQ 310, at p. 313.
5. See Fletcher, Law of Bankruptcy (1978) at pp. 301—304 for a description of certain legal restraints to which a discharged bankrupt remains subject at English law.

6. For a comparative survey of the bankruptcy laws of the Member States, see L. Ganshof, Le Droit de la faillite dans les Etats de la CEE (Brussels, 1969); J. Van der Gucht, Droit de la Faillite dans les six pays (La Jurisprudence de Bruxelles, 1964); J.H. Dalhuizen, International Insolvency and Bankruptcy (New York, 1980), vol. I, part II, and the same author's Compositions in Bankruptcy (Amsterdam, 1968); Houin (1961) 76 Journal des Tribunaux 345.

7. For a survey of the relevant legal provisions of all the (then) Member States of the EEC, specifically related to proceedings which will be governed by the Bankruptcy Convention, see J. Bonell, I. Fletcher and M. Fontaine, Les Conditions d'Ouverture des Procédures de Faillite et des Procédures Analogues (Brussels, EEC Commission, 1979), EEC Doc. III/D/223/80-FR (2 volumes, English-language version pending).

8. See the comparative survey prepared by Professor M. Sauveplanne (October, 1963) EEC Comm. Doc. 8838/IV/63-E.

9. For further appraisal of the problems caused by diversity of rules in private international law concerning insolvency, see L. Blom-Cooper, Bankruptcy in Private International Law (London, 1954) (also published in (1955) 4 ICLQ 170); M. Trochu, Conflits de lois et conflits de juridictions en matière de faillite (Paris, 1967); Dalhuizen, *op. cit. supra* n. 6, vol. I, part III; Fletcher, *op. cit. supra* n. 5, ch. 14; Ganshof (1971) CDE 146; Dicey and Morris, The Conflict of Laws (10th edn. 1980), ch. 26. See also the Noël-Lemontey Report, refd. to *infra* n. 16.

10. *cf.* Nadelmann (1966) 41 Tul. L. Rev. 75.

11. *cf.* Nadelmann (1970) Riv. Dir. Int. Priv. e Proc. 501 (also published in English in K. Nadelmann, Conflict of Laws, International and Interstate (1972) at p. 340); same author, (1946) 9 M.L.R. 154 (also reproduced in Conflict of Laws (1972) at p. 273); same author, (1946) 11, Law and Contemp. Prob. 696 (reproduced in A.A.L.S. Selected Readings in Conflict of Laws (1956) at p. 1073).

12. For a review of past history, see Nadelmann (1944) 93 U. Pa. L. Rev. 58 (reproduced in *op. cit. supra* n. 11, at p. 299); same author, (1961) 10 ICLQ 70; and (1943—44) 5 U. Tor. L. J. 324. For English and French language versions of the extant, bilateral conventions relating, wholly or partially, to bankruptcy, see Dalhuizen, *op. cit. supra* n. 6, vol. II. See also comments in Noël-Lemontey Report, refd. to *infra* n. 16, at pp. 9—10.

13. For texts, see respectively 155 LNTS (1935) 116 (Eng. and Fr. translation at p. 133); (1943) 37 AJIL, Supp. at p. 138; and 86 LNTS (1929) 112, at p. 362 (Eng. translation).

14. Actes de la 5e Conférence de d.i.p. (La Haye, 1925). See also Actes de la 6e Conférence (1928).

15. Doc. 3.327/1/XIV/70-F, dated 16 February 1970. An agreed English version, dated August 1974, was subsequently published as Doc. 3.327/1/XIV/70-E, and may be found published as App. 10 to the Report of the Dept. of Trade Advisory Committee (Chairman, Mr. Kenneth Cork), presented to Parliament, August 1976 (Cmnd. 6602), hereafter referred to as the "Cork Report". The Draft is also published as Appendix C in K. Lipstein (Ed.) Harmonisation of Private International Law by the EEC (1978).

16. The Report is published as E. Comm. Doc. 16.775/XIV/70-F (original French version); an English translation has been published under the same coded reference number, substituting the suffix-letter "E" in place of "F". The Report is hereafter referred to as the "Noël-Lemontey" or "N-L" Report, page references being to the English version.

17. See Hunter (1972) 21 ICLQ 682, and (1976) 25 ICLQ 310; Nadelmann, *op. cit. supra* n. 11, at p. 340; same author, (1977) 52 NYULR 1, at pp. 27—32; Coppens, in Idées Nouvelles dans le droit de la Faillite (4ème Journée d'études juridiques Jean Dabin, 17 Mai 1968) (Bruxelles, 1969), Part III; K. Lipstein, The Law of the European Economic Community (1974) p. 284; Fletcher in K. Lipstein (Ed.), *op. cit. supra* n. 15, at p. 119

(also published in (1977) 2 ELR 15); Farrar [1972] JBL 256, [1977] JBL 320; L. Ganshof, *op. cit. supra* n. 6, Part IV, and (1971) CDE 146; Hirsch (1970) CDE 50; Jähr (1972) 36 Rabels Z. 620; Noël (1976) RTDE 159; Lemontey (1975) RTDE 172; Noël and Lemontey (1968) RTDE 703; Hillman (1974) Am. Bankr. L.J. 369; Cork Report, Cmnd. 6602, *passim*, and especially the note of reservations by Mr. A.E. Anton at pp. 105—28.

18. Contrast the position of the Judgments Convention (*ante*, Chapter 4) at the date of accession of the three new Member States. However, important amendments were made to the substance of this Convention also, during the course of negotiations for the accession thereto of the new Member States: see *ante* pp. 103, 110.

19. Additional doubts were introduced during the period of so-called "renegotiation" of the terms of United Kingdom membership of the Community during 1974—75.

20. Comments upon this latest version of the Draft are now beginning to appear: see Thieme (1981) 45 Rabels Z. 459.

21. See N-L Report at pp. 10—11.

22. See further *infra*, esp. at pp. 213—14, 222—23, 228—34.

23. See Chapter 4 *ante*.

24. A. 1 (1). The rejection of any significant role to be played by the factor of nationality is a further instance of the important decision to transcend the more limited notion of principle contained in A. 220 ECT: see Chapter 4 *ante* at p. 106.

25. See Arts. 56, 60, 61 and 62 (1).

26. A. 63, together with A. XI of the Protocol.

27. As with regard to the "nationality" factor (see n. 24), the Convention arguably transcends the strict requirements of A. 220 ECT by including rules of jurisdiction and choice of law. But it is submitted that this enhanced approach is capable of justification in terms of the overall spirit and purposes both of A. 220 ECT itself, and more generally of the Treaty as a whole.

28. *q.v. ante*, Chapter 4, esp. at pp. 133—38 (in relation to Title III of the Judgments Convention).

29. See the references to this text, and commentaries thereon, in notes 15, 16 and 17 *supra*.

30. See Blom-Cooper, *op. cit. supra* n. 9; Hirsch (1970) CDE 50; Ganshof (1971) CDE 146; Nadelmann (1944) 93 U. Pa. L. Rev. 58, (1943—44) 5 U. of Tor. L.J. 324, (1961) 10 ICLQ 70; Dalhuisen, *op. cit. supra* n. 6, vol. I, section 2.02 (3).

31. See *infra* in relation to the effects of Arts. 5, 10, 66 and also 43.

32. See *infra* in relation to Title VI (Arts. 70—74).

33. See *infra* in relation to Arts. 55—66 and 70—74.

34. *cf*, the mechanical reasoning processes which led to the notorious decision in *M'Elroy* v. *M'Allister*, 1949 S.C. 110. The issue of justice versus certainty was also canvassed in *Gallie* v. *Lee* [1969] 2 Ch. 17 (C.A.). [1971] A.C. 1004 (H.L.).

35. See *infra* in relation to Arts. 3—14 and 57—59.

36. See *infra* in relation to A. 62 (2) (b).

37. See *infra* in relation to Arts. 71 and 73.

38. See *infra* in relation to Arts. 3—14 and 57 and 59.

39. *cf*. N-L Report at pp. 1, 3.

40. See *infra* pp. 207—13 for possible instances of such occurrences.

41. See Chapter 4 *ante* in relation to A. 1 (2) of the Judgments Convention.

42. A. 1(1) together with A. 1 (a) of the Protocol.

43. A. 1 (2) together with A. 1 (b) of the Protocol.

44. See A. 1 (a) of the Protocol.

45. See further *infra* p. 204 in relation to jurisdiction generally.

46. See N-L Report, p. 12. *cf*. the apparent incorporation of such a precondition to

the application of the Judgments Convention (*ante*, Chapter 4, p. 111), and observations in the Jenard Report in E.C. Bull. Supp. 12/1972, at pp. 25—27.
47. See Chapter 4 *ante*, p. 106, and also the Jenard Report, *loc. cit. supra* n. 46.
48. *cf.* N-L Report at p. 21.
49. See, especially A. 3.
50. See, especially A. 5.
51. See Draft Directive on the co-ordination of laws, regulations and administrative provisions governing the winding-up of direct insurance undertakings.
52. See A. 1 (3), second paragraph.
53. However, s. 119 of the Bankruptcy Act 1914 (together with rules 285 and 288 of the Bankruptcy Rules, 1952) enables the partners to be made bankrupt upon a petition brought against them in the firm name: a receiving order made against a firm operates as a receiving order against each person who is a partner at the date of the order, and thereafter each partner may be adjudicated bankrupt pursuant to the receiving order. The position is different in Scotland, where the law confers upon a partnership a legal personality distinct from the members of which it is composed. Therefore, under Scots law a partnership is liable to be made notour bankrupt and to undergo sequestration: see Partnership Act 1890, ss. 4 (2) and 47, and generally, J.B. Miller, Partnership (1973), ch. 13.
54. Thus, the Channel Islands, the Isle of Man and Gibraltar, together with any non-European, dependent territories of the United Kingdom, must each be specifically "contracted in" if the Convention is to apply.
55. A. II of the Protocol states that, for the purposes of A. 2 of the Convention, the effective date of the "opening" of bankruptcy in England and Wales shall be the date of the receiving order; and that in the case of a creditors' voluntary winding-up in both the United Kingdom and in the Republic of Ireland it shall be the date of the passing of a resolution by the company for voluntary winding-up. See also A. 52, which determines the effective date of "opening" in cases where one type of proceedings in A. I (a) or (b) of the Protocol is replaced by a different type of proceedings from among those listed in A. I (b): the date applicable for determining the *situs* of property referred to in Arts. 45, 46 and 49 is to be the date upon which the *last* of the proceedings was opened.
56. See *infra* in relation to Arts. 5, 10, 65 and 66. While A. 2 contains no reference to these "special cases", A. 34 (concerning the effect upon property of the debtor's bankruptcy) and A. 56 (concerning recognition as of right) do so expressly.
57. A. 34, for example, makes no mention of the effects which are to be considered to take place with regard to the debtor's assets situated *outside* the territory of the Contracting States.
58. *cf.* the provisions of A. 6 (1) with A. 7; A. 43 (1) with (2); and see also A. 47 (1). The implications of Arts. 3—5 (on jurisdiction) should also be considered from this aspect (see *infra*).
59. Contrast the ostensible position currently maintained at English law, under the provisions of the Bankruptcy Act 1914, ss. 18 (1) and 167, which purport to create effects in relation to property of every kind situated anywhere in the world. Such extravagant assertions are largely empty rhetoric today: see Fletcher, *op. cit. supra* n. 5, ch. 14, at pp. 375—79.
60. Arts. 3 and 4. The possibility formerly arising under the 1970 version of the Draft, whereby Community-wide effect would have been enjoyed by a bankruptcy opened against a debtor who had neither his centre of administration nor any establishment anywhere within the EEC, has now been excluded from the amended version of A. 5, which declares that such bankruptcies do not fall within the scope of the Convention, and hence enjoy territorial effect only (see *infra*).
61. See Chapter 4 *ante* at pp. 117—20.

62. One possible way of developing the idea advanced in the text might be to create the means by which Community-wide recognition could be accorded to bankruptcies opened in non-Member States whose courts *in fact* had opened proceedings in accordance with jurisdictional principles equivalent to those made mandatory for the Contracting States. If necessary, an additional requirement of reciprocity of recognition between the Community States and the third State could be included. It would then be a relatively simple matter for the Community from time to time to conclude formal agreements with such third States to provide for the recognition and enforcement of each other's judgments.

63. A. 5. *cf.* the previous version of A. 5 (1970 text, references *supra* n. 15), criticised by Fletcher, *loc. cit. supra* n. 17, at pp. 122—24/19—21. See also Cork Report at paras. 119—21, and Note of dissent by Anton, para. 17 (pp. 110—11).

64. A. 9 provides that in relation to deceased debtors, or debtors who die before the court becomes seized of the matter, the jurisdictional criteria of Arts. 3—8 are required to have been fulfilled on the part of the debtor at the date of death.

65. See A. 13 (1).

66. See criticisms of the expression "centre of administration", and of the definition, by Hunter (1972) 21 ICLQ at pp. 686—87, and (1976) 25 ICLQ at pp. 315—19; Fletcher, *loc. cit. supra* n. 17, at pp. 122—23/19—20; Cork Report at paras 103—18, and Note of Reservations by Anton at p. 107. See also Appendix 9 of the Report for proposed alternative definitions, and *cf*, N-L Report at pp. 26—32.

67. *cf.* N-L Report at pp. 26—29.

68. A. 3 (3).

69. *cf.* 1970 version of A. 4, which contained no definition of "establishment", and see the criticisms of Hunter (1976) 25 ICLQ at p. 317; Fletcher, *loc. cit. supra* n. 17, at pp. 121—24/18—21; Cork Report at para. 105, together with Appendix 8 containing alternative definitions; N-L Report at pp. 33—35.

70. See also A. 6 (2), whereby if a first (or subsequent) bankruptcy has been opened against the debtor and has not been closed, a second or subsequent bankruptcy may be opened in the same State even where the grounds of jurisdiction laid down in Arts. 3 and 4 are no longer satisfied in that State, and A. 6 (3), allowing the courts of a State where one of the proceedings listed in A. I (b) of the Protocol has been opened, to substitute any other proceeding referred to in the Convention in the same circumstances, unless in the meantime any court which has acquired jurisdiction under Arts. 3 or 4 has opened a bankruptcy or other proceedings against the debtor.

71. The appellate proceedings which are relevant for this purpose are specified in A. XII of the Protocol.

72. See A. 2, and also A. 58.

73. See the combined effects of Arts. 13, 57 and 58.

74. See Fletcher, *loc. cit. supra* n. 17, at pp. 123—24/20—21.

75. See *loc. cit.* in n. 74 *supra* for further criticisms of this subsidiary rule.

76. See A. 13 (1), (2).

77. The alternative procedure of a reference made under A. 73 by a "competent authority" of a Contracting State seems incapable of resolving the difficulty here envisaged, because A. 73 (2) expressly declares that the Court's ruling in such a case shall not affect the inconsistent judgments which gave rise to the request for interpretation.

78. See It. C.C. A. 2083.

79. While some debtors may contrive to exploit a personal immunity from bankruptcy to some advantage, it should not be forgotten that bankruptcy is also capable of providing a debtor with much-needed relief from pressures of many kinds: such relief is of course denied to persons governed by the laws herein referred to.

80. Failing the existence of any establishment abroad, it would seem that the debtor

could undergo "piecemeal adjudication" in other Member States in accordance with A. 5, provided their local requirements for the opening of proceedings could be met.

81 In order to do so, however, they (and, indeed, any other creditors from other Member States) would be obliged under the "hotchpot" rule to surrender the fruits of any private diligence effected within the debtor's "bankruptcy haven", and to make the proceeds available to the general body of creditors: *cf.* Fletcher, *op. cit. supra* n. 5, at pp. 370—79, Nadelmann (1948) 11 Law and Contemp. Probl. 696, (1952) 1 ICLQ 484.

82. *cf.* principles of English Law discussed in Fletcher, *op. cit. supra* n. 5, at pp. 375—79.

83. See further Chapter 4 *ante* pp. 111—33.

84. A. 12 provides that the liquidator of a company or firm shall claim on behalf of the general body of creditors in the bankruptcy of any person whose liability arises under A. 11.

85. *cf.* Companies Act 1948, ss. 332, 333.

86. A. 67.

87. *cf.* the original provisions of Arts. 10, 11 and 12 in the 1970 Draft, which would have empowered the court of bankruptcy of the company or firm to exercise jurisdiction also to adjudicate the persons concerned, irrespective of where their own centre of administration was situated. (See N-L Report at pp. 40—47; Cork Report at paras. 133—51.)

88. See the full text of A. 15 in Appendix C *post*.

89. *cf.* Judgments Convention, Chapter 4 *ante*, especially in relation to Arts. 2 and 16 of that Convention.

90. *cf.* Cork Report, paras. 155 and 156; Fletcher, *loc. cit. supra* n. 17, at pp. 125—26/22—23.

91. *cf.* Bankruptcy Act 1914, s. 54. See Fletcher, *op. cit. supra* n. 5, at pp. 166—67.

92. See Judgments Convention (Chapter 4 *ante*) Arts. 5 (1), 16 (1). *Cf.* A. 19 of the Bankruptcy Convention.

93. See Bonell, Fletcher and Fontaine, *op. cit. supra* n. 7, *passim*; Dalhuisen, *op. cit. supra* n. 6 vol. I, part II. For a survey of the laws of the original Six Member States, see the relevant sections of the respective works of Ganshof, Van der Gucht, and Trochu, *cit. supra* notes 6 and 9.

94. See Fletcher, *loc. cit. supra* n. 17, at p. 126/23. A more sanguine — indeed, complacent — view of the significance of disparities between the laws of the original Six is to be found in the N-L Report at pp. 63—65; an altogether more disturbing picture — leading to conclusions similar to those drawn in the text above — is painted in the Cork Report at paras. 169—72.

95. Subject to such specific exceptions as arise by virtue of Arts. 10, 65 and 66.

96. See A. 26, *infra*. It should be remembered that the effects embraced by A. 20 will not be operative in any State where the bankruptcy is denied recognition by virtue of either A. 10 or Arts. 65—66.

97. Companies Act 1948, s. 244.

98. Bankruptcy (Scotland) Act 1913, ss. 44, 70. See, however, s. 41.

99. *cf.* Bankruptcy (Scotland) Act 1913, s. 107. The protection of s. 45 of the Bankruptcy Act 1914 is applicable only to payments made *before* the date of the receiving order, and the position of persons who deal with a debtor between that date and the date of gazetting the order of adjudication has not been fully protected by means of s. 4 of the Bankruptcy (Amendment) Act 1926: see Fletcher *op. cit. supra* n. 5, at pp. 201—206.

100. A. 22 (1), (4). See also A. 22 (3) in relation to actions for recovery of movable property which have already commenced.

101. Such acts could consist of the formal initiation of civil proceedings by service of the writ of summons, or the formal exercise of an option to purchase.

102. See *infra*.

103.   A. 26 (2), (3). The relevant Gazettes for all the Member States are listed in A. VII of the Protocol.

104.   For the provisions of Arts. III, IV and VI concerning the United Kingdom (*inter alia*) see Appendix C *post.*

105.   A. 27 (2).

106.   A. 33 (3) also provides for an expeditious hearing before a local court at the *situs* of any property with respect to which the trustee is taking protective measures, or effecting disposal, so that any creditor or third party, or the debtor himself, may raise objection to prevent irreversible steps being taken before the matter can be considered by the court which enjoys substantive jurisdiction.

107.   A. 29 (2), together with the specimen form contained in the Annex to the Protocol.

108.   A. 30, together with A. IX of the Protocol, which establishes a uniform procedure for notification of the postal authorities in the other Contracting States. On the redirection of the bankrupt's letters under the law of England and Wales, see Bankruptcy Act 1914, s. 24.

109.   This form of words suggests that a letter written from Wales in the Welsh language must be considered receivable, since although it is not one of the official languages of the Community, use of the Welsh language is officially sanctioned within certain parts of the United Kingdom.

110.   A. 31.

111.   See *supra* p. 213, and *infra* pp. 234–37, in relation to Arts. 10 (2) and 66.

112.   This provision was included at the behest of the United Kingdom: *cf.* Bankruptcy Act 1914, s. 38 (1).

113.   This provision mainly pertains to the position under German law, whereby after-acquired property is excluded from the effects of bankruptcy (section 1 (1), K.O.).

114.   The list of such items varies under the laws of the different Member States. For English law, see Bankruptcy Act 1914, s. 38 (2), and for comments thereon see Fletcher, *op. cit. supra* n. 5, at pp. 188–89.

115.   For example, under English law the total value of the excluded property in any one case is presently not permitted to exceed £ 250: Bankruptcy Act 1914, s. 38 (2), as amended by Insolvency Act 1976, s. 1 and Schedule I, Part 1.

116.   Sometimes the presumption is applied to property belonging to the wife only (Belgium, Luxembourg); sometimes to that belonging to either spouse (Italy, Netherlands). The Mucian presumption is not applied in French or German law, nor under the laws of any part of the United Kingdom, or Ireland or Denmark. See N-L Report at pp. 84–85; Cork Report, paras. 195–98; Ganshof, *op. cit. supra* n. 6, at pp. 115–19; Trochu, *op. cit. supra* n. 9, at pp. 210–18.

117.   That is, if the spouses' matrimonial property rights are regulated by Belgian or Dutch or Italian or Luxembourg law, property situated in France or Germany will nonetheless be subjected to the Mucian presumption if bankruptcy is opened in any of the four Member States in which that presumption is operative, whether or not that State happens to be the one whose law regulates the spouses' property rights.

118.   A. 35 (1) together with A. 1 of Annex I. This would enable oral evidence to be receivable, and not merely proof by written or notarially-attested evidence, as required (formerly) under French law, and presently still under Dutch law.

119.   It is submitted that the arguments in favour of the prevalence of the *lex concursus* over such questions, advanced, for example, by Trochu, *op. cit.* at pp. 211–18, are excessively influenced by the notion (true for only four of the Member States) that personal bankruptcy is confined to cases of traders (*commerçants*), and seems to ignore altogether the possibility that evolving personal circumstances, over which the other spouse

may have little or no control, may produce the result that bankruptcy (whether of a trader or non-trader) may occur in a jurisdiction other than that by which matrimonial rights were and are regulated.

120. See *supra* pp. 195—97, criteria (ii) and (iii).

121. For the text of A. 2 of Annex I, see Appendix C *post*.

122. See 1970 version of the Draft (refs. *supra* n. 15), Arts. 35, 76 (1), and Annex I, A. 4. The latter provision has altogether disappeared from the Uniform Law in its latest version.

123. One example is the so-called Paulian Action. See N-L Report at pp. 88—97; Cork Report, paras. 333—63. For comparable types of action under the laws of the United Kingdom, see Law of Property Act 1925, ss. 172, 173; Scottish Act Against Fraudulent Alienations of 1621, c. 18.

124. Convention of 19 June 1980, discussed in Chapter 5 *ante*.

125. *cf.* Cork Report, para. 221.

126. See *supra* p. 215 for comment upon certain latent difficulties to which A. 15, as currently expressed, may give rise in practice.

127. See Chapter 5 *ante*. *cf.* N-L Report at pp. 106—109 for justification of the original decision to draft this provision in favour of the application of the *lex concursus*, and see Cork Report, paras. 224—26.

128. Reservation of title clauses are commonly referred to in the United Kingdom as "Romalpa Clauses", after the name of the case in which the validity of such clauses was judicially upheld: *Aluminium Industrie Vaassen B.V.* v. *Romalpa Aluminium Ltd.* [1976] 2 All E.R. 552, [1976] L1. Rep. 443 (C.A.). See also *Borden (U.K.) Ltd.* v. *Scottish Timber Products Ltd.* [1979] 3 All E.R. 961 (C.A.); *Re Bond Worth Ltd.* [1979] 3 All E.R. 919 (Ch. D.). See, in general, Goode (1976) 92 L.Q.R. 401 and 528, esp. at pp. 547—60.

129. This variant is associated with a provision contained in A. 3 of Annex I (Uniform Law), which would require the laws of all Contracting States to recognise the validity of reservation of title clauses, subject to certain, standard conditions: see the text of A. 3, incorporated in the Draft of A. 41 contained in Appendix C *post*.

130. At present, the definition of "proper law" is here to be specially construed as being, in the case of the buyer's bankruptcy, the Contracting State in which the property, which is affected by any reservation of title clause, is situated at the opening of bankruptcy. It is further specified that, in the event of the seller's bankruptcy occurring after delivery of the thing sold, the bankruptcy shall not be a ground for rescinding the contract and shall not prevent the buyer from acquiring ownership of the thing sold: see A. 41 (2), Second Variant, reproduced in Appendix C *post*.

131. See the Comparative Study prepared by Professor M. Sauveplanne, E. Comm. Doc. 8838/IV/63-E (October 1963), which formed the basis for this conclusion reached by the Committee of Experts at an early stage.

132. See N-L Report at pp. 113—28. For a mainly critical appraisal of these provisions, together with much instructive discussion, see Cork Report, Ch. 4 (paras. 244—78). See also Fletcher (1977) 2 E.L.R. at pp. 27—29 (also in Harmonisation (Ed. Lipstein, 1978) at pp. 130—32); Hunter (1972) 21 ICLQ at p. 693, and (1976) 25 ICLQ at pp. 322—24.

133. See, however, the provisions of A. 51 (*infra*) in relation to registered property.

134. A. 44(1). It is presently uncertain whether fiscal and similar debts will be included in the scope of this provision, or whether they will be limited to being satisfied out of the assets situated in the Contracting State in which the debts in question were actually incurred.

135. A. 44 (2). See *infra* for discussion of A. 50. Note also the effects of A. 54, where-

by any extension of time for the payment or compounding of his debts which is accorded to the debtor by virtue of the opening of any analogous procedure listed in A. I (b) of the Protocol is not allowed to enjoy validity, in Contracting States other than the *forum concursus*, against creditors for the debts referred to in A. 44 (2), or against those creditors whose debts are preferential or secured by a charge over property.

136.   A. 44 (3). If it is finally decided to confer upon debts of this kind the advantaged position accorded under A. 44 (1) (see n. 134 *supra*), the words "or after" will be deleted, leaving A. 44 (3) applicable only to debts of this kind which are incurred *before* bankruptcy opens.

137.   *Government of India* v. *Taylor* [1955] A. C. 491.

138.   The same considerations militate against permitting the continuation of the use of prerogative or executive powers of direct recovery which may be exercised even after the opening of bankruptcy by the authorities in certain Member States. The continued use of such methods of privileged self-help is expressly sanctioned by A. 23 in its present form.

139.   A typical example of a widely-respected, preferential claim is one for wages owed to employees of the bankrupt. *cf.* Bankruptcy Act 1914 (as amended), s. 33 (1) (b); Companies Act 1948, s. 319. The present maximum figure allowed to be recovered as a preferential debt by each creditor for wages or salary owed is £ 800 (see Insolvency Act 1976, s. 1 and Schedule 1, Part I).

140.   A. 50 (1), first indent.

141.   If three sub-estates, A, B and C, were involved, each allowing different maximum amounts of, say, £ 800, £ 400 and £ 300, the three estates would contribute in the proportions of 8/15, 4/15 and 3/15, respectively. Thus, if all three estates had sufficient funds, the creditor's £ 800 payment would be composed of (in round figures) amounts of £ 427 (A); £ 213 (B); and £ 160 (C).

142.   A. 50 (1), second indent. Thus, to take the example given in n. 141 *supra*, if estate B contained but £ 100, while the other two estates had assets of £ 2,000 and £ 6,000 respectively, a deficit of £ 113 would emerge from the first "round" representing the amount by which the assets in B fell short of the contribution (£ 213) for which that estate was proportionally liable. On the second "round", that deficit would be made up by further contributions from estates A and C, this time contributing in proportions established as between themselves (i.e. 8/11 : 3/11). Thus, estate A would supply (in round figures) £ 82 and estate C £ 31, totalling £ 113.

143.   For the date of opening, see A. 52, and also A. II of the Protocol, both referred to *supra*, n. 55.

144.   See *infra*.

145.   It is of course foreseeable that in many cases ships might be on the high seas at the date of opening of the bankruptcy, and for some time thereafter. The whereabouts of aircraft at the relevant moment could also be somewhat elusive to determine.

146.   At some point, the nettle must be grasped of declaring that the competitive advantages which are capable of being derived from the use of "flag of convenience" registrations are impermissible in the case of any enterprise whose centre of operations lies within the EEC.

147.   A. 47 (3) declares that the law which is applicable by virtue of A. 47 (1) shall also determine any issue of the relative priority to be accorded to these two classes of rights.

148.   Discussed *supra*.

149.   Arts. 5 and 10 (2) are discussed *supra*, p. 213; A. 66 is discussed *infra*, pp. 234—37.

150.   Therefore, for example, an order for the arrest of a debtor made pursuant to s. 23 of the Bankruptcy Act 1914 would not enjoy full faith and credit by virtue of A. 55.

151.   *cf.* Judgments Convention, A. 26 (Chapter 4 *ante*).

152.   *supra*, pp. 208—11.

153.   See Judgments Convention, as amended (Chapter 4 *ante*) esp. Arts. 31—45.

154.   These grounds are reproduced in full in Appendix C *post*.

155.   A. 62 (2) (b): this ground has already been noted *supra*, p. 211, in relation to jurisdiction. Hence, all challenges to the assumption of jurisdiction in bankruptcy are confined to the *forum concursus*.

156.   A. 62 (2) (d): see further the discussion at p. 213 *supra* concerning the effects of A. 10.

157.   A. 63. The courts so designated are, for England and Wales, the High Court of Justice; for Scotland, the Court of Session; and for Northern Ireland, the High Court of Justice in Northern Ireland: see A. XI of the Protocol. Within the United Kingdom, the jurisdiction of these three courts is the subject of internal arrangements so that only one of them will exercise jurisdiction in any given case, while its resulting decision will take effect throughout the whole of the United Kingdom: A. 63 (2).

158.   A. 64. The petitioning creditor may be joined as a party to the action to challenge the bankruptcy. See also Arts. 68 and 69 for provisions to minimise formalities in relation to the lodging of security for costs, and in relation to the reception of documents, in proceedings brought under A. 61.

159.   See A. 26, discussed *supra*, p. 220, in relation to the requirements for advertisement.

160.   A. 65 (4).

161.   A. 65 (1), (2).

162.   A. 65 (3).

163.   For other exceptions, see Arts. 5 and 10 (2), discussed *supra*, p. 213.

164.   See *supra* p. 234.

165.   See Chapter 4 *ante*.

166.   *cf.* the different procedure formerly specified in the 1970 version of the Draft, and contained in Arts. 61—67 thereof together with A. XI of the Protocol. Since the procedure was essentially the same as that for which the Judgments Convention provides, the economy and neatness of the present provision is to be commended.

167.   See, especially, Arts. 31—45 of the Judgments Convention, described in Chapter 4 *ante* at pp. 133—38.

168.   See A. 70.

169.   *q.v. ante* Chapter 4, pp. 139—41. The general comments made *ibid*, regarding the desirability of enabling references to be made by courts of first instance are, it is submitted, capable of being addressed with equal validity to the case of the Bankruptcy Convention.

170.   A. 71 (c) contains a cross-reference to A. 37 of the Judgments Convention, to provide for the cases governed by A. 67 of the Bankruptcy Convention.

171.   A. 82.

172.   See the 1970 version, refs. given *supra*, n. 15.

173.   *supra*, p. 193.

174.   The Three Articles of the Uniform Law have been discussed in relation to the specific Articles of the Convention upon which they have a significant bearing: see comments *supra* upon Arts. 35, 36 and 41, respectively.

CHAPTER 7

Conventions in the Field of Company Law

A. The Convention of 29 February 1968 on the Mutual Recognition of Companies and Bodies Corporate

1. Preliminary

The Community Convention on the Mutual Recognition of Companies and Bodies Corporate was signed on behalf of the original Six Member States at Brussels on 29 February 1968.[1] It was subsequently ratified by all of its signatories apart from the Netherlands, and in consequence has not yet entered into force. However, as one of the Conventions provided for in A. 220 ECT, the Convention is among those to which the new Member States expressly undertook to accede.[2] Accordingly, but somewhat desultorily, negotiations have taken place with a view to such accession being accomplished, although at the time of writing no clear indication is available of the extent to which these negotiations will effect any changes of substance to the original text of the Convention. The following commentary is therefore based upon the published text of the Convention as originally adopted and signed, and also upon the published text of the Protocol of 3 June 1971 on the Jurisdiction of the Court of Justice, which is similarly not yet in force.[3]

2. Justification for the Convention

The legal justification for the Convention is contained in the third indent to A. 220 ECT, which requires that the Member States enter into negotiations with each other with a view to securing for the benefit of their nationals "the mutual recognition of companies or firms within the meaning of the second paragraph of A. 58, the retention of legal personality in the event of transfer of their seat from one country to another, and the possibility of mergers between companies or firms governed by the laws of different countries".[4] The paragraph of A. 58 ECT referred to supplies the following definition of the two terms "companies or firms" as used in A. 220: " 'companies or firms' means companies or firms constituted under civil or commercial law, including co-operative societies, and other legal persons governed by public or private law, save for those which are non-profit-making".

The incorporation by reference of the definition contained in A. 58 ECT, which forms part of Chapter 2, Title III of Part Two of the Treaty,[5] supplies the clue also to the logical justification for this Convention, since it would be impossible to realise the full requirements of Title III with regard to free movement of persons, services and capital (including the right of establishment, with which Chapter 2 is concerned), unless the Member States' rules of private international law applicable to legal persons first underwent harmonisation. This is because of the fundamental differences of approach which are entertained within the laws of the States in question towards the vital questions of which country's law shall control the creation, continuation of existence, and finally the extinction of companies and other types of legal person. Broadly speaking, on these matters the laws of the Member States fall into two camps, namely the "state of incorporation" theory and the "real seat" theory. According to the former view, a company is considered to have been validly formed provided that its formation took place in accordance with the legal requirements relating to corporate formations which, at the time of the alleged formation, were in force in the country under whose law the company purported to be formed.[6] As a corollary to this proposition, the proponents of the "state of incorporation" theory also maintain that a company, once validly formed under the law of a given country, is thereafter perpetually subject to that country's company law, which is alone capable of supplying the legal basis for the company's continued existence, and which also finally controls the processes by which, if at all, that corporate existence and legal personality shall be terminated and cease to exist. There is, however, no impediment in principle to the free migration of a company's organs of management and operation across frontiers, according to the dictates of policy or expediency. The contrasting position, adopted by the adherents of the "real seat" theory, is one of insistence that a company, at the moment of its formation and also subsequently, must comply with the requirements for incorporation which are in force in the country where the company is *in reality* "domiciled" by virtue of the fact that its principal seat of corporate activity (its "head office" or "*siège réel*", also referred to as "*siège social*") is situated in that country. Thereafter, the maintenance of the company's legal personality is dependent upon its continuing to fulfil the legal requirement imposed by the law of the country where its "real seat" is situated, and a very testing conceptual problem is posed whenever it becomes possible to assert that a company's actual seat of central management has removed from the country in which the company was originally incorporated, to some other place. On the most extreme view, such a migration of its head office would bring about the automatic extinction of the company as a legal creature, and it would be necessary for those concerned in its management to undertake the lengthy — and costly — procedure of formally liquidating the company under the law of its original formation, and thereafter of re-incorporating under the law of its new principal seat. Less drastic formulations of the real seat theory would at any rate require that the company should begin to comply with the company law requirements of the country to which its seat has migrated.[7]

The two theories are not in fact mutually irreconcilable, because a company formed in circumstances which would meet the criteria for recognition imposed by the real seat theory would have no difficulty in gaining recognition from any Court employing the state of incorporation theory. Difficulties arise, however, where a company is formed in circumstances which would still satisfy the adherents of the state of incorporation theory, but which would fail to meet the more restrictive criteria of the 'real seat" school of thought. Further problems would arise wherever a company, even though initially commanding recognition under the respective tests applied by both theories, undergoes a development which results in its principal seat of corporate activity emigrating from the jurisdiction in which it was situated at the date of the company's first formation. According to the tenets of the state of incorporation theory, such a development in no way alters the fact that the company is considered in law to be domiciled in the country under whose laws it was originally incorporated, a fact which is, indeed, held to be immutable. On the other hand, this selfsame development would lead any Court applying the real seat theory to the conclusion that the company's domicile had moved away from the country under whose laws the legal personality of the company was acquired, thereby putting in question the very survival of that legal personality. An added complication, which could in theory arise even as between legal systems of two States, each of which employs the real seat theory, would result from any failure of the Courts of the respective countries to agree upon the whereabouts of the real seat of a given company formed under a given law. If one Court concludes that the company's seat is located at the place of incorporation, while the other Court concludes that it lies in some other jurisdiction, the company will possess a "limping" identity even though the question of its recognition has been referred to the same general theory by both the Courts concerned.

In truth, each of the theories has its own particular merits and con-
comitant disadvantages: the real seat theory is highly effective in preventing
a company from being run in such a way as to avoid (or evade) the application of the company law provisions of the country in which in reality it is
functioning, but on the other hand makes no concessions to the possibility
that a company may over time experience logical and legitimate developments which carry its "centre of gravity" outside the country of first formation. The state of incorporation theory, with its greater flexibility, conveniently allows for such commercial realities to be accommodated, but does
so admittedly at the expense of facilitating the exploitation of the "Delaware syndrome" by those desirous of so doing.

By and large, the countries which adhere to the state of incorporation
theory belong to the Common law world, though with the notable addition,
within the EEC, of the Netherlands.[8] The adherents of the real seat theory
are generally those countries of the continent of Europe (and their juristic
descendants throughout the world) which trace their legal traditions more
directly back to Roman law,[9] and which constituted a majority among the
original Six Member States of the EEC, as indeed they continue to do within
the Community of Ten. It is pertinent to add, however, that A. 58 ECT itself
is evidently composed upon the premises associated with the state of incorporation theory: A. 58(1) states that "companies or firms *formed in accordance with the law of a Member State* and having their registered office,
central administration, or principal place of business *within the Community*
shall, for the purposes of (Arts. 52—58) be treated in the same way as
natural persons who are nationals of Member States".[10] Thus, the bare
essentials which suffice to confer upon legal persons an eligibility to enjoy
the right of free movement analogously to natural persons who are nationals
of any of the Member States are: formation under the law of one of the
Member States, and the maintenance of at least *one* of the three alternative
forms of contact *somewhere* within the EEC, but not necessarily within the
State of incorporation. Indeed, the inclusion of the company's registered
office (*siège statutaire*) as one of the three possible types of sufficient contact is further proof that A. 58(1) is intended to espouse the "state of
incorporation" theory as the basis for the attribution of the right of free
movement. Nor, indeed, could the draughtsmen of the Treaty have proceeded to do otherwise, since the "real seat" theory, on its own terms, is incompatible with the exercise of the right of free movement across traditional
jurisdictional boundaries by legal entities which must, perforce, commence
their existence by undergoing formation under the auspices of a given system
of law. To be sure, the real seat theory has the notable virtue of preventing

one species of "distortion" which, as has been argued already,[11] offends against the fundamental tenets of Community law. But the "Delaware syndrome" can and will be cured, within the EEC at least, in consequence of the completion of the programme of harmonisation of the company laws of the Member States which is already well under way.[12] The inbuilt restrictions of the real seat theory therefore offer no long-term advantages from the aspect of the wider concerns of Community law, but on the other hand they do militate against the realisation of one of the "basic freedoms" of the Common Market, namely the free movement of both legal as well as natural persons. Hence, in framing the provisions of the Convention on Mutual Recognition, the dominant consideration for the participating States was the need to bring about the discontinuation of the use of the real seat theory of recognition, at least in relation to companies formed under the law of any Member State of the EEC and fulfilling any of the contract requirements enumerated in A. 58(1) ECT. Furthermore, in order to obviate the utilisation by certain Member States of "parallel" sets of rules of private international law in relation to the recognition of companies, it was additionally desirable for agreement to have been reached upon a single set of rules to govern recognition of all companies, whether formed inside or outside the EEC, but perhaps containing certain safeguards to prevent the exploitation of many advantages offered by the company laws of non-Member States to companies whose primary destiny and purpose *ab initio* was to function and to compete within the EEC itself. As we shall see, the concluded provisions of the Convention on Mutual Recognition of Companies have succeeded in accomplishing these objectives, albeit with rather more concessions towards the prevailing doctrines of the real seat school of opinion than may have been either necessary or desirable. Indeed, the extent to which the final text is so evidently the result of a considerable exercise in the art of compromise may be in no small part responsible for the fact that the Convention has still not received the essential sixth ratification — significantly that of the Netherlands, which alone of the original Six had developed a preference for the state of incorporation theory — and so has still not entered into force despite the lapse of more than thirteen years since the date on which it was originally signed.

3. Commentary

The Convention was prepared by a Committee of Experts under the chairmanship of Professor Berthold Goldman, who was also the author of the explanatory Report published at the time of the original signing of the Convention in 1968. [13] The Committee's work was conducted between 1962 and 1968, and resulted in a text containing only 19 Articles together with a Protocol containing three Joint Declarations. The Convention is solely concerned with the juridical question of the recognition of companies and other bodies corporate as validly-formed, legal persons. The other matters specifically mentioned in A. 220(3) ECT, which also bear closely upon the exercise of the rights of free movement and establishment by legal persons within the EEC, namely the question of the retention of legal personality in the event of transfer of the corporate seat from one country to another, and the question of international mergers between companies, were both omitted from the provisions of this Convention and left to become the subject-matter of two further projected Conventions. [14] The Preamble to the Convention confirms that it has been concluded by the High Contracting Parties to the Treaty establishing the EEC in implementation of the provision of A. 220 ECT, and further proclaims the conviction that the mutual recognition of companies or firms within the meaning of A. 58(2) ECT should be as liberal as possible, without prejudice to the application to companies of the other provisions of the Treaty. This open espousal of a liberal policy of recognition not only signifies that the Convention is the product of a victory for the state of incorporation theory over the real seat theory, but also furnishes in a more general way the watchword which should inspire those to whom it subsequently falls to interpret and apply its provisions.

(a) Scope of the Convention

The title of the Convention indicates that its subject-matter is the mutual recognition of "companies and bodies corporate", but it is necessary to examine the provisions of the Convention with some care in order to discover precisely which kinds of company and other bodies corporate actually fall within its scope and thus may qualify for recognition as of right throughout the EEC. [15] The first indication of the scope of the Convention *ratione personae* is contained in A. 1, which states that recognition is to be accorded to "companies under civil or commercial law, including co-operative societies, established in accordance with the law of a Contracting State which grants them the capacity of persons having rights and duties, and having their statutory registered office in the territories to which the present Convention applies". Here at once we may notice two significant points of divergence between this definition and the terms of A. 58(1) ECT[16] which purport to designate the entities which are to enjoy the rights of free movement and establishment under Community law. On the one hand, the latter provision offers two additional factors of territorial contact with the EEC as alternatives to the location of the company's statutory registered office within the Community, namely the maintenance of the company's central administration or of its principal place of business within the Community, while, on the other hand, A. 58(1) makes no mention of any requirement that the law of the Member State under which the company is incorporated must grant to the company the capacity of a person having rights and duties. These discrepancies are explicable on account of the policy-shift in favour of the state of incorporation theory of recognition which effectively becomes the basic approach required of the courts of all Member States: the earlier draftsmen who were responsible for devising the terms of the Treaty establishing the EEC presumably did not wish to pre-judge this question, and hence framed the ambivalent provisions of A. 58 in such a way as to accommodate the essential requirements of both rival philosophies within a single paragraph. On the other hand, there is a further, notable omission from A. 1 of the Convention when considered against the basic definition of "companies or firms" supplied by A. 58(2) ECT,[17] since the latter provision concludes with the words "save for those which are non-profit-making", an exception omitted from the terms of A. 1. It therefore appears to be the case that any type of company under civil or commercial law, including a co-operative society, which fulfils the "contact" requirements imposed by A. 1 will fall within the ambit of the Convention whether or not it has a profit-making objective.[18] The profit-making objective does however enter into the provisions of A. 2, which has the effect of further extending the scope of the Convention *ratione personae*. This it does by creating an otherwise broadly-defined, additional category of corporate entities whose legal personality is also required to be recognised as of right. A. 2 refers to "Bodies corporate under public or private law, other than the companies specified under A. 1, which fulfil the conditions stipulated in the said Article", and hence complements the phrase employed in A. 58(2) ECT, which refers to "other legal persons governed by public or private law". This time, however, the restrictive terms of the final phrase of A. 58(2) ECT, excluding non-profit-making entities from enjoying the rights otherwise conferred upon companies and firms, are fully respected and incorporated into the substance of A. 2, which stipulates that recognition shall be confined to these bodies corporate which, in addition to the fact that they meet the "contact requirements" imposed by A. 1, "have as their main or accessory object an economic activity normally exercised for reward, or which, without infringing the law under which they are established, do in fact continuously exercise such activity". Conse-

quently, the remunerated economic activity may be the principal, or merely an incidental, object of the company as formed, or alternatively it may be
an activity which the company simply engages in on a continuous basis
subsequently to its formation, provided that in the latter case such business
activities do not in fact infringe the law under which the company was
established. It is furthermore interesting that the mode of drafting employed
in A. 2 ensures that all such companies will enjoy recognition as of right
provided that the activity in which they engage constitutes a "business activity" in the sense that it is "an economic activity normally exercised for
reward", [19] irrespective of whether the company itself does actually operate
profitably either in relation to its business activities or overall. Among the
primary beneficiaries of the basis of recognition supplied by A. 2 will be
those nationalised companies which engage in any form of business activity.

A further, important refinement is imparted to the combined effects of
Arts. 1 and 2 by the provision in A. 8 that the capacity, rights and powers of
a company recognised by virtue of the present Convention may not be
denied or restricted for the *sole* reason that the law in accordance with
which it was established does not grant it the legal status of a body corporate. [20] Therefore, all that is necessary in order that a company may
become entitled to recognition under the Convention is that the law under
which it is formed should grant it, in the words of A. 1, the capacity of a
person having rights and duties. On this basis, a number of entities which do
not enjoy a fully separate legal *persona* — such as partnerships formed under
English law — will nevertheless command recognition throughout the EEC
by virtue of the fact that, in some sense, they may hold assets and incur
liabilities, and may sue and be sued in their own name, as distinct from their
members. [21] Two specific types of body are indeed made the subject of a
special Joint Declaration in the Protocol to the Convention, which expressly
states that A. 1 shall apply to the *società semplice* in Italian law and to the
vennootschap onder firma in Dutch law. [22]

Finally, it may be noted that the provisions of Arts. 1 and 2 produce the
result that any company which purports to have been formed under the law
of a non-Member State of the EEC, or one whose statutory registered office is
located outside the territories to which the Convention applies, will fall
outside the scope of the Convention *ratione personae*, regardless of whether
its principal (or "real") seat of administration or any place of business is
situated inside or outside the Community.

The scope of the Convention *ratione loci* is expressed by A. 12, which
states that the Convention shall apply to the European territories of the
Contracting States, to the French overseas *Départements*, and to the French

overseas territories. There is also an optional facility whereby any Contracting State may by declaration cause the Convention to be extended in its application to any country or countries, or to the territory or territories specifically indicated within the declaration, whose international relations it governs. This Article is noticeably more succinct in its wording than are the equivalent provisions in the other Community Conventions whose texts have been more recently concluded or revised, [23] and hence some expansion of A. 12 may be envisaged, to take account of the precise legal arrangements which the new Member States of the EEC in particular are likely to regard as essential.

The scope of the Convention *ratione temporis* is a matter of no little interest. A. 14 effectively provides that the Convention itself shall not come into force until the process of ratification, as required by A. 13, has been completed by all of the signatory States, and even then only on the first day of the third month following the deposit with the Secretary-General of the Council of the European Communities of the instrument of ratification by the last signatory State to complete this formality. When the Convention actually does come into force, A. 17 declares it to be concluded for an indefinite period. But nowhere in the Convention does there appear any provision limiting the effectiveness of the Convention, once it has finally entered into force, either forwards of backwards in time from the moment in question. It is submitted that the most liberal construction of the Convention would also be the most logical and appropriate one in the circumstances, and hence it is suggested that recognition should be accorded to any company which satisfies the criteria for recognition laid down in the Convention, irrespective of when the company in question was originally formed. Indeed, since in many of the Member States there are companies whose uninterrupted legal existence commenced well over a century ago, it would be frankly absurd if it were to be insisted that such companies, together of course with many others which happen to have been formed at any time up until the very day on which the Convention at last enters into effect, were to be obliged to undergo re-incorporation purely for the purpose of ensuring that the automatic effects of this Convention become applicable to them.

(b) Recognition and its Effects

The material words of both A. 1 and A. 2 declare than any company or body corporate which falls within the scope of the Convention *ratione personae* "shall be recognised as of right". Consequently, no procedure or formality (such as registration, or an application to the authorities of the country concerned for some sort of confirmatory declaration) is required as a precondition to the according of full recognition of the legal personality, capacity, rights and powers of any company which qualifies for recognition under the terms of the Convention. A. 6 imparts a specific dimension to the effects of recognition by stating that (subject to the application of A. 4)[24] all companies or bodies corporate recognised by virtue of the Convention shall have the capacity accorded to them by the law under which they were established. Thus, a uniform conflicts rule is introduced with the effect of submitting the question of the precise legal capacity of a company to the law of its state of incorporation, which also happens to be the law which is selected to determine the very validity of that formation. The broad terms of A. 6 must, however, be set alongside those of A. 7,[25] but it is important to emphasize that, whatever inroads into the final *quantum* of the company's capacities, rights and powers may be sanctioned by this latter provision, it does, at any rate, serve to establish an irreducible minimum notion of the capacity which any company is to enjoy in law, namely the capacity to hold assets, to enter into contracts, and to engage in litigation and to accomplish other legal acts.[26]

(c) Limitations and Exceptions to Recognition

The foregoing description of the effects of the Convention must be read in the light of the important and substantial exceptions and limitations established by Arts. 3, 4, 7 and 9 (together with Arts. 5 and 10). These provisions, either in combination or singly, will seriously denude the *corpus* of rights and capacities accorded to some companies under the law of some of the Contracting States, and in the case of certain companies will lead to a denial of their corporate personality under the laws of certain of the States concerned.

Perhaps the mildest of the limiting provisions is that contained in A. 7, which is permissive in nature. It allows any State in which recognition is sought to refuse to accord to the company or body corporate in question any rights or powers specified which it does not grant to entities of a similar type which are governed by its own laws. This "subtractive" facility is, as has already been mentioned, subject to a proviso that the exercise of this power may not result in the withdrawal from any company or body corporate of the minimum capacity, as a person having rights and duties, to hold assets, enter into contracts, or to accomplish other legal acts including the capacity to sue or be sued. The second paragraph of A. 7 also contains the important, additional provision that any restriction visited upon companies or bodies corporate by virtue of A. 7 may not be invoked by the entities themselves. This rule, whereby a company is estopped from pleading its own want of capacity incurred by virtue of A. 7, is essential to preclude the possibility of a form of *ultra vires* defence becoming available to the company.[27] For example, a company which had engaged in banking or insurance activities in a country in which it was not incorporated might otherwise seek to plead that, by the law of the country in question, it lacked the legal capacity to engage in such business. Although A. 7(2) denies the company in such circumstances any means of avoiding liability for its actions, the reverse would not necessarily be true in any case in which the company attempted to sue another party in respect of liabilities arising from actions which, by virtue of A. 7, the company lacked the capacity to perform under the law of the State in question. The defendant should, in principle, be entitled to invoke the company's want of capacity incurred in this manner, and thereby resist the enforcement of any liability alleged to have been incurred towards the company.

A potentially more far-reaching encroachment upon the application of the Convention in specific cases is constituted by A. 9, which introduces the concept of public policy as a ground upon which each Contracting State may refuse to accord the recognition to which a given company would ostensibly be entitled by virtue of the fact that in other respects its circumstances conform to the criteria already described. The drafting of this provision must be studied with some care, however, and it should be noted that A. 9 permits such waiver by a Contracting State only when the company or body corporate invoking the Convention contravenes by its object, its purpose or the activity which it actually exercises the principles or rules which the Contracting State in question considers as being a matter of public policy *as defined in private international law* (emphasis added). Thus, the waiver by a Contracting State must always be directed at a specific company on account of its intrinsic attributes or activities, and may never be invoked merely on account of the form or origin of the company. Moreover, as is shown by the words to which emphasis has been added above, the concept of public policy which is permitted to be invoked is not the internal policy of the State concerned (*ordre public interne*), but the more generalised concept of public policy as understood by private international law (*ordre public international*). This "universal and immutable"[28] standard of scrutiny seems especially apt to undergo interpretation by the European Court of Justice in due course. At any rate, it should not be lightly or easily invoked by Member States as a gound for refusal of recognition, but should be reserved for genuine cases where a company is discovered to be in serious violation of fundamental international standards of propriety in relation to corporate activity or behaviour. However, it is evident that, where this ground is legitimately invoked by any Contracting State, the net result will, or may, be the denial of recognition of its juridical personality to the entity in question by the State concerned.

Two further matters should be noted in relation to the exception based upon public policy. The first is that, by A. 9(2), no Contracting State may consider the norms of public policy to have been violated by a company for the sole reason that the company is a "single proprietorship" (the so-called "one-man company") provided that the company may be validly formed as such under the law of the state of its incorporation. [29] Secondly, A. 10 expressly provides that principles or rules contrary to the provisions of the Treaty establishing the EEC may not be deemed a matter of public policy within the meaning of A. 9. Thus, once again, the notion of *ordre public Communautaire* asserts its characteristic, paramount authority. [30]

The third, and by far the most extensive and regrettable, group of provisions derogating from the general effects of the Convention are those contained in Arts. 3 and 4. These two Articles together constitute a major concession to the position hitherto maintained by those who subscribe to the real seat theory. Both Articles afford to any State which becomes a Contracting Party to this Convention the facility of lodging a declaration either at the time of depositing its instrument of ratification or before, [31] to the effect that it will not apply the Convention, or will only do so in a modified form, in each of two separate, and carefully defined, situations.

The first such situation, specified in A. 3, is where a company or body corporate which otherwise fulfils the requirements of A. 1 or A. 2 [32] has its real registered office (its *siège réel*) outside the territories to which the Convention applies, and furthermore has no genuine link with the economy of at least one of the said territories. Under such circumstances, a State lodging a declaration under A. 3 may refuse to apply the Convention *in toto*, and hence recognition may be refused to such bodies by States which continue to adhere to the real seat theory. The Convention supplies no definition of what constitutes a "genuine link", nor does it establish any criteria whereby the existence of such links, or their "genuineness", are to be ascertained. This in itself is unsatisfactory, but worse still is the prospect that companies originally formed within the EEC, but whose natural growth subsequently leads to a translation of their central seat of administration into a non-Member State of the EEC, may suddenly discover that their legal personality has become cancelled in the eyes of several Member States' laws.

The second situation arises where a company or body corporate which fulfils the requirements of A. 1 or A. 2 has its real registered office (its *siège réel*) in the territory of a Contracting State which has lodged a separate declaration pursuant to the terms of A. 4. By virtue of such a declaration, the Contracting State in question may proclaim its intention to apply any provisions of its own legislation which it deems essential to any corporate entity whose real seat lies within its jurisdiction, even though the entity in question has been established in accordance with the law of another Contracting State. Thus, the "mandatory rules" (*lois impératives*) of the country in which the real seat is located may be applied pursuant to a declaration lodged, at the latest, at the time of ratification of the Convention. [33] The second paragraph of A. 4 further provides that the suppletory, or directory, provisions (*lois supplétives*) of the legislation of the State making the declaration may also be applied to companies affected by the terms of A. 4, but in only one of two specifically-defined cases. These are: either (i) if the memorandum and articles of association so permit, if necessary by an express general reference to the law in accordance with which the company or body corporate has been established; or (ii) if, the memorandum and articles of association so permitting, the company or body corporate fails to show that it has actually exercised its activity for a reasonable time in the Contracting State in accordance with the law under which it was established. [34]

In view of the significance of the expression "real registered office" in the context of Arts. 3 and 4, it should be noted that A. 5 ventures to define this as meaning "the place where the company's central administration is established". Presumably, the invocation of A. 3 or A. 4 (according to the circumstances) will be triggered by a finding by some court of the State in which the real seat is alleged to be located that it is indeed located within that jurisdiction. Presumably, also, the court will base such a finding upon the application of the standards and techniques with which it is accustomed to work when dealing with such questions. This surely lays the way open to considerable unevenness of practice in relation to the discovery of the "true" whereabouts of the company's real seat, even as A. 5 attempts to define it. The complex and sophisticated techniques of modern corporate management threaten to expose the gaucheness of the somewhat rudimentary notion of the "real seat" of the company. For example, the use of telecommunications facilities between the individuals involved in the administration of a company may impart such a degree of fluidity and flexibility to their activities that the only possible conclusion may be that the "centre of administration" is dispersed among several countries (which would seem a contradiction in terms), or alternatively that it exists at no single identifiable place (which would be equally stultifying). Faced with such possibilities, there must be a genuine likelihood that on some occasions the courts of more than one Contracting State will each solemnly conclude that the real seat of a given company lies within their own jurisdiction, and will accordingly proceed to attempt to apply the provisions of A. 3 or A. 4 (as the case may be) simultaneously, with unfortunate, and possibly damaging results.[35] While it is necessary to admit that it may be reasonable for any State to seek to take steps to prevent companies which are primarily engaged in operating within their jurisdiction from exploiting the possibilities of out-of-State incorporation so as to evade those provisions of domestic company law which may impose a competitive disadvantage upon domestically-formed companies, the application of such measures to companies formed under the law of sister-States of the EEC surely contradicts and offends against the fundamental notion of a Common Market. On the other hand, the practical force of A. 4 at least may be expected to dwindle over time, as the harmonisation of the Member States' company laws by means of Community Directives[36] becomes progressively more of an accomplished reality.

Finally, it may be noted that A. 15(2) permits the withdrawal of any declaration, formally lodged pursuant to A. 3 or A. 4, to be effected by any of the Contracting States at any time. One hopes that in due course those States which originally availed themselves of this facility in the Convention will see fit to renounce the instruments by which they did so.

4. Conflicts of Conventions

The purpose of A. 11 is to avert any possibility that conflict between the provisions of the present Convention and those of any other Conventions to which the Contracting States are or may become parties give rise to uncertainties prejudicial to the interests of the companies and bodies corporate for whose benefit the Conventions have supposedly been concluded. The primary thrust of A. 11(1) is to the effect that the present Convention shall apply notwithstanding any conflicting provisions concerning the recognition of companies or bodies corporate contained in other Conventions.[37] However, this proper insistence upon the prevalence of the Community-based regime for recognition should not be allowed to impede the introduction of more liberal arrangements for according recognition of the juridical personality of companies or other bodies corporate. Accordingly, A. 11(2) adds the proviso that any rules of municipal law, or any provisions of international Conventions, which either are or will be in force and which provide for recognition in other cases or with wider effects shall not be precluded from operating, provided that such recognition or effects are compatible with the Treaty establishing the EEC. Thus, the present Convention is to be seen as creating *minimum* standards and conditions for the according of recognition, and does not hinder the conclusion of more favourable provisions. Conversely, if the exemptions to the according of recognition which are presently contained within the Convention should themselves become the object of new arrangements which effectively restrict their scope, these latter arrangements should prevail over the original terms of the Convention because their effect will be to liberalise the practice of recognition in fidelity to the primary spirit and policy of the Convention, as described above. [38]

It may further be noted that, while A. 17 declares the Convention to be concluded for an indefinite period, A. 18 provides for the convening of a revision conference at the request of any Contracting State at any future time. Such a conference could certainly be convened whenever serious apprehensions arise concerning the compatibility of the Convention with emerging or developed practices in the realm of corporate activity and the law relating thereto.

5. Interpretation by the Court of Justice

The Protocol on Interpretation by the Court of Justice, concluded in response to the statement of intention contained in Joint Declaration No. 3 to the Convention as originally signed, was opened for signature at Luxembourg on 3 June 1971. [39] As with the Convention to which it relates, the Protocol has so far been ratified by only five of the original six signatories and so has not yet come into force. Its terms have a certain interest, however, when compared with the equivalent provisions of other, subsequently-concluded Community Conventions, particularly those of the Judgments Convention of 27 September 1968. [40] Although the Protocols to the two Conventions of 1968 were both signed on the same day, 3 June 1971, a comparison between their texts reveals several striking discrepancies, both in substance and in philosophy. In particular, the Protocol to the Convention on Mutual Recognition of Companies is much more closely modelled on the provisions of A. 177 ECT, to the extent that by A. 2 a full, discretionary jurisdiction to refer questions for interpretation by the European Court of Justice is conferred upon "any court or tribunal of the Contracting States" before which is raised a question relating to the interpretation of the Convention and the present Protocol itself, and upon which the Court in question considers that a decision is necessary to enable it to give judgment. Thus, unlike the other

Community Conventions negotiated to date, no attempt is made to confine the power of reference to the appellate courts of the Contracting States. Similarly, and again in close imitation of the wording of A. 177 ECT, A. 2(2) of the Protocol imposes upon any national court of final resort before which such interpretative questions are raised, the binding obligation to refer the question to the European Court of Justice for a preliminary ruling. Conversely, there is no provision in this Protocol for a reference to the Court of Justice to be requested "in the interests of the law" by any specified public officials of the Member States. [41] It will be interesting to see to what extent the foregoing provisions are modified, if at all, in consequence of the negotiations currently in hand to enable the new Member States of the Community to accede to the Convention and Protocol. It is submitted that the substance of the original text should not be altered, because it is in fact more appropriate than that of the versions subsequently adopted in respect of the other Community Conventions.

B.   Draft Convention on Company Mergers

In response to the reference in A. 220(3) ECT to the problems engendered by international mergers between companies, a Convention has been in preparation since 1965 to make provision for the possibility of mergers between companies or firms governed by the laws of different countries. A Draft of this Convention was submitted to the Council of Ministers of the EEC by the Commission on 29 June 1973. [42] In view of the current uncertainty concerning prospects of progress towards a finalisation of this project, the status of the published draft text remains unclear. Consequently, it has not been thought worthwhile at the present time to engage in a detailed analysis of the published provisions. Suffice it to say that A. 1 of the Draft forges a connection with the Convention on Mutual Recognition of Companies by specifying that the later Convention shall only apply in cases of mergers between companies which are accorded recognition by the Contracting States by virtue of the Convention of 1968. Moreover, A. 2 would further refine the scope of the Convention by limiting its application to mergers between companies belonging to the category of "public, joint stock, limited liability companies". [43] By A. 3, a functional distinction is drawn between two forms of merger, namely merger by acquisition of one (or several) company or companies by another (covered in detail within Arts. 4—40 of the Draft); and merger by formation of a new company (covered by Arts. 41—52). Among the final provisions, Arts. 57—60 notably create a procedure for references to be made to the European Court of Justice for interpretation of the Convention, along the by-now familiar lines. [44]

C Projected Convention on International Transfer of the Company's Principal Office

Again in response to the requirements of A. 220(3) ECT, a projected Convention has been in contemplation since 1960 to make arrangements for "the retention of legal personality in the event of the transfer of (the company's) seat from one country to another". [45] This conceptual difficulty presents itself in its fullest form only in the imagination of those who subscribe to the "real seat" theory of recognition of corporate identity and capacity, [46] and it may well be that this project has been allotted a low order of priority in view of the fact that in the Convention on Mutual Recognition of Companies, the "state of incorporation" theory has emerged as the preferred, primary approach to be adopted by the Member States. It is also true that with the progressive harmonisation of the company law of the EEC, the "conflicts" between the supposedly-applicable national company laws will largely be converted into "false" ones. In due course, therefore, the actual need for the completion of this further project may disappear, or it may become, at most, a convention to furnish safeguards against the evasion of any significant rules of domestic company law which happen to remain unharmonised.

NOTES

1. For the text, see Appendix D *post*. The text is also published in E.C. Bull. Supp. 2/1969; in Encyclopaedia of European Community Law Vol. B.II, Bll—036; in E. Stein, Harmonisation of European Company Laws (1971), Annex II; in A. Campbell (Ed.), Common Market Law (1973), vol. 3, ch. 9, Annex 2 (p. 522); and in C. Schmitthof, European Company Law Texts (1974) at p. 273. (Note: of the English translations just cited, apart from those contained in the works by Stein and Campbell, an important mistranslation occurs in A. 2, where the words "and which" are wrongly supplied instead of "or which", to translate the French "ou". For the French version of the text, see (1968) RTDE at p. 400.

2. See A. 3(2) of the Act of Accession of 22 January 1972, and A. 3(2) of the Act of Accession of 28 May 1979.

3. For the text of the Protocol, see Appendix D *post*. The text is also published in E.C. Bull. Supp. 7/1971; in Encyclopaedia of European Community Law, Vol. B.II,

Bll-077; in Stein, *op. cit. supra* n. 1, at Annex II; and in Schmitthof, *op. cit. supra* n. 1, at p. 279.

For published comments on the Convention and Protocol, see Stein, *op. cit.* at pp. 394—424; B. Goldman, European Commercial Law (1973), paras. 853—67 (see also paras. 136—69); K. Lipstein, The Law of the EEC (1974) at pp. 148—51; Goldsmith, in A. Campbell (Ed.) Common Market Law (1973), vol. 3, ch. 9, at pp. 473—76; Goldman (1968) RTDE 400, (1968—69) 6 CML Rev. 104, (1967) 31 Rabels Z. 201; Dieu (1968) 4 CDE 532; Cerexhe (1968) Rev. M.C. 578; Houin (1968) RTDE 131; Drobnig (1966) 129 ZHR 93; Fikentscher and Grossfeld (1964—65) 2 CML Rev. 259; Grossfeld (1967) 31 Rabels Z. 1; Scholten (1966—67) 4 CML Rev. 377; Beitzke (1968) 14 BBAWD 91, (1964) ZHR 127; Morse [1972] JBL 195; Loussouarn (1974) Rev. Crit. D.I.P. 248; Diephuis (1980) 27 NILR 347; Timmermans (1980) 27 NILR 357. See also C. Schmitthof (Ed.), Harmonisation of European Company Law (1973), *passim.*

4. The projects for conventions to provide in a more detailed way for the transfer of the corporate seat and for transnational mergers are discussed in Sections B and C *infra.*

5. Part II, Title III ECT, comprising Arts. 48—73 inclusive, is concerned with the rights of free movement of persons, services and capital.

6. For the position under English Law, see A. Farnsworth, The Residence and Domicile of Corporations (1939); Dicey and Morris, The Conflict of Laws (10th edn. 1980), rules 136—39 and commentary thereto: Cheshire and North, Private International Law (10th edn. 1979) at pp. 188—92, and 620—26; M. Wolff, Private International Law (2nd edn. 1950), ch. XXI.

7. *cf.* the celebrated Belgian case of *Lamot* v. *Société "Lamot" Ltd.'*, Cass. Nov. 12, 1965; Pa. 1966 I. 366; comments in (1967) Rev. Crit. D.I.P. 506 (Loussouarn) and in (1967) Clunet 140, also discussed by Conard in C. Schmitthof (Ed.), Harmonisation of European Community Laws (1973), p. 45 at p. 57.

8. Law of 25 July 1959, Official Gazette 1959, at p. 256.

9. See E. Rabel, The Conflict of Laws, a Comparative Study (2nd edn. 1960), vol. 2, p. 27 *et seq.*, esp. pp. 125—172. The following Member States currently adhere to the "real seat" theory: Belgium, Denmark, France, Germany, Greece, Italy, Luxembourg.

10. Emphasis has been added in each case to draw attention to the revealing use of language in this text. *cf.* Institute of International Law, Rules adopted 10 September 1965 and recommended for adoption by States "in order to resolve the conflicts of law with regard to companies formed *under* municipal law", (1965) 51 II, Institut de Droit International, A. 1: "A company is governed by the law *under which* it has been incorporated." (Text also in (1966) 60 A.J.I.L. 523; for commentary see Drucker (1968) 17 ICLQ 28.) See also the Hague Convention of 1 June 1956 Concerning the Recognition of the Legal Personality of Companies, A. 1: "The legal personality acquired by a company, association or foundation by virtue of the law of the Contracting State where the formalities of registration or of publicity have been fulfilled, and where its statutory seat is situated, shall be automatically recognised in the other Contracting States." (This Convention has not yet entered into force.)

11. See Chapter 2 *ante* at pp. 45—56.

12. For this programme of Directives, based upon A. 54(3)(g) ECT, see Ficker in Schmitthof, *op. cit. supra* n. 7, at pp. 66—72; Stein, *op. cit. supra* n. 1, chapters 5—8 and annex I; Schmitthof, European Company Law Texts (1974); D. Lasok, The Law of the Economy of the European Communities (1980) at pp. 401—409. For the collected texts of the Directives, as and when enacted, see Encyclopaedia of European Community Law, vol. CII, part C3.

13. See Goldman (1968) RTDE 400 (Text in French) and 405 (Report). See also Beitzke (1964) 1 ZHR 127.

14. These two projects currently remain in draft form, and are discussed in Sections B and C *infra*.

15. See A. 14 *infra* for the indication that the Convention's coming into force is conditional upon its receiving ratification by all the Member States.

16. The text of this provision is quoted in full on p. 254 *supra*.

17. The text of this provision is quoted in full on p. 252 *supra*.

18. *cf.* Goldman, *European Commercial Law* (1973), para. 055, where it is argued that *in fact* the Convention entertains such a widely-defined notion of "profit-making object" that any entity with the legal form of a company necessarily has a profit-making object for this purpose.

19. *cf.* A. 60 ECT, which speaks of "services ... normally provided for remuneration," and which appears to have furnished the inspiration for the wording employed in the Convention. See Goldman (1968–69) 6 CML Rev. at p. 115, and in (1968) RTDE at pp. 409–411.

20. Emphasis added. It is not clear whether this reason, taken in combination with some other reasons, may become sufficient for denial of recognition, or whether it is intended that some further reason must be found which is sufficient in itself for denial of recognition to a company which, as it happens, is not accorded the legal status of a body corporate by the law under which it was formed. See also A. 9(2) *infra*, which precludes the use of the "public policy" exception to recognition against "one-man companies" which are validly formed under the law of the State of their incorporation.

21. Other examples at English law could be joint tenancies and tenancies in common (suggested by Lipstein, *op. cit. supra* n. 3, at p. 149) and "special register" trade unions, as defined by the Trade Union and Labour Relations Act, 1974, s. 30. In other Member States, the French société civile (C.C. Arts. 1832–1873, and société en participation (C. de Comm. Arts. 42–45) and Groupement d'Intérêt Economique (Ord. 67–821, 23 September 1967), and the German Gesellschaft des bürgerlichen Rechts (B.G.B. ss. 705–740), the offene Handelsgesellschaft, the Kommanditgesellschaft, and the Stille Gesellschaft (H.G.B. ss. 105–60, 161–77 and 335–42, respectively) would all seem to qualify.

22. Joint Declaration No. 1.

23. *cf.* A. 60 of the Judgments Convention (as amended), A. 27 of the Contracts Convention, and A. 79 of the Draft Bankruptcy Convention, discussed *ante* in Chapters 4, 5 and 6, respectively.

24. *q.v. infra*, next section.

25. Further discussed *infra*, next Section.

26. A. 7(1), second sentence.

27. *cf.* the provisions of the First Directive on harmonisation of company law, Dir. 68/151 EEC, O.J. 1968 L65/8 (O.J. Sp. Ed. 1968 I, 41), Arts. 7–9 of which have the general effect of eliminating the doctrine of *ultra vires*, as traditionally understood and applied, from the company laws of the Member States. (See, however, the European Communities Act 1972, s. 9, and comments thereon by Prentice (1973) 89 LQR 518 at pp. 523–30, to the effect that the steps so far taken to incorporate the provisions of the First Directive into English Law have not been fully satisfactory. See also Wyatt (1978) 94 LQR 182.)

28. *cf.* M. Wolff, *op. cit. supra* n. 6, § 159.

29. For example, under Belgian law hitherto, a foreign "one-man company", though permitted to be formed in its country of origin, has been considered to be contrary to public policy: Cass. 5 January 1911, Clunet 1912, 912.

30. See Lipstein, *op. cit. supra* n. 3, at p. 151, for criticism of the mode of drafting employed in A. 10.

31. See A. 15.
32. Discussed *supra*.
33. All of those five Member States which have ratified the Convention so far, have availed themselves of the facility to lodge declarations under Arts. 3 and 4.
34. See Stein, *op. cit. supra* n. 1, at pp. 409—12; Goldman (1968) RTDE at p. 413.
35. For other criticisms of the provisions in Arts. 3 and 4, see Goldman (1968—69) 6 CML Rev. at pp. 120—26.
36. See references *supra*, notes 12 and 27.
37. Such as the Hague Convention of 1 June 1956 concerning the recognition of the legal personality of companies, associations and foundations. This convention is not yet in force, but it has been ratified by Belgium, France and the Netherlands, and signed by Luxembourg and Spain. Important differences exist between the provisions of this Convention and those of the Community Convention under discussion in the present Chapter, e.g. in relation to the extent to which the adherents of the "real seat" theory are allowed to refuse to accord recognition to a company whose real seat is situated outside the State under whose law it has been incorporated: see A. 2 of the Hague Convention.
38. *cf.* Goldman (1968) RTDE at p. 419, to the same effect.
39. For references, see *supra* n. 3.
40. See the Protocol of 3 June 1971 on the Interpretation of the Judgments Convention, discussed in Chapter 4 *ante*, and the provisions of Arts. 70—74 of the Bankruptcy Convention (*ante*, Chapter 6). It is expected that the Contracts Convention (*ante*, Chapter 5) will eventually be accompanied by a Protocol drafted along similar lines.
41. *cf.* Protocol on the Interpretation of the Judgments Convention, A. 4.
42. E.C. Bull. Supp. 13/1973, together with Report thereon by Professor Goldman at pp. 31—123, Parliamentary Question (European Parliament) No. 8/71, J.O. 1971 C50/10. For comment on the Draft, see Goldsmith in Campbell, Common Market Law, Supplement (1975), ch. 9 at pp. 483—91; Stein, *op. cit. supra* n. 1, at pp. 364—94. See also Conard (1966) 14 AJCL 573; Beitzke in Probleme des Europäischen Rechts (Festschrift Hallstein, 1966) at p. 14. On the question of the imposition of a Community law regime to control mergers and concentrations within the EEC, see Draft Regulation under A. 235 ECT, submitted to Council by Commission on 20 July 1973, OJ. 1973 C92/1 (31 October 1973), note, Van Kraay (1977) 26 ICLQ 468.
43. Specifically the Société Anonyme (France, Belgium, Luxembourg), the Aktiengesellschaft (Germany), the Naamloze Vennootschap (Netherlands) and the Società per Azioni (Italy). Presumably the Public Limited Company under the company laws of the United Kingdom and the Republic of Ireland, and the Aktieselskab under Danish law would be added to any updated version of the Draft.
44. *cf.* the provision of the Protocol on Interpretation of the Judgments Convention, discussed in Chapter 4 *ante* at p. 139 *et seq.*
45. See, for example, 5th General Report of the Commission of the European Communities, 1971, p. 117, section 163.
46. See *supra* pp. 252—55.

CHAPTER 8

Results and Prospects

At the time of writing (April 1981) the fate of the programme of Community Conventions is very much in the balance. Not only is it uncertain whether further work will take place to produce additional Conventions to set along-side those whose provisions have been described in the preceding chapters of this book, but also there is no complete assurance that all of the Conventions which have so far been elaborated will be adopted and brought into force within all nine (and, indeed, all ten) Member States of the EEC. Despite the elapse of more than 22 years since the Commission first encouraged the Member States to begin the task of fulfilling their obligations under A. 220 ECT, only the Judgments Convention[1] has yet entered into force, even among the original Six. There are, however, encouraging grounds for believing that developments in the near future will see the Judgments Convention enter into force among all nine States which have so far negotiated to become parties to it, and that almost simultaneously the Contracts Convention[2] will similarly enter into force. It may take some further time before the Member States duly sign and ratify the Bankruptcy Convention,[3] but once again there are hopeful portents that they will do so. Negotiations are also known to be taking place between the original Six and the new Member States with a view to bringing the Convention on Mutual Recognition of Companies[4] into effect among all Nine. But it is not possible to be more than moderately optimistic about the likelihood of much progress regarding this particular Convention, in view of the less-than-wholehearted reception accorded to it even by the original Six, and by academic and professional opinion generally.

It is to be expected that Greece, and any other States which subsequently become Members of the Community, will, following the necessary negotiations,[5] accede to those Conventions which have already been concluded, and will thereafter participate fully in any further negotiations which may take place for the conclusion of Community Conventions in the field of private international law. However, it must be conceded that the current prospects for further multilateral negotiations to conclude additional Conventions to those which have been produced so far are, frankly, not very promising. Despite the theoretically favourable conditions in which the negotiations for the "first generation" of Community Conventions took place, the picture which emerges from a close survey of their evolution is one of steadily deepening disillusion and exasperation on all sides. As a medium for bringing about the harmonisation of the laws of Member States, the international Convention has proved to be unsuitable in the majority of respects. First, by reason of its character as a "non-Community act",[6] each Convention has, throughout its protracted gestation, been kept under the close control of the Member States. The "Experts" who were responsible for the preparation and drafting of each successive version of the texts were governmentally-appointed, and as such seem in some instances to have gone to extraordinary lengths to maintain a cherished, "national" position, as opposed to seeking the ideal, "Community" solution which was ostensibly the object of the exercise. Thus, the negotiations were excessively protracted, were vulnerable to fluctuations in international (and, especially, inter-governmental and inter-ministerial) relations among the Member States, and were frequently beset by deadlock which could only be resolved, if at all, by means of some compromise in which principle and logic, and even the best interests of justice itself, were invariably sacrificed to expediency. Moreover, the relatively subordinate role which was allotted to the Commission throughout these negotiations made it difficult to achieve full co-ordination between the policies and rules being formulated within the Conventions on the one hand, and those being developed on the other hand as part of the general programme for the approximation of laws, over whose content and direction the Commission has a far greater degree of control.

The above-mentioned factors may go a long way to explaining why, in many respects, each of the Conventions seems to contain flaws and inconsistencies not only internally and *vis-à-vis* the other Conventions, but also in relation to the provisions of other Community legislation with which it ought to interact in a complementary fashion.[7] One further, unsatisfactory aspect of the way in which the preparation and negotiation of the Conventions has been carried out is the atmosphere of secrecy and confidentiality with which the Draft Projects have been surrounded, at the insistence of the Governments involved (or, at least, of some of them). This factor, together with the length of time over which negotiations have been extended, has effectively ensured that the healthy and beneficial stimulus which could have been gained from an inflow, at each vital stage, of rigorous criticism from outside academic, and other, commentators has been sadly absent over long stretches of the evolution of the texts. Moreover, the lack of any systematic or formalised interplay between negotiating authorities and external commentators has probably contributed to the sense of frustration which seems to have built up around these projects over time, to the extent that the very many favourable and positive aspects of the programme have been increasingly overlooked or ignored. What needs to be reaffirmed is the enormous advance which has already been achieved by means of the four extant Conventions, both in general terms and in numerous matters of detail, towards the attainment of the overall goal of clearing away the present jungle that is private international law, and replacing it, throughout Western Europe at least, with a planned and orderly legal parkland. It cannot be denied that in many respects the work might have been better done, and also more quickly done. But the important fact at this juncture, surely, is that so much has been done at all.

The first priority must therefore be to ensure that the governments of the Member States do not allow the expenditure of so much effort over many years to be dissipated through failure, at the highest levels, to ensure that the final stages of ratification and implementation are completed with reasonable dispatch. Thereafter, on the basis of the empirical evidence to be gained from a period of operating the Conventions, it would become possible to form an assessment of whether the advantages accruing from them are such as to justify the further commitment of intellectual and administrative resources which would be needed if their number is to be added to in the near future. In that event, high among the list of priorities would undoubtedly come the concluding of a Convention to unify the Member States' conflicts rules regarding arbitration agreements, including choice of law clauses and *forum* clauses within such agreements, and also to make provisions for the recognition and enforcement of arbitral awards. These important matters were omitted from the scope of the Contracts Convention and the Judgments Convention respectively,[8] yet there is an urgent need to bring about this harmonisation within the Community, in view of the great significance of arbitration in the context of the international commercial activities which are so fundamental to the operation of the Common Market.

Even allowing that the Member States might bestir themselves to take some action in the field of arbitration, it is not clear that there will be any further Conventions produced after that. That it would be desirable, for example, to harmonise the Member States' rules of private international law in relation to non-contractual obligations is undoubtedly true. But that to do so would require a disproportionately-large amount of time and effort to be devoted to the task by already over-extended personnel is equally true. The decision[9] to exclude questions of non-contractual liability from the final version of what thereby became the Contracts Convention was a practical and realistic one, based upon an awareness that the delays which would be necessitated by any attempt to produce acceptable and workable final provisions in the field of delictual liability (to say nothing of the further field of restitution) would entail the indefinite postponement of the enactment of those provisions concerning contracts on which agreement had begun to emerge. The original proposals relating to non-contractual obligations were much criticised,[10] and it is impossible to be sanguine about the prospects of any consensus emerging among the representatives of ten negotiating States in relation to this, one of the most controversial and intractable of all topics in the conflict of laws. Nor does there seem to be much enthusiasm at present for taking up any of the alternative projects which were formerly envisaged for inclusion within the programme of Conventions, such as the law applicable to corporeal and incorporeal property, the law applicable to the form of legal transactions and evidence, and general matters such as *renvoi*, classification, application of foreign law, public policy, capacity, representation and so forth.

The truth is that the practical difficulties inherent in the conduct of multinational, multilingual negotiations for the harmonisation of private international law by means of Conventions, even where there is an abundance of zeal and a general willingness to achieve results, have now become too great. While progress was reasonably attainable between Six negotiating States, all of whom, broadly speaking, belonged to the same legal tradition, it rapidly became apparent that the augmentation of numbers up to nine, taking in representatives of the Common law tradition, had introduced a severe impediment to the maintenance of any sort of momentum, even in an ideal political climate. The further increase in membership of the Community up to and (soon) beyond ten merely confirms the sheer impracticality of pursuing further negotiations in this field, once the current programme of work has been seen through to its completion. Indeed, had it not been for the tenacity and persistence of certain individual members of the Working Parties of Experts, and of the Commission, the programme of work which has brought at least four Conventions to a state of completion might long ago have sunk into the sands of apathy and been lost without trace.

Nevertheless, the fact remains that private international law within the EEC must undergo further harmonisation, as a matter of legal necessity. The author remains convinced of the validity of the thesis, argued in Part I of this book, wherein such harmonisation was seen to be required as part of the overall working-out of the legal implications of the basic Treaties, and of the legal cosmology they have engendered. The question is therefore not so much *whether* the private international law of the Member States shall continue to undergo harmonisation, but rather *how* such harmonisation may expediently be brought about. The answer would appear to lie in the further use of Community Directives and Regulations, based either on A. 100 or on A. 235 ECT, in which either specific areas of private international law are harmonised on their own, or (and, perhaps, more appropriately), specific areas of private international law are harmonised together with the areas of substantive law to which they properly relate.[11] What needs to be established, however, is some more "open" and receptive preparatory process on the part of the Commission during the formative stages of the creation of such legislative proposals. Too often, it must be said, Draft Directives and Regulations emerge from the Commission, rather like Athena bounding from the head of Zeus, in a fully-developed state. Shock and resentment thereafter tend to ensue from many interested quarters, to be transformed subsequently into the negative, obstructionist activities, aimed at preventing the measures from gaining the force of law, which are the bane of Community political life. Perhaps a more suitable way of working would be through procedures analogous to those developed by the English and Scottish Law Commissions, whereby Working Papers are produced at an early stage of exploring a particular topic being considered for reform, in order that interested parties may communicate their views before any firm proposals are actually formulated. Thereafter, when the "feedback" has been digested, further dialogue can take place, so that the final, published proposals are often the product of a dynamic interplay of ideas, and can frequently (though not invariably) command a wide spectrum of support and endorsement at what is still the pre-legislative stage. If the future harmonisation of private international law within the Community is to be carried out, *faute de mieux*, by means of acts of Community secondary legislation over whose formulation the Commission will have primary control, let it be by means of some such widely-consultative processes at the formative phase as have been adumbrated above.

Conclusions

Historically, the fortunes of the programme of Community Conventions in the field of private international law have tended to mirror those of the European Community itself, albeit in microcosm. During the early years of the 1960s, the energy and enthusiasm with which the various projects for Conventions were pursued resembled the prevailing mood of euphoria in which European integration generally was taking place under the combined auspices of the Treaties of Rome and the Treaty of Paris. Subsequently, the reaction which was registered on a far larger canvas when national pride and prestige began to be asserted against the encroaching claims of the Community, notably in the political sphere, also produced its consequences in the sphere of legal harmonisation. A general slowing down of all programmes of legal harmonisation took place from the late 1960s, and various *causes célèbres* arose in which fervent resistance was offered to the merging of national legal identities in the "common pool" of the Community's synthesised system of law. Nor is this altogether to be deplored. Laws must, after all, reflect the deep-seated convictions and preferences of the governed, and will ultimately cease to command that quality of respect which gives them their very force as law, unless the requisite popular consensus is forthcoming. It is not realistic to expect that proud, self-respecting peoples with deeply-engrained legal and social traditions will, of an instant, relinquish those traditions in favour of some neutral, impersonal and untried substitute which is the product of negotiations whose primary objective may not infrequently have been to arrive at the solution which is merely the least offensive to the susceptibilities of the largest number of participants, rather than one which positively commands the enthusiasm of the populations whom they purport to represent.

When considered against the above background, the "first generation" of private international law Conventions may be adjudged as a modest success. Though flawed in some respects, each of the four extant Conventions is capable of producing considerable practical benefits which would amply justify such price as may have to be paid in terms of the repeal (or discontinuation from use) of certain, familiar rules of national law. With their coming into effect, large and important areas of the conflict of laws will have been transformed, within the Community at least, in ways in which are mostly for the better. It would surely be unrealistic to have entertained hopes that, in the first instance, they might have achieved more. Informed, constructive criticism, allied to working experience, surely offers the best hope that these Conventions will gradually be modified and improved where necessary, and that their provisions will in time be complemented by further developments, whatever their form, to continue the process of harmonisation of private international law within the EEC. Rome was not built in a day; neither will the Treaty of Rome be fully and properly implemented within a single generation of legal activity.

NOTES

1. Described in Chapter 4 *ante*.
2. Described in Chapter 5 *ante*.
3. Described in Chapter 6 *ante*.
4. Described in Chapter 7 *ante*.
5. *cf.* A. 3(2) of the Act of Accession of 28 May 1979, whereby Greece, on becoming a Member of the Community, undertook to accede to the Conventions provided for in A. 220 ECT.
6. See the comments in Chapter 4 *ante*, p. 109, on the significance of the rubric in each of the Conventions to the effect that the representatives of the signatory States purported to meet "in the Council" and not "as" the Council.
7. *cf.* the lack of logical correspondence between the choice of law rules of the Contracts Convention relating to insurance, and the choice of law rules contained in the Draft Directive on Non-Life Insurance Services, mentioned in Chapter 5 *ante*, p. 154. *cf.* also the seemingly un-coordinated approaches to such concepts as the "domicile" of an individual, the "seat" of a company and the "centre of administration" of an individual or of a company, in the four Conventions described in Chapters 4—7 inclusive.
8. See Chapters 5 and 4, respectively, on the question of the scope of each of the Conventions referred to.
9. This decision is mentioned in Chapter 5 *ante*, p. 150.
10. These proposals, comprising Arts. 10—14 of the Preliminary Draft Convention may be found published together with the other provisions of the 1970 version of the Draft Convention, at the references supplied in n. 9 of Chapter 5 *ante*. For comments upon these provisions, see: contributions by Karsten, Morse and Collier to Harmonisation (Ed. Lipstein) at pp. 51, 63 and 81, respectively; contributions by Sundstrom, Von Overbeck and Volken, Lipstein, and Hartley to EPILO (Ed. Lando) at pp. 214, 165 and 112 respectively; Van der Elst (1975) RTDE 187; Nadelmann (1976) 24 AJCL 1; Bourel, in The Influence of the European Communities on Private International Law of the Member States, ed. by P. Bourel and others (Brussels, 1981) at pp. 97-123.
11. Here, the inclusion of choice of law rules within the Draft Non-Life Insurance Services Directive (see the first part of n. 7 *supra*, and references therein) is probably a portent of things to come.

APPENDIX A

Convention on Jurisdiction and the Enforcement of Judgments in Civil and Commercial Matters

CONVENTION

on jurisdiction and the enforcement of judgments in civil and commercial matters (*)

PREAMBLE

THE HIGH CONTRACTING PARTIES TO THE TREATY ESTABLISHING THE EUROPEAN ECONOMIC COMMUNITY,

Desiring to implement the provisions of Article 220 of that Treaty by virtue of which they undertook to secure the simplification of formalities governing the reciprocal recognition and enforcement of judgments of courts or tribunals;

Anxious to strengthen in the Community the legal protection of persons therein established;

Considering that it is necessary for this purpose to determine the international jurisdiction of their courts, to facilitate recognition and to introduce an expeditious procedure for securing the enforcement of judgments, authentic instruments and court settlements;

Have decided to conclude this Convention and to this end have designated as their Plenipotentiaries:

HIS MAJESTY THE KING OF THE BELGIANS:

Mr Pierre HARMEL,

Minister for Foreign Affairs;

THE PRESIDENT OF THE FEDERAL REPUBLIC OF GERMANY:

Mr Willy BRANDT,

Vice-Chancellor,

Minister for Foreign Affairs;

THE PRESIDENT OF THE FRENCH REPUBLIC:

Mr Michel DEBRÉ,

Minister for Foreign Affairs;

THE PRESIDENT OF THE ITALIAN REPUBLIC:

Mr Giuseppe MEDICI,

Minister for Foreign Affairs;

(*) Text as amended by the Convention of Accession.

HIS ROYAL HIGHNESS THE GRAND DUKE OF LUXEMBOURG:

Mr Pierre GRÉGOIRE,

Minister for Foreign Affairs;

HER MAJESTY THE QUEEN OF THE NETHERLANDS:

Mr J.M.A.H. LUNS,

Minister for Foreign Affairs;

WHO, meeting within the Council, having exchanged their Full Powers, found in good and due form,

HAVE AGREED AS FOLLOWS:

TITLE I

SCOPE

Article 1

This Convention shall apply in civil and commercial matters whatever the nature of the court or tribunal. It shall not extend, in particular, to revenue, customs or administrative matters (¹).

The Convention shall not apply to:

1. the status or legal capacity of natural persons, rights in property arising out of a matrimonial relationship, wills and succession;

2. bankruptcy, proceedings relating to the winding-up of insolvent companies or other legal persons, judicial arrangements, compositions and analogous proceedings;

3. social security;

4. arbitration.

TITLE II

JURISDICTION

Section 1

General provisions

Article 2

Subject to the provisions of this Convention, persons domiciled in a Contracting State shall, whatever their nationality, be sued in the courts of that State.

(¹) Second sentence added by Article 3 of the Convention of Accession.

Persons who are not nationals of the State in which they are domiciled shall be governed by the rules of jurisdiction applicable to nationals of that State.

Article 3

Persons domiciled in a Contracting State may be sued in the courts of another Contracting State only by virtue of the rules set out in Sections 2 to 6 of this Title.

In particular the following provisions shall not be applicable as against them:

— in Belgium: Article 15 of the civil code (Code civil — Burgerlijk Wetboek) and Article 638 of the judicial code (Code judiciaire — Gerechtelijk Wetboek),

— in Denmark: Article 248 (2) of the law on civil procedure (Lov om rettens pleje) and Chapter 3, Article 3 of the Greenland law on civil procedure (Lov for Grønland om rettens pleje),

— in the Federal Republic of Germany: Article 23 of the code of civil procedure (Zivilprozeßordnung),

— in France: Articles 14 and 15 of the civil code (Code civil),

— in Ireland: the rules which enable jurisdiction to be founded on the document instituting the proceedings having been served on the defendant during his temporary presence in Ireland,

— in Italy: Articles 2 and 4, Nos 1 and 2 of the code of civil procedure (Codice di procedura civile),

— in Luxembourg: Articles 14 and 15 of the civil code (Code civil),

— in the Netherlands: Articles 126 (3) and 127 of the code of civil procedure (Wetboek van Burgerlijke Rechtsvordering),

— in the United Kingdom: the rules which enable jurisdiction to be founded on:

(a) the document instituting the proceedings having been served on the defendant during his temporary presence in the United Kingdom; or

(b) the presence within the United Kingdom of property belonging to the defendant; or

(c) the seizure by the plaintiff of property situated in the United Kingdom (¹).

Article 4

If the defendant is not domiciled in a Contracting State, the jurisdiction of the courts of each Contracting State shall, subject to the provisions of Article 16, be determined by the law of that State.

As against such a defendant, any person domiciled in a Contracting State may, whatever his nationality, avail himself in that State of the rules of jurisdiction there in force, and in particular those specified in the second paragraph of Article 3, in the same way as the nationals of that State.

Section 2

Special jurisdiction

Article 5

A person domiciled in a Contracting State may, in another Contracting State, be sued:

1. in matters relating to a contract, in the courts for the place of performance of the obligation in question;

2. in matters relating to maintenance, in the courts for the place where the maintenance creditor is domiciled or habitually resident or, if the matter is ancillary to proceedings concerning the status of a person, in the court which, according to its own law, has jurisdiction to entertain those proceedings, unless that jurisdiction is based solely on the nationality of one of the parties (²);

3. in matters relating to tort, delict or quasi-delict, in the courts for the place where the harmful event occurred;

4. as regards a civil claim for damages or restitution which is based on an act giving rise to criminal proceedings, in the court seised of those proceedings, to the extent that that court has jurisdiction under its own law to entertain civil proceedings;

5. as regards a dispute arising out of the operations of a branch, agency or other establishment, in the courts for the place in which the branch, agency or other establishment is situated;

6. as settlor, trustee or beneficiary of a trust created by the operation of a statute, or by a written instrument, or created orally and evidenced in writing, in the courts of the Contracting State in which the trust is domiciled (³);

7. as regards a dispute concerning the payment of remuneration claimed in respect of the salvage of a cargo or freight, in the court under the authority of which the cargo or freight in question:

(a) has been arrested to secure such payment, or

(b) could have been so arrested, but bail or other security has been given;

provided that this provision shall apply only if it is claimed that the defendant has an interest in the cargo or freight or had such an interest at the time of salvage (⁴);

Article 6

A person domiciled in a Contracting State may also be sued:

1. where he is one of a number of defendants, in the courts for the place where any one of them is domiciled;

(¹) Second paragraph as modified by Article 4 of the Convention of Accession.

(²) No 2 as amended by Article 5 (3) of the Convention of Accession.
(³) No 6 added by Article 5 (4) of the Convention of Accession.
(⁴) No 7 added by Article 5 (4) of the Convention of Accession.

2. as a third party in an action on a warranty or guarantee or in any other third party proceedings, in the court seised of the original proceedings, unless these were instituted solely with the object of removing him from the jurisdiction of the court which would be competent in his case;

3. on a counter-claim arising from the same contract or facts on which the original claim was based, in the court in which the original claim is pending.

Article 6a (¹)

Where by virtue of this Convention a court of a Contracting State has jurisdiction in actions relating to liability arising from the use or operation of a ship, that court, or any other court substituted for this purpose by the internal law of that State, shall also have jurisdiction over claims for limitation of such liability.

Section 3

Jurisdiction in matters relating to insurance

Article 7

In matters relating to insurance, jurisdiction shall be determined by this Section, without prejudice to the provisions of Articles 4 and 5 (5).

Article 8 (²)

An insurer domiciled in a Contracting State may be sued:

1. in the courts of the State where he is domiciled, or

2. in another Contracting State, in the courts for the place where the policy-holder is domiciled, or

3. if he is a co-insurer, in the courts of a Contracting State in which proceedings are brought against the leading insurer.

An insurer who is not domiciled in a Contracting State but has a branch, agency or other establishment in one of the Contracting States shall, in disputes

arising out of the operations of the branch, agency or establishment, be deemed to be domiciled in that State.

Article 9

In respect of liability insurance or insurance of immovable property, the insurer may in addition be sued in the courts for the place where the harmful event occurred. The same applies if movable and immovable property are covered by the same insurance policy and both are adversely affected by the same contingency.

Article 10

In respect of liability insurance, the insurer may also, if the law of the court permits it, be joined in proceedings which the injured party has brought against the insured.

The provisions of Articles 7, 8 and 9 shall apply to actions brought by the injured party directly against the insurer, where such direct actions are permitted.

If the law governing such direct actions provides that the policy-holder or the insured may be joined as a party to the action, the same court shall have jurisdiction over them.

Article 11

Without prejudice to the provisions of the third paragraph of Article 10, an insurer may bring proceedings only in the courts of the Contracting State in which the defendant is domiciled, irrespective of whether he is the policy-holder, the insured or a beneficiary.

The provisions of this Section shall not affect the right to bring a counterclaim in the court in which, in accordance with this Section, the original claim is pending.

Article 12 (³)

The provisions of this Section may be departed from only by an agreement on jurisdiction:

1. which is entered into after the dispute has arisen, or

(¹) Article added by Article 6 of the Convention of Accession.
(²) Text as amended by Article 7 of the Convention of Accession.

(³) Text as amended by Article 8 of the Convention of Accession.

2. which allows the policy-holder, the insured or a beneficiary to bring proceedings in courts other than those indicated in this Section, or

3. which is concluded between a policy-holder and an insurer, both of whom are at the time of conclusion of the contract domiciled or habitually resident in the same Contracting State, and which has the effect of conferring jurisdiction on the courts of that State even if the harmful event were to occur abroad, provided that such an agreement is not contrary to the law of that State, or

4. which is concluded with a policy-holder who is not domiciled in a Contracting State, except in so far as the insurance is compulsory or relates to immovable property in a Contracting State, or

5. which relates to a contract of insurance in so far as it covers one or more of the risks set out in Article 12a.

Article 12a (¹)

The following are the risks referred to in Article 12 (5):

1. Any loss of or damage to

    (a) sea-going ships, installations situated off-shore or on the high seas, or aircraft, arising from perils which relate to their use for commercial purposes,

    (b) goods in transit other than passengers' baggage where the transit consists of or includes carriage by such ships or aircraft;

2. Any liability, other than for bodily injury to passengers or loss of or damage to their baggage,

    (a) arising out of the use or operation of ships, installations or aircraft as referred to in (1) (a) above in so far as the law of the Contracting State in which such aircraft are registered does not prohibit agreements on jurisdiction regarding insurance of such risks,

    (b) for loss or damage caused by goods in transit as described in (1) (b) above;

3. Any financial loss connected with the use or operation of ships, installations or aircraft as referred to in (1) (a) above, in particular loss of freight or charter-hire;

4. Any risk or interest connected with any of those referred to in (1) to (3) above.

Section 4 (²)

Jurisdiction over consumer contracts

Article 13

In proceedings concerning a contract concluded by a person for a purpose which can be regarded as being outside his trade or profession, hereinafter called 'the consumer', jurisdiction shall be determined by this Section, without prejudice to the provisions of Articles 4 and 5 (5), if it is:

1. a contract for the sale of goods on instalment credit terms, or

2. a contract for a loan repayable by instalments, or for any other form of credit, made to finance the sale of goods, or

3. any other contract for the supply of goods or a contract for the supply of services, and

    (a) in the State of the consumer's domicile the conclusion of the contract was preceded by a specific invitation addressed to him or by advertising, and

    (b) the consumer took in that State the steps necessary for the conclusion of the contract.

Where a consumer enters into a contract with a party who is not domiciled in a Contracting State but has a branch, agency or other establishment in one of the Contracting States, that party shall, in disputes arising out of the operations of the branch, agency or establishment, be deemed to be domiciled in that State.

This Section shall not apply to contracts of transport.

Article 14

A consumer may bring proceedings against the other party to a contract either in the courts of the

---

(¹) **Article added by Article 9 of the Convention of Accession.**

(²) **Text as amended by Article 10 of the Convention of Accession.**

Contracting State in which that party is domiciled or in the courts of the Contracting State in which he is himself domiciled.

Proceedings may be brought against a consumer by the other party to the contract only in the courts of the Contracting State in which the consumer is domiciled.

These provisions shall not affect the right to bring a counter-claim in the court in which, in accordance with this Section, the original claim is pending.

Article 15

The provisions of this Section may be departed from only by an agreement:

1. which is entered into after the dispute has arisen, or

2. which allows the consumer to bring proceedings in courts other than those indicated in this Section, or

3. which is entered into by the consumer and the other party to the contract, both of whom are at the time of conclusion of the contract domiciled or habitually resident in the same Contracting State, and which confers jurisdiction on the courts of that State, provided that such an agreement is not contrary to the law of that State.

Section 5

Exclusive jurisdiction

Article 16

The following courts shall have exclusive jurisdiction, regardless of domicile:

1. in proceedings which have as their object rights *in rem* in, or tenancies of, immovable property, the courts of the Contracting State in which the property is situated;

2. in proceedings which have as their object the validity of the constitution, the nullity or the dissolution of companies or other legal persons or associations of natural or legal persons, or the decisions of their organs, the courts of the Contracting State in which the company, legal person or association has its seat;

3. in proceedings which have as their object the validity of entries in public registers, the courts of the Contracting State in which the register is kept;

4. in proceedings concerned with the registration or validity of patents, trade marks, designs, or other similar rights required to be deposited or registered, the courts of the Contracting State in which the deposit or registration has been applied for, has taken place or is under the terms of an international convention deemed to have taken place;

5. in proceedings concerned with the enforcement of judgments, the courts of the Contracting State in which the judgment has been or is to be enforced.

Section 6

Prorogation of jurisdiction

Article 17 (¹)

If the parties, one or more of whom is domiciled in a Contracting State, have agreed that a court or the courts of a Contracting State are to have jurisdiction to settle any disputes which have arisen or which may arise in connection with a particular legal relationship, that court or those courts shall have exclusive jurisdiction. Such an agreement conferring jurisdiction shall be either in writing or evidenced in writing or, in international trade or commerce, in a form which accords with practices in that trade or commerce of which the parties are or ought to have been aware. Where such an agreement is concluded by parties, none of whom is domiciled in a Contracting State, the courts of other Contracting States shall have no jurisdiction over their disputes unless the court or courts chosen have declined jurisdiction.

The court or courts of a Contracting State on which a trust instrument has conferred jurisdiction shall have exclusive jurisdiction in any proceedings brought against a settlor, trustee or beneficiary, if relations between these persons or their rights or obligations under the trust are involved.

Agreements or provisions of a trust instrument conferring jurisdiction shall have no legal force if they are contrary to the provisions of Article 12 or 15, or if the courts whose jurisdiction they purport to exclude have exclusive jurisdiction by virtue of Article 16.

If an agreement conferring jurisdiction was concluded for the benefit of only one of the parties, that party shall retain the right to bring proceedings in any other court which has jurisdiction by virtue of this Convention.

(¹) Text as amended by Article 11 of the Convention of Accession.

Article 18

Apart from jurisdiction derived from other provisions of this Convention, a court of a Contracting State before whom a defendant enters an appearance shall have jurisdiction. This rule shall not apply where appearance was entered solely to contest the jurisdiction, or where another court has exclusive jurisdiction by virtue of Article 16.

Section 7

Examination as to jurisdiction and admissibility

Article 19

Where a court of a Contracting State is seised of a claim which is principally concerned with a matter over which the courts of another Contracting State have exclusive jurisdiction by virtue of Article 16, it shall declare of its own motion that it has no jurisdiction.

Article 20

Where a defendant domiciled in one Contracting State is sued in a court of another Contracting State and does not enter an appearance, the court shall declare of its own motion that it has no jurisdiction unless its jurisdiction is derived from the provisions of this Convention.

The court shall stay the proceedings so long as it is not shown that the defendant has been able to receive the document instituting the proceedings or an equivalent document in sufficient time to enable him to arrange for his defence, or that all necessary steps have been taken to this end (¹).

The provisions of the foregoing paragraph shall be replaced by those of Article 15 of the Hague Convention of 15 November 1965 on the service abroad of judicial and extrajudicial documents in civil or commercial matters, if the document instituting the proceedings or notice thereof had to be transmitted abroad in accordance with that Convention.

Section 8

Lis Pendens — related actions

Article 21

Where proceedings involving the same cause of action and between the same parties are brought in

---

(¹) Second paragraph as amended by Article 12 of the Convention of Accession.

the courts of different Contracting States, any court other than the court first seised shall of its own motion decline jurisdiction in favour of that court.

A court which would be required to decline jurisdiction may stay its proceedings if the jurisdiction of the other court is contested.

Article 22

Where related actions are brought in the courts of different Contracting States, any court other than the court first seised may, while the actions are pending at first instance, stay its proceedings.

A court other than the court first seised may also, on the application of one of the parties, decline jurisdiction if the law of that court permits the consolidation of related actions and the court first seised has jurisdiction over both actions.

For the purposes of this Article, actions are deemed to be related where they are so closely connected that it is expedient to hear and determine them together to avoid the risk of irreconcilable judgments resulting from separate proceedings.

Article 23

Where actions come within the exclusive jurisdiction of several courts, any court other than the court first seised shall decline jurisdiction in favour of that court.

Section 9

Provisional, including protective, measures

Article 24

Application may be made to the courts of a Contracting State for such provisional, including protective, measures as may be available under the law of that State, even if, under this Convention, the courts of another Contracting State have jurisdiction as to the substance of the matter.

TITLE III

RECOGNITION AND ENFORCEMENT

Article 25

For the purposes of this Convention, 'judgment' means any judgment given by a court or tribunal of a

Contracting State, whatever the judgment may be called, including a decree, order, decision or writ of execution, as well as the determination of costs or expenses by an officer of the court.

involving the same cause of action and between the same parties, provided that this latter judgment fulfils the conditions necessary for its recognition in the State addressed (²).

Section 1

Recognition

Article 26

A judgment given in a Contracting State shall be recognized in the other Contracting States without any special procedure being required.

Any interested party who raises the recognition of a judgment as the principal issue in a dispute may, in accordance with the procedures provided for in Sections 2 and 3 of this Title, apply for a decision that the judgment be recognized.

If the outcome of proceedings in a court of a Contracting State depends on the determination of an incidental question of recognition that court shall have jurisdiction over that question.

Article 27

A judgment shall not be recognized:

1. if such recognition is contrary to public policy in the State in which recognition is sought;

2. where it was given in default of appearance, if the defendant was not duly served with the document which instituted the proceedings or with an equivalent document in sufficient time to enable him to arrange for his defence (¹);

3. if the judgment is irreconcilable with a judgment given in a dispute between the same parties in the State in which recognition is sought;

4. if the court of the State in which the judgment was given, in order to arrive at its judgment, has decided a preliminary question concerning the status or legal capacity of natural persons, rights in property arising out of a matrimonial relationship, wills or succession in a way that conflicts with a rule of the private international law of the State in which the recognition is sought, unless the same result would have been reached by the application of the rules of private international law of that State;

5. if the judgment is irreconcilable with an earlier judgment given in a non-Contracting State

Article 28

Moreover, a judgment shall not be recognized if it conflicts with the provisions of Section 3, 4 or 5 of Title II, or in a case provided for in Article 59.

In its examination of the grounds of jurisdiction referred to in the foregoing paragraph, the court or authority applied to shall be bound by the findings of fact on which the court of the State in which the judgment was given based its jurisdiction.

Subject to the provisions of the first paragraph, the jurisdiction of the court of the State in which the judgment was given may not be reviewed; the test of public policy referred to in Article 27 (1) may not be applied to the rules relating to jurisdiction.

Article 29

Under no circumstances may a foreign judgment be reviewed as to its substance.

Article 30

A court of a Contracting State in which recognition is sought of a judgment given in another Contracting State may stay the proceedings if an ordinary appeal against the judgment has been lodged.

A court of a Contracting State in which recognition is sought of a judgment given in Ireland or the United Kingdom may stay the proceedings if enforcement is suspended in the State in which the judgment was given by reason of an appeal (³).

Section 2

Enforcement

Article 31

A judgment given in a Contracting State and enforceable in that State shall be enforced in another

---

(¹) 2 as amended by Article 13 (1) of the Convention of Accession.

(²) 5 added by Article 13 (2) of the Convention of Accession.

(³) Second paragraph added by Article 14 of the Convention of Accession.

Contracting State when, on the application of any interested party, the order for its enforcement has been issued there.

However, in the United Kingdom, such a judgment shall be enforced in England and Wales, in Scotland, or in Northern Ireland when, on the application of any interested party, it has been registered for enforcement in that part of the United Kingdom (¹).

Article 32

The application shall be submitted:

— in Belgium, to the tribunal de première instance or rechtbank van eerste aanleg,

— in Denmark, to the underret,

— in the Federal Republic of Germany, to the presiding judge of a chamber of the Landgericht,

— in France, to the presiding judge of the tribunal de grande instance,

— in Ireland, to the High Court,

— in Italy, to the corte d'appello,

— in Luxembourg, to the presiding judge of the tribunal d'arrondissement,

— in the Netherlands, to the presiding judge of the arrondissementsrechtbank,

— in the United Kingdom:

1. in England and Wales, to the High Court of Justice, or in the case of a maintenance judgment to the Magistrates' Court on transmission by the Secretary of State;

2. in Scotland, to the Court of Session, or in the case of a maintenance judgment to the Sheriff Court on transmission by the Secretary of State;

3. in Northern Ireland, to the High Court of Justice, or in the case of a maintenance judgment to the Magistrates' Court on transmission by the Secretary of State (²).

The jurisdiction of local courts shall be determined by reference to the place of domicile of the party against whom enforcement is sought. If he is not domiciled in the State in which enforcement is sought, it shall be determined by reference to the place of enforcement.

(¹) Second paragraph added by Article 15 of the Convention of Accession.
(²) First paragraph as amended by Article 16 of the Convention of Accession.

Article 33

The procedure for making the application shall be governed by the law of the State in which enforcement is sought.

The applicant must give an address for service of process within the area of jurisdiction of the court applied to. However, if the law of the State in which enforcement is sought does not provide for the furnishing of such an address, the applicant shall appoint a representative *ad litem*.

The documents referred to in Articles 46 and 47 shall be attached to the application.

Article 34

The court applied to shall give its decision without delay; the party against whom enforcement is sought shall not at this stage of the proceedings be entitled to make any submissions on the application.

The application may be refused only for one of the reasons specified in Articles 27 and 28.

Under no circumstances may the foreign judgment be reviewed as to its substance.

Article 35

The appropriate officer of the court shall without delay bring the decision given on the application to the notice of the applicant in accordance with the procedure laid down by the law of the State in which enforcement is sought.

Article 36

If enforcement is authorized, the party against whom enforcement is sought may appeal against the decision within one month of service thereof.

If that party is domiciled in a Contracting State other than that in which the decision authorizing enforcement was given, the time for appealing shall be two months and shall run from the date of service, either on him in person or at his residence. No extension of time may be granted on account of distance.

Article 37 (²)

An appeal against the decision authorizing enforcement shall be lodged in accordance with the rules governing procedure in contentious matters:

— in Belgium, with the tribunal de première instance or rechtbank van eerste aanleg,

---

(²) Text as amended by Article 17 of the Convention of Accession.

— in Denmark, with the landsret,

— in the Federal Republic of Germany, with the Oberlandesgericht,

— in France, with the cour d'appel,

— in Ireland, with the High Court,

— in Italy, with the corte d'appello,

— in Luxembourg, with the Cour supérieure de justice sitting as a court of civil appeal,

— in the Netherlands, with the arrondissementsrechtbank,

— in the United Kingdom:

1. in England and Wales, with the High Court of Justice, or in the case of a maintenance judgment with the Magistrates' Court;

2. in Scotland, with the Court of Session, or in the case of a maintenance judgment with the Sheriff Court;

3. in Northern Ireland, with the High Court of Justice, or in the case of a maintenance judgment with the Magistrates' Court.

The judgment given on the appeal may be contested only:

— in Belgium, France, Italy, Luxembourg and the Netherlands, by an appeal in cassation,

— in Denmark, by an appeal to the højesteret, with the leave of the Minister of Justice,

— in the Federal Republic of Germany, by a Rechtsbeschwerde,

— in Ireland, by an appeal on a point of law to the Supreme Court,

— in the United Kingdom, by a single further appeal on a point of law.

Article 38

The court with which the appeal under the first paragraph of Article 37 is lodged may, on the application of the appellant, stay the proceedings if an ordinary appeal has been lodged against the judgment in the State in which that judgment was given or if the time for such an appeal has not yet expired; in the latter case, the court may specify the time within which such an appeal is to be lodged.

Where the judgment was given in Ireland or the United Kingdom, any form of appeal available in the State in which it was given shall be treated as an ordinary appeal for the purposes of the first paragraph (¹).

The court may also make enforcement conditional on the provision of such security as it shall determine.

Article 39

During the time specified for an appeal pursuant to Article 36 and until any such appeal has been determined, no measures of enforcement may be taken other than protective measures taken against the property of the party against whom enforcement is sought.

The decision authorizing enforcement shall carry with it the power to proceed to any such protective measures.

Article 40

If the application for enforcement is refused, the applicant may appeal:

— in Belgium, to the cour d'appel or hof van beroep,

— in Denmark, to the landsret,

— in the Federal Republic of Germany, to the Oberlandesgericht,

— in France, to the cour d'appel,

— in Ireland, to the High Court,

— in Italy, to the corte d'appello,

— in Luxembourg, to the Cour supérieure de justice sitting as a court of civil appeal,

— in the Netherlands, to the gerechtshof,

— in the United Kingdom:

1. in England and Wales, to the High Court of Justice, or in the case of a maintenance judgment to the Magistrates' Court;

2. in Scotland, to the Court of Session, or in the case of a maintenance judgment to the Sheriff Court;

3. in Northern Ireland, to the High Court of Justice, or in the case of a maintenance judgment to the Magistrates' Court (²).

(¹) Second paragraph added by Article 18 of the Convention of Accession.

(²) First paragraph as amended by Article 19 of the Convention of Accession.

The party against whom enforcement is sought shall be summoned to appear before the appellate court. If he fails to appear, the provisions of the second and third paragraphs of Article 20 shall apply even where he is not domiciled in any of the Contracting States.

Article 41 (¹)

A judgment given on an appeal provided for in Article 40 may be contested only:

— in Belgium, France, Italy, Luxembourg and the Netherlands, by an appeal in cassation,

— in Denmark, by an appeal to the højesteret, with the leave of the Minister of Justice,

— in the Federal Republic of Germany, by a Rechtsbeschwerde,

— in Ireland, by an appeal on a point of law to the Supreme Court,

— in the United Kingdom, by a single further appeal on a point of law.

Article 42

Where a foreign judgment has been given in respect of several matters and enforcement cannot be authorized for all of them, the court shall authorize enforcement for one or more of them.

An applicant may request partial enforcement of a judgment.

Article 43

A foreign judgment which orders a periodic payment by way of a penalty shall be enforceable in the State in which enforcement is sought only if the amount of the payment has been finally determined by the courts of the State in which the judgment was given.

Article 44 (²)

An applicant who, in the State in which the judgment was given, has benefited from complete or partial

legal aid or exemption from costs or expenses, shall be entitled, in the procedures provided for in Articles 32 to 35, to benefit from the most favourable legal aid or the most extensive exemption from costs or expenses provided for by the law of the State addressed.

However, an applicant who requests the enforcement of a decision given by an administrative authority in Denmark in respect of a maintenance order may, in the State addressed, claim the benefits referred to in the first paragraph if he presents a statement from the Danish Ministry of Justice to the effect that he fulfils the economic requirements to qualify for the grant of complete or partial legal aid or exemption from costs or expenses.

Article 45

No security, bond or deposit, however described, shall be required of a party who in one Contracting State applies for enforcement of a judgment given in another Contracting State on the ground that he is a foreign national or that he is not domiciled or resident in the State in which enforcement is sought.

Section 3

Common provisions

Article 46

A party seeking recognition or applying for enforcement of a judgment shall produce:

1. a copy of the judgment which satisfies the conditions necessary to establish its authenticity;

2. in the case of a judgment given in default, the original or a certified true copy of the document which establishes that the party in default was served with the document instituting the proceedings or with an equivalent document (³).

Article 47

A party applying for enforcement shall also produce:

1. documents which establish that, according to the law of the State in which it has been given, the judgment is enforceable and has been served;

(¹) Text as amended by Article 20 of the Convention of Accession.

(²) Text as amended by Article 21 of the Convention of Accession.

(³) 2 as amended by Article 22 of the Convention of Accession.

2. where appropriate, a document showing that the applicant is in receipt of legal aid in the State in which the judgment was given.

Article 48

If the documents specified in Articles 46 (2) and 47 (2) are not produced, the court may specify a time for their production, accept equivalent documents or, if it considers that it has sufficient information before it, dispense with their production.

If the court so requires, a translation of the documents shall be produced; the translation shall be certified by a person qualified to do so in one of the Contracting States.

Article 49

No legalization or other similar formality shall be required in respect of the documents referred to in Article 46 or 47 or the second paragraph of Article 48, or in respect of a document appointing a representative *ad litem*.

TITLE IV

AUTHENTIC INSTRUMENTS AND COURT SETTLEMENTS

Article 50

A document which has been formally drawn up or registered as an authentic instrument and is enforceable in one Contracting State shall, in another Contracting State, have an order for its enforcement issued there, on application made in accordance with the procedures provided for in Article 31 *et seq.* The application may be refused only if enforcement of the instrument is contrary to public policy in the State in which enforcement is sought.

The instrument produced must satisfy the conditions necessary to establish its authenticity in the State of origin.

The provisions of Section 3 of Title III shall apply as appropriate.

Article 51

A settlement which has been approved by a court in the course of proceedings and is enforceable in the State in which it was concluded shall be enforceable in the State in which enforcement is sought under the same conditions as authentic instruments.

TITLE V

GENERAL PROVISIONS

Article 52

In order to determine whether a party is domiciled in the Contracting State whose courts are seised of a matter, the Court shall apply its internal law.

If a party is not domiciled in the State whose courts are seised of the matter, then, in order to determine whether the party is domiciled in another Contracting State, the court shall apply the law of that State.

The domicile of a party shall, however, be determined in accordance with his national law if, by that law, his domicile depends on that of another person or on the seat of an authority.

Article 53

For the purposes of this Convention, the seat of a company or other legal person or association of natural or legal persons shall be treated as its domicile. However, in order to determine that seat, the court shall apply its rules of private international law.

In order to determine whether a trust is domiciled in the Contracting State whose courts are seised of the matter, the court shall apply its rules of private international law (¹).

TITLE VI

TRANSITIONAL PROVISIONS (²)

Article 54

The provisions of this Convention shall apply only to legal proceedings instituted and to documents formally drawn up or registered as authentic instruments after its entry into force.

However, judgments given after the date of entry into force of this Convention in proceedings instituted before that date shall be recognized and enforced in accordance with the provisions of Title III if jurisdiction was founded upon rules which accorded

---

(¹) Second paragraph added by Article 23 of the Convention of Accession.

(²) Transitional provisions for the Convention of Accession are to be found in Title V of that Convention.

with those provided for either in Title II of this Convention or in a convention concluded between the State of origin and the State addressed which was in force when the proceedings were instituted.

TITLE VII

RELATIONSHIP TO OTHER CONVENTIONS

Article 55

Subject to the provisions of the second paragraph of Article 54, and of Article 56, this Convention shall, for the States which are parties to it, supersede the following conventions concluded between two or more of them:

— the Convention between Belgium and France on jurisdiction and the validity and enforcement of judgments, arbitration awards and authentic instruments, signed at Paris on 8 July 1899,

— the Convention between Belgium and the Netherlands on jurisdiction, bankruptcy, and the validity and enforcement of judgments, arbitration awards and authentic instruments, signed at Brussels on 28 March 1925,

— the Convention between France and Italy on the enforcement of judgments in civil and commercial matters, signed at Rome on 3 June 1930,

— the Convention between the United Kingdom and the French Republic providing for the reciprocal enforcement of judgments in civil and commercial matters, with Protocol, signed at Paris on 18 January 1934 (¹),

— the Convention between the United Kingdom and the Kingdom of Belgium providing for the reciprocal enforcement of judgments in civil and commercial matters, with Protocol, signed at Brussels on 2 May 1934 (¹),

— the Convention between Germany and Italy on the recognition and enforcement of judgments in civil and commercial matters, signed at Rome on 9 March 1936,

— the Convention between the Federal Republic of Germany and the Kingdom of Belgium on the mutual recognition and enforcement of judgments, arbitration awards and authentic instruments in civil and commercial matters, signed at Bonn on 30 June 1958,

— the Convention between the Kingdom of the Netherlands and the Italian Republic on the recognition and enforcement of judgments in civil and commercial matters, signed at Rome on 17 April 1959,

— the Convention between the United Kingdom and the Federal Republic of Germany for the reciprocal recognition and enforcement of judgments in civil and commercial matters, signed at Bonn on 14 July 1960 (¹),

— the Convention between the Kingdom of Belgium and the Italian Republic on the recognition and enforcement of judgments and other enforceable instruments in civil and commercial matters, signed at Rome on 6 April 1962,

— the Convention between the Kingdom of the Netherlands and the Federal Republic of Germany on the mutual recognition and enforcement of judgments and other enforceable instruments in civil and commercial matters, signed at The Hague on 30 August 1962,

— the Convention between the United Kingdom and the Republic of Italy for the reciprocal recognition and enforcement of judgments in civil and commercial matters, signed at Rome on 7 February 1964, with amending Protocol signed at Rome on 14 July 1970 (²),

— the Convention between the United Kingdom and the Kingdom of the Netherlands providing for the reciprocal recognition and enforcement of judgments in civil matters, signed at The Hague on 17 November 1967 (²),

and, in so far as it is in force:

— the Treaty between Belgium, the Netherlands and Luxembourg on jurisdiction, bankruptcy, and the validity and enforcement of judgments, arbitration awards and authentic instruments, signed at Brussels on 24 November 1961.

Article 56

The Treaty and the conventions referred to in Article 55 shall continue to have effect in relation to matters to which this Convention does not apply.

They shall continue to have effect in respect of judgments given and documents formally drawn up or registered as authentic instruments before the entry into force of this Convention.

(¹) Fourth, fifth and ninth indents added by Article 24 of the Convention of Accession.

(²) 12th and 13th indents added by Article 24 of the Convention of Accession.

Article 57 (¹)

This Convention shall not affect any conventions to which the Contracting States are or will be parties and which, in relation to particular matters, govern jurisdiction or the recognition or enforcement of judgments (²).

This Convention shall not affect the application of provisions which, in relation to particular matters, govern jurisdiction or the recognition or enforcement of judgments and which are or will be contained in acts of the institutions of the European Communities or in national laws harmonized in implementation of such acts.

Article 58

This Convention shall not affect the rights granted to Swiss nationals by the Convention concluded on 15 June 1869 between France and the Swiss Confederation on Jurisdiction and the enforcement of judgments in civil matters.

Article 59

This Convention shall not prevent a Contracting State from assuming, in a convention on the recognition and enforcement of judgments, an obligation towards a third State not to recognize judgments given in other Contracting States against defendants domiciled or habitually resident in the third State where, in cases provided for in Article 4, the judgment could only be founded on a ground of jurisdiction specified in the second paragraph of Article 3.

However, a Contracting State may not assume an obligation towards a third State not to recognize a judgment given in another Contracting State by a court basing its jurisdiction on the presence within that State of property belonging to the defendant, or the seizure by the plaintiff of property situated there:

1. if the action is brought to assert or declare proprietary or possessory rights in that property, seeks to obtain authority to dispose of it, or arises from another issue relating to such property, or,

2. if the property constitutes the security for a debt which is the subject-matter of the action (³).

TITLE VIII

FINAL PROVISIONS (⁴)

Article 60 (⁵)

This Convention shall apply to the European territories of the Contracting States, including Greenland, to the French overseas departments and territories, and to Mayotte.

The Kingdom of the Netherlands may declare at the time of signing or ratifying this Convention or at any later time, by notifying the Secretary-General of the Council of the European Communities, that this Convention shall be applicable to the Netherlands Antilles. In the absence of such declaration, proceedings taking place in the European territory of the Kingdom as a result of an appeal in cassation from the judgment of a court in the Netherlands Antilles shall be deemed to be proceedings taking place in the latter court.

Notwithstanding the first paragraph, this Convention shall not apply to:

1. the Faroe Islands, unless the Kingdom of Denmark makes a declaration to the contrary;

2. any European territory situated outside the United Kingdom for the international relations of which the United Kingdom is responsible, unless the United Kingdom makes a declaration to the contrary in respect of any such territory.

Such declarations may be made at any time by notifying the Secretary-General of the Council of the European Communities.

Proceedings brought in the United Kingdom on appeal from courts in one of the territories referred to in subparagraph 2 of the third paragraph shall be deemed to be proceedings taking place in those courts.

Proceedings which in the Kingdom of Denmark are dealt with under the law on civil procedure for the

---

(¹) Text as amended by Article 25 (1) of the Convention of Accession.
(²) Implementing provisions for this paragraph are laid down in Article 25 (2) of the Convention of Accession.

(³) Second paragraph added by Article 26 of the Convention of Accession.
(⁴) Final provisions for the Convention of Accession are to be found in Title VI of that Convention.
(⁵) Text as amended by Article 27 of the Convention of Accession.

Faroe Islands (lov for Faeroerne om rettens pleje) shall be deemed to be proceedings taking place in the courts of the Faroe Islands.

Article 61

This Convention shall be ratified by the signatory States. The instruments of ratification shall be deposited with the Secretary-General of the Council of the European Communities.

Article 62 (¹)

This Convention shall enter into force on the first day of the third month following the deposit of the instrument of ratification by the last signatory State to take this step.

Article 63

The Contracting States recognize that any State which becomes a member of the European Economic Community shall be required to accept this Convention as a basis for the negotiations between the Contracting States and that State necessary to ensure the implementation of the last paragraph of Article 220 of the Treaty establishing the European Economic Community.

The necessary adjustments may be the subject of a special convention between the Contracting States of the one part and the new Member States of the other part.

Article 64

The Secretary-General of the Council of the European Communities shall notify the signatory States of:

(¹) For the entry into force of the Convention of Accession, see Article 39 of that Convention.

(a) the deposit of each instrument of ratification;

(b) the date of entry into force of this Convention;

(c) any declaration received pursuant to Article 60 (²);

(d) any declaration received pursuant to Article IV of the Protocol;

(e) any communication made pursuant to Article VI of the Protocol.

Article 65

The Protocol annexed to this Convention by common accord of the Contracting States shall form an integral part thereof.

Article 66

This Convention is concluded for an unlimited period.

Article 67

Any Contracting State may request the revision of this Convention. In this event, a revision conference shall be convened by the President of the Council of the European Communities.

Article 68 (³)

This Convention, drawn up in a single original in the Dutch, French, German and Italian languages, all four texts being equally authentic, shall be deposited in the archives of the Secretariat of the Council of the European Communities. The Secretary-General shall transmit a certified copy to the Government of each signatory State.

(²) (c) as amended by Article 28 of the Convention of Accession.
(³) See also the second paragraph of Article 37 of the Convention of Accession which provides that the Danish, English and Irish texts are equally authentic.

In witness whereof, the undersigned Plenipotentiaries have signed this Convention.

Done at Brussels this twenty-seventh day of September in the year one thousand nine hundred and sixty-eight.

For His Majesty the King of the Belgians,
    Pierre HARMEL

For the President of the Federal Republic of Germany,
    Willy BRANDT

For the President of the French Republic,
    Michel DEBRÉ

For the President of the Italian Republic,
    Giuseppe MEDICI

For His Royal Highness the Grand Duke of Luxembourg,
    Pierre GRÉGOIRE

For Her Majesty the Queen of the Netherlands,
    J.M.A.H. LUNS

PROTOCOL (*)

The High Contracting Parties have agreed upon the following provisions, which shall be annexed to the Convention:

Article I

Any person domiciled in Luxembourg who is sued in a court of another Contracting State pursuant to Article 5 (1) may refuse to submit to the jurisdiction of that court. If the defendant does not enter an appearance the court shall declare of its own motion that it has no jurisdiction.

An agreement conferring jurisdiction, within the meaning of Article 17, shall be valid with respect to a person domiciled in Luxembourg only if that person has expressly and specifically so agreed.

Article II

Without prejudice to any more favourable provisions of national laws, persons domiciled in a Contracting State who are being prosecuted in the criminal courts of another Contracting State of which they are not nationals for an offence which was not intentionally committed may be defended by persons qualified to do so, even if they do not appear in person.

However, the court seised of the matter may order appearance in person; in the case of failure to appear, a judgment given in the civil action without the person concerned having had the opportunity to arrange for his defence need not be recognized or enforced in the other Contracting States.

Article III

In proceedings for the issue of an order for enforcement, no charge, duty or fee calculated by reference to the value of the matter in issue may be levied in the State in which enforcement is sought.

Article IV

Judicial and extrajudicial documents drawn up in one Contracting State which have to be served on persons in another Contracting State shall be transmitted in accordance with the procedures laid down in the conventions and agreements concluded between the Contracting States.

Unless the State in which service is to take place objects by declaration to the Secretary-General of the Council of the European Communities, such documents may also be sent by the appropriate public officers of the State in which the document has been drawn up directly to the appropriate public officers of the State in which the addressee is to be found. In this case the officer of the State of origin shall send a copy of the document to the officer of the State applied to who is competent to forward it to the addressee. The document shall be forwarded in the manner specified by the law of the State applied to. The forwarding shall be recorded by a certificate sent directly to the officer of the State of origin.

Article V

The jurisdiction specified in Articles 6 (2) and 10 in actions on a warranty or guarantee or in any other third party proceedings may not be resorted to in the Federal Republic of Germany. In that State, any person domiciled in another Contracting State may be sued in the courts in pursuance of Articles 68, 72, 73 and 74 of the code of civil procedure (*Zivilprozeßordnung*) concerning third-party notices.

Judgments given in the other Contracting States by virtue of Article 6 (2) or 10 shall be recognized and enforced in the Federal Republic of Germany in accordance with Title III. Any effects which judgments given in that State may have on third parties by application of Articles 68, 72, 73 and 74 of the code of civil procedure (*Zivilprozeßordnung*) shall also be recognized in the other Contracting States.

Article Va (¹)

In matters relating to maintenance, the expression 'court' includes the Danish administrative authorities.

(*) Text as amended by the Convention of Accession.

(¹) Articles added by Article 29 of the Convention of Accession.

Article Vb (¹)

In proceedings involving a dispute between the master and a member of the crew of a sea-going ship registered in Denmark or in Ireland, concerning remuneration or other conditions of service, a court in a Contracting State shall establish whether the diplomatic or consular officer responsible for the ship has been notified of the dispute. It shall stay the proceedings so long as he has not been notified. It shall of its own motion decline jurisdiction if the officer, having been duly notified, has exercised the powers accorded to him in the matter by a consular convention, or in the absence of such a convention has, within the time allowed, raised any objection to the exercise of such jurisdiction.

Article Vc (¹)

Articles 52 and 53 of this Convention shall, when applied by Article 69 (5) of the Convention for the European patent for the common market, signed at Luxembourg on 15 December 1975, to the provisions relating to 'residence' in the English text of that Convention, operate as if 'residence' in that text were the same as 'domicile' in Articles 52 and 53.

Article Vd (¹)

Without prejudice to the jurisdiction of the European Patent Office under the Convention on the grant of European patents, signed at Munich on 5 October 1973, the courts of each Contracting State shall have exclusive jurisdiction, regardless of domicile, in proceedings concerned with the registration or validity of any European patent granted for that State which is not a Community patent by virtue of the provisions of Article 86 of the Convention for the European patent for the common market, signed at Luxembourg on 15 December 1975.

Article VI

The Contracting States shall communicate to the Secretary-General of the Council of the European Communities the text of any provisions of their laws which amend either those articles of their laws mentioned in the Convention or the lists of courts specified in Section 2 of Title III of the Convention.

(¹) **Articles added by Article 29 of the Convention of Accession.**

In witness whereof, the undersigned Plenipotentiaries have signed this protocol.

Done at Brussels this twenty-seventh day of September in the year one thousand nine hundred and sixty-eight.

For His Majesty the King of the Belgians,

Pierre HARMEL

For the President of the Federal Republic of Germany,

Willy BRANDT

For the President of the French Republic,

Michel DEBRÉ

For the President of the Italian Republic,

Giuseppe MEDICI

For His Royal Highness the Grand Duke of Luxembourg,

Pierre GRÉGOIRE

For Her Majesty the Queen of the Netherlands,

J.M.A.H. LUNS

JOINT DECLARATION

The Governments of the Kingdom of Belgium, the Federal Republic of Germany, the French Republic, the Italian Republic, the Grand Duchy of Luxembourg and the Kingdom of the Netherlands;

On signing the Convention on jurisdiction and the enforcement of judgments in civil and commercial matters;

Desiring to ensure that the Convention is applied as effectively as possible;

Anxious to prevent differences of interpretation of the Convention from impairing its unifying effect;

Recognizing that claims and disclaimers of jurisdiction may arise in the application of the Convention;

Declare themselves ready:

1. to study these questions and in particular to examine the possibility of conferring jurisdiction in certain matters on the Court of Justice of the European Communities and, if necessary, to negotiate an agreement to this effect;

2. to arrange meetings at regular intervals between their representatives.

In witness whereof, the undersigned Plenipotentiaries have signed this Joint Declaration.

Done at Brussels this twenty-seventh day of September in the year one thousand nine hundred and sixty-eight.

Pierre HARMEL   Willy BRANDT   Michel DEBRÉ

Giuseppe MEDICI   Pierre GRÉGOIRE   J.M.A.H. LUNS

PROTOCOL

on the interpretation by the Court of Justice of the Convention of 27 September 1968 on jurisdiction and the enforcement of judgments in civil and commercial matters (*)

THE HIGH CONTRACTING PARTIES TO THE TREATY ESTABLISHING THE EUROPEAN ECONOMIC COMMUNITY,

Having regard to the Declaration annexed to the Convention on jurisdiction and the enforcement of judgments in civil and commercial matters, signed at Brussels on 27 September 1968,

Have decided to conclude a Protocol conferring jurisdiction on the Court of Justice of the European Communities to interpret that Convention, and to this end have designated as their Plenipotentiaries:

HIS MAJESTY THE KING OF THE BELGIANS:

Mr Alfons VRANCKX,

Minister of Justice;

THE PRESIDENT OF THE FEDERAL REPUBLIC OF GERMANY:

Mr Gerhard JAHN,

Federal Minister of Justice;

THE PRESIDENT OF THE FRENCH REPUBLIC:

Mr René PLEVEN,

Keeper of the Seals,

Minister of Justice;

THE PRESIDENT OF THE ITALIAN REPUBLIC:

Mr Erminio PENNACCHINI,

Under Secretary of State in the Ministry of Justice;

HIS ROYAL HIGHNESS THE GRAND DUKE OF LUXEMBOURG:

Mr Eugène SCHAUS,

Minister of Justice,

Deputy Prime Minister;

HER MAJESTY THE QUEEN OF THE NETHERLANDS:

Mr C.H.F. POLAK,

Minister of Justice;

WHO, meeting within the Council, having exchanged their Full Powers, found in good and due form,

HAVE AGREED AS FOLLOWS:

(*) Text as amended by the Convention of Accession.

Article 1

The Court of Justice of the European Communities shall have jurisdiction to give rulings on the interpretation of the Convention on jurisdiction and the enforcement of judgments in civil and commercial matters and of the Protocol annexed to that Convention, signed at Brussels on 27 September 1968, and also on the interpretation of the present Protocol.

The Court of Justice of the European Communities shall also have jurisdiction to give rulings on the interpretation of the Convention on the accession of the Kingdom of Denmark, Ireland and the United Kingdom of Great Britain and Northern Ireland to the Convention of 27 September 1968 and to this Protocol (¹).

Article 2

The following courts may request the Court of Justice to give preliminary rulings on questions of interpretation:

1. — in Belgium: la Cour de Cassation — het Hof van Cassatie and le Conseil d'État — de Raad van State,

— in Denmark: højesteret,

— in the Federal Republic of Germany: die obersten Gerichtshöfe des Bundes,

— in France: la Cour de Cassation and le Conseil d'État,

— in Ireland: the Supreme Court,

— in Italy: la Corte Suprema di Cassazione,

— in Luxembourg: la Cour supérieure de Justice when sitting as Cour de Cassation,

— in the Netherlands: de Hoge Raad,

— in the United Kingdom: the House of Lords and courts to which application has been made under the second paragraph of Article 37 or under Article 41 of the Convention (²);

2. the courts of the Contracting States when they are sitting in an appellate capacity;

3. in the cases provided for in Article 37 of the Convention, the courts referred to in that Article.

(¹) Second paragraph added by Article 30 of the Convention of Accession.
(²) (1) as amended by Article 31 of the Convention of Accession.

Article 3

1. Where a question of interpretation of the Convention or of one of the other instruments referred to in Article 1 is raised in a case pending before one of the courts listed in Article 2 (1), that court shall, if it considers that a decision on the question is necessary to enable it to give judgment, request the Court of Justice to give a ruling thereon.

2. Where such a question is raised before any court referred to in Article 2 (2) or (3), that court may, under the conditions laid down in paragraph 1, request the Court of Justice to give a ruling thereon.

Article 4

1. The competent authority of a Contracting State may request the Court of Justice to give a ruling on a question of interpretation of the Convention or of one of the other instruments referred to in Article 1 if judgments given by courts of that State conflict with the interpretation given either by the Court of Justice or in a judgment of one of the courts of another Contracting State referred to in Article 2 (1) or (2). The provisions of this paragraph shall apply only to judgments which have become *res judicata*.

2. The interpretation given by the Court of Justice in response to such a request shall not affect the judgments which gave rise to the request for interpretation.

3. The Procurators-General of the Courts of Cassation of the Contracting States, or any other authority designated by a Contracting State, shall be entitled to request the Court of Justice for a ruling on interpretation in accordance with paragraph 1.

4. The Registrar of the Court of Justice shall give notice of the request to the Contracting States, to the Commission and to the Council of the European Communities; they shall then be entitled within two months of the notification to submit statements of case or written observations to the Court.

5. No fees shall be levied or any costs or expenses awarded in respect of the proceedings provided for in this Article.

Article 5

1. Except where this Protocol otherwise provides, the provisions of the Treaty establishing the European Economic Community and those of the Protocol on the Statute of the Court of Justice annexed thereto, which are applicable when the Court is requested to give a preliminary ruling, shall also apply to any proceedings for the interpretation of

the Convention and the other instruments referred to in Article 1.

2. The Rules of Procedure of the Court of Justice shall, if necessary, be adjusted and supplemented in accordance with Article 188 of the Treaty establishing the European Economic Community.

Article 6 (¹)

This Protocol shall apply to the European territories of the Contracting States, including Greenland, to the French overseas departments and territories, and to Mayotte.

The Kingdom of the Netherlands may declare at the time of signing or ratifying this Protocol or at any later time, by notifying the Secretary-General of the Council of the European Communities, that this Protocol shall be applicable to the Netherlands Antilles.

Notwithstanding the first paragraph, this Convention shall not apply to:

1. the Faroe Islands, unless the Kingdom of Denmark makes a declaration to the contrary,

2. any European territory situated outside the United Kingdom for the international relations of which the United Kingdom is responsible, unless the United Kingdom makes a declaration to the contrary in respect of any such territory.

Such declarations may be made at any time by notifying the Secretary-General of the Council of the European Communities.

Article 7

This Protocol shall be ratified by the signatory States. The instruments of ratification shall be deposited with the Secretary-General of the Council of the European Communities.

Article 8 (²)

This Protocol shall enter into force on the first day of the third month following the deposit of the instrument of ratification by the last signatory State to take this step; provided that it shall at the earliest enter into force at the same time as the Convention of 27 September 1968 on jurisdiction and the enforcement of judgments in civil and commercial matters.

Article 9

The Contracting States recognize that any State which becomes a member of the European Economic Community, and to which Article 63 of the Convention on jurisdiction and the enforcement of judgments in civil and commercial matters applies, must accept the provisions of this Protocol, subject to such adjustments as may be required.

Article 10

The Secretary-General of the Council of the European Communities shall notify the signatory States of:

(a) the deposit of each instrument of ratification;

(b) the date of entry into force of this Protocol;

(c) any designation received pursuant to Article 4 (3);

(d) any declaration received pursuant to Article 6 (³).

Article 11

The Contracting States shall communicate to the Secretary-General of the Council of the European Communities the texts of any provisions of their laws which necessitate an amendment to the list of courts in Article 2 (1).

Article 12

This Protocol is concluded for an unlimited period.

Article 13

Any Contracting State may request the revision of this Protocol. In this event, a revision conference shall be convened by the President of the Council of the European Communities.

Article 14 (⁴)

This Protocol, drawn up in a single original in the Dutch, French, German and Italian languages, all four texts being equally authentic, shall be deposited in the archives of the Secretariat of the Council of the European Communities. The Secretary-General shall transmit a certified copy to the Government of each signatory State.

(¹) Text as amended by Article 32 of the Convention of Accession.
(²) For the entry into force of the Convention of Accession, see Article 39 thereof.

(³) (d) as amended by Article 33 of the Convention of Accession.
(⁴) See also the second paragraph of Article 37 of the Convention of Accession which provides that the Danish, English and Irish texts are equally authentic.

In witness whereof, the undersigned Plenipotentiaries have signed this Protocol.

Done at Luxembourg this third day of June in the year one thousand nine hundred and seventy-one.

For His Majesty the King of the Belgians,

Alfons VRANCKX

For the President of the Federal Republic of Germany,

Gerhard JAHN

For the President of the French Republic,

René PLEVEN

For the President of the Italian Republic,

Erminio PENNACCHINI

For His Royal Highness the Grand Duke of Luxembourg,

Eugène SCHAUS

For Her Majesty the Queen of the Netherlands,

C.H.F. POLAK

JOINT DECLARATION

The Governments of the Kingdom of Belgium, the Federal Republic of Germany, the French Republic, the Italian Republic, the Grand Duchy of Luxembourg and the Kingdom of the Netherlands;

On signing the Protocol on the interpretation by the Court of Justice of the Convention of 27 September 1968 on jurisdiction and the enforcement of judgments in civil and commercial matters;

Desiring to ensure that the provisions of that Protocol are applied as effectively and as uniformly as possible;

Declare themselves ready to organize, in cooperation with the Court of Justice, an exchange of information on the judgments given by the courts referred to in Article 2 (1) of that Protocol in application of the Convention and the Protocol of 27 September 1968.

In witness whereof, the undersigned Plenipotentiaries have signed this Joint Declaration.

Done at Luxembourg this third day of June in the year one thousand nine hundred and seventy-one.

For His Majesty the King of the Belgians,
Alfons VRANCKX

For the President of the Federal Republic of Germany,
Gerhard JAHN

For the President of the French Republic,
René PLEVEN

For the President of the Italian Republic,
Erminio PENNACCHINI

For His Royal Highness the Grand Duke of Luxembourg,
Eugène SCHAUS

For Her Majesty the Queen of the Netherlands,
C.H.F. POLAK

Convention on the Law Applicable to Contractual Obligations

II

(Acts whose publication is not obligatory)

COUNCIL

CONVENTION

ON THE LAW APPLICABLE TO CONTRACTUAL OBLIGATIONS

opened for signature in Rome on 19 June 1980

(80/934/EEC)

PREAMBLE

THE HIGH CONTRACTING PARTIES to the Treaty establishing the European Economic Community,

ANXIOUS to continue in the field of private international law the work of unification of law which has already been done within the Community, in particular in the field of jurisdiction and enforcement of judgments,

WISHING to establish uniform rules concerning the law applicable to contractual obligations,

HAVE AGREED AS FOLLOWS:

TITLE I

SCOPE OF THE CONVENTION

Article 1

Scope of the Convention

1. The rules of this Convention shall apply to contractual obligations in any situation involving a choice between the laws of different countries.

2. They shall not apply to:

(a) questions involving the status or legal capacity of natural persons, without prejudice to Article 11;

(b) contractual obligations relating to:

— wills and succession,

— rights in property arising out of a matrimonial relationship,

— rights and duties arising out of a family relationship, parentage, marriage or affinity, including maintenance obligations in respect of children who are not legitimate;

(c) obligations arising under bills of exchange, cheques and promissory notes and other negotiable instruments to the extent that the obligations under such other negotiable instruments arise out of their negotiable character;

(d) arbitration agreements and agreements on the choice of court;

(e) questions governed by the law of companies and other bodies corporate or unincorporate such as the creation, by registration or otherwise, legal capacity, internal organization or winding up of companies and other bodies corporate or unincorporate and the personal liability of officers and members as such for the obligations of the company or body;

(f) the question whether an agent is able to bind a principal, or an organ to bind a company or body corporate or unincorporate, to a third party;

(g) the constitution of trusts and the relationship between settlors, trustees and beneficiaries;

(h) evidence and procedure, without prejudice to Article 14.

3. The rules of this Convention do not apply to contracts of insurance which cover risks situated in the territories of the Member States of the European Economic Community. In order to determine whether a risk is situated in these territories the court shall apply its internal law.

4. The preceding paragraph does not apply to contracts of re-insurance.

Article 2

Application of law of non-contracting States

Any law specified by this Convention shall be applied whether or not it is the law of a Contracting State.

TITLE II

UNIFORM RULES

Article 3

Freedom of choice

1. A contract shall be governed by the law chosen by the parties. The choice must be expressed or demonstrated with reasonable certainty by the terms of the contract or the circumstances of the case. By their choice the parties can select the law applicable to the whole or a part only of the contract.

2. The parties may at any time agree to subject the contract to a law other than that which previously governed it, whether as a result of an earlier choice under this Article or of other provisions of this Convention. Any variation by the parties of the law to be applied made after the conclusion of the contract shall not prejudice its formal validity under Article 9 or adversely affect the rights of third parties.

3. The fact that the parties have chosen a foreign law, whether or not accompanied by the choice of a foreign tribunal, shall not, where all the other elements relevant to the situation at the time of the choice are connected with one country only, prejudice the application of rules of the law of that country which cannot be derogated from by contract, hereinafter called 'mandatory rules'.

4. The existence and validity of the consent of the parties as to the choice of the applicable law shall be determined in accordance with the provisions of Articles 8, 9 and 11.

Article 4

Applicable law in the absence of choice

1. To the extent that the law applicable to the contract has not been chosen in accordance with Article 3, the contract shall be governed by the law of the country with which it is most closely connected. Nevertheless, a severable part of the contract which has a closer connection with another country may by way of exception be governed by the law of that other country.

2. Subject to the provisions of paragraph 5 of this Article, it shall be presumed that the contract is most closely connected with the country where the party who is to effect the performance which is characteristic of the contract has, at the time of conclusion of the contract, his habitual residence, or, in the case of a body corporate or unincorporate, its central administration. However, if the contract is entered into in the course of that party's trade or profession, that country shall be the country in which the principal place of business is situated or, where under the terms of the contract the performance is to be effected through a place of business other than the principal place of business, the country in which that other place of business is situated.

3. Notwithstanding the provisions of paragraph 2 of this Article, to the extent that the subject matter of the contract is a right in immovable property or a right to use immovable property it shall be presumed that the contract is most closely connected with the country where the immovable property is situated.

4. A contract for the carriage of goods shall not be subject to the presumption in paragraph 2. In such a

contract if the country in which, at the time the contract is concluded, the carrier has his principal place of business is also the country in which the place of loading or the place of discharge or the principal place of business of the consignor is situated, it shall be presumed that the contract is most closely connected with that country. In applying this paragraph single voyage charter-parties and other contracts the main purpose of which is the carriage of goods shall be treated as contracts for the carriage of goods.

5. Paragraph 2 shall not apply if the characteristic performance cannot be determined, and the presumptions in paragraphs 2, 3 and 4 shall be disregarded if it appears from the circumstances as a whole that the contract is more closely connected with another country.

Article 5

Certain consumer contracts

1. This Article applies to a contract the object of which is the supply of goods or services to a person ('the consumer') for a purpose which can be regarded as being outside his trade or profession, or a contract for the provision of credit for that object.

2. Notwithstanding the provisions of Article 3, a choice of law made by the parties shall not have the result of depriving the consumer of the protection afforded to him by the mandatory rules of the law of the country in which he has his habitual residence:

— if in that country the conclusion of the contract was preceded by a specific invitation addressed to him or by advertising, and he had taken in that country all the steps necessary on his part for the conclusion of the contract, or

— if the other party or his agent received the consumer's order in that country, or

— if the contract is for the sale of goods and the consumer travelled from that country to another country and there gave his order, provided that the consumer's journey was arranged by the seller for the purpose of inducing the consumer to buy.

3. Notwithstanding the provisions of Article 4, a contract to which this Article applies shall, in the absence of choice in accordance with Article 3, be governed by the law of the country in which the consumer has his habitual residence if it is entered into in the circumstances described in paragraph 2 of this Article.

4. This Article shall not apply to:

(a) a contract of carriage;

(b) a contract for the supply of services where the services are to be supplied to the consumer exclusively in a country other than that in which he has his habitual residence.

5. Notwithstanding the provisions of paragraph 4, this Article shall apply to a contract which, for an inclusive price, provides for a combination of travel and accommodation.

Article 6

Individual employment contracts

1. Notwithstanding the provisions of Article 3, in a contract of employment a choice of law made by the parties shall not have the result of depriving the employee of the protection afforded to him by the mandatory rules of the law which would be applicable under paragraph 2 in the absence of choice.

2. Notwithstanding the provisions of Article 4, a contract of employment shall, in the absence of choice in accordance with Article 3, be governed:

(a) by the law of the country in which the employee habitually carries out his work in performance of the contract, even if he is temporarily employed in another country; or

(b) if the employee does not habitually carry out his work in any one country, by the law of the country in which the place of business through which he was engaged is situated;

unless it appears from the circumstances as a whole that the contract is more closely connected with another country, in which case the contract shall be governed by the law of that country.

Article 7

Mandatory rules

1. When applying under this Convention the law of a country, effect may be given to the mandatory rules of the law of another country with which the situation has a close connection, if and in so far as, under the law of the latter country, those rules must be applied whatever the law applicable to the contract. In considering whether to give effect to these mandatory rules, regard shall be had to their nature and purpose and to the consequences of their application or non-application.

2. Nothing in this Convention shall restrict the application of the rules of the law of the forum in a

situation where they are mandatory irrespective of the law otherwise applicable to the contract.

Article 8

Material validity

1. The existence and validity of a contract, or of any term of a contract, shall be determined by the law which would govern it under this Convention if the contract or term were valid.

2. Nevertheless a party may rely upon the law of the country in which he has his habitual residence to establish that he did not consent if it appears from the circumstances that it would not be reasonable to determine the effect of his conduct in accordance with the law specified in the preceding paragraph.

Article 9

Formal validity

1. A contract concluded between persons who are in the same country is formally valid if it satisfies the formal requirements of the law which governs it under this Convention or of the law of the country where it is concluded.

2. A contract concluded between persons who are in different countries is formally valid if it satisfies the formal requirements of the law which governs it under this Convention or of the law of one of those countries.

3. Where a contract is concluded by an agent, the country in which the agent acts is the relevant country for the purposes of paragraphs 1 and 2.

4. An act intended to have legal effect relating to an existing or contemplated contract is formally valid if it satisfies the formal requirements of the law which under this Convention governs the contract or of the law of the country where the act was done.

5. The provisions of the preceding paragraphs shall not apply to a contract to which Article 5 applies, concluded in the circumstances described in paragraph 2 of Article 5. The formal validity of such a contract is governed by the law of the country in which the consumer has his habitual residence.

6. Notwithstanding paragraphs 1 to 4 of this Article, a contract the subject matter of which is a right in immovable property or a right to use immovable property shall be subject to the mandatory requirements of form of the law of the country where the property is situated if by that law those requirements are imposed irrespective of the country where the contract is concluded and irrespective of the law governing the contract.

Article 10

Scope of the applicable law

1. The law applicable to a contract by virtue of Articles 3 to 6 and 12 of this Convention shall govern in particular:

(a) interpretation;

(b) performance;

(c) within the limits of the powers conferred on the court by its procedural law, the consquences of breach, including the assessment of damages in so far as it is governed by rules of law;

(d) the various ways of extinguishing obligations, and prescription and limitation of actions;

(e) the consequences of nullity of the contract.

2. In relation to the manner of performance and the steps to be taken in the event of defective performance regard shall be had to the law of the country in which performance takes place.

Article 11

Incapacity

In a contract concluded between persons who are in the same country, a natural person who would have capacity under the law of that country may invoke his incapacity resulting from another law only if the other party to the contract was aware of this incapacity at the time of the conclusion of the contract or was not aware thereof as a result of negligence.

Article 12

Voluntary assignment

1. The mutual obligations of assignor and assignee under a voluntary assignment of a right against another

person ('the debtor') shall be governed by the law which under this Convention applies to the contract between the assignor and assignee.

2. The law governing the right to which the assignment relates shall determine its assignability, the relationship betweeen the assignee and the debtor, the conditions under which the assignment can be invoked against the debtor and any question whether the debtor's obligations have been discharged.

Article 13

Subrogation

1. Where a person ('the creditor') has a contractual claim upon another ('the debtor'), and a third person has a duty to satisfy the creditor, or has in fact satisfied the creditor in discharge of that duty, the law which governs the third person's duty to satisfy the creditor shall determine whether the third person is entitled to exercise against the debtor the rights which the creditor had against the debtor under the law governing their relationship and, if so, whether he may do so in full or only to a limited extent.

2. The same rule applies where several persons are subject to the same contractual claim and one of them has satisfied the creditor.

Article 14

Burden of proof, etc.

1. The law governing the contract under this Convention applies to the extent that it contains, in the law of contract, rules which raise presumptions of law or determine the burden of proof.

2. A contract or an act intended to have legal effect may be proved by any mode of proof recognized by the law of the forum or by any of the laws referred to in Article 9 under which that contract or act is formally valid, provided that such mode of proof can be administered by the forum.

Article 15

Exclusion of renvoi

The application of the law of any country specified by this Convention means the application of the rules of law in force in that country other than its rules of private international law.

Article 16

'Ordre public'

The application of a rule of the law of any country specified by this Convention may be refused only if such application is manifestly incompatible with the public policy ('ordre public') of the forum.

Article 17

No retrospective effect

This Convention shall apply in a Contracting State to contracts made after the date on which this Convention has entered into force with respect to that State.

Article 18

Uniform interpretation

In the interpretation and application of the preceding uniform rules, regard shall be had to their international character and to the desirability of achieving uniformity in their interpretation and application.

Article 19

States with more than one legal system

1. Where a State comprises several territorial units each of which has its own rules of law in respect of contractual obligations, each territorial unit shall be considered as a country for the purposes of identifying the law applicable under this Convention.

2. A State within which different territorial units have their own rules of law in respect of contractual obligations shall not be bound to apply this Convention to conflicts solely between the laws of such units.

Article 20

Precedence of Community law

This Convention shall not affect the application of provisions which, in relation to particular matters, lay down choice of law rules relating to contractual obligations and which are or will be contained in acts of the institutions of the European Communities or in national laws harmonized in implementation of such acts.

Article 21

Relationship with other conventions

This Convention shall not prejudice the application of international conventions to which a Contracting State is, or becomes, a party.

Article 22

Reservations

1. Any Contracting State may, at the time of signature, ratification, acceptance or approval, reserve the right not to apply:

(a) the provisions of Article 7 (1);

(b) the provisions of Article 10 (1) (e).

2. Any Contracting State may also, when notifying an extension of the Convention in accordance with Article 27 (2), make one or more of these reservations, with its effect limited to all or some of the territories mentioned in the extension.

3. Any Contracting State may at any time withdraw a reservation which it has made; the reservation shall cease to have effect on the first day of the third calendar month after notification of the withdrawal.

TITLE III

FINAL PROVISIONS

Article 23

1. If, after the date on which this Convention has entered into force for a Contracting State, that State wishes to adopt any new choice of law rule in regard to any particular category of contract within the scope of this Convention, it shall communicate its intention to the other signatory States through the Secretary-Geneal of the Council of the European Communities.

2. Any signatory State may, within six months from the date of the communication made to the Secretary-General, request him to arrange consultations between signatory States in order to reach agreement.

3. If no signatory State has requested consultations within this period or if within two years following the communication made to the Secretary-General no agreement is reached in the course of consultations, the Contracting State concerned may amend its law in the manner indicated. The measures taken by that State shall be brought to the knowledge of the other signatory States through the Secretary-General of the Council of the European Communities.

Article 24

1. If, after the date on which this Convention has entered into force with respect to a Contracting State, that State wishes to become a party to a multilateral convention whose principal aim or one of whose principal aims is to lay down rules of private international law concerning any of the matters governed by this Convention, the procedure set out in Article 23 shall apply. However, the period of two

years, referred to in paragraph 3 of that Article, shall be reduced to one year.

2. The procedure referred to in the preceding paragraph need not be followed if a Contracting State or one of the European Communities is already a party to the multilateral convention, or if its object is to revise a convention to which the State concerned is already a party, or if it is a convention concluded within the framework of the Treaties establishing the European Communities.

Article 25

If a Contracting State considers that the unification achieved by this Convention is prejudiced by the conclusion of agreements not covered by Article 24 (1), that State may request the Secretary-General of the Council of the European Communities to arrange consultations between the signatory States of this Convention.

Article 26

Any Contracting State may request the revision of this Convention. In this event a revision conference shall be convened by the President of the Council of the European Communities.

Article 27

1. This Convention shall apply to the European territories of the Contracting States, including

Greenland, and to the entire territory of the French Republic.

2. Nothwithstanding paragraph 1:

(a) this Convention shall not apply to the Faroe Islands, unless the Kingdom of Denmark makes a declaration to the contrary;

(b) this Convention shall not apply to any European territory situated outside the United Kingdom for the international relations of which the United Kingdom is responsible, unless the United Kingdom makes a declaration to the contrary in respect of any such territory;

(c) this Convention shall apply to the Netherlands Antilles, if the Kingdom of the Netherlands makes a declaration to that effect.

3. Such declarations may be made at any time by notifying the Secretary-General of the Council of the European Communities.

4. Proceedings brought in the United Kingdom on appeal from courts in one of the territories referred to in paragraph 2 (b) shall be deemed to be proceedings taking place in those courts.

Article 28

1. This Convention shall be open from 19 June 1980 for signature by the States party to the Treaty establishing the European Economic Community.

2. This Convention shall be subject to ratification, acceptance or approval by the signatory States. The instruments of ratification, acceptance or approval shall be deposited with the Secretary-General of the Council of the European Communities.

Article 29

1. This Convention shall enter into force on the first day of the third month following the deposit of the seventh instrument of ratification, acceptance or approval.

2. This Convention shall enter into force for each signatory State ratifying, accepting or approving at a later date on the first day of the third month following the deposit of its instrument of ratification, acceptance or approval.

Article 30

1. This Convention shall remain in force for 10 years from the date of its entry into force in accordance with

Article 29 (1), even for States for which it enters into force at a later date.

2. If there has been no denunciation it shall be renewed tacitly every five years.

3. A Contracting State which wishes to denounce shall, not less than six months before the expiration of the period of 10 or five years, as the case may be, give notice to the Secretary-General of the Council of the European Communities. Denunciation may be limited to any territory to which the Convention has been extended by a declaration under Article 27 (2).

4. The denunciation shall have effect only in relation to the State which has notified it. The Convention will remain in force as between all other Contracting States.

Article 31

The Secretary-General of the Council of the European Communities shall notify the States party to the Treaty establishing the European Economic Community of:

(a) the signatures;

(b) the deposit of each instrument of ratification, acceptance or approval;

(c) the date of entry into force of this Convention;

(d) communications made in pursuance of Articles 23, 24, 25, 26, 27 and 30;

(e) the reservations and withdrawals of reservations referred to in Article 22.

Article 32

The Protocol annexed to this Convention shall form an integral part thereof.

Article 33

This Convention, drawn up in a single original in the Danish, Dutch, English, French, German, Irish and Italian languages, these texts being equally authentic, shall be deposited in the archives of the Secretariat of the Council of the European Communities. The Secretary-General shall transmit a certified copy thereof to the Government of each signatory State.

Til bekræftelse heraf har undertegnede behørigt befuldmægtigede underskrevet denne konvention.

Zu Urkund dessen haben die hierzu gehörig befugten Unterzeichneten ihre Unterschriften unter dieses Übereinkommen gesetzt.

In witness whereof the undersigned, being duly authorized thereto, have signed this Convention.

En foi de quoi, les soussignés, dûment autorisés à cet effet, ont signé la présente convention.

Dá fhianú sin, shínigh na daoine seo thíos, arna n-údarú go cuí chuige sin, an Coinbhinsiún seo.

In fede di che, i sottoscritti, debitamente autorizzati a tal fine, hanno firmato la presente convenzione.

Ten blijke waarvan, de ondergetekenden, daartoe behoorlijk gemachtigd, hun handtekening onder dit Verdrag hebben geplaatst.

Udfærdiget i Rom, den nittende juni nitten hundrede og firs.

Geschehen zu Rom am neunzehnten Juni neunzehnhundertachtzig.

Done at Rome on the nineteenth day of June in the year one thousand nine hundred and eighty.

Fait à Rome, le dix-neuf juin mil neuf cent quatre-vingt.

Arna dhéanamh sa Róimh, an naoú lá déag de Mheitheamh sa bhliain míle naoi gcéad ochtó.

Fatto a Roma, addì diciannove giugno millenovecentoottanta.

Gedaan te Rome, de negentiende juni negentienhonderd tachtig.

Pour le royaume de Belgique
Voor het Koninkrijk België

På kongeriget Danmarks vegne

Für die Bundesrepublik Deutschland

Pour la République française

Thar ceann na hÉireann

Per la Repubblica italiana

Pour le grand-duché de Luxembourg

Voor het Koninkrijk der Nederlanden

For the United Kingdom of Great Britain and Northern Ireland

PROTOCOL

The High Contracting Parties have agreed upon the following provision which shall be annexed to the Convention:

Notwithstanding the provisions of the Croatian Dammak may retain the rules contained in Søloven (Statute on Maritime Law) paragraph 169 concerning the applicable law in matters relating to carriage of goods by sea and may revise these rules without following the procedure prescribed in Article 23 of the Convention.

Til bekræftelse heraf har undertegnede behørigt befuldmægtigede underskrevet denne protokol.

Zu Urkund dessen haben die hierzu gehörig befugten Unterzeichneten ihre Unterschriften unter dieses Protokoll gesetzt.

In witness whereof the undersigned, being duly authorized thereto, have signed this Protocol.

En foi de quoi, les soussignés, dûment autorisés à cet effet, ont signé le présent protocole.

Dá fhianú sin, shínigh na daoine seo thíos, arna n-údarú go cuí chuige sin, an Prótacal seo.

In fede di che, i sottoscritti, debitamente autorizzati a tal fine, hanno firmato il presente protocollo.

Ten blijke waarvan, de ondergetekenden, daartoe behoorlijk gemachtigd, hun handtekening onder dit Protocol hebben geplaatst.

Udfærdiget i Rom, den nittende juni nitten hundrede og firs.

Geschehen zu Rom am neunzehnten Juni neunzehnhundertachtzig.

Done at Rome on the nineteenth day of June in the year one thousand nine hundred and eighty.

Fait à Rome, le dix-neuf juin mil neuf cent quatre-vingt.

Arna dhéanamh sa Róimh, an naoú lá déag de Mheitheamh sa bhliain míle naoi gcéad ochtó.

Fatto a Roma, addì diciannove giugno millenovecentoottanta.

Gedaan te Rome, de negentiende juni negentienhonderd tachtig.

Pour le royaume de Belgique
Voor het Koninkrijk België

På kongeriget Danmarks vegne

Für die Bundesrepublik Deutschland

Pour la République française

Thar ceann na hÉireann

Per la Repubblica italiana

Pour le grand-duché de Luxembourg

Voor het Koninkrijk der Nederlanden

For the United Kingdom of Great Britain and Northern Ireland

JOINT DECLARATION

At the time of the signature of the Convention on the law applicable to contractual obligations, the Governments of the Kingdom of Belgium, the Kingdom of Denmark, the Federal Republic of Germany, the French Republic, Ireland, the Italian Republic, the Grand Duchy of Luxembourg, the Kingdom of the Netherlands and the United Kingdom of Great Britain and Northern Ireland,

I. anxious to avoid, as far as possible, dispersion of choice of law rules among several instruments and differences between these rules,

express the wish that the institutions of the European Communities, in the exercise of their powers under the Treaties by which they were established, will, where the need arises, endeavour to adopt choice of law rules which are as far as possible consistent with those of this Convention;

II. declare their intention as from the date of signature of this Convention until becoming bound by Article 24, to consult with each other if any one of the signatory States wishes to become a party to any convention to which the procedure referred to in Article 24 would apply;

III. having regard to the contribution of the Convention on the law applicable to contractual obligations to the unification of choice of law rules within the European Communities, express the view that any State which becomes a member of the European Communities should accede to this Convention

Til bekræftelse heraf har undertegnede behørigt befuldmægtigede underskrevet denne fælleserklæring.

Zu Urkund dessen haben die hierzu gehörig befugten Unterzeichneten ihre Unterschriften unter diese gemeinsame Erklärung gesetzt.

In witness whereof the undersigned, being duly authorized thereto, have signed this Joint Declaration.

En foi de quoi, les soussignés, dûment autorisés à cet effet, ont signé la présente déclaration commune.

Dá fhianú sin, shínigh na daoine seo thíos, arna n-údarú go cuí chuige sin, an Dearbhu Comhphaírteach seo.

In fede di che, i sottoscritti, debitamente autorizzati a tal fine, hanno firmato la presente dichiarazione comune.

Ten blijke waarvan, de ondergetekenden, daartoe behoorlijk gemachtigd, hun handtekening onder deze Verklaring hebben geplaatst.

Udfærdiget i Rom, den nittende juni nitten hundrede og firs.

Geschehen zu Rom am neunzehnten Juni neunzehnhundertachtzig.

Done at Rome on the nineteenth day of June in the year one thousand nine hundred and eighty.

Fait à Rome, le dix neuf juin mil neuf cent quatre vingt.

Arna dhéanamh sa Róimh, an naoú lá déag de Mheitheamh sa bhliain míle naoi gcéad ochtó.

Fatto a Roma, addì diciannove giugno millenovecentoottanta.

Gedaan te Rome, de negentiende juni negentienhonderd tachtig.

Pour le gouvernement du royaume de Belgique
Voor de Regering van het Koninkrijk België

På kongeriget Danmarks vegne

Für die Regierung der Bundesrepublik Deutschland

Pour le gouvernement de la République française

Thar ceann Rialtas na hÉireann

Per il governo della Repubblica italiana

Pour le gouvernement du grand-duché de Luxembourg

Voor de Regering van het Koninkrijk der Nederlanden

For the Government of the United Kingdom of Great Britain and Northern Ireland

JOINT DECLARATION

The Governments of the Kingdom of Belgium, the Kingdom of Denmark, the Federal Republic of Germany, the French Republic, Ireland, the Italian Republic, the Grand Duchy of Luxembourg, the Kingdom of the Netherlands, and the United Kingdom of Great Britain and Northern Ireland,

On signing the Convention on the law applicable to contractual obligations;

Desiring to ensure that the Convention is applied as effectively as possible;

Anxious to prevent differences of interpretation of the Convention from impairing its unifying effect;

Declare themselves ready:

1. to examine the possibility of conferring jurisdicition in certain matters on the Court of Justice of the European Communities and, if necessary, to negotiate an agreement to this effect;

2. to arrange meetings at regular intervals between their representatives.

Til bekræftelse heraf har undertegnede behørigt befuldmægtigede underskrevet denne fælleserklæring.

Zu Urkund dessen haben die hierzu gehörig befugten Unterzeichneten ihre Unterschriften unter diese gemeinsame Erklärung gesetzt.

In witness whereof the undersigned, being duly authorized thereto, have signed this Joint Declaration.

En foi de quoi, les soussignés, dûment autorisés à cet effet, ont signé la présente déclaration commune.

Dá fhianú sin shínigh na daoine seo thíos, arna n-údarú go cuí chuige sin, an Dearbhu Comhpháirteach seo.

In fede di che, i sottoscritti, debitamente autorizzati a tal fine, hanno firmato la presente dichiarazione comune.

Ten blijke waarvan, de ondergetekenden, daartoe behoorlijk gemachtigd, hun handtekening onder deze Verklaring hebben geplaatst.

Udfærdiget i Rom, den nittende juni nitten hundrede og firs.

Geschehen zu Rom am neunzehnten Juni neunzehnhundertachtzig.

Done at Rome on the nineteenth day of June in the year one thousand nine hundred and eighty.

Fait à Rome, le dix-neuf juin mil neuf cent quatre-vingt.

Arna dhéanamh sa Róimh, an naoú lá déag de Mheitheamh sa bhliain míle naoi gcéad ochtó.

Fatto a Roma, addì diciannove giugno millenovecentoottanta.

Gedaan te Rome, de negentiende juni negentienhonderd tachtig.

Pour le gouvernement du royaume de Belgique
Voor de Regering van het Koninkrijk België

Pā kongeriget Danmarks vegne

Für die Regierung der Bundesrepublik Deutschland

Pour le gouvernement de la République française

Thar ceann Rialtas na hÉireann

Per il governo della Repubblica italiana

Pour le gouvernement du grand-duché de Luxembourg

Voor de Regering van het Koninkrijk der Nederlanden

For the Government of the United Kingdom of Great Britain and Northern Ireland

Draft Convention on Bankruptcy, Winding-up, Arrangements, Compositions and Similar Proceedings

PREAMBLE

The High Contracting Parties to the Treaty establishing the European Economic Community;

Desiring to implement the provisions of Article 220 of that Treaty by virtue of which they undertook to secure the simplification of formalities governing the reciprocal recognition and enforcement of judgments, of Courts or Tribunals;

Anxious to strengthen in the Community the legal protection of persons therein established;

Considering that it is necessary for this purpose to determine the jurisdiction of their courts or authorities with regard to bankruptcy, winding-up, arrangements, compositions and similar proceedings and to facilitate the recognition and enforcement of judgments given in such matters;

Have decided to conclude this Convention and to this end have designated as their Plenipotentiaries:

HIS MAJESTY THE KING OF THE BELGIANS

HER MAJESTY THE QUEEN OF DENMARK

THE PRESIDENT OF THE FEDERAL REPUBLIC OF GERMANY

THE PRESIDENT OF THE FRENCH REPUBLIC

THE PRESIDENT OF IRELAND

THE PRESIDENT OF THE ITALIAN REPUBLIC

HIS ROYAL HIGHNESS THE GRAND DUKE OF LUXEMBOURG

HER MAJESTY THE QUEEN OF THE NETHERLANDS

HER MAJESTY THE QUEEN OF THE UNITED KINGDOM OF GREAT
BRITAIN AND NORTHERN IRELAND

Who, meeting in the Council, having exchanged their Full Powers, found in
good and due form,

HAVE AGREED AS FOLLOWS:

TITLE I

SCOPE OF THE CONVENTION AND GENERAL PROVISIONS

Article 1 — Scope of the Convention

(1) This Convention shall apply, irrespective of the nationality of the persons concerned, to the proceedings (hereinafter called "bankruptcy"), specified in Article I(a) of the Protocol to this Convention, and to the arrangements, compositions and other proceedings listed in Article I(b) of the
Protocol.
     (2) In so far as is not otherwise provided, the provisions of this Conven-
tion relating to bankruptcy shall apply by analogy to the arrangements,
compositions and other proceedings listed in Article I(b) of the Protocol.
     (3) Nevertheless, this Convention shall apply to the bankruptcy and to

arrangements, compositions and the other proceedings listed in Article I(b) of the Protocol, as well as to the [special compulsory[1]] winding-up procedure, of insurance undertakings only when the Directive dealing with the co-ordination of national laws in this respect has been brought into force and in so far as this Directive does not otherwise provide.

It shall, however, apply to bankruptcies, arrangements, compositions and other proceedings listed in Article I(b) of the Protocol which are opened in respect of undertakings which are engaged only in re-insurance, with the exception however of mutual re-insurance companies which have entered into agreements with mutual insurance companies involving the complete re-insurance of the insurance contracts of those mutual insurance companies or the substitution of the assignee undertaking for the assigning undertaking for the fulfilment of obligations arising from the said contracts.

Article 2 — Unity of the bankruptcy

The proceedings to which this Convention applies shall, when opened in one of the Contracting States, have effect *ipso jure* in the other Contracting States and so long as they have not been closed, shall preclude the opening of any other such proceedings in those other States.

TITLE II

JURISDICTION

Section I

General Provisions

Article 3 — Jurisdiction based on the centre of administration

(1) Where the centre of administration of the debtor is situated in one of the Contracting States, the courts of that State shall have exclusive jurisdiction to declare the debtor bankrupt.

---

[1] The panel of experts has put the words "special compulsory" in brackets to indicate that in the present state of its work it considered that it is not appropriate to anticipate the terminology which will be used in the final text of the proposed directive mentioned in the first part of paragraph 3 of Article 1).

(2)   The centre of administration means the place where the debtor usually administers his main interests. In the case of firms, companies or legal persons that place shall be presumed, for the purposes of this Convention and until the contrary is proved, to be their registered office, if any.

(3)   Notwithstanding the second sentence of paragraph (2), in the case of firms, companies and legal persons which have been granted authorisation to carry on the business of insurance or credit institutions, the centre of administration shall always be the place where the registered office is situated.

Article 4 — Jurisdiction based on the existence of an establishment

(1)   Where the centre of administration is not situated in a Contracting State, the courts of any Contracting State in which the debtor has an establishment shall have jurisdiction to declare the debtor bankrupt.

(2)   For the purposes of this Convention, an establishment exists in a place where an activity of the debtor comprising a series of transactions is carried on by him or on his behalf.

Article 5 — Jurisdiction based on national law

Where neither the centre of administration nor any establishment is situated in a Contracting State, this Convention will not affect the competence of the courts of any Contracting State to declare the debtor bankrupt if its law so permits. A bankruptcy thus declared shall not fall within the scope of this Convention.

Article 6 — Transfer of the centre of administration to another Contracting State

(1)   Where the debtor has, within the six months next before the date when the court becomes seised of the matter, transferred his centre of administration to another Contracting State, both the courts of the latter State and those of the State where the centre of administration was previously situated shall have jurisdiction to declare the debtor bankrupt.

(2)   The courts of a Contracting State in which there has been opened one of the proceedings referred to in Article I(a) of the Protocol to this Convention, shall retain jurisdiction, so long as those proceedings have not been closed, to open subsequent bankruptcy or other proceedings referred to in this Convention against the same debtor even where the requirements laid down in Articles 3 and 4 as to jurisdiction are no longer satisfied.

(3)   The courts of a Contracting State in which there has been opened, in accordance with this Convention, one of the proceedings referred to in Article I(b) of the Protocol to this Convention, shall retain jurisdiction to substitute for the proceeding opened any other proceeding referred to in the Convention, even when the requirements laid down in Articles 3 and 4 as to jurisdiction are no longer satisfied. However, so long as such substitution has not taken place, any court which has acquired jurisdiction under Articles 3 or 4 may, if an arrangement or composition is already being implemented, open bankruptcy or other proceedings in respect of debts incurred after the approval of the arrangement or composition. When such bankruptcy or other proceedings have been opened the courts which previously had jurisdiction shall cease to have jurisdiction to effect such substitution as is referred to above.

Article 7 — Transfer of the centre of administration to a non-Contracting State

Where the debtor has transferred his centre of administration to a non-Contracting State, the courts of the Contracting State in which the centre of administration was previously situated shall retain jurisdiction if they become seised of the matter within twelve months after the transfer.

Article 8 — Transfer or closure of an establishment

(1)   Where the jurisdiction of the courts of a Contracting State is based on the existence of an establishment, Articles 6(1) and 7 shall apply *mutatis mutandis* in relation to the transfer thereof.

(2)   In the case of closure of the establishment, Article 6(1) shall apply *mutatis mutandis* if there remains another establishment within the Community; otherwise Article 7 shall apply *mutatis mutandis*.

Article 9 — Bankruptcy of the estate of a deceased person

Articles 3—8 shall also apply to the bankruptcy of the estate of a deceased person or to the bankruptcy of a debtor who dies before the Court becomes seised of the matter, if the conditions prescribed in these articles were fulfilled on the part of the debtor at the time of his death.

Section II

Special provisions

Article 10 — Particular capacity of the debtor

(1)   Where the courts of a Contracting State, which have jurisdiction under the provisions of the foregoing Section, are unable to open any of the proceedings listed in Article I of the Protocol by reason of their national law and of the capacity of the debtor, a bankruptcy may be declared by the courts of one of the other Contracting States if the debtor has an establishment in that State and if the law of that State so permits.

(2)   Judgments given under the rules of jurisdiction laid down in paragraph (1) shall not take effect in the Contracting State in which the debtor's centre of administration is situated.

Article 11 — Managers of firms, companies or legal persons. Members whose liability for the debts is unlimited

The Courts of the Contracting State in which the bankruptcy of a firm, company or legal person has been opened shall have exclusive jurisdiction to determine actions concerning

(a)   the liability incurred in consequence of their direction or management by persons who have directed or managed the affairs of that firm, company or legal person to pay compensation for loss or damage suffered by the general body of creditors, or, where the law of the Contracting State in which the bankruptcy has been opened so allows, for loss or damage sustained by the company;

(b)   liability for its debts by members whose joint and several liability in respect thereof is unlimited.

Article 12 — Claims on behalf of a firm, company or legal person in the bankruptcy of a person who has directed or managed its affairs or of a member whose liability for its debts is unlimited

Where a person to whom Article 11 applies has been declared bankrupt, the liquidator of the firm, company or legal person shall claim in the bankruptcy of that person in the name and on behalf of the general body of creditors.

Section III

Rules to prevent conflicts of jurisdiction

Article 13 — Concurrent jurisdiction

(1) Where the courts of different Contracting States are considering whether to open bankruptcy proceedings in respect of the same debtor, and the jurisdiction of one of those courts prevails under the provisions of this Convention, the other courts shall, if necessary of their own motion, either declare that they have no jurisdiction or stay the proceedings. They shall maintain this position so long as the judgment delivered by the court whose jurisdiction prevails, whereby the bankruptcy is opened, can be the subject of any of the appeal proceedings set out in Article XII of the Protocol hereto.

(2) Where the courts of different Contracting States which have concurrent jurisdiction under the provisions of this Convention are considering whether to open bankruptcy proceedings in respect of the same debtor, and one of those courts actually opens the bankruptcy, the other courts shall stay proceedings so long as the judgment opening the bankruptcy can be the subject of any of the appeal proceedings set out in Article XII of the Protocol hereto.

Article 14 — Conflicting disclaimers of jurisdiction

(1) Where there exist circumstances of such a nature that the jurisdiction of the courts of another Contracting State prevails over that of the Court already seised of the matter, the latter court shall, if necessary of its own motion, either stay proceedings and grant time to enable the applicant to bring proceedings in the former courts, or decline jurisdiction.

(2) Where, by a judgment which is no longer subject to any of the forms of appeal specified in Article XII of the Protocol, the court of a Contracting State has, under paragraph (1), declined jurisdiction, the courts of the other Contracting States may not decline jurisdiction on the ground that in the first-mentioned State there exists a basis of jurisdiction which the courts of that State have refused to acknowledge.

Section IV

Actions arising from the bankruptcy

Article 15 — Actions arising from the bankruptcy

The courts of the State in which the bankruptcy has been opened shall have exclusive jurisdiction to entertain proceedings concerning:

(1) Claims as to the invalidity as against the general body of creditors of transactions carried out by the debtor before or after the opening of the bankruptcy, even if those transactions relate to immovable property;

(2) Claims for payment or for recovery of property which are based on the allegation that the transaction referred to in paragraph (1) are void as against the general body of creditors or on the allegation that they should be set aside where those claims are made against the party who transacted with the debtor;

(3) Complaints concerning the capacity or powers of the liquidator, subject to the provisions of Article 33(3);

(4) Disputes relating to the validity of disposals by the liquidator, of the movable property of the bankrupt, which involve an allegation that there has been a breach of the rules determining the powers of the liquidator in that respect, subject to the provisions of Article 33(3);

(5) Claims against the general body of creditors in respect of movable property;

(6) Actions brought against the spouse of the bankrupt in which a particular provision of bankruptcy law is invoked;

(7) Actions relating to the admission of debts; but this rule shall not:

(a) as regards fiscal debts or debts similarly recoverable, social security debts and debts arising under a contract of employment, affect the jurisdiction of those courts and authorities which are in the ordinary way competent to determine whether a debt exists and, if so, the amount thereof, and whether it is preferential and, if so, to what extent;

(b) as regards debts which are covered by general or special preferential rights over property which is subject to registration or by secured rights over property which is subject to registration, affect the jurisdiction of those courts in the Contracting State in which the property is situated which are in the ordinary way competent to determine what secured rights or general or special preferential rights exist over it;

(8) Actions brought for the purpose of terminating current contracts under a provision of bankruptcy law, with the exception of contracts of

employment and contracts relating to immovable property;

(9) Actions based on the personal liability of the liquidator acting in his capacity as such and disputes relating to the submission of his accounts.

Article 16

The rules contained in Article 15(7)(a) and (b) shall not affect the jurisdiction of the court which opened the bankruptcy to determine whether a debt is to be admitted.

TITLE III

APPLICABLE LAW

Article 17 — Requirements for the opening of a bankruptcy

The requirements for the opening of a bankruptcy shall be determined by the internal law of the Contracting State in which the court having jurisdiction in accordance with this Convention is situated.

Article 18 — Procedure and effects of the bankruptcy

(1) The internal law of the State in which the bankruptcy has been opened shall determine the procedure to be followed.

(2) Subject to the provisions to the contrary contained in Title IV, the law of the State in which the bankruptcy has been opened, including where appropriate its rules of private international law, shall determine the effects of the bankruptcy and also the conditions under which the bankruptcy is effective against third parties.

Article 19 — Characterisation of property

For purposes of the application of this Convention, the lex situs shall determine whether property is movable or immovable.

TITLE IV

GENERAL EFFECTS OF THE BANKRUPTCY

Section I

Effects of the bankruptcy independently of advertisement

Article 20 — Cessation of debtor's power to deal with his property

Independently of the provisions for advertisement contained in Article 26 the bankruptcy shall take effect against the debtor in each Contracting State, and in particular with respect to the cessation of his power to deal with his property.

Article 21 — Prohibition of proceedings brought by individual creditors, including enforcement measures

In the Contracting States other than that in which the bankruptcy has been opened the bankruptcy shall, independently of the provisions for advertisement contained in Article 26 preclude the commencement against the debtor of any proceedings, including enforcement measures, affecting the property included in the assets in the bankruptcy, on the part of creditors whose debts arose before the bankruptcy was opened and are not secured by a charge on movable or immovable property. This prohibition shall take effect on the date laid down in the law of the State in which the bankruptcy has been opened.

Article 22 — Stay of proceedings brought by individual creditors, including enforcement measures

(1) In accordance with the conditions laid down in Article 21, the bankruptcy shall operate to stay all actions affecting the property included in the assets in the bankruptcy which were commenced before the bankruptcy was opened. However, if it is necessary to continue the action, the court previously seised shall remain competent to determine it if, in the course of the proceedings, an order has been made on any point in dispute other than one of jurisdiction.

(2) In accordance with the conditions laid down in Article 21, the bankruptcy shall operate to stay all enforcement measures against the debtor

which were commenced before the bankruptcy was opened. However, such measures shall not be stayed where, at the date of the judgment opening the bankruptcy, they have reached such a stage that, under the law of the Contracting State where they were commenced, the judgment opening the bankruptcy would no longer have any staying effect.

(3) Actions for recovery of movable property may be continued only in the courts having jurisdiction under Article 15(5), unless the court previously seised has already made an order on any point in dispute other than one of jurisdiction.

(4) The conditions under which proceedings which have been suspended in accordance with the preceding paragraphs may be continued shall be determined by the law of the State in which the bankruptcy has been opened.

Article 23

The provisions of Articles 21 and 22 shall not affect the rights of authorities and agencies to collect in their territory fiscal debts and debts similarly recoverable.

Article 24 — Interruption of periods of limitation

Notwithstanding Articles 20, 21 [and 22,] acts done by third parties after the opening of the bankruptcy and before it has taken effect against them in accordance with Article 27 shall interrupt any periods of limitation enuring as regards the general body of creditors, and shall prevent the latter from relying on any loss of rights resulting from any failure to perform acts which are to be effected within a compulsory time.

[Article 25 — Time limits for the exercise of certain legal remedies

(1) Where the applicant has neither his centre of administration nor his "domicile" nor his residence in the State in which the bankruptcy has been opened, but one or more of them is situated in another contracting State any such application to set aside the judgment opening the bankruptcy as may be allowed under national law to third parties who were not party to the proceedings may be brought within a period of at least thirty-one days following the day which under that law initiated the period.

(2) The law of the State in which the bankruptcy has been opened shall determine the conditions for the extension of that period, where it expires

on a Saturday or Sunday, or on a day which according to that law is a public holiday.]

Section II

Effects of the bankruptcy dependent upon advertisement

Article 26 — Requirements as to advertisement

(1) It shall be for the liquidator to advertise the bankruptcy by the insertion in the *Official Journal of the European Communities* of an extract of the judgment opening it. The liquidator must cause this insertion to be made in cases where an establishment of the bankrupt is situated in a Contracting State other than that in which the bankruptcy has been opened, and also in all cases where the court which has opened the bankruptcy has so ordered. He may in all other cases effect such advertisement if he thinks fit. These provisions shall also apply to the decisions listed in Article IV of the Protocol to this Convention.

(2) In the Contracting States other than that in which the bankruptcy has been opened, the liquidator must make sure that the bankruptcy judgment is entered in the trade or company registers in which the bankrupt is registered.

(3) In the Contracting States other than that in which the bankruptcy has been opened, the liquidator may advertise the bankruptcy judgment in the Official Gazettes listed in Article VII of the Protocol to this Convention and may, if need be, further advertise the judgment as he thinks fit.

[(4) The requirements as to advertisement laid down in paragraphs (1)–(3) shall as necessary apply to the other decisions listed in Article IV of the Protocol to this Convention. The particulars to be advertised in respect of each category of decision are listed in Articles III and VI of that Protocol. It shall be for the liquidator to effect such advertisement.]

5) The law of the State in which the bankruptcy has been opened may provide for some other person or authority to carry out the requirements as to advertisement prescribed in this Article.

Article 27 — Effects of the bankruptcy as against third parties

(1) In the Contracting States other than that in which the bankruptcy has been opened the bankruptcy shall take effect in full against third parties from the eighth day following its advertisement in the *Official Journal of the*

European Communities. Acts done after the expiry of that period shall be void as against the general body of creditors if they cause detriment to the latter.

(2) Acts done before the aforesaid advertisement or within seven days thereafter shall also be voidable as against the general body of creditors if, when the act was done, the third party knew or ought reasonably to have known of the opening of the bankruptcy.

(3) The rules of the State in which the bankruptcy has been opened which relate to the invalidity as against the general body of creditors of certain acts done by the debtor before the bankruptcy was opened may, however, be applied to acts done during the period between the opening of the bankruptcy and the eighth day following its advertisement in the *Official Journal of the European Communities.*

(4) This article shall apply subject to the provisions of Article 28.

Article 28 — Effects with regard to property subject to registration

The effects of the bankruptcy on rights relating to property which is subject to registration in a public register and on rights and securities subject to such registration shall, with regard to, inter alia, establishment, modification, transfer or termination, be determined by the law of the Contracting State in which the register is kept as if the bankruptcy had been opened in that State.

Section III

Powers and functions of authorities administering the bankruptcy

Article 29 — Powers of the liquidator

(1) In the Contracting States the liquidator shall have the powers which are vested in him by the law of the State in which the bankruptcy has been opened, or which have been conferred on him by the competent authority of that State. In this connection, the procedural means to be followed by the liquidator shall be determined by the law of the Contracting State where the exercise of those powers produces its effects. He shall have power in relation to the matters covered in Article 28 to apply for the registrations required by the laws of the other Contracting State where the register is kept.

(2) The appointment of the liquidator shall be evidenced by a certificate drawn up in accordance with the specimen form attached to the Protocol to this Convention.

(3) Where the law of the State in which the bankruptcy has been opened permits the appointment of more than one liquidator, one or more of them may be chosen from among persons who, in the territories of the other Contracting States, are authorised to act as liquidators. Where the law of the State in which the bankruptcy has been opened permits the delegation of certain powers of the liquidator to other persons, such persons may be chosen from among those who, in the territories of the other Contracting States, are authorised to act as liquidators.

Article 30 — Redirection of mail

(1) Where the law of the State in which the bankruptcy has been opened provides that mail may be redirected to the liquidator and the bankrupt is "domiciled" or resident or has an establishment or postal address in a Contracting State other than that in which the bankruptcy has been opened, mail addressed to the bankrupt shall be redirected to the liquidator by the postal authorities of that State. Such redirection of mail may take place only as a result of an order to that effect made either by the court which has opened the bankruptcy or by the "juge-commissaire". This order shall be valid for a maximum period of six months and may be renewed for a similar period from time to time until the closure of the proceedings, under the conditions laid down by the law of the State in which the bankruptcy has been opened.

(2) Article IX of the Protocol to this Convention specifies the manner in which postal authorities are to be informed of the bankruptcy and of the duration of the duty placed upon them pursuant to paragraph (1).

(3) When mail addressed to the bankrupt is sent to him by the liquidator, it shall bear the liquidator's name, capacity and signature.

Article 31 — Lodging of claims

(1) Where the law of the State in which the bankruptcy has been opened requires that claims should be lodged, known creditors who reside in a Contracting State other than that in which the bankruptcy has been opened shall be individually notified of the opening of the bankruptcy. The notification shall indicate
— whether creditors whose claims are preferential or secured need prove in the bankruptcy and
— the manner in which the true nature of the claim must be affirmed if this formality is required.

(2) Subject to any necessary formality as to affirmation, creditors who reside in a contracting State other than that in which the bankruptcy has been opened may lodge their claims by writing informally in a letter written in one of the official languages of the Contracting States to the bankruptcy authorities specified in Article X of the Protocol to this Convention which shall, where necessary, provide for translation. The claim shall indicate the date, the amount of the debt and whether or not the debt is preferential or secured and shall be accompanied by a copy of such supporting documents as exist.

Article 32 — Continuance of business

The competent authority under the law of the State in which the bankruptcy has been opened shall have power to authorize the continuance of the business in the other Contracting States.

Article 33 — Realisation of the assets

(1) The Liquidator shall without further formality take such protective measures and effect such disposals as are within the scope of the powers conferred upon him, either by the law of the State in which the bankruptcy has been opened, or by an authorisation granted by the competent authorities administering the bankruptcy. In this connection, the procedural means to be followed by the liquidator shall be determined by the law of the Contracting State in which the property is situated. However, the Liquidator may himself dispose of property, which is subject to a charge in a Contracting State other than that in which the bankruptcy has been opened only if this is permitted under the law of the State in which the property is situated.

(2) Where the law of the State in which the bankruptcy has been opened or the court which has opened the bankruptcy, requires a particular form of realisation, such as public auction, the way in which it is to be effected shall be determined by the law of the place where the property is situated.

(3) Where the debtor, a creditor or a third party has an objection to a protective measure or disposal undertaken by the liquidator in a Contracting State other than that in which the bankruptcy has been opened, any of them may apply to the local court of that State having jurisdiction in accordance with the procedure for urgent matters. That court may order, either that the objection be dismissed, or that there be a stay of execution with sufficient time granted to enable an application to be made to the court having substantive jurisdiction in accordance with the law of the State in which the bankruptcy has been opened.

Section IV

Effects of the bankruptcy on the estate of the debtor

Article 34 — Universality of the bankruptcy

(1)   Subject to Article 10(2) and Article 66, a bankruptcy opened in conformity with this Convention shall take effect with respect to the whole of the debtor's assets situated in the Contracting States. Property held by the debtor in the capacity of trustee on behalf of other persons shall not be considered part of the debtor's assets.

(2)   The bankruptcy shall not however take effect with respect to assets to which the debtor becomes entitled subsequent to the opening of the bankruptcy, where the law of the State in which the bankruptcy has been opened excludes such assets.

(3)   Paragraph 1 shall not apply to property which is excluded from the bankruptcy by virtue of the law of the Contracting State in which it is situated for a reason other than that the debtor became entitled to that property subsequent to the opening of the bankruptcy.

Article 35 — Rights of spouses

(1)   If the law of the State in which the bankruptcy has been opened presumes, in the event of bankruptcy, that the property of the spouse has been acquired with the funds of the bankrupt, this presumption shall not apply to property situated in Contracting States whose law does not include such a presumption, unless the law governing matrimonial property rights includes such a presumption. Any such presumption may be rebutted in the manner provided by Article 1 of Annex I.

(2)   The bankruptcy provisions of the law of the State in which the bankruptcy has been opened shall determine to what extent "les avantages matrimoniaux" and disposals of property to a spouse without valuable consideration are to be held valid as against the general body of creditors.

Section V

Effects of the bankruptcy on past acts and on current contracts

Article 36 — Set-off

The law of the Contracting States must allow set-off in the event of bankruptcy, at least in the cases referred to in Article 2 of Annex I.

Article 37 — Recovery actions

When, according to the law of the State in which the bankruptcy has been opened, a recovery action, brought in the interest of the general body of creditors, in respect of an act done by the debtor in fraud of the rights of the creditors is provided for only by provisions of law other than bankruptcy law, the conditions regulating the setting aside shall be those applicable under the law of the State which governs the transaction as if the bankruptcy had been opened in that State.

Article 38 — Contracts of employment

(1) The effects of the bankruptcy on a contract of employment shall be governed by the law applicable to that contract, where that law is the law of a Contracting State.

(2) In other cases the law of the State in which the bankruptcy has been opened shall apply.

Article 39 — Contracts of leases and hiring

The effects of the bankruptcy on leases or tenancies of immovable property shall be governed by the law of the place where that property is situated. The same shall apply where the lease or tenancy relates both to movable and immovable property.

Article 40 — Contracts of sale

The effects of the bankruptcy on contracts for the sale of immovable property shall be governed by the law of the place where the property is situated. The same shall apply to contracts of lease/sale, "crédit-bail" or leasing of immovables and to combined sales of immovable and movable property.

Article 41 — Contracts of sale of movable property with reservation of title

1. *First Variant*
The validity of sales with reservation of title shall be governed by the law designated in accordance with the rules of private international law of the State in which the bankruptcy has been opened.

Second Variant
The validity of sales with reservation of title shall be determined by the law governing the contract.

Third Variant
[No provisions at all in this Convention; as a consequence the law of the State in which the bankruptcy has been opened shall apply in accordance with Article 18 of this Convention.]

2. *First Variant*
In the event of the bankruptcy of the buyer or seller, the validity as against the general body of creditors of clauses containing a reservation of title shall be governed by the provisions of Article 3 of Annex I.

Article 3 of Annex I
   (1) The law of the State in which the bankruptcy has been opened shall at least admit that clauses containing a reservation of title in the thing sold and guaranteeing payment of the price, are valid as against the creditors of the buyer, provided they are stipulated, before delivery and by written agreement, [telegram] telex or by oral agreement confirmed in writing by the buyer. The writing shall not be subject to any particular requirements as to form. The liquidator may prove by any means the fraudulent or inaccurate character of the writing or of the date thereof.
   (2) The bankruptcy of the seller occuring after the thing sold has been delivered shall not be a ground for rescinding the contract and shall not prevent the buyer from acquiring ownership of the thing sold.

Second Variant
In the event of the bankruptcy:
— of the buyer, the applicable law for determining the validity of the reservation of title clauses as against the general body of creditors, shall be the law of the contracting State in whose territory the property, being the subject of these reservation of title clauses, is situated at the time of the opening of the bankruptcy.

— of the seller occuring after the thing sold has been delivered, the bankruptcy shall not be a ground for rescinding the contract and shall not prevent
the buyer from acquiring ownership of the thing sold.

Third Variant
[No provisions at all in this Convention; as a consequence the law of the State
in which the bankruptcy has been opened shall apply in accordance with
Article 18 of this Convention.]

Article 42 — Rights of preferential creditors

The provisions of this section do not apply to the system of preferential
claims, secured claims and claims by creditors in respect of debts incurred by
the general body of creditors (créances de masse) which is governed by
Section VI of this title.

Section VI

**Preferential claims, secured claims, claims by creditors in respect of debts
incurred by the general body of creditors (créances de masse)**

Article 43 — Sub-estates for accounting purposes

(1)   For the purposes of the distribution of the assets pursuant to the provisions of this section, a sub-estate shall be formed for accounting purposes in
relation to each Contracting State in which assets to be realised are situated.
    (2)   Assets recovered in a non-Contracting State, or the proceeds of their
realisation, shall be aggregated with the sub-estate situated in the State in
which the bankruptcy has been opened.

*Article 44 — Rights of creditors in respect of debts incurred on behalf of the
general body of creditors or who have general rights of preference*

(1)   Creditors in respect of debts incurred after the opening of the bankruptcy [other than fiscal debts and debts similarly recoverable][1] will be satisfied

---

[1]   In regard to fiscal debts and debts similarly recoverable incurred after the opening
of the bankruptcy and which are liabilities of the general body of creditors, governments
have the choice of two alternatives as follows:

→

out of the assets situated in each of the Contracting States where they are
considered to be liabilities of the general body of creditors. The contributions of each sub-estate towards the payment of these debts will be made,
according to the ranking laid down in the law of the Contracting State
concerned, in proportion to the assets available for that purpose.

(2) In civil and commercial matters, creditors in respect of debts incurred
before the opening of the bankruptcy may invoke, in respect of assets situated in each of the Contracting States the rights against the general body of
creditors or the rights of preference as the law of that State attaches to these
debts. Debts which, even though incurred before the opening of the bankruptcy are deemed by the law of one Contracting State to be debts incurred
by the general body of creditors and which, in the other Contracting States
enjoy general rights of preference, shall be satisfied in accordance with Article 50 out of the assets available respectively in all the sub-estates.

(3) In matters other than civil and commercial, and particularly in fiscal
or social security matters, the public authorities, government departments
and other public agencies of a Contracting State, may exercise their right to
payment of a debt incurred before [or after] the opening of the bankruptcy
on behalf of the general body of creditors or the right of preference to which
they are entitled in that State only in relation to assets situated there. To the
extent that they have not obtained full satisfaction in that State and irrespective of whether their rights are preferential or not, they shall be entitled,
subject always to the acts of the European Communities and to bilateral
agreements concluded between Contracting States, to claim as unsecured
creditors in any other Contracting State, provided the (unsecured) debt
would have been admitted to proof in a bankruptcy opened in their own
State.

Article 45 — Law applicable to general rights of preference

For the purposes of distributing the proceeds of realisation of the assets in
bankruptcy, the subject-matter, extent and ranking of general preferences

---

First variant
Satisfaction of the said debts out of the assets situated in *each* of the contracting States.
In that case the words in brackets in paragraphs (1) and (3) will be deleted.

Second variant
The said debts are to be satisfied only out of the assets situated in the contracting State in
which these debts were incurred. In that case the brackets in paragraphs (1) and (3) will
be deleted and the words "other than fiscal debts and debts similarly recoverable" and
"or after", respectively, will be retained.

shall be determined by the law of the Contracting State in which the assets were situated at the time when the bankruptcy was opened.

Article 46 — Law applicable to secured rights and special rights of preference

For the purposes of distributing the proceeds of realisation of the assets in bankruptcy, the subject-matter, extent and ranking of secured rights and special rights of preference shall be determined by the law of the Contracting State in which the property charged with such a secured right or special right of preference was situated at the time when the bankruptcy was opened.

Article 47 — Law applicable to rights secured upon ships, boats and aircraft; determination of the place where those assets are situated

(1) For the purposes of distributing the proceeds of realisation of the assets, the subject matter, extent and ranking of unregistrable special rights of preference over a ship or aircraft shall be determined by the law of the Contracting State in which the ship or aircraft is situated when it is sold. If at the time of sale the ship or aircraft is situated in a non-Contracting State, the law of the State in which it is registered shall apply.

(2) For the purposes of distributing the proceeds of realisation of the assets, the subject matter, extent and ranking of registered secured rights over a ship or aircraft, such as "hypothèques" and mortgages, shall be determined by the law of the State in which the ship or aircraft is registered. [The same shall apply in the case of unregisterable special rights of preference and registered secured rights over an inland navigation vessel registered in a Contracting State[1] (subject however to the rights of preference arising under the law of the Contracting State in which attachment or forced sale is carried out)[2] (if the law of the State where the vessel is registered authorises or recognises such rights of preference)].

(3) The law applicable under paragraph 1 shall determine the ranking as between, on the one hand, the rights of special preference referred to in paragraphs (1) [and (2)] and, on the other hand, the registered secured rights referred to in paragraph (2).

---

[1] The German delegation requested that these words be retained but the Netherlands delegation requested that all the text which follows the words "registered in a contracting State" be deleted.

(2) The German delegation requested that these words be deleted if its request concerning the problem raised in note 1 above is satisfied.

(4) The provisions of the foregoing paragraphs shall also apply to ships and aircraft [and boats] under construction if they have been registered.

(5) Property referred to in this Article shall, for the purposes of Articles 43, 44 and 45 be deemed to be situated in the State whose law is applicable under paragraph (3) above.

Article 48 — Rights of lien

The right to a lien on property shall be governed by the law of the Contracting State in which the property is held.

Article 49 — Ranking as between (1) general rights of preference and claims in respect of debts incurred by the general body of creditors (créances de masse), and (2) secured rights and special rights of preference

Ranking as between general rights of preference and claims against the general body of creditors on the one hand and secured rights and special rights of preference on the other shall be determined by the law of the Contracting State in which the property is situated when the bankruptcy is opened.

Article 50 — Principles governing distribution where general rights of preference apply in relation to more than one Contracting State

(1) Where a general right of preference attaches to a debt, within the meaning of the first sentence of Article 44(2), which may be satisfied simultaneously out of a number of sub-estates, the following procedure shall be adopted:
— where a general right of preference attaches to a debt in each of the Contracting States in which there are sub-estates, for a like amount in each, the debt shall be borne in equal shares by those sub-estates. However, where the assets available in one or more sub-estates are insufficient to discharge the debt, the remainder shall be divided in equal shares between the other sub-estates to the extent that they contain sufficient available assets.
— where a general right of preference attaches to a debt in each of the States in which there are sub-estates, for different amounts because the extent of preference is not the same in all the States, the debt shall be borne by each sub-estate up to the amount of the most extensive right of preference in proportion to the sums to which the general right of preference attaches in each State and up to the amount of those sums. If the

preferential debt is not wholly discharged thereby, one or more further distributions shall be made on the same principles from the assets remaining available in each sub-estate.

(2)   In the cases provided for in the foregoing paragraph, where a general right of preference attaching to a debt is effective in relation to more than one sub-estate and other preferential debts rank equally with the first debt in some of those sub-estates, the amount available from the sub-estates in which a number of debts rank equally shall be distributed in proportion to those debts, and contribution from the sub-estates for the discharge of the first-mentioned preferential debt shall not exceed the amount of the share available for such distribution.

(3)   If, due to the fact that the ranking within different sub-estates varies to such an extent that it will be impossible simultaneously to satisfy a general preference from different sub-estates, that debt shall be first borne by the sub-estate where the debt has the highest ranking. If after this in order to satisfy another right of general preference, assets are simultaneouly available from more than one sub-estate, the rules mentioned in paragraphs (1) and (2) of this Article shall be applied.

Article 51 — Determination of the place where certain property is situated

For the purposes of Articles 43, 44, 45, 46 and 49:
—   movable property including incorporeal property, but excluding that referred to in Article 47, which is registered, inscribed or recorded in a national public register of a Contracting State shall be deemed to be situated in that State;
—   incorporeal property which is registered, inscribed or recorded only in an international public register, shall be deemed to be situated in the State in which the bankruptcy has been opened.

Article 52 — Date applicable for determining the place where property is situated in a bankruptcy which follows upon other proceedings

Where either a bankruptcy or any of the proceedings listed in Article I(b) of the Protocol to this Convention has been opened superseding any of the other proceedings listed in Article I(b) of the said Protocol; the date applicable for determining where the property referred to in Articles 45, 46 and 49 is situated shall be the date upon which the last of the proceedings was opened.

Section VII

Effects of the bankruptcy on the personal capacity of the debtor

Article 53 — Disabilities, disqualification and restrictions of rights

It shall be a matter for the law of each Contracting State to determine whether, and to what extent, disabilities, disqualifications and restrictions of rights will be entailed, within its jurisdiction, by the opening of bankruptcy in any Contracting State.

Section VIII

Special provisions applying to certain proceedings other than bankruptcy

Article 54 — Invalidity, as against preferential or secured creditors, of extensions of time for payment and compounding of debts

Extensions of the time for payment or compounding of debts allowed to the debtor in one of the forms of proceeding listed in Article I(b) of the Protocol to this Convention shall in Contracting States other than that in which the proceeding has been opened be invalid as against the creditors for the debts referred to in the second sentence of Article 44(2) as well as those creditors whose debts are preferential or secured by a charge over property.

TITLE V

RECOGNITION AND ENFORCEMENT

Article 55 — Judgments

For the purposes of this Convention, "judgment" means any judgment given by a court, tribunal or authority of a Contracting State, whatever the judgment may be called, including a decree, decision, order or writ of execution, as well as the determination of costs or expenses by an officer of the court, and includes the decisions listed in Article V of the Protocol.

Section I

Recognition of judgments concerning the opening and course of the proceedings

Article 56 — Recognition as of right

Subject to the provisions of Articles 5, 10(2) and 66, as well as of this Section, judgments concerning the opening and procedure of one of the forms of proceeding listed in Article I of the Protocol to this Convention, including judgments under Article 15(3), and arrangements and compositions approved by a court, made in a Contracting State shall be recognised in the other Contracting States without any special procedure being required. These provisions shall not apply to judgments concerning the liberty of the individual.

Article 57 — Recognition in cases of conflict between non-co-ordinate jurisdictions

Where a bankruptcy has been opened against the same debtor by the courts of different Contracting States, and where the jurisdiction of one of those courts prevails under this Convention, the judgment given by the court whose jurisdiction prevails shall alone take effect, even in the States where the other judgments have been given.

Article 58 — Recognition in cases of conflict between coordinate jurisdictions

(1) Where a bankruptcy has been opened against the same debtor by the courts of different Contracting States, being courts of coordinate jurisdiction under this Convention, the judgment of the Court which first gave judgment shall alone take effect, even in the States where the other judgments have been given.

(2) Where, in the case provided for in paragraph (1), more than one judgment has been given on the same day, the alphabetical order of the place-names of the courts shall determine which takes precedence. The relevant place-name for this purpose shall be that given to the place where the court sits in the State in which it is situated.

Article 59 — Validity of Acts

Acts performed in accordance with a judgment referred to in Article 57 or 58 and before that judgment has been rendered ineffective by the operation of the aforesaid articles, shall not on that ground cease to be valid.

Section II

Enforcement of judgments concerning the opening and course of the proceedings

Article 60 — Enforcement as of right

Judgments and arrangements and compositions approved by a court, which are recognized under the provisions of the foregoing Section, shall take effect as of right and shall be enforced in the other Contracting States.

Section III
Proceedings to challenge the bankruptcy

Article 61 — Action to challenge the bankruptcy

In each Contracting State other than that in which the bankruptcy proceedings have been opened, an action to challenge the judgment opening the bankruptcy may be brought in the cases specified in Article 62.

Article 62 — Cases in which an action to challenge the bankruptcy may be brought

(1) An action to challenge the bankruptcy may be brought only in the following cases:
  (a) if, as a result of circumstances for which he cannot be held responsible, the debtor did not have knowledge of the proceedings in sufficient time, either to prepare his defence, or to avail himself of any legal remedy against the judgment opening the bankruptcy;
  (b) if recognition of the judgment opening the bankruptcy is contrary to the public policy of the State in which the action to challenge the bankruptcy is brought.
  (2) The action may not however be brought on the basis that the judgment is contrary to public policy on any of the following grounds:

(a) that the proceeding in question is unknown in the law of that State, if such proceeding is listed in Article I of the Protocol to this Convention;

(b) that the court which opened the bankruptcy had no jurisdiction;

(c) that the judgment could not have been given in the State where the action to challenge the bankruptcy is brought, by reason of its own law governing the requirements for opening of a bankruptcy;

(d) that the judgment has been given against a natural person or an association of natural or legal persons under private law, who or which could not have been declared bankrupt in the State where the action to challenge the bankruptcy has been brought, so long as such person or association of persons has not or no longer had his or its centre of administration in that State;

(e) that the judgment has been given on the court's own motion or *ex parte*.

Article 63 — Courts with jurisdiction to entertain actions to challenge the bankruptcy

(1) An action to challenge the bankruptcy shall be brought in each Contracting State before the Court designated in Article XI of the Protocol to this Convention.

(2) In the United Kingdom of Great Britain and Northern Ireland, an action to challenge the bankruptcy shall be brought only in one of the three designated courts, according to which is appropriate. The decision given by that court shall take effect in the whole of the United Kingdom.

Article 64 — Parties to such action and time limits

(1) The action to challenge the bankruptcy shall be brought against the person or persons having the powers of the liquidator according to Article 29(2) of this Convention. It may be brought by the "ministère public", the debtor or any other interested party, with the exception of the person who brought the bankruptcy proceedings. The petitioning creditor may be joined as a party to the action.

(2) The action may not be brought after the expiration of a period of three months from the date of advertisement of the bankruptcy judgment in the *Official Journal of the European Communities* or, in the absence of such advertisement, from the date when the person bringing the action had knowledge of the judgment. In no circumstances may the action be brought more than six months after the date on which the bankruptcy is opened nor after it has been closed.

Article 65 — Effects of an action to challenge the bankruptcy and legal remedies

(1) The bringing of an action to challenge the bankruptcy shall not operate to stay enforcement of the judgment opening the bankruptcy.

(2) The Court seised of such an action may nevertheless decide to stay enforcement in the State where such action is raised, in whole or in part, until it has decided the action. Courts with jurisdiction to decide matters of urgency shall also have power to stay enforcement in that State in whole or in part if they lay down a time limit within which an application is to be made to the court having substantive jurisdiction to entertain an action challenging the bankruptcy. Judgments ordering such a stay may also order measures to protect the estate situated in that State. The time limit thus set shall not operate to extend that applicable under Article 64(2). Upon expiry of the time limit, the judgment imposing the stay of execution shall cease to have effect if the court having substantive jurisdiction has not been seised of an action challenging the bankruptcy.

(3) A judgment declaring the bankruptcy invalid when it is *res judicata* shall, in the State in which it is given, take effect *erga omnes* and shall be advertised there in the same manner as a bankruptcy judgment. This judgment shall also be advertised in the *Official Journal of the European Communities* by the authority which advertised the bankruptcy judgment. A judgment in an action to challenge the bankruptcy shall be subject to appeal in the same way as a bankruptcy judgment.

(4) A judgment which has been successfully challenged shall cease to be recognised or to have effect in the State where the action to challenge the bankruptcy has been brought. The same shall apply accordingly to judgments given in the actions referred to in Article 11, in any of the proceedings set out in Article 15, as well as to any other judgments given in the course of the bankruptcy proceedings. In neither case, however, shall acts performed prior thereto in accordance with a judgment which has been declared invalid and rendered ineffective on that ground cease to be valid.

Article 66 — Territorial bankruptcy in the case of successful challenge

Where the judgment opening the bankruptcy in one Contracting State has been successfully challenged in an action brought in another Contracting State, a bankruptcy may be opened in the latter State. A bankruptcy so opened shall have no effect in the other Contracting States.

Section IV

Recognition and enforcement of other judgments

Article 67 — Application of the Brussels Convention of 27 September 1968

(1)   The recognition and enforcement of judgments and of settlements approved by a Court or made before a judge, other than those referred to in Article 56 of this Convention, shall be governed by the Brussels Convention of 27 September 1968 on Jurisdiction and the Enforcement of Judgments in Civil and Commercial Matters, as amended by the Convention of Accession of 9 October 1978. The same shall apply to instruments for enforcement delivered to creditors in bankruptcy proceedings in accordance with the law of the State in which the proceedings have been opened.

(2)   The provisions of paragraph (1) shall not apply to judgments concerning the liberty of the individual.

Section V

General provisions

Article 68 — Dispensing with security

No security, bond or deposit, however described, shall be required of a party bringing an action under Article 61, either on the ground that he is a foreign national, or on the ground that he is not domiciled or resident in the State in which the action is brought.

Article 69 — Dispensation from legalisation

No legalisation or similar formality shall be required in respect of documents produced in actions brought under Article 61.

TITLE VI

INTERPRETATION BY THE COURT OF JUSTICE

Article 70 — Jurisdiction of the Court of Justice

The Court of Justice of the European Communities shall have jurisdiction to

give rulings on the interpretation of this Convention, of the Protocol hereto
and of Annex I.

Article 71 — National Courts able to request interpretation

The following courts may request the Court of Justice to give preliminary
rulings on questions of interpretation:

(a) in Belgium: la Cour de Cassation — het Hof van Cassatie,
    in Denmark: the HÖJESTERET,
    in the Federal
    Republic of
    Germany: die obersten Gerichtshöfe des Bundes,
    in France: la Cour de Cassation and le Conseil d'Etat,
    in Ireland: the Supreme Court,
    in Italy: la Corte Suprema di Cassazione,
    in Luxembourg: [la Cour supérieure de Justice, when sitting as Cour
                         de Cassation],
    in the
    Netherlands: de Hoge Raad,
    in Great   The House of Lords and, in England and Wales the
    Britain and   Court of Appeal where no appeal lies against its deci-
    Northern   sion; in Scotland similarly the Inner House of the
    Ireland: Court of Session; and in Northern Ireland similarly
                         the Court of Appeal in Northern Ireland.

(b) the courts of the Contracting States when they are sitting in an
appellate capacity;

(c) in the cases provided for in Article 67 of this Convention, the courts
referred to in Article 37 of the Brussels Convention of 27 September 1968,
as amended by the Convention of Accession of 9 October 1978.

Article 72 — Preliminary rulings by the Court of Justice

(1) Where a question of interpretation of the Convention or of one of the
other instruments referred to in Article 70 is raised in a case pending before
one of the courts listed in Article 71(a), that court shall, if it considers that a
decision on the question is necessary to enable it to give judgment, request
the Court of Justice to give a ruling thereon.

(2) Where such a question is raised before any court referred to in Article
71(b) and (c), that court may, under the conditions laid down in paragraph
(1), of this Article request the Court of Justice to give a ruling thereon.

Article 73 — Other cases where the Court of Justice is seised

(1) The competent authority of a Contracting State may request the Court of Justice to give a ruling on a question of interpretation of the Convention or of one of the other instruments referred to in Article 70 if judgments given by courts of that State conflict with the interpretations given either by the Court of Justice or in a judgment of one of the courts of another Contracting State referred to in Article 71(a) and (b). The provisions of this paragraph shall apply only to judgments which have become *res judicata*.

(2) The interpretation given by the Court of Justice in response to such a request shall not affect the judgments which gave rise to the request for interpretation.

(3) The Procurators-General of the Courts of Cassation of the Contracting States, or any other authority designated by a Contracting State, shall be entitled to request the Court of Justice for a ruling on interpretation in accordance with paragraph (1).

(4) The Registrar of the Court of Justice shall give notice of the request to the Contracting States, to the Commission and to the Council of the European Communities; they shall then be entitled within two months of the notification to submit statements of case or written observations to the Court.

(5) No fees shall be levied or any costs or expenses awarded in respect of the proceedings provided for in this Article.

Article 74 — Application of provisions relating to the Court of Justice

(1) Except where this title otherwise provides, the provisions of the Treaty establishing the European Economic Community and those of the Protocol on the Statute of the Court of Justice annexed thereto, which are applicable when the Court is requested to give a preliminary ruling, shall also apply to any proceedings for the interpretation of the Convention and the other instruments referred to in Article 70.

(2) The Rules of Procedure of the Court of Justice shall, if necessary, be adjusted and supplemented in accordance with Article 188 of the Treaty establishing the European Economic Community.

TITLE VII

TRANSITIONAL PROVISIONS

Article 75 — Time for Commencement

The provisions of this Convention shall apply only to proceedings opened after its entry into force.

TITLE VIII

RELATIONSHIP TO OTHER CONVENTIONS

Article 76 — Substitution for existing Conventions between the Contracting States

When this Convention applies, it shall, in respect of the matters referred to therein, supersede, as between the States which are party to it, the following Conventions concluded between two or more of those States:
— The Convention between Belgium and France on Jurisdiction and the Validity and Enforcement of Judgments, Arbitration Awards and Authentic Instruments, signed in Paris on 8 July 1899;
— The Convention between Belgium and the Netherlands on Jurisdiction, Bankruptcy, and the Validity and Enforcement of Judgments, Arbitration Awards and Authentic Instruments, signed in Brussels on 28 March 1925;
— The Convention between France and Italy on the Enforcement of Judgments in Civil and Commercial Matters, signed in Rome on 3 June 1930;
— The Convention between the Kingdom of the Netherlands and the Federal Republic of Germany on the Mutual Recognition and Enforcement of Judgments and other Enforceable Instruments in Civil and Commercial Matters, signed in The Hague on 30 August 1962;
— The Convention between the United Kingdom and the Kingdom of Belgium providing for the reciprocal enforcement of judgments in civil and commercial matters, with protocol, signed at Brussels on 2 May 1934.

Article 77 — Continuance in force of existing Conventions between the Contracting States

The Conventions referred to in Article 76 shall continue to have effect in relation to matters to which this Convention applies, so far as concerns proceedings opened before the entry into force of the latter.

Article 78 — Conventions concluded with non-Member States

This Convention shall not apply:
— in any Contracting State to the extent that it is irreconcilable with the obligations arising in relation to bankruptcy resulting from another Convention concluded by that State with one or more non-Member States before the entry into force of this Convention;
— and in the United Kingdom of Great Britain and Northern Ireland, to the extent that it is irreconcilable with the obligations arising in relation to bankruptcy and the winding-up of insolvent companies, resulting from any Commonwealth arrangements which still remain in force at the time of the entry into force of this Convention.

TITLE IX

FINAL PROVISIONS

Article 79 — Territorial scope

(1) This Convention shall apply to the European territories of the Contracting States, including Greenland, to the French overseas departments and territories, and to Mayotte.

(2) The Kingdom of the Netherlands may declare at the time of signing or ratifying this Convention or at any later time, by notifying the Secretary-General of the Council of the European Communities, that this Convention shall be applicable to the Netherlands Antilles. In the absence of such declaration, proceedings taking place in the European territory of the Kingdom as a result of an appeal in cassation from the judgment of a court in the Netherlands Antilles shall be deemed to be proceedings taking place in the latter court.

(3) The United Kingdom may declare at the time of signing or ratifying this Convention or at any later time, by notifying the Secretary-General of the Council of the European Communities, that this Convention shall be applicable to any of its dependent territories. In the absence of such declaration, proceedings brought in the United Kingdom on appeal from courts of these dependent territories shall be deemed to be proceedings taking place in those courts.

(4)   Notwithstanding the first paragraph, this Convention shall not apply to:

(a)   the Faroe Islands, unless the Kingdom of Denmark makes a declaration to the contrary,

(b)   any European territory situated outside the United Kingdom for the international relations of which the United Kingdom is responsible, unless the United Kingdom makes a declaration to the contrary in respect of any such territory.

Such declarations may be made at any time by notifying the Secretary-General of the Council of the European Communities.

(5)   Proceedings brought in the United Kingdom on appeal from courts in one of the territories referred to in subparagraph (b) of paragraph (4) shall be deemed to be proceedings taking place in those courts.

(6)   Proceedings which in the Kingdom of Denmark are dealt with under the law on civil procedure for the Faroe Islands (lov for Færøerne om rettens pleje) shall be deemed to be proceedings taking place in the courts of the Faroe Islands.

Article 80 — Ratification and entry into force

(1)   This Convention shall be ratified by the signatory States. The instruments of ratification shall be deposited with the Secretary-General of the Council of the European Communities.

(2)   This Convention shall enter into force on the first day of the sixth month following the deposit of the instrument of ratification by the last signatory State to take this step.

Article 81 — Incorporation of the uniform law into national legislation

(1)   Each Contracting State shall, not later than the date on which this Convention enters into force, incorporate into its own legislation relating to the forms of bankruptcy proceedings listed in Article I(a) of the Protocol to this Convention provisions in conformity with the uniform law laid down in Annex I [and also if need be provisions in conformity with Article 41].

(2)   Paragraph (1) shall also apply to the proceedings listed in Article I(b) of the Protocol to the extent that those provisions are capable of applying thereto.

(3)   Those Contracting States whose laws do not include the presumption referred to in Article 35(1) shall not be required to incorporate therein the provisions of Article 1 of Annex I.

(4) At the time of signing or ratifying this Convention, the Contracting States named in Annex II may, by a declaration addressed to the Secretary-General of the Council of the European Communities, make the reservations therein provided for. Such reservations may be withdrawn at any time.

Article 82 — Accession to the Convention

(1) The Contracting States recognise that any State which becomes a member of the European Economic Community shall be required to accept this Convention as a basis for the negotiations between the Contracting States and that State necessary to ensure the implementation of the last paragraph of Article 220 of the Treaty establishing the European Economic Community.

(2) The necessary adjustments may be the subject of a special convention between the Contracting States of the one part and the new Member State of the other part.

Article 83 — Notification by the Council of the European Communities

The Secretary-General of the Council of the European Communities shall notify the signatory States of:
(a)   the deposit of each instrument of ratification;
(b)   the date of entry into force of this Convention;
(c)   any declaration received pursuant to Article 79;
(d)   any declaration received pursuant to Article 81(4), or pursuant to Article VIII(2) of the Protocol to this Convention;
(e)   any communication made pursuant to Article XIII or XIV of the Protocol to this Convention.

Article 84 — Protocol to the Convention

The Protocol annexed to this Convention by common accord of the Contracting States shall form an integral part thereof.

Article 85 — Duration of the Convention

This Convention is concluded for an unlimited period.

Article 86 — Revision of the Convention

Any Contracting State may request the revision of this Convention. In this event, a revision conference shall be convened by the President of the Council of the European Communities.

Article 87 — Deposit of the Convention

This Convention, drawn up in a single original in the Danish, Dutch, English, French, German, Irish and Italian languages, all seven texts being equally authentic, shall be deposited in the archives of the Secretariat of the Council of the European Communities. The Secretary-General shall transmit a certified copy to the Government of each signatory State.

In witness whereof, the undersigned Plenipotentiaries have signed this Convention.

Done at Brussels this

ANNEX I

UNIFORM LAW

Article 1 — Proof of the spouse's claim to property

All modes of proof shall be admissible to rebut a presumption that the property of the spouse was acquired with the funds of the bankrupt.

Article 2 — Set-off

(1) The bankruptcy shall not preclude set-off where the creditor's claim and the debt to be set off existed in the same estate at the date when the bankruptcy was opened.

(2) The bankruptcy shall not preclude set-off where at the time of the opening of the bankruptcy, the debts to be set off, or one of them, were payable at a future date, or the claim of the creditor of the bankrupt was not expressed in money, or was expressed in currency other than that of the State in which the bankruptcy was opened. Such debts shall be valued as at the date of the opening of the bankruptcy, and in accordance with any other provisions of the law of the State where the bankruptcy was opened.

[*Article 3 — Contracts of Sale with reservation of title*

see Article 41, paragraph (2), First Variant.]

ANNEX II

At the time of signing or ratifying this Convention:
The Federal Republic of Germany may declare that it reserves the right not to introduce into its own legislation the right of the "Ministère Public" to bring an action to challenge the bankruptcy in pursuance of Article 64(1).

JOINT DECLARATION

The Governments of the Kingdom of Belgium, the Kingdom of Denmark, the Federal Republic of Germany, the French Republic, Ireland, the Italian Republic, the Grand Duchy of Luxembourg, the Kingdom of the Netherlands, and the United Kingdom of Great Britain and Northern Ireland.

On signing the Convention on Bankruptcy, Winding-up, Arrangements, Compositions and Similar Proceedings.

Desirous of ensuring that the Convention is applied as effectively as possible.

Declare themselves ready:

(1) to arrange meetings at regular intervals between their representatives;

[(2) to take appropriate measures to remove discrepancies existing between this Convention and the conventions into which they have previously entered with non-Member States;]

[(3) to organise, in co-operation with the Court of Justice, an exchange of information, on judgments given by the Courts referred to in Article 71(a) of this Convention.]

In witness whereof, the undersigned Plenipotentiaries have signed the Joint Declaration.

Done at Brussels on

PROTOCOL

THE HIGH CONTRACTING PARTIES have agreed upon the following provisions, which shall be annexed to the Convention:

ARTICLE I

In accordance with Article 1(1) of the Convention, the Convention shall apply:

(a) to the following bankruptcy proceedings:
   in Belgium:
   to "faillite" — "faillissement";
   in Denmark:
   to "konkurs";
   in the Federal Republic of Germany:
   to "Konkurs";
   in France:
   to "liquidation des biens";
   in Ireland:
   to "bankruptcy"
   to "winding-up in bankruptcy of partnerships"
   to "compulsory winding-up of companies";
   to "creditors' voluntary winding-up";
   in Italy:
   to "fallimento"
   in Luxembourg:
   to "faillite";
   in the Netherlands:
   to "faillissement";
   in the United Kingdom of Great Britain and Northern Ireland:
   to "compulsory winding-up"
   to "winding-up under the supervision of the court"
   to "bankruptcy" (England, Wales and Northern Ireland)
   to the "administration in bankruptcy of the estate of persons dying insolvent" (England, Wales and Northern Ireland)
   to "sequestration" (Scotland).
(b) to the other proceedings listed below:
   in Belgium:
   to "concordat judiciaire" — "gerechtelijk akkoord"
   to "sursis de paiement" — "uitstek van betaling"
   in Denmark:
   to "tvangsakkord"
   to "likvidation af banker og sparekasser, der har standset deres betalinger"

to "likvidation af pensionskasser"
to "likvidation af begravelseskasser"
to "betalingsstandsning"
in the Federal Republic of Germany:
to "gerichtliches Vergleichsverfahren"
to "nachfolgendes Verfahren bei freiwilliger Unterwerfung des Schuldners unter die Überwachung durch einen Sachwalter"
to "Verfahren des Vergleichsgerichts nach Aufhebung des Vergleichsverfahrens über die Feststellung der mutmasslichen Höhe einer bestreittenen Forderung oder des Ausfalls einer teilweise gedeckten Forderung"
to "Massnahmen der Aufsichtsbehörden für Kreditinstitute und Versicherungsunternehmen zur Vermeidung des Konkurses";
in France:
to "règlement judiciaire"
to "procédure de suspension provisoire des poursuites et d'apurement collectif du passif de certaines entreprises"
in Ireland:
to "arrangements under the control of the Court"
to "arrangements, reconstructions and compositions of companies whether or not in the course of liquidation where the sanction of the court is required and creditors' rights are involved"
in Italy:
to "concordato preventivo"
to "amministrazione controllata"
to "liquidazione coatta amministrativa"
to "ammistrazione straordinaria delle grandi imprese in crisi"
in Luxembourg:
to "concordat préventif de la faillite"
to "sursis de paiement"
to "régime spécial de liquidation applicable aux notaires"
to "gestion contrôlée"
in the Netherlands:
to "surséance van betaling"
to "regeling, vervat in de wet op de vergadering van houders van schuldbrieven aan toonder"
to "noodregeling, wet toezicht Kredietwezen van 13 April 1978"
in the United Kingdom of Great Britain and Northern Ireland:
to "creditors' voluntary winding-up"
to "compositions and schemes of arrangement" (England and Wales)

to "compositions" (Northern Ireland)
to "arrangements under the control of the court" (Northern Ireland)
to "deeds of arrangement approved by the court" (Northern Ireland)
to "judicial compositions" (Scotland)

ARTICLE II

For the purposes of Article 2 of the Convention, the effective date of the opening of a "bankruptcy" in England and Wales shall be the date of the receiving order; in the case of Creditors' voluntary winding-up proceedings in the Republic of Ireland as well as in the United Kingdom of Great Britain and Northern Ireland, that date is the date of the passing of the resolution by the company for voluntary winding-up.

ARTICLE III

(1) The extract of a judgment opening a bankruptcy, or of a judgment in one of the proceedings listed in Article I(b), which is to be advertised in the Official Journal of the European Communities in accordance with Article 26(1) and [(4)] of the Convention, shall contain the following particulars:

(a) the surname, forenames and business address of the bankrupt or, if he has no business address, the address of his "domicile"; in the case of an association, with or without legal personality, its name and the address of its registered or head office; in the case of the bankruptcy of a deceased person or a deceased's estate, the surname, forenames and business address of the deceased or, if he had no business address, the address of his last "domicile";

(b) the order made on the judgment, the date thereof and the court which gave it;

(c) the date of the cessation of payments, if the judgment specifies it;

(d) the name of the "juge-commissaire", if any;

(e) the name and address of the person or persons acting as liquidator, curator, or administrator, and of the persons referred to in Article 29(3) of the Convention;

(f) any other particulars which are considered to be useful.

(2) Changes in the particulars of persons referred to in paragraph 1 (d) and (e) shall also be advertised in the Official Journal of the European Communities.

(3) As regards judgments which have clearly been made on the basis of Article 10 of the Convention, the notice thereof in the Official Journal of

the European Communities shall indicate the Contracting State or States in which the judgment is without effect. In the case of judgments made on the basis of Article 66 of the Convention, the notice shall indicate the State in which the judgment takes effect.

ARTICLE IV

In accordance with Article 26(1) of the Convention there shall be advertised in the *Official Journal of the European Communities*, as well as the judgments opening the bankruptcy the following judgments, acts and notices which:

in Belgium:
1. *in cases of "faillite"*
— fix, subsequent to the opening of the bankruptcy, the date of the cessation of payments,
— close the proceedings;
2. *in cases of "concordat judiciaire"*
— propose the composition,
— convene the meeting of creditors, or notify the creditors of the proposals for the composition;
— record approval of the composition;
3. *in cases of "sursis de paiement"*
— convene the creditors,
— grant an interim or permanent stay of proceedings, or extend a stay;

in Denmark:
1. *in cases of "konkurs"*
— convene the meeting of creditors,
— request the creditors to declare their claims,
— concern advertisement of the draft composition,
— convene the creditors for the purpose of studying the draft composition,
— close the bankruptcy proceedings;
2. *in cases of "tvangsakkord"*
— open negotiations,
— convene a new meeting for the purpose of amending the draft composition,
— concern publication of the results of negotiations;
3. *in cases of "likvidation af pensionskasser"*
— concern publication of the liquidation;

4. *in cases of "likvidation af begravelseskasser"*
— concern publication of the liquidation;
5. *in cases of "likvidation af banker og sparekasser, der har standset deres betalinger"*
— concern publication of the liquidation;

in the Federal Republic of Germany:
1. *in cases of "Konkursverfahren"*
— convene a meeting of creditors and specify what business is to be transacted, if the meeting is not merely the continuation of a previous adjourned meeting or the new date for resumption of such adjourned meeting has not already been announced at the previous meeting,
— appoint a meeting to verify the creditors' claims, if the meeting is not merely the continuation of a previous adjourned meeting for that purpose or the new date for resumption of such adjourned meeting has not already been announced at the previous meeting,
— announce the appointment of a new liquidator, giving his name and address,
— appoint a hearing for a composition,
— discontinue or close the proceedings, after the decision has become *res judicata*, or which re-open the proceedings;
2. *in cases of "gerichtliches Vergleichsverfahren"*
— announce the receipt of an application for a composition, giving the name and address of the interim administrator,
— disallow the opening of composition proceedings and decline to open a bankruptcy, after the decision has become *res judicata*,
— impose on or remove from the debtor a general restraint as regards the disposal of his property,
— refuse the approval of a composition and decline to open a bankruptcy, after the decision has become *res judicata*,
— close the proceedings,
— discontinue the "gerichtliches Vergleichsverfahren" and decline to open a bankruptcy, after the decision has become *res judicata*;

in France:
1. *in cases of "liquidation des biens" or "règlement judiciaire"*
— close the proceedings,
— set aside a decision opening a "liquidation des biens" or a "règlement judiciaire", or a judgment closing the proceedings;
2. *in cases of "règlement judiciaire"*

— open a "règlement judiciaire",
— approve, annul or set aside a composition,
— convert a "règlement judiciaire" into a "liquidation des biens";
3. *in cases of "suspension provisoire des poursuites et d'apurement collectif du passif de certaines entreprises"*
— grant or put an end to an interim stay of proceedings,
— sanction a scheme for the collective discharge of the liabilities of the bankrupt, or set it aside;

in Ireland:
1. *in cases of "winding-up by the Court under Sections 213, 344 and 345 of the Companies Act 1963"*
— contain the decision relating to the "arrangement, reconstruction or composition" in accordance with Section 201 of the Companies Act 1963.
2. *in cases of "bankruptcy"*
— give notice of the meeting specifying the precise offer of "composition to be made".
3. *in cases of "creditors' voluntary winding-up"*
— Resolution by the Company and by the meeting of creditors for the appointment of a "liquidator";

in Italy:
1. *in cases of "fallimento"*
— set aside a judgment opening a bankruptcy,
— close, or order the re-opening of, the bankruptcy,
— propose a composition, where individual notification is particularly difficult because of the number of persons to be notified,
— approve the composition or record its complete implementation and order the release of the securities given and the entry of satisfaction notices as regards the mortgages registered as security;
2. *in cases of "concordato preventivo"*
— declare the opening of the proceedings,
— record approval of the "concordato preventivo";
3. *in cases of "amministrazione controllata"*
— admit to the proceedings,
— determine the powers of the court's receiver and entrust to him, in whole or in part, the management of the undertaking and the administration of the property of the debtor,
— close the proceedings;

4. *in cases of "liquidazione coatta amministrativa" [and of "amministra-zione straordinaria]*
— declare the debtor insolvent and make an order for liquidation,
— concern the lodging of the final balance sheet of the liquidation, the statement of affairs and the scheme for distribution,
— approve the "concordato";

in Luxembourg:
1. *in cases of "faillite"*
— fix, subsequent to the opening of the bankruptcy, the date of the cessation of payments,
— close the proceedings;
2. *in cases of "concordat préventif de la faillite"*
— propose the composition,
— convene the meeting of creditors, or notify the creditors of the proposals for the composition,
— record approval of the composition;
3. *in cases of "sursis de paiement"*
— convene the creditors,
— grant an interim or permanent stay of proceedings, or extend a stay;
4. *in cases of "gestion contrôlée"*
— appoint one or more commissaires to supervise the administration of the applicant's estate,
— contain either a proposal for the reorganization of the applicant's business or a proposal for the realization and distribution of the assets, drawn up the commissaires,
— approve by order of the court the proposal made by the commissaires;

in the Netherlands:
1. *in cases of "faillissement"*
— declare the annulment, the discontinuance or the closure of the bankruptcy,
— declare the annulment of an approved composition and at the same time re-open the bankruptcy,
— fix the time limit for the submission of claims and the date of the meeting for their verification;
2. *in cases of "surséance van betaling"*
— provisionally grant the "surséance van betaling" and fix the date for the hearing at which the application will be examined,
— certify that a draft agreement has been filed with the court registry, and

fix the date for the examination of that agreement,
— finally, confirm or set aside the "surséance van betaling";
3. *in cases of "noodregeling", "wet toezicht van kredietwezen" of 13 April 1978*
— contain the declaration that the credit institution is in a situation which necessitates some special measures in the interest of the whole body of creditors,
— concern the transfer of obligations and the modifications of the terms of the contracts from which the obligations flow, in accordance with Article 36 of the "wet toezicht kredietwezen",
— concern the closure of the liquidation as well as the extension or the withdrawal of the above-mentioned declaration;

in the United Kingdom of Great Britain and Northern Ireland:
1. *in cases of "compulsory winding-up"*
— contain the decision relating to the "arrangement, reconstruction or composition" in accordance with Section 206 of the Companies Act 1948 or Section 197 of the Companies Act (Northern Ireland) 1960;
2. *in cases of "bankruptcy" (England, Wales and Northern Ireland)*
— contain the authorisation relating to the "composition or scheme of arrangement";
— declare the annulment of the bankruptcy;
— "certify" by the "Department of Trade" the appointment of a "trustee in bankruptcy" or "a trustee under a composition or scheme of arrangement" in England or Wales;
— "certify" by the "High Court of Justice in Northern Ireland" the appointment of a "trustee in bankruptcy" or "a trustee under a composition or a scheme of arrangement" in Northern Ireland;
3. *in cases of "sequestration" (Scotland)*
— contain the authorisation relating to the "composition or deed of arrangement";
4. *in cases of "creditors' voluntary winding-up"*
— contain the resolution by the meeting of creditors for the appointment of a "liquidator".

AND any other particulars which are considered to be useful.

ARTICLE V

Article 55 of the Convention shall likewise apply in respect of the following non-judicial decisions:

in Ireland:
— Company resolution for voluntary winding-up in a "creditors' voluntary winding-up";
— Resolution by the Company and by the meeting of creditors for the appointment of a "liquidator" in a "creditors' voluntary winding-up";

in Italy:
in cases of "liquidazione coatta amministrativa" and "amministrazione straordinaria"
— the list of claims drawn up by the "commissario" and filed with the court registry;
— the final balance sheet of the liquidation the accounts of the administrator and the scheme for distribution;

in the Netherlands:
— the transfer of obligations and the modification of the terms of the contracts from which the obligations flow, in accordance with Article 36 of the "wet toezicht kredietwezen" made in the case of a "noodregeling" mentioned in Article I(b) under the heading "in the Netherlands".

in the United Kingdom of Great Britain and Northern Ireland:
— Company resolution for voluntary winding-up in a "creditors' voluntary winding-up";
— Resolution by the meeting of creditors for the appointment of a "liquidator" in a "creditors' voluntary winding-up".

ARTICLE VI

The extracts of the decisions, acts and notices listed in Article IV which are to be advertised in the *Official Journal of the European Communities* in accordance with Article 26 of the Convention shall contain the particulars referred to in Article III(a), (b) and (f).

ARTICLE VII

(1) The gazetting provided for by Article 26(3) of the Convention shall appear:
— in Belgium, in the *Moniteur belge — Belgisch Staatsblad.*
— in Denmark, in the *Statstidende,*
— in the Federal Republic of Germany, in the *Bundesanzeiger,*
— in France, in the *Bulletin Officiel des Annonces Commerciales,*
— in Ireland, in the *Iris Oifigiuil,*
— in Italy, in the *Foglio degli Annunci legali della Pronvincia* and in the case of companies in the *Bollettino Ufficiale delle Società per azioni e a responsabilità limitata,*
— in Luxembourg, in the *Mémorial,* edition B,
— in the Netherlands, in the *Nederlandse Staatscourant,*
— in the United Kingdom of Great Britain and Northern Ireland,
    in the *London Gazette* (England and Wales)
    in the *Edinburgh Gazette* (Scotland)
    in the *Belfast Gazette* (Northern Ireland)

(2) The particulars or extracts to be gazetted shall be furnished by the liquidator in the official language or one of the official languages of the authority concerned.

ARTICLE VIII

(1) Judicial and extrajudicial documents drawn up in one Contracting State which have to be served on persons in another Contracting State shall be transmitted in accordance with the procedures laid down in the conventions and agreements concluded between the Contracting States.

(2) Unless the State in which service is to take place objects by declaration to the Secretary-General of the Council of the European Communities, such documents may also be sent by the appropriate public officers of the State in which the instrument has been drawn up directly to the appropriate public officers of the State in which the addressee is to be found. In this case, the officer of the State of origin shall send a copy of the document to the officer of the State applied to who is competent to forward it to the addressee. The document shall be forwarded in manner required by the law of the State applied to. The forwarding shall be recorded by a certificate sent directly to the officer of the State of origin.

ARTICLE IX

(1) The liquidator shall inform the postal authorities of the Contracting States other than that in which the bankruptcy has been opened of the duty placed upon them by Article 30 of the Convention, by sending them an office copy of the judgment ordering the re-direction of mail. This shall be accompanied, either by an extract, provided by the registrar of the court, of the judgment appointing the liquidator or liquidators, or by a copy of the Official Journal of the European Communities, or of the official gazette of the State whose postal authorities are concerned, containing the advertisement of the bankruptcy. The office copy and the extract referred to above shall be accompanied by a certified translation in the official language or one of the official languages of the postal authority concerned.

(2) The duty under Article 30 of the Convention shall terminate with the sending to the postal authorities, in the same manner as in the foregoing paragraph, of the extract of the judgment declaring the closure of the bankruptcy proceedings or bringing to an end the re-direction of mail to the liquidator.

ARTICLE X

In accordance with Article 31 of the Convention, creditor claims shall be submitted:

in Belgium:
    to the "juge-commissaire", – to the "rechter-commissaris"
in Denmark:
    in cases of "konkurs", to the "skifteretten"
    in cases of "tvangsakkord", to the "skifteretten"
    in cases of "likvidation af banker og sparekasser, der har standset deres betalinger", likvidation af pensionskasser" and "likvidation af begravelseskasser", to the "likvidator";

in the Federal Republic of Germany:
    in cases of "Konkursverfahren" to the "Konkursgericht" ("Amtsgericht")
    in cases of "gerichtliches Vergleichsverfahren", to the "Vergleichsgericht" ("Amtsgericht");
in France:
    to the "syndic";
in Ireland:
    in cases of "bankruptcy", to the "Official Assignee in bankruptcy",

in cases of "procedures under the Companies Act 1963" to the "Official Liquidator";

in Italy:
in cases of "fallimento" and of "concordato preventivo", to the "giudice delegato"
in cases of "amministrazione controllata", of "liquidazione coatta amministrativa" and of "amministrazione straordinaria" to the "commissario";

in Luxembourg:
to the "greffier du tribunal de commerce";

in the Netherlands:
in cases of "faillissement", to the "Curator",
in cases of "surséance van betaling" to the "Bewindvoerder";

in the United Kingdom of Great Britain and Northern Ireland:
to the "official receiver", the "provisional liquidator" the "liquidator" or the "trustee" as the case may be (England and Wales),
to the "trustee", the "judicial factor" or the "liquidator" as the case may be (Scotland),
to the "official assignee", the "provisional liquidator", the "liquidator", or the "trustee" according to the case (Northern Ireland);

ARTICLE XI

Actions to challenge the bankruptcy shall be brought in accordance with Article 63 of the Convention:

in Belgium:
before the "Président du Tribunal de Commerce" — "voorzitter van de rechtbank van koophandel" in Brussels who shall give judgment according to the procedure for matters of urgency;

in Denmark:
before the "Sø-og handelsretten" in Copenhagen;

in the Federal Republic of Germany:
before the "Amtsgericht" in Wiesbaden, which shall give judgment according to the "Beschlussverfahren";

in France:
before the "Président du Tribunal de grande instance" in Paris, who shall give judgment according to the procedure for matters of urgency;

in Ireland:
before the "High Court" (in Dublin);

in Italy:
   before the "Tribunale di Roma";
in Luxembourg:
   before the "Président du Tribunal d'arrondissement de Luxembourg" who
   shall give judgment according to the procedure for matters of urgency;
in the Netherlands:
   before the "arrondissementsrechtbank" in the Hague;
in the United Kingdom of Great Britain and Northern Ireland:
   in England and Wales: before the "High Court of Justice", (in London);
   in Scotland: before the "Court of Session", (in Edinburgh);
   in Northern Ireland: before the "High Court of Justice" (in Belfast);

ARTICLE XII

(a)   The proceedings referred to in Article 13 of the Convention shall be:

in Belgium:
— "appel" — "hoger beroep"
— "opposition" — "verzet"
— "pourvoi en cassation" — "voorziening in cassatie"

in Denmark:
— "anke"
— "kaerer"

in the Federal Republic of Germany:
— "die sofortige Beschwerde"
— "die weitere sofortige Beschwerde"
— "die Erinnerung";

in France:
— "l'appel" or "le contredit"
— "le pourvoi en cassation"

in Ireland:
— "Appeals to the Supreme Court"

in Italy:
— "oppossizione"
— "appello"

— "ricorso per cassazione"
— "regolamento di competenza"

in Luxembourg:
— "l'appel"
— "l'opposition"
— "le pourvoi en cassation";

in the Netherlands:
— "verzet"
— "hoger beroep"
— "beroep in cassatie"

in the United Kingdom of Great Britain and Northern Ireland:
— "Appeals" to the "House of Lords" and, in England and Wales, the "Court of Appeal" where no appeal lies against its decision; in Scotland similarly the "Inner House of the Court of Session"; and in Northern Ireland similarly the "Court of Appeal in Northern Ireland".

(b) The proceedings referred to in Article 14(2) of the Convention shall be:

in Belgium:
— "appel" — "hoger beroep"
— "opposition — "verzet"
— "pourvoi en cassation" — "voorziening in cassatie"

in Denmark:
— "anke"
— "kaerer";

in the Federal Republic of Germany:
— "die sofortige Beschwerde"
— "die weitere sofortige Beschwerde"
— "die Erinnerung";

in France:
— "le contredit"
— "le pourvoi en cassation"

in Ireland:
— Appeals to the Supreme Court

in Italy:
— "oppossizione"
— "appello"
— "ricorso per cassazione"
— "regolamento di competenza"

in Luxembourg:
— "l'appel"
— "l'opposition"
— "le pourvoi en cassation";

in the Netherlands:
— "hoger beroep"
— "beroep in cassatie"

in the United Kingdom of Great Britain and Northern Ireland:
— "Appeals" to the "House of Lords" and, in England and Wales, the "Court of Appeal" where no appeal lies against its decision; in Scotland similarly the "Inner House of the Court of Session"; and in Northern Ireland similarly the "Court of Appeal in Northern Ireland".

ARTICLE XIII

Each contracting State shall communicate to the Secretary-General of the Council of the European Communities the text of any significant amendments introduced into its own legislation on bankruptcy, winding-up, arrangements, compositions and similar proceedings and also, to the extent that it deems necessary, any proposed reforms in these fields which are likely to affect the application of the Convention.

ARTICLE XIV

Each contracting State may, by a declaration addressed to the Secretary-General of the Council of the European Communities, amend those particulars listed in relation to that State which are contained in the Articles IV, V, VI, VII, X, XI and XII indicating the date on which such amendment is to come into force.

In witness whereof the undersigned Plenipotentiaries have signed this Protocol.

Done at Brussels this

ANNEX TO THE PROTOCOL

Form of certificate provided for in Article 29 of the Convention

Passport or Identity Card No........

Certificate

provided for in Article 29 of the Convention

of...

on bankruptcy, winding-up, arrangements, compositions and similar proceedings

Photograph

I, the undersigned, (1) ....
in (2) ....
certify that a judgment given on (3) .... by (3a) ....
declared (4) ....
of (5) .... (of the estate ....)
of (6) ....
(last known address)
and appointed (7) ....
address (8) ....
as (9) ....
Date ....

(seal) .... (signature)
.... (Designation of signatory —
Department of Trade or
Registrar of the Court)

---

(1)   Function of signatory
(2)   Place and State in which the court or authority sits
(3)   Date of the judgment
(3a) Name of the court or authority which gave the judgment
(4)   Nature of the judgment
(5)   Name of the bankrupt or of the debtor (of the deceased)
(6)   Address of the bankrupt or of the debtor
(7)   Name and forenames of the person appointed
(8)   Address of the person appointed
(9)   Capacity of the person appointed

Convention on the Mutual Recognition of Companies and Bodies Corporate (*)

PREAMBLE

The High Contracting Parties to the Treaty establishing the European Economic Community,

Being desirous of implementing the provisions of Article 220 of the said Treaty concerning the mutual recognition of companies within the meaning of Article 58, second paragraph,

Whereas the mutual recognition of companies or firms within the meaning of Article 58, second paragraph, should be as liberal as possible, without prejudice to the application to companies of the other provisions of the Treaty,

Have decided to conclude the present Convention on the mutual recognition of companies and bodies corporate and have for this purpose nominated as plenipotentiaries:

HIS MAJESTY THE KING OF THE BELGIANS:
M. Pierre Harmel, Minister for Foreign Affairs;

THE PRESIDENT OF THE FEDERAL REPUBLIC OF GERMANY:
M. Willy Brandt, Vice-Chancellor and Minister for Foreign Affairs;

THE PRESIDENT OF THE FRENCH REPUBLIC:
M. Maurice Couve de Murville, Minister for Foreign Affairs;

THE PRESIDENT OF THE ITALIAN REPUBLIC:
M. Amintore Fanfani, Minister for Foreign Affairs;

(*) Signed on 29 February 1968.

HIS ROYAL HIGHNESS THE GRAND–DUKE OF LUXEMBOURG:
M. Pierre Grégoire, Minister for Foreign Affairs;

HER MAJESTY THE QUEEN OF THE NETHERLANDS:
M. J.M.A.H. Luns, Minister for Foreign Affairs;

Who, meeting in the Council, having exchanged their Full Powers, found in good and due form,

HAVE AGREED AS FOLLOWS:

CHAPTER I

RECOGNITION: SCOPE AND CONDITIONS

Article 1

Companies under civil or commercial law, including co-operative societies, established in accordance with the law of a Contracting State which grants them the capacity of persons having rights and duties, and having their statutory registered office in the territories to which the present Convention applies, shall be recognised as of right.

Article 2

Bodies corporate under public or private law, other than the companies specified in Article 1, which fulfil the conditions stipulated in the said Article, which have as their main or accessory object an economic activity normally exercised for reward, or which, without infringing the law under which they were established, do in fact continuously exercise such activity, shall also be recognised as of right.

Article 3

Notwithstanding the foregoing, any Contracting State may declare that it will not apply the present Convention to any companies or bodies corporate specified in Articles 1 and 2 which have their real registered office outside the territories to which the present Convention applies, if such companies or bodies corporate have no genuine link with the economy of one of the said territories.

Article 4

Any Contracting State may also declare that it will apply any provisions of its own legislation which it deems essential, to the companies or bodies corporate specified in Articles 1 and 2 having their real registered offices on its territory, even if these have been established in accordance with the law of another Contracting State.

The suppletory provisions of the legislation of the State making such a declaration shall apply in only one of the following two cases:

(i) If the memorandum and articles of association so permit, if necessary by an express general reference to the law in accordance with which the company or body corporate has been established,

(ii) If, the memorandum and articles of association so permitting, the company or body corporate fails to show that it has actually exercised its activity for a reasonable time in the Contracting State in accordance with the law under which it was established.

Article 5

For the purpose of this Convention, the real registered office of a company or body corporate shall mean the place where its central administration is established.

CHAPTER II

RECOGNITION: EFFECTS

Article 6

Without prejudice to the application of Article 4, all companies or bodies corporate recognised by virtue of this Convention shall have the capacity accorded to them by the law under which they were established.

Article 7

Any State in which recognition is sought may refuse such companies or bodies corporate any rights and powers specified which it does not grant to companies or bodies corporate of a similar type which are governed by its own laws. However, the exercise of this power may not result in the withdrawal from such companies or bodies corporate of their capacity, as persons having rights and duties, to award contracts, or to accomplish other legal acts or to sue or be sued.

The companies or bodies corporate referred to in Articles 1 and 2 may not invoke the restrictions on their rights and powers specified in this Article.

Article 8

The capacity, rights and powers of a company recognised by virtue of this Convention may not be denied or restricted for the sole reason that the law in accordance with which it was established does not grant it the legal status of a body corporate.

CHAPTER III

PUBLIC POLICY

Article 9

In each Contracting State, the application of this Convention may only be waived when the company or body corporate invoking it contravenes by its object, its purpose or the activity which it actually exercises the principles or rules which the said State considers as being a matter of public policy as defined in private international law.

If the law under which a single proprietorship is established allows it to possess the status of a company, such company may not for that reason alone be considered by a Contracting State as conflicting with public policy as defined in private international law.

Article 10

Principles or rules contrary to the provisions of the Treaty establishing the European Economic Community may not be deemed a matter of public policy within the meaning of Article 9.

CHAPTER IV

FINAL PROVISIONS

Article 11

In relations between the Contracting States, this Convention shall apply notwithstanding any conflicting provisions concerning recognition of companies or bodies corporate contained in other conventions to which the Contracting States are or will be parties.

However, the present Convention shall be without prejudice:
(i) To those rules of municipal law
(ii) And to those provisions of international conventions
which are or will be in force and which provide for recognition in other cases or with wider effects, provided that such recognition or such effects are compatible with the Treaty Establishing the European Economic Community.

Article 12

This Convention shall apply to the European territories of the Contracting States, to the French Overseas Departments and to the French Overseas Territories.

Any Contracting State may declare by notification to the Secretary-General of the Council of the European Communities that this Convention applies to the country or countries, or to the territory or territories indicated in the said declaration, whose international relations it governs.

Article 13

This Convention shall be ratified by the signatory States. The instruments of ratification shall be deposited with the Secretary-General of the Council of the European Communities.

Article 14

This Convention shall come into force on the first day of the third month following deposit of the instrument of ratification by the last signatory State to complete this formality.

Article 15

The declarations specified in Articles 3 and 4 must be made for each signatory State no later than the time when its instrument of ratification of this Convention is deposited. They shall take effect on the day this Convention comes into force. If the declaration specified in Article 12, second paragraph, is made no later than the time when the sixth instrument of ratification of this Convention is deposited, it shall take effect on the day this Convention comes into force; if the declaration is made at a later date, it shall take effect on the first day of the third month following receipt of its notification.

Any Contracting State may at any time withdraw either or both of the declarations made by virtue of Articles 3 and 4. The withdrawal shall take effect on the first day of the third month following the receipt of its notification by the Secretary-General of the Council of the European Communities. It shall be final.

Article 16

The Secretary-General of the Council of the European Communities shall notify the signatory States of:
(i)   The deposit of every instrument of ratification;
(ii)   The date of entry into force of this Convention;
(iii)   The declarations and notifications received in pursuance of Articles 3, 4, 12, second paragraph, and 15, second paragraph;
(iv)   The dates when these declarations and notifications take effect.

Article 17

This Convention shall be concluded for an indefinite period.

Article 18

Any Contracting State may request the revision of the present Convention. In this event, a revision conference shall be convened by the President of the Council of the European Communities.

Article 19

This Convention, drawn up in one original only, in German, French, Italian and Dutch, the four texts being equally authentic, shall be deposited in the archives of the Secretariat of the Council of the European Communities. The Secretary-General shall supply a certified true copy to the Government of each signatory State.

In witness whereof, the undersigned plenipotentiaries have affixed their signatures to this Convention.

Done at Brussels, on the twenty-ninth day of February, nineteen hundred and sixty-eight.

For His Majesty the King of the Belgians,
    Pierre HARMEL.

For the President of the Federal Republic of Germany,
    Willy BRANDT.

For the President of the French Republic,
    Maurice COUVE DE MURVILLE.

For the President of the Italian Republic,
    Amintore FANFANI.

For His Royal Highness the Grand-Duke of Luxembourg,
    Pierre GRÉGOIRE.

For Her Majesty the Queen of the Netherlands,
    Joseph M.A.H. LUNS.

PROTOCOL

Upon signing the text of the Convention on the mutual recognition of companies and bodies corporate, the plenipotentiaries of the High Contracting Parties to the Treaty establishing the European Economic Community adopted the texts of the following three declarations:

JOINT DECLARATION No. 1

The Governments of the Kingdom of Belgium, the Federal Republic of

Germany, the French Republic, the Italian Republic, the Grand Duchy of Luxembourg and the Kingdom of the Netherlands,

Declare that Article 1 of this Convention applies to the *società semplice* in Italian law and the *vennootschap onder firma* in Netherlands law.

JOINT DECLARATION No. 2

The Governments of the Kingdom of Belgium, the Federal Republic of Germany, the French Republic, the Italian Republic, the Grand Duchy of Luxembourg and the Kingdom of the Netherlands,

Declare themselves ready to engage, as may be necessary under association agreements, in negotiations with any Associated State of the European Economic Community with a view to the mutual recognition of companies and bodies corporate within the meaning of Articles 1 and 2 of the aforesaid Convention.

JOINT DECLARATION No. 3

The Governments of the Kingdom of Belgium, the Federal Republic of Germany, the French Republic, the Italian Republic, the Grand Duchy of Luxembourg and the Kingdom of the Netherlands,

Being desirous of ensuring that the Convention is applied as effectively as possible,

Being anxious to prevent differences of interpretation from impairing the unity of the Convention,

Declare themselves ready to study ways and means of achieving these ends, notably by examining the possibility of conferring certain powers on the Court of Justice of the European Communities, and, as appropriate, to negotiate an agreement to this effect.

In witness whereof, the undersigned plenipotentiaries have affixed their signatures to this Protocol.

Done at Brussels, on the twenty-ninth day of February, nineteen hundred and sixty-eight.

For His Majesty the King of the Belgians,
    Pierre HARMEL.

For the President of the Federal Republic of Germany,
Willy BRANDT.
For the President of the French Republic,
Maurice COUVE DE MURVILLE.

For the President of the Italian Republic,
Amintore FANFANI.

For His Royal Highness the Grand-Duke of Luxembourg,
Pierre GRÉGOIRE.

For Her Majesty the Queen of the Netherlands,
Joseph M.A.H. LUNS.

PROTOCOL OF 3 JUNE 1971 ON INTERPRETATION BY THE COURT OF JUSTICE OF THE CONVENTION OF 29 FEBRUARY 1968

The High Contracting Parties to the Treaty establishing the European Economic Community, having regard to the Joint Declaration No. 3 appearing in the Protocol annexed to the Convention on the Mutual Recognition of Companies and Legal Persons, signed at Brussels on 29 February 1968, have decided to conclude a Protocol bestowing powers on the Court of Justice of the European Communities to interpret the said Convention and to this end have designated as Plenipotentiaries:

HIS MAJESTY THE KING OF THE BELGIANS:
Mr Alfons Vranckx, Minister of Justice;

THE PRESIDENT OF THE FEDERAL REPUBLIC OF GERMANY:
Mr Gerhard Jahn, Federal Minister of Justice;

THE PRESIDENT OF THE FRENCH REPUBLIC:
Mr René Pleven, Keeper of the Seals, Minister of Justice;

THE PRESIDENT OF THE ITALIAN REPUBLIC:
Mr Erminio Pennacchini, Deputy State Secretary, Ministry of Justice and Pardons;

HIS ROYAL HIGHNESS THE GRAND DUKE OF LUXEMBOURG:
Mr Eugène Schaus, Minister of Justice, Deputy Prime Minister;

HER MAJESTY THE QUEEN OF THE NETHERLANDS:
Mr C.H.F. Polak, Minister of Justice;

Who, being met within the Council, having exchanged their Full Powers, found in good and true form, have agreed upon the following provisions:

Article 1

The Court of Justice of the European Communities shall have jurisdiction to give preliminary rulings concerning the interpretation of the Convention on the Mutual Recognition of Companies and Legal Persons and the Joint Declaration No. 1 appearing in the Protocol annexed to that Convention, signed at Brussels on 29 February 1968, and concerning the interpretation of this Protocol.

Article 2

(1) Where a question relating to the interpretation of the Convention and the other texts mentioned in Article 1 is raised before any court or tribunal of one of the Contracting States, that court or tribunal may, if it considers that a decision on the question is necessary to enable it to give judgment, request the Court of Justice to give a ruling thereon.

(2) Where such a question is raised in a case pending before a court or tribunal of a Member State, from whose decisions there is no possibility of appeal under internal law, that court or tribunal shall be bound to bring the matter before the Court of Justice.

Article 3

(1) Except where this Protocol provides otherwise, the provisions of the Treaty establishing the European Economic Community and those of the Protocol on the Statute of the Court of Justice annexed thereto, which are applicable when the Court is required to give a preliminary ruling, shall apply also to the procedure for the interpretation of the Convention and the other texts mentioned in Article 1.

(2) The Rules of Procedure of the Court of Justice shall be adapted and supplemented, as necessary, in conformity with Article 188 of the Treaty establishing the European Economic Community.

Article 4

This Protocol shall apply to the European territory of the Contracting States, to the French Overseas Departments and to the French Overseas Territories.

The Kingdom of the Netherlands may, at the time of signing or of ratifying this Protocol, or at any time subsequently, by notifying the Secretary-General of the Council of the European Communities, declare that this Protocol shall apply to Surinam and to the Netherlands Antilles.

Article 5

This Protocol shall be ratified by the Signatory States. The instruments of ratification shall be deposited with the Secretary-General of the Council of the European Communities.

Article 6

This Protocol shall come into force on the first day of the third month following the deposit of the instrument of ratification of the last Signatory State to complete this formality. However, its entry into force shall occur at the earliest at the same time as that of the Convention of 29 February 1968 on the Mutual Recognition of Companies and Legal Persons.

Article 7

The Secretary-General of the Council of the European Communities shall notify the Signatory States of:
    (a) the deposit of any instrument of ratification;
    (b) the date of entry into force of this Protocol;
    (c) the declarations received pursuant to Article 4, second paragraph.

Article 8

This Protocol shall be concluded for an unlimited period.

Article 9

Each Contracting State may ask for this Protocol to be revised. In that event, a revision conference shall be convened by the President of the Council of the European Communities.

Article 10

This Protocol, drawn up in a single original in the German, French, Italian and Dutch languages, all four texts being equally authentic, shall be deposited in the archives of the Secretariat of the Council of the European Communities. The Secretary-General shall transmit a certified copy to the Government of each of the Signatory States.

JOINT DECLARATION

The Governments of the Kingdom of Belgium, the Federal Republic of Germany, the French Republic, the Italian Republic, the Grand Duchy of Luxembourg and the Kingdom of the Netherlands, at the time of signing the Protocol concerning the interpretation by the Court of Justice of the Convention of 29 February 1968 on the Mutual Recognition of Companies and Legal Persons, wishing to ensure that these provisions are applied as effectively and as uniformly as possible, declare that they are willing, in co-operation with the Court of Justice, to organise an exchange of information on the decisions made by the courts and tribunals mentioned in Article 2(2) of the said Protocol in application of the Convention of 29 February 1968 and of the Joint Declaration No. 1 appearing in the Protocol annexed to that Convention.

Index